P9-CNC-037

THE JUVENILE SEX OFFENDER

The Juvenile
Sex Offender

EDITED BY

Howard E. Barbaree
William L. Marshall
Stephen M. Hudson

THE GUILFORD PRESS
New York   London

44.00

©1993 The Guilford Press
A Division of Guilford Publications, Inc.
72 Spring Street, New York, NY 10012

Printed in the United States of America

This book is printed on acid-free paper.

Last digit is print number: 9   8   7

Library of Congress Cataloging-in-Publication Data

The Juvenile sex offender / edited by Howard E. Barbaree, William
    L. Marshall, Stephen M. Hudson
        p.   cm.
    Includes bibliographical references and index.
    ISBN 0-89862-120-8
    1. Teenage sex offenders.   I. Barbaree, H. E.   II. Marshall,
William L.   III. Hudson, Stephen M.
        [DNLM: 1. Sex Offenses.   2. Psychosexual Disorders—in
        adolescence.   3. Psychosexual Disorders—therapy.   4.
        Juvenile Delinquency—psychology.   5. Mental Disorders—in
        adolescence.   WS 463 J975   1993]
RJ506.S48J88   1993
364.1'53'0835—dc20
DNLM/DLC
for Library of Congress   93-5209
                                                                CIP

*To our children and grandchildren
as they pass through adolescence.*

Contributors

GENE ABEL, Ph.D., Behavioral Medicine Institute, Atlanta, Georgia

NICHOLAS BALA, LL.M., Faculty of Law, Queen's University, Kingston, Ontario, Canada

HOWARD E. BARBAREE, Ph.D., Department of Psychology, Queen's University, Kingston, Ontario, Canada

JUDITH BECKER, Ph.D., Department of Psychiatry, College of Medicine, The University of Arizona Health Sciences Center, Tuscon, Arizona

JOHN M. W. BRADFORD, M.B., Department of Psychiatry, Forensic Program, University of Ottawa, Ottawa, Ontario, Canada

WILLIAM BRENDER, Ph.D., Department of Psychology, Concordia University, Montreal, Canada

WILLIAM BUKOWSKI, Ph.D., Department of Psychology, Concordia University, Montreal, Quebec, Canada

FRANCA A. CORTONI, M.A., Queen's University, Kingston, Ontario, Canada

ANTHONY ECCLES, Ph.D., Forensic Behavior Service, Kingston, Ontario, Canada

KAREN FRANCE, Ph.D., Department of Psychology, University of Canterbury, Christchurch, New Zealand

ALISON STICKROD GRAY, M.S., Center for Prevention Services, Underhill Center, Vermont

GRANT T. HARRIS, Ph.D., Oakridge Mental Health Center, Penetanguishene, Ontario, Canada

SHARON HODKINSON, M.A., Forensic Behavior Service, Kingston, Ontario,
Canada

STEPHEN M. HUDSON, Ph.D., Department of Psychology, University of Canterbury, Christchurch, New Zealand

MEG S. KAPLAN, Ph.D., Department of Sexual Behavior Clinic, New York
State Psychiatric Institute, New York, New York

RAYMOND A. KNIGHT, Ph.D., Department of Psychology, Brandeis University, Waltham, Massachusetts

MARY P. KOSS, Ph.D., Department of Family and Community Medicine,
University of Arizona Medical School, Tuscon, Arizona

LYNN O. LIGHTFOOT, Ph.D., Forensic Behavior Service, Kingston, Ontario,
Canada

WILLIAM L. MARSHALL, Ph.D., Department of Psychology, Queen's University, Kingston, Ontario, Canada

CANDICE A. OSBORN, M.A., Behavioral Medical Institute, Atlanta, Georgia

WILLIAM D. PITHERS, Ph.D., Vermont Center for Prevention and Treatment
of Sexual Abuse, Waterbury, Vermont

ROBERT PRENTKY, Ph.D., Massachusetts Treatment Center, Bridgewater,
Massachusetts

VERNON QUINSEY, Ph.D., Department of Psychology, Queen's University,
Kingston, Ontario, Canada

KELLY S. REID, M.A., Department of Psychology, Queen's University, Kingston, Ontario, Canada

MARNIE E. RICE, Ph.D., Oakridge Mental Health Center, Penetanguishene,
Ontario, Canada

IRA SCHWARTZ, Ph.D., Center for Study of Youth Policy, School of Social
Work, University of Michigan, Ann Arbor, Michigan

MICHAEL C. SETO, M.A., Department of Psychology, Queen's University, Kingston, Ontario, Canada

PETER SHERIDAN, M.A., Doctoral Candidate, York University, Toronto, Ontario, Canada

LORRIE SIPPOLA, M.A., Department of Psychology, Concordia University, Montreal, Quebec, Canada

LANA STERMAC, Ph.D., Department of Applied Psychology, The Ontario Institute for Studies in Education, Toronto, Ontario, Canada

DEBORAH A. TWIGG, M.S., Behavioral Medicine Institute, Atlanta, Georgia

JACQUELYN W. WHITE, Ph.D., Department of Psychology, University of North Carolina at Greensboro, Greensboro, North Carolina

Acknowledgments

The editors would like to thank Jim Breiling at NIMH for the support and encouragement he has provided for this project.

We wish to express our appreciation to everyone at The Guilford Press for the professional and businesslike way in which they have handled the publication of this book. Special thanks to Seymour Weingarten, Editor-in-Chief, for his sage advice and for his enthusiasm for the project from the beginning, and to Gerald Feldman and Jodi Creditor for seeing to the details of production.

We are deeply indebted to Jennifer DeTombe who served so capably as an "administrative assistant" to us during the period in which chapters were being solicited, written, submitted, edited, returned to authors, revised and finalized. She kept track of all the various drafts of chapters, the numerous figures and tables, and kept them all straight and in order.

As editors, we want to express our sincere thanks to the authors who contributed chapters to the book. Mostly, we want to thank them for the high quality of the chapters, but we also want to express our appreciation for their patience with our editing and with the inevitable delays in production.

Finally, we wish to acknowledge the financial support we received while we worked on this project. Thanks to the Correctional Services of Canada and the Ontario Ministry of Corrections for their financial support during this period.

HOWARD E. BARBAREE
WILLIAM L. MARSHALL
STEPHEN M. HUDSON

Preface

The impetus for this book was given us by Jim Breiling. Jim is a psychologist with the Violence and Traumatic Stress Branch of the U.S. National Institute of Mental Health. One of us (H. B.) had the privilege of spending part of a sabbatical leave with Jim in Rockville in the spring of 1988. As part of his duties with the Institute, Jim was responsible for overseeing research projects funded by NIMH, and for encouraging and facilitating research which was potentially fundable. Jim has a long standing interest in the assessment and treatment of the sex offender, and his interest, enthusiasm, and advice have been appreciated over the years by many of us in the area.

That spring, he frequently expressed his unhappiness with the research on the juvenile sex offender, mainly in terms of the lack of such research, but also in terms of the quality of the research which had been reported. Specifically, with respect to his duties at NIMH, Jim felt that the area was so badly underdeveloped that hopeful researchers submitting proposals were disadvantaged by the lack of knowledge and background information. The vast majority of these proposals failed to gain funding, thereby ensuring that the needed research would not be done. The well known "Catch 22" was in effect. Jim encouraged us to organize the writing of this book as a way of providing future researchers with a thorough and critical description of the current research literature and a guided tour of the areas of investigation that we thought would be most important and fruitful.

Of course, there are a small number of academics, clinicians, and researchers who have made the juvenile sex offender their topic of research and clinical work. We tried to include as many as possible as contributors to this book. In spite of their valiant efforts over many years, the lack of quality research in this area has remained.

Besides this small group, however, there are a great many individuals who have a potential interest in the area. The juvenile sex offender as a research topic is an intersection between two other more mature and developed areas, namely: (1) sexual deviation in the adult offender, and (2) disordered or troubled youth and families. As a consequence, there are at least two large, broadly defined but distinct groups of academics and professionals who come in frequent contact with the juvenile sex offender and who have an interest in the research on this topic. The first group includes those of us who have been primarily interested in the adult sexual offender. We will refer to these professionals as coming from a "sexual deviance" perspective. The other group will be those whose primary interest is in children, the adolescent, or the family, and who come into contact with the juvenile sexual offender because these offenders are found among the boys and young men they assess or treat. We will refer to these professionals as coming from a "child and family" perspective.

These two distinct groups have much to learn from one another. For example, it is clear that the juvenile sex offender is not simply a smaller or younger adult sex offender, and he should not be treated as such. The professional who has experience in working with the adult sex offender will be most comfortable treating the juvenile using the same strategies and methods that have worked for them with the adult. In some instances these methods may be exactly the right things to use. In other instances, they may be a very bad choice. By the same token, professionals who work with troubled youth but who have no experience with deviant sexuality may be most comfortable dealing with the young sexual offender as if he were simply a conduct disordered or emotionally disturbed youngster expressing his disorder through his sexuality. For some of these boys, this may be entirely appropriate, and for others, it may not.

We, as editors, have approached the organization of this book from our perspective, the "deviant sexuality" perspective. No doubt the book will reflect that perspective, and we make no apologies for it. Even so, we have tried to include—wherever possible and appropriate—contributors and topics from the "child and family" perspective.

In the past two decades, there has been a veritable explosion in interest in sexual assault, prompted in no small part by the women's movement. The increased public awareness of sexual assault and its harmful effects on victims has led to changes in the law; the availability of services for victims, including sexual assault crisis centres, and treatment programs for offenders, both adult and juvenile. This increased interest in sexual assault has been reflected in a large volume of published research and theory on sexual assault in both the academic and the more popular media. Several books have been published, including numerous edited volumes, presenting a broad and comprehensive perspective on the characteristics of the sex offender, theories concerning the nature of sexual assault, and descriptions of programs of clinical treatment and assessment. But this focus has been almost exclusively on the adult offender. In contrast, little attention has been paid to the juvenile or adolescent offender, either as a subject of study in his own right, or in an effort to understand the developmental processes which lead to sexually assaultive behavior in the adult. As far as we know, our book is the only book of its kind, providing, we hope, a comprehensive and detailed examination of the juvenile sex offender and the development of sexually assaultive behavior.

The chapters fall into four main subject areas. Chapters 1–3 focus on a definition of terms and concepts, and an outline of the research, professional, and legal issues facing the professional dealing with the juvenile sex offender. Chapter 3 proposes salient historical, personality, and behavioral characteristics which may differentiate various important subgroupings of these offenders.

Chapters 4–8 take a developmental approach to the juvenile sex offender, examining the development of sexuality in the normal teenager, the development of deviant sexuality in adolescence and its continuation in adulthood, the development of deviant sexual arousal and preferences, and the developmental processes involving social bonds and influences in the development of deviant sexuality.

Chapters 9–12 attempt to characterize the juvenile sex offender in more detail by examining factors that are perhaps causally related to juvenile sexual assault, or features of the offender that may accompany sexual aggression and complicate the assessment and treatment of the offender. Chapter 9 examines the social influences arising from dating in a society which condones and supports male sexual dominance and aggression in heterosexual relationships. The remaining chapters in this section examine the role of substance abuse, impulsiveness or conduct disorders, and developmental disabilities in sexual assault by juveniles.

Finally, Chapters 13–16 examine the ways that society might respond to prevent or control the occurrence of sexual assault by juveniles. Chapter 13 examines a comprehensive approach to treatment of the juvenile offender in the context of the criminal justice and mental health systems. The remaining chapters examine cognitive-behavioral interventions, pharmacological approaches to treatment, and relapse prevention and supervision.

It is our hope that this book will provide an impetus to further research and encouragement to clinicians and researchers who are determined to follow their interest in and commitment to the juvenile sexual offender.

HOWARD E. BARBAREE
WILLIAM L. MARSHALL
STEPHEN M. HUDSON

Contents

    Normative Sexuality from a
    Developmental Perspective   84
    William M. Bukowski, Lorrie Sippola, and
    William Brender

    Sexuality, Synthesis, and Development: What is
        Sexual Development?   **85**
    Sexuality in Childhood   **88**
    Sexuality in Adolescence: What Changes?   **92**
    Summary and Conclusion   **99**
    Acknowledgment   **100**
    References   **100**

5   **Sexual Assault through the Life Span:**
    Adult Offenders with Juvenile Histories   104
    Gene G. Abel, Candice A. Osborn, and
    Deborah A. Twigg

    Sexual Development   **105**
    Etiology of Sexual Deviance   **105**
    Do Some Adolescents Have Paraphilias?   **106**
    The Age of Onset of Paraphilias   **107**
    Paraphiliacs Who Were Adolescents When
        Evaluated   **109**
    Adult Paraphiliacs Reporting the Onset of Paraphilic
        Interest Prior to Age 18   **112**
    Summary and Conclusion   **114**
    References   **116**

6   **Pavlovian Conditioning Processes in Adolescent**
    Sex Offenders   118
    William L. Marshall and Anthony Eccles

    The Nature of Conditioning Theories   **119**
    Evidence for Conditioning   **122**
    A Multifaceted Theory of Adolescent Sex
        Offending   **131**
    Conclusion   **136**
    References   **137**

CHAPTER 1

Sexual Assault in Society: The Role of the Juvenile Offender

Howard E. Barbaree
Stephen M. Hudson
Michael C. Seto

This chapter is intended to place juvenile sex offenders in a context, in terms of their relation to the problem of sexual assault in our society, their relation to adult offenders, and their place in our society's attempt to prevent sexual assault.

Sexual assault is now recognized as one of the more severe problems in modern Western society, ranking with nonsexual crime, poverty, environmental damage and substance abuse as a societal ill. The increasing concern over sexual assault has been both reflected and enhanced by the international media coverage of recent prosecutions of William Kennedy Smith and Mike Tyson for rape. Feminist authors have raised our consciousness on this issue, and their concern for victims has resulted in the proliferation of sexual assault crisis centers in almost all urban centers. As well, society's newly developed determination to prevent sexual assault has resulted in the development of numerous treatment services for the sexual offender in the communities and correctional institutions of North America. Scientific research into the causes of sexual assault, attempts to provide effective clinical interventions, and innovative developments in legal and criminal justice approaches to the problem

1

have led to the publication of hundreds of journal articles and book chapters, though the area of inquiry is only in its infancy. While some observers may complain that society's concern is still not sufficient, and that the funding available for treatment services is still not adequate, there is a remarkable contrast between today's awareness and concern, on the one hand, and society's denial and ignorance of a single decade ago, on the other.

The severity of the problem of sexual assault is the result of the number of individuals who are victimized and the degree of harm they suffer by their victimization. Koss, Gidycz, and Wisniewski (1987) administered the Sexual Experiences Survey to a national sample of 6,159 women and men enrolled in 32 institutions representative of the diversity of higher education settings across the United States. The Sexual Experiences Survey is a ten-item instrument reflecting various degrees of sexual aggression and violence. Their sampling procedures allowed the authors to generalize their findings to postsecondary students, a group that represents 26% of all persons aged 18–24 in the United States. Therefore, the survey allowed for the determination of the prevalence of sexual aggression in a subgroup of the male and female population of young adults, and the incidence of sexual aggression among these individuals during the previous year.

Over half of the women surveyed reported some form of sexual victimization since age 14. The percentage of women who reported being raped was 15.4%, and 12.1% had experienced an attempted rape. Over one quarter of the men reported having been involved in some form of sexual aggression, with 4.4% reporting that they had raped, and an additional 3.3% reported that they had attempted rape. The incidence of rape reported for the previous 12-month period was 353 rapes involving 207 victims in a total population of 3,187 women. Gavey (1991) has reported the results of a study using the same instrument showing almost identical prevalence rates for a New Zealand undergraduate population.

Finkelhor, Hotaling, Lewis, and Smith (1989) surveyed 1,145 male and 1,481 female adults concerning their histories of childhood sexual abuse. Twenty-seven percent of women and 16% of men reported childhood sexual abuse. On average, the abuse occurred at age 10 for both males and females. Boys were more often abused by older men or boys whom they did not know, whereas girls were more often abused by male family members or friends of the family.

The effects of sexual victimization are severe, numerous, and long-lasting (Browne & Finkelhor, 1986; Roth & Lebowitz, 1988; Cohen & Roth, 1987) and seem to be similar whether the victim is male or female (Finkelhor, 1990). Browne and Finkelhor (1986) distinguish between the initial effects and the long-term effects of sexual victimization. The initial effects of child sexual abuse include emotional disturbance including feelings of anxiety and fear (DeFrancis, 1969; Anderson, Bach, & Griffith, 1981); the physical symptoms of anxiety and fear, such as sleep and eating disturbances (Peters, 1976); anger and hostility (Tufts, 1984, cited in Browne & Finkelhor, 1986); inappropriate sexual behavior including open masturbation, excessive sexual curiosity, and frequent exposure of genitals (Tufts, 1984); and behavioral and social problems including truancy, running away from home, and early marriage (Herman, 1981).

The long-term effects of child sexual abuse include symptoms of depression (Bagley & Ramsay, 1985; Briere & Runtz, 1989; Sedney & Brooks, 1984), anxiety and tension (Bagley & Ramsay, 1985; Briere, 1984; Sedney & Brooks, 1984), and lowered self-esteem and negative self-concept (Bagley & Ramsay, 1985; Courtois, 1979; Herman, 1981). Some of the more serious and long-lasting effects of sexual victimization include disturbances of social interaction and affiliation. As adults, women who were abused as children report problems in their relations with others, continuing problems with their parents, and difficulties in fulfilling their roles as parents (Browne & Finkelhor, 1986; DeYoung, 1982; Meiselman, 1978; Herman, 1981). Victims of sexual assault have serious problems in trusting others and in the development of intimate relationships (Briere, 1984; Courtois, 1979; Meiselman, 1978). As well, victims of sexual abuse seem to be more vulnerable to later revictimization (Fromuth, 1983).

As one would expect, victims report great difficulties in sexual adjustment (Meiselman, 1978; Langmade, 1983; Briere, 1984). Victims of child sexual abuse show an increased rate of sexual behavior as adults (Courtois, 1979; DeYoung, 1982; Herman, 1981), a behavioral effect often described by them as promiscuity (Browne & Finkelhor, 1986), although this effect may be due to the victims' being more likely to label their sexual activity as promiscuous (Fromuth, 1983). Victims of child sexual abuse may be more likely to enter into prostitution (James & Meyerding, 1977), and they are more likely to develop substance abuse problems (Briere, 1984).

As we come to more fully appreciate the prevalence of sexual assault and its victims, and as we understand more completely the effects of victimization, it becomes apparent how sexual assault has important impacts on our society. It may go without saying that prevention of sexual assault will depend on the extent to which we can stop men from committing these crimes. Therefore, as a first step in prevention, we should examine what we know about the men who commit sexual assaults and the factors that motivate their behavior.

MEN WHO COMMIT SEXUAL CRIMES

In this discussion, we will concentrate on issues relating to the more dangerous sex offender. These include men who have raped or sexually assaulted adult women, and men who have molested or sexually assaulted children. We will not consider men who have committed less intrusive offenses or who engage in nuisance sexual deviations, such as exhibitionism, frotteurism, voyeurism, or making obscene telephone calls, unless these are adjunct behaviors with the more serious assaults.

In this chapter, we define rapists as men who have committed sexual assaults against women above the age of consent. These men are most often in their teens, their 20s, or their early 30s. They usually have a varied criminal background including such crimes as break and enter, theft, and physical assault, and they usually begin their criminal careers at an early age (Amir, 1971; Christie, Marshall, & Lanthier, 1979; Cohen, Garafalo, Boucher, & Seghorn, 1971; Gebhard, Gagnon, Pomeroy & Christenson, 1965).

In this chapter, we define child molesters as men who have been convicted of a sexual assault against a child. The upper age of the "child" category of victim varies across jurisdictions and research studies, depending on the legal age of consent. Also, the definition of a child molester usually requires that the offender is 5 years older than the victim. Among incarcerated sex offenders, child molesters are more likely to be older than rapists. They do not show the same diversity of nonsexual offenses in their criminal history, compared with rapists, and they are not likely to have begun their criminal career as early as the rapists (Baxter, Marshall, Barbaree, Davidson, & Malcolm, 1984). Beyond these generalizations, this group of men is heterogeneous in many respects. For example, in terms of scholastic achievement (Bard et al., 1987) and intelligence (Marshall, Barbaree, & Christophe, 1986), the distribution of scores of child molesters has a greater variance than that of rapists due primarily to the existence of a large group of individuals at the lower end of each scale. Indeed, this low IQ subgroup among the child molesters requires special consideration in the planning of treatment and in the assessment of dangerousness (Barbaree & Marshall, 1988, 1989; Marshall et al., 1986).

Child molesters have been categorized according to the nature of their offense. It is usual to distinguish between incest offenders who have offended against their own children (primarily their own daughters and stepdaughters), and nonfamilial child molesters, who molest children with whom they have no familial or legal relationship. Child molestation by stepfathers is most often included in the incest category, as is the molestation perpetrated by a common-law husband of the victim's mother. Nonfamilial child molesters have been subdivided according to the gender of their victims, and it has become common to refer to these subgroups as heterosexual and homosexual child molesters, but this may be a misnomer. We have found that classifying men who molest boys according to their relative laboratory arousal to adult male and female stimuli results in heterosexuals outnumbering homosexuals by a ratio of 2 to 1 (Marshall, Barbaree & Butt, 1988).

There have been a number of attempts to classify sex offenders further according to the behavioral topography of the offense and the inferred motivation of the offensive behavior. Notable among these recent efforts is the work of Knight and Prentky and their associates at the Massachusetts Treatment Center (Knight & Prentky, 1990). These authors have devised two separate taxonomies: one for child molesters and one for rapists. These taxonomies are complex, multifactorial arrangements of dichotomous and multilevel variables that represent salient features of the offender groups in question. In the child molester taxonomy, Knight and Prentky (1990) classify offenders on two separate axes. Axis I classifies offenders using two independent dichotomous decisions, yielding four types, as in a 2 × 2 contingency table. In the first decision, offenders are classified as either high or low in fixation on children. Highly fixated subjects are those whose thoughts and social interactions focus primarily on children. These men would be referred to as pedophiles in the typology from the third revised edition of the *Diagnostic and Statistical Manual of Mental Disorders* (DSM-III-R) (American Psychiatric Association, 1987). Offenders low in fixation do not show the same focus on children. In the second decision, social competence is judged as high or low, depending on the offender's success in employment, adult relationships, and social responsibilities.

Axis II classifies offenders according to the nature of their contact with children using a series of independent dichotomous decisions, yielding six separate types. In the first decision, the offender is classified according to the amount of contact he has with children. Offenders who have a great deal of contact are further subdivided according to the meaning of the contact: interpersonal or narcissistic. Interpersonal contact signifies contact with children in a broad range of activities, not simply sexual interactions, and that the sexual interactions are not primarily directed toward orgasm. Narcissistic contact is primarily sexual and directed toward orgasm. Offenders who do not have a great deal of contact with children are further subdivided into four subtypes, based on two independent dichotomous decisions. The first distinguishes men who have caused a high degree of physical injury to victims from those who have not. The second distinguishes men who have sadistic fantasies or exhibit sadistic behaviors from those who do not.

In the rapist taxonomy, Knight and Prentky (1990) first classify men according to four primary motivations for raping, and according to these motivations rapists are either opportunistic, pervasively angry, sexually motivated, or vindictive. For the opportunistic rapist, the offense results from poor impulse control, and the sexual offense is only one of many instances of unsocialized behaviors. The offense does not involve anger, nor any more violence than is required to counter resistance on the part of the victim, but the offenders are indifferent to the harm they do their victims. The pervasively angry rapist often inflicts serious victim injury, resulting in death in the extreme cases. For these men, anger is generalized and the targets of their anger are not restricted to women, but the anger and violence are independent of their sexual arousal and motivation. The sexually motivated rapists are characterized by predominant sexual fantasies and preoccupations and are subdivided into sadists and non-sadists. For the sadist, the sexual and aggressive motivations are not only undifferentiated; they are mutually facilitating or synergistic, with anger increasing sexual arousal, and sexual arousal increasing anger and hostility. For these men, violence is an important component of their sexual fantasies. For the nonsadist, nonconsenting sex is an outlet for sexual gratification, but they do not use violence to accomplish the act. Of all the rapist subtypes, this group is regarded as the least aggressive in both sexual and nonsexual contexts. Finally, the vindictive rapists are men whose anger is focused exclusively on women. Their assaults are characterized by verbal abuse and physical violence, usually result in victim harm, and often include the additional elements of degradation and humiliation. Knight and Prentky (1990) further subdivide the opportunistic, sexual nonsadistic, and vindictive rapists into two subgroups according to levels of social competence, defined as it was for the child molesters, in terms of success in employment, adult relationships, and social responsibilities. It is hoped that this approach to classification will greatly increase our ability to predict both response to treatment and recidivism among these men (Knight, Rosenberg, & Schneider, 1985).

Sexual murderers are very rarely seen in treatment programs for sex offenders. Although these offenses attract a great deal of media and public attention (Quinsey, 1984), they are extremely rare (Swigert, Farrell, & Yoels, 1976). Among a sample of rapists and child molesters, the amount of force used in the commission of offenses varied from subterfuge and verbal threats to severe physical assault (Christie et al., 1979; Marshall & Christie, 1981). In the extreme, the assaults may result in the death of the victims and in this regard, sexual murder may be seen as an extension of the processes and dimensions relevant to less severe sexual assaults. Some writers, however, have regarded sexual murder as a category apart from other sexual assaults (Quinsey, 1984); these offenses might be better understood when factors relating to hostility and aggression are given greater consideration (Megargee, 1984), although in at least some cases the murder might be aimed at silencing the victim. Unfortunately, the scientific literature on sexual murderers is restricted to clinical impressions and psychoanalytic case histories (Brittain, 1970; Howell, 1972; Revitch, 1965; Thornton & Pray, 1975; Williams, 1964), and the bulk of descriptions of the treatment of sex offenders do not differentiate murderers from others.

Alcohol intoxication is frequently implicated in the commission of sexual offenses. On the basis of rapist's and victim's self-report, it is estimated that between 30% and 80% of rapists are intoxicated at the time of their offense (Christie et al., 1979; Gebhard et al., 1965; Johnson, Gibson, & Linden, 1978; Scully & Marolla, 1984; Wormith, 1983); between 33% (Groth, 1979) and 77% (Wormith, 1983) of child molesters report having been intoxicated at the time of the offense. However, it is suspected that offenders' self-report of intoxication is often exaggerated in an attempt to reduce their culpability in the offense (Quinsey, 1984).

As could be expected, the psychological difficulties experienced by sex offenders are not restricted to the direction of their sexual motives. In a study of incarcerated sex offenders, Christie et al. (1979) found that 57% of child molesters and 44% of rapists had received psychiatric attention for other problems such as anxiety, depression, and psychotic episodes. The psychiatric disturbance was described as being severe "at one time or another" in the case of 26% of the child molesters and 32% of the rapists. It is not known whether these difficulties were present at the time of the offense, although no doubt these difficulties were brought on, at least in part, by the stress of institutional life as experienced by sex offenders. Similarly, in a study of 300 incarcerated sex offenders, a sample that included less dangerous offenders than we are considering here, Brancale, Ellis, and Doorbar (1952) found that only 14% were diagnosed as being psychologically "normal." Almost 65% were found to be neurotic, 8% borderline psychotic, 2% frankly psychotic, 5% organically brain damaged, 3% psychopathic, and 4% mentally deficient.

While it is not known what statistics would result if modern diagnostic criteria (e.g., DSM-III-R; APA, 1987) were to be systematically applied to the population, some educated guesses are possible from our own experiences, and from observations reported by other researchers. It is quite clear that apart from the paraphilias, serious mental disorders on Axis I are infrequently observed in sex offenders. Abel, Mittleman, and Becker (1985) report that serious diagnosable mental disorders are found in less than 25% of sex offenders seen in an outpatient treatment setting. Laws (1981, cited in Knopp, 1984) reports that no more than 10% of incarcerated offenders exhibit serious mental disorders. The DSM-III-R describes the essential feature of the paraphilias as "recurrent intense sexual urges and sexually arousing fantasies generally involving either (1) nonhuman objects, (2) the suffering or humiliation of oneself or one's partner (not merely simulated), or (3) children or other nonconsenting persons." Therefore, obviously, a significant number of sex offenders would be diagnosed as "paraphiliacs." According to Abel et al. (1985), 100% of child molesters can be diagnosed as "pedophiles." Among rapists, diagnosis is not so straightforward. The only paraphilia presently listed in DSM-III-R that relates to rape is sexual sadism, but it would apply only to those rapists who appear to gain sexual pleasure from the suffering of their victim.

A larger proportion of sex offenders, however, would be diagnosed as having an antisocial personality disorder. For example, Abel et al. (1985) estimate that approximately 30% of rapists and 12% of child molesters can be so diagnosed. Using the Psychopathy Checklist (Hare, 1980, 1985) and a cutoff score of 29 (out of a possible 40), Serin, Malcolm, Khanna, and Barbaree (in press) have found 7.5% of child molesters and 12.2% of rapists in a prison setting were found to be "psychopaths." Higher proportions have been found in earlier studies (Prentky & Knight, 1986) of sex offenders in a psychiatric setting.

Some studies of incarcerated sex offenders using standardized psychological tests have found a high rate of clinical symptoms. For example, Hall, Maiuro, Vitaliano, and Proctor (1986) examined the Minnesota Multiphasic Personality Inventory (MMPI) profiles of 406 institutionalized child molesters and found elevated means on all of the clinical scales. Sixty-five percent of the sample had a T-score over 70 on the Psychopathic Deviate Scale. Similarly, approximately 50% of the sample had elevated scores on both the Schizophrenia Scale and the Depression Scale. Other reviews of the literature (Quinsey, 1984, 1986) point out that both child molesters and rapists show a peak on the Psychopathic Deviate Scale (Langevin, 1983; Panton, 1979) but that this pattern of results is not different from that obtained by other groups of incarcerated offenders.

In summary, sex offenders appear to show a significant degree of psychopathology, but the role of this disturbance in their offenses is not understood at present; psychological disturbance may have preceded and contributed to the offense, or it may have been a consequence of the arrest and incarceration. More likely, some level of psychological disturbance was a contributing factor in the offense of many incarcerated sex offenders, and this disturbance was exacerbated by the judicial process and the stresses of incarceration. However, it is also very clear that significant psychological disturbance is not a necessary condition for sexual aggression, since many offenders cannot be diagnosed with any mental disorder except, perhaps, "paraphilia."

Rapists and child molesters have a number of features in common. They are often the products of large families and live in a disturbed home environment, as indicated by high rates of family psychiatric history, criminal history, and substance abuse (Bard et al., 1987). Offenders report having been both sexually (Seghorn, Boucher, & Prentky, 1987) and nonsexually abused as children, and neglected (Bard et al., 1987). A small but significant proportion report having been the victim of some kind of sexual deviation in the childhood home, including sodomy or child pornography, or having grown up in a home where either promiscuity or unusual sexual practices occurred (Bard et al., 1987). The offender's own victimization in sexual abuse is often used to account for later offending. However, our estimates of the prevalence of this victimization is based on offenders' self-reports. These self-reports are self-serving in the sense that they seem to attenuate the offender's responsibility for their crimes. We should use caution in interpreting these reports unless independent corroboration of the offender's victimization is available.

Social psychologists (Koss & Dinero, 1988; Malamuth, 1986, 1988) have argued that clinical studies of sex offenders may bias our understanding of sexual assault because they include only a small subset of sex offenders, the detected cases. Using their prevalence data, and comparing these with the numbers of men who have been convicted of sexual crimes, they argue that the vast majority of sex offenders are unconvicted and therefore unidentified. It follows that, by studying only convicted cases, we may be biasing our understanding of sexual assault. To combat this bias, these authors have attempted to survey undetected cases using anonymous questionnaires. There have been no direct comparisons between detected and undetected cases. However, a comparison of the research on detected and undetected cases reveals a remarkable similarity in conclusions. In a recent special issue of the *Journal of Consulting and Clinical Psychology*, two articles focused on the factors that lead to rape. In one of these, Malamuth, Sockloskie, Koss, and Tonaka (1991) analyzed data from a large anonymous survey (Koss et al., 1987) and identified a number of salient features in a statistical model predictive of sexual aggression, including delinquency, sexual promiscuity, hostile masculinity, social isolation, and attitudes supportive of violence. In the model, the final common pathway to sexual aggression combined delinquent sexuality with hostile masculinity. In the second of these articles, Prentky and Knight (1991) described the factors or variables that differentiate the subtypes of convicted rapists in their rapist typology. These authors identified a number of salient factors that help to differentiate among rapist subgroups, including lifestyle impulsivity or antisocial personality, amount and meaning of aggression, social competence, and sexual fantasies. Considering these factors, we (Barbaree & Serin, 1993) have cast the Massachusetts Treatment Center typology into a two-dimensional table, with the two defining dimensions being the amount and meaning of aggression and criminal personality. It is remarkable that the factors found to be strongly related to sexual aggression from studies using anonymous questionnaire methodologies, and from those studies using a clinical methodology are so similar. It is true that there still may be important differences between detected and undetected cases. In the end we may learn much about sexual assault from these differences, but it is also true that the study of both detected and undetected cases may provide converging evidence on the issue of sexual assault.

When convicted, rapists and child molesters often face prison terms ranging from several months to several years, depending upon the jurisdiction, the number of previous offenses, and the severity of the current sexual assault. Mentally disordered sex-offender statutes (Weiner, 1985) in the United States, and dangerous offender legislation in Canada, have provided for indefinite sentences for many sex offenders. The vast majority of sex offenders in most jurisdictions do not receive treatment, although some are treated in the prison setting or in a secure mental hospital. Less frequently, they are treated in a community-based setting while on probation or parole. Often, treatment is part of a release plan and precedes parole or release to the community. The offender's willingness to involve himself in treatment is typically a consequence of pressure brought to bear on him by the correctional or mental health system. Often, he feels added pressure from his family. To a man entering treatment, the outcome of treatment seems to have a bearing on his chances for parole or release. Similarly, when a man enters a community-based treatment setting with criminal charges pending, involvement in treatment may influence whether or not he will be sentenced to a jail term rather than probation, it may influence the length of a jail term, or in some cases treatment may lead to the avoidance of prosecution altogether.

JUVENILES WHO COMMIT SEXUAL CRIMES

Over the past 20 years, we have seen a surge of interest in the juvenile sex offender. A search of our large data base of published literature on sex offenders indicated that, prior to 1970, only 9 major papers were published on the adolescent offender. During the 1970s, only 10 additional papers were published. However, from 1981 to 1985, 28 papers were published, and during the 5 years just prior to the preparation of this book, over 60 papers were published. While interest in the sexually assaultive behavior of juveniles has a long history (Atcheson & Williams, 1954; Cook, 1934; Doshay, 1943; Waggoner & Boyd, 1941), our views on the significance of their behavior has undergone a marked change. Prior to the early 1980s, the predominant view of the sexual offenses committed by this age group was that they constituted nuisance value only, reflecting a "boys-will-be-boys" attitude and a discounted estimate of the severity of harm produced (e.g., Roberts, Abrams, & Finch, 1973). This view held sway despite early studies that suggested that these offenders posed a long-term risk (Mohr, Turner, & Jerry, 1964). Frequently, the sexually offensive behavior was not seen as assaultive; instead, these acts were seen as examples of experimentation and therefore as innocent. They were seen as being a byproduct of the normal aggressiveness of sexually maturing adolescents, or as a result of the marginal status of the adolescent male and the consequent restriction of his permitted sexual outlets (Finklehor, 1979; Gagnon, 1965; Maclay, 1960; Markey, 1950; Reiss, 1960; Roberts et al., 1973). Often, the sexual assaults committed by juveniles were not seen as problems in their own right. Instead, the sex offending was seen as reflecting a more general problem of antisocial behavior, such as juvenile delinquency, conduct disorder, substance abuse, or adjustment disorder. Underlying the misapprehension was a profound lack of knowledge concerning social and psychological aspects of sexual development in adolescence. An additional factor that encouraged the minimization of juvenile offenses was the greater likelihood, with a juvenile offender, that the victim was a family member (Becker, 1988; Knopp, 1982). All of these factors were exacerbated by the notion that these offenders rarely repeated their offenses (Chatz, 1972).

The tendency to minimize the sexual crimes of juveniles has been reduced substantially over the past decade, for several reasons. First, there has been increased awareness of the numbers of juvenile sex offenders. Ageton (1983) estimated that 2%–4% of juvenile males have reported committing sexually assaultive behavior. Second, a substantial proportion of all sexual offenses can be attributed to adolescents. The best available estimates suggest that approximately 20% of all rapes and between 30% and 50% of child molestations are perpetrated by adolescent males (Becker, Kaplan, Cunningham-Rathner, & Kavoussi, 1986; Brown, Flanagan, & McLeod, 1984; Deisher, Wenet, Paperny, Clark, & Fehrenbach, 1982; Groth, Longo, & McFadin, 1982). From 1986 arrest statistics, males under 19 years of age committed 18% of all violent crimes, 19% of forcible rapes, 18% of all other sexual offenses (excluding prostitution), and 14% of all aggravated assaults (Federal Bureau of Investigation, 1987). From a different perspective, Ageton's (1983) national probability study of 13- to 19-year-old male adolescents suggested the rate of sexual assault (victim contact crimes) was between 5 and 16 per 1,000. Knopp (1982) suggested that 450,000 sexual assaults were committed by juveniles in the United States in 1976. From yet another perspective, Abel et al., (1984) claimed that the average adolescent sex offender will, without treatment, go on to commit 380 sexual crimes during his lifetime. Finally, professionals working with adult sexual offenders have become increasingly aware of the proportions of their clients who began their deviant careers in adolescence (Abel et al., 1985; Becker, Kaplan, et al., 1986; Longo & Groth, 1983; Longo, & McFadin, 1981; McConaghy, Blaszczynski, Armstrong, & Kidson, 1989; Ryan, Lane, Davis, & Issac, 1987). It is estimated that approximately 50% of adult sex offenders report sexually deviant behavior in adolescence (Abel et al., 1985; Becker & Abel, 1985; Longo & Groth, 1983; Groth et al., 1982). If treatment is effective in reducing deviant behaviors among juvenile offenders, then treatment of the juvenile could go a long way toward reducing the impact of sexual assault in our society. The literature not only suggests a progression from less to more serious offending but also provides an appalling picture of the damage being perpetrated by these young men. The argument that treatment should be directed toward the juvenile offender is made more potent by the suggestion that early intervention might be more efficacious, as it has the potential to treat the problem in an individual before the behavior becomes more entrenched in adulthood (Green, 1987; Stenson & Anderson, 1987). In addition, despite the very limited success in predicting who will reoffend (Smith & Monastersky, 1986), juvenile sex offenders as a group manifest developmental adjustment problems and histories of traumatic adjustment to their own victimization experiences (Smets & Cebula, 1987), which make them a "high-risk group" independent of their offense histories.

The term *adolescence* is a developmental construct referring to the developmental stage that serves as a transition period between childhood and adulthood. In contrast, the term *juvenile* is a legal term referring, in most jurisdictions to individuals between the ages of 13 and 18. Juvenile status is a transition period with respect to the law. Children less than 13 years of age are not often held accountable for criminal offenses, whereas 16- to 19-year olds are seen as being more responsible, and may more often be treated as adults by the courts, thereby holding them fully accountable for criminal acts. The seriousness of the offense, considerations of community protection, the presence of aggression and premeditation, and the strength of the prosecution's case, all serve to increase the probability that an offense will be dealt with in adult court (National Adolescent Perpetrator Network, 1988).

In this chapter, data from all these groups—juveniles, adolescents, and children—will be considered. Defining what constitutes sexual abuse is less clear. The usual dimensions that apply to adult offenders, with respect to degree of intrusiveness (noncontact offenses such as exhibitionism through to forcible rape) and amount of coercion used, apply equally well to adolescent offenders. However, the traditional criterion of age difference (i.e., 5 years) between perpetrator and victim cannot be applied in a straightforward manner. Any age difference becomes more difficult to apply as the offender becomes younger, especially with the abuse-reactive child. For example, Johnson and Berry (1989) used a 2-year age difference in the admission criteria to their Support Program for Abuse Reactive Kids (SPARK) designed for 13-year-olds or younger, and yet they noted the older child was not necessarily the perpetrator. The use of age differences is a reflection of our lack of adequate knowledge as to what constitutes "normal" adolescent sexual behavior. In any event, with the juvenile offender, it seems more constructive to examine the behaviors involved, particularly in terms of the degree of coercion, than to rely on essentially arbitrary age-difference criteria.

Adolescent offenders seem to show all of the same variations of sexually abusive behavior as do older offenders. Fehrenbach, Smith, Monastersky, and Deisher (1986) examined 305 offenders 18 years of age or younger. Within the 279 male offenders the most common offense was fondling (59%), then rape (23%), exhibitionism (11%), and other noncontact offenses (7%). Wasserman and Kappel, (1985) examined the sexual behaviors in the offenses of 161 (149 male) under 19-year-old or younger offenders. Some form of penetration was involved in 59% of offenses, while 31% involved intercourse, 12% oral-genital contact, and 16% genital fondling; 12% were judged to be noncontact offenses. Intercourse becomes more common as the age of both offender and victim increases. When the victims were children who were younger than the adolescent offender, rape occurred in 21%–24% of instances compared to 67% of offenses involving same-age or older victims (Groth 1977; Wasserman & Kappel, 1985). Awad and Saunders's (1989) sample of 11- to 16-year-old child molesters had mainly fondled their victims, whereas Smith, Monastersky, and Deisher's (1987) older sample of 262 juvenile sex offenders (mean age = 15.3 years) had raped, or attempted to rape, in 77.5% of cases. Level of reported coercion varies as a function of who is doing the reporting and age of the victim. Victims report higher levels of coercion than offenders, and younger victims seem to be subject to less force (Davis & Leitenberg, 1987). Groth (1977) reported that 43% of offenses against a peer or older victim involved a weapon, whereas when the victim was a much younger child no weapons were involved. Both Wasserman and Kappel (1985) and Fehrenbach et al. (1986) found a low rate of weapon usage (4–8%), but in approximately half of their cases some form of threat was used. McDermott and Hindelang (1981) suggest that, in general, less violence is used by adolescent than by adult offenders. In the case of rape, a victim of an adolescent offender is one-third as likely to have had a weapon used against her and one-half as likely to be physically injured compared to a similar assault by an adult. Nevertheless, one-third of offenses perpetrated by adolescents result in physical injury (McDermott & Hindelang, 1981).

There is some debate as to what extent females are represented among juvenile sex offenders. An early study (Roberts, McBee, & Bettis, 1969) examined juvenile sex offenders (less than 16 years of age) and reported that 43% of their sample was female, compared to only 20% in a comparison group of non-sex-offender juveniles. However, more recent data suggest that while females account for 18% of all under 18-year-old arrests, they constitute only 7% of sex offenders (excluding prostitution) and only 2% of rapists (Brown et al., 1984). Early prejudicial attitudes regarding what was appropriate sexual behavior for males compared with females may complicate this issue. For example, in Markey's (1950) report on 25 male and 25 female juvenile offenders, the predominant offense for females was simply "having intercourse"; at least two of these female "sex delinquents" would be seen more recently to be the victims of an incestuous sexual assault. There have been no studies specifically comparing female and male offenders. Typically, survey studies (e.g., Fehrenbach et al., 1986) identify the proportion of females in the sample but then only discuss the predominantly male part of the sample. More recently, however, Fehrenbach and Monstersky (1988) exclusively examined female adolescent offenders. This report noted that, in contrast to adult female sex offenders who frequently offend in conjunction with a male cooffender, female adolescent offenders are more likely to perpetrate serious offenses on their own, typically against young female children (mean age 5.2 years) whom they are babysitting. Studies of adult female sex offenders note that none of their subjects reported being sexually abusive during adolescence (McCarty, 1986).

Groth et al., (1982) reported the modal age for first offense in 83 rapists as 16 years (range 9–47), whereas the 54 child molesters showed a bimodal distribution, peaking in early adolescence around 14 years of age, and again in the early 30s. Longo (1982) found 14.3 years was the mean age of first sexual assault among adult offenders. Lewis, Shankok, and Pincus (1979) found that both juvenile violent offenders and juvenile sex offenders had committed deviant acts by 6 years of age.

Among all of the offenses reported by the FBI that were committed by adolescents, 74% of the offenders were white; for sexual offenses this figure drops to 64%, and for forcible rape it decreases to 42% (Brown et al., 1984). In individual studies, race is rarely reported (e.g., Awad & Saunders, 1989; Awad, Saunders, & Levene, 1984; Fehrenbach et al., 1986; Lewis et al., 1979; Shoor, Speed, & Bartelt, 1966). In studies that report race as a demographic variable, between 33.0% and 55.2% of the subjects were black, 21–32% were Hispanic and 12–46% were white (Becker, Cunningham-Rathner, & Kaplan, 1986; Becker, Kaplan, et al., 1986; Van Ness, 1984; Vinogradov, Dishotsky, Doty, & Tinklenberg, 1988).

As we reported earlier for the adult sex offender, family instability, frequent violence, high rates of disorganization (Awad et al., 1984; Deisher et al., 1982; Fehrenbach et al., 1986; Lewis et al., 1979; Longo, 1982; Smith, 1988), and both sexual and physical abuse (Awad & Saunders, 1989; Becker, Kaplan, et al., 1986; Becker, Cunningham-Rathner, & Kaplan, 1986; Fehrenbach et al., 1986; Lewis et al., 1979; Longo, 1982; Robertson, 1990; Smith, 1988; Van Ness, 1984) have commonly been observed as prevalent in the histories of juvenile sex offenders. These factors are thought to play an important contributory role in both the development of their offending and the seriousness of their assaults (Smith, 1988). In a recent study, Blaske, Borduin, Hengeler, and Mann (1989) suggest that the family relations of both sex offenders and violent offenders are generally low in positive affect and correspondingly high in negative affect.

The distribution of juvenile sex offenders among the various social classes is unclear, most likely because of considerable variation in the source, composition, and age of the samples studied. Awad et al. (1984) compared a group of 24 juvenile sex offenders aged 11–16 years, all of whom had been adjudicated (41% rape or attempted rape), with 24 nonsexual delinquents. They found the juvenile sex offenders were more likely to come from the middle-class backgrounds. Similarly, Awad and Saunders (1989) found middle-class status overrepresented in their sample of 29 juvenile child molesters referred to a Canadian Family Court clinic. However Roberts et al., (1969) found juvenile sex offenders (less than 16 years of age) to be from significantly lower socioeconomic status backgrounds than other delinquents.

As has been the case with the literature on adult sex offenders, many investigators and clinicians have suggested that deficiencies in social competence may be causally linked to offending. However, the search for a set of unique deficits in social competencies that separate adult sex offenders from nonsexual offenders has not been remarkably successful (Segal & Marshall, 1985a, 1985b; Stermac & Quinsey, 1986). A lack of assertiveness in social interaction (Becker & Abel, 1985), deficiencies in intimacy skills (Groth, 1977; Marshall, 1989), and social isolation (Fehrenbach et al., 1986; Shoor et al.,

1966) have been suggested, and to some extent identified, in adolescent sex offenders. As yet there is little evidence that these are unique deficiencies compared to other adolescents, especially those who offend in nonsexual ways. Consistent with this later possibility, both Awad et al. (1984) and Lewis et al. (1979) found an equally high prevalence of psychiatric symptoms in both juvenile non–sex offenders and juvenile sex offenders. Similarly, academic performance is typically poorer than average in juvenile sex offenders, but in most studies this is not discriminably different from the case of other delinquents (Fehrenbach et al., 1986; Lewis et al., 1979; Tarter, Hegedus, Alterman, & Katz-Garris, 1983). A more recent study (Awad & Saunders, 1989) has found significantly greater social isolation and serious chronic learning problems in a sample of court-referred adolescent child molesters, compared to other male delinquents matched for age, socioeconomic status, and time of referral.

As mentioned earlier in this chapter, the presence of other forms of disordered conduct suggests to some that the index offense happens to be a sex crime and is simply one way of acting out (Davis & Leitenburg, 1987). This may well be true for the majority of young female sex offenders who, historically at least, have been prosecuted on morality grounds (e.g., see Markey, 1950). Moreover, in young men, it is not unusual to find high levels of coincidental behavior problems. The most common indicators of this disordered behavior are taken to be a history of delinquency, prior arrests for both sexual and nonsexual crimes, and psychiatric diagnoses such as conduct disorder and oppositional disorder. A history of delinquency is common in juvenile sex offenders (Saunders, Awad, & White, 1986). Among juvenile sex offenders, a prior nonsexual offense was found in 28–50% of cases (Becker, Cunningham-Rathner, & Kaplan, 1986; Becker, Kaplan, et al., 1986; Fehrenbach et al., 1986); a prior sexual offense in 46–90% of cases (Awad et al., 1984; Becker, Kaplan et al., 1986; Pierce & Pierce, 1987); aggressive acts and other antisocial behavior in 50–86% of cases (Awad & Saunders, 1989; Shoor et al., 1966; Van Ness, 1984); and arrests and incarceration in 33% of child molesters (Shoor et al., 1966) and 50% of adolescent incest offenders (Becker, Cunningham-Rathner, & Kaplan, 1986).

As in the case of the adult sex offender, a psychiatric history is frequently found in the juvenile sex offender. Psychiatric problems have been found in between 70–87% of juvenile offenders (Awad & Saunders, 1989; Awad et al., 1984; Lewis et al., 1979); prior psychiatric treatment in 33% of young offenders (Awad & Saunders, 1989); conduct disorder in 48% of young offenders, with rapists (75%) being more likely than child molesters (38%) to receive this diagnosis (Kavoussi, Kaplan, & Becker, 1988); and substance abuse in over 10% of these juveniles (Kavoussi et al., 1988). Similar to adult sex offenders, juvenile offenders have exhibited high rates of emotional problems (Deisher et al., 1982; Groth, 1977; Shoor et al., 1966; Van Ness, 1984). In addition,

Friedrich and Luecke's (1988) sexually abusing children (4–11 years old) not only generally met the criteria for DSM-III-R diagnosis of conduct or oppositional disorder, they also had academic and social competency deficits and histories involving long-standing parental neglect and abuse. In a recent well-designed study comparing matched groups of adolescent sex offenders, assaultive and nonviolent offenders, and nondelinquent youths, Blaske et al. (1989) found disturbed emotional functioning and disrupted peer relations among the sex offenders, who displayed greater anxiety and estrangement and less emotional bonding to peers than seen in other juveniles. This is of particular interest given Fehrenbach et al.'s (1986) finding that the severity of the crimes of these young sex offenders was a function of social isolation.

It may be obvious to say that juvenile sexual offenders display a disordered or dysfunctional sexuality. What is not obvious, however, is the nature of the sexual disorder or dysfunction. In adults, deviant sexual arousal (Abel, Blanchard, & Jackson, 1974; Freund, 1967) has been seen to be an important motivation for sexual assaults. However, in adolescents, few studies have been done and none have compared juvenile offenders with nonoffenders. One explanation of juvenile sex offenses, which again minimizes the seriousness of these behaviors, is that they represent misguided and inept attempts at sexual relations by inexperienced or poorly informed individuals. The existing data do not support this hypothesis, since between 59% and 86% of juvenile sex offenders report having previous, consensual intercourse (Becker, Cunningham-Rathner, & Kaplan, 1986; Groth, 1977; Longo, 1982). There seems to be no literature comparing the level of sexual knowledge and experience of adolescent offenders with nonoffenders. Many (19%–54%) adolescent sex offenders have experienced sexual abuse (Becker, Cunningham-Rathner, & Kaplan, 1986; Becker, Kaplan et al., 1986; Fehrenbach et al., 1986; Longo, 1982; Pierce & Pierce, 1987). Clinical experience suggests that even higher rates can be found in male adolescents who molest younger boys (Davis & Leitenberg, 1987); one sample of incarcerated homosexual pedophiles reported a 73% prevalence of sexually abusive experience as children (Robertson, 1990). Friedrich and Luecke (1988) studied a group of school-age children (4–11 years, mean = 7.3 years) who had behaved in a sexually abusive way (genital contact involving coercion) and found even more severe sex abuse in their histories than expected in a random sample of sexually abused children. In a similar study looking at 6- to 13-year-old perpetrators, Johnson (1988) found an inverse relationship between a history of sexually abusive experience and age, with over three-quarters of those under 6 years of age having been abused themselves.

In all likelihood, the population of juvenile sex offenders is every bit as heterogeneous as the population of adult sex offenders (Knight et al., 1985). Perhaps we will understand sexual aggression in the juvenile more fully when we have conducted the research required to develop meaningful typologies of offenders. As with the adult population, typologies may divide the large heterogeneous population of juvenile offenders into meaningful subgroups within which common factors and psychological processes contribute to the sexual aggression we observe.

THE VICTIMS OF THE JUVENILE SEX OFFENDER

Typically the victims of assaults by juvenile sex offenders are younger children. Fehrenbach et al. (1986) found that 62% of the victims of their sample of abusers were less than 12 years of age, with 44% less than 6. The victims of the female perpetrators in this sample were all less than 6 years old. In both Deisher et al. 's (1982) and Wasserman and Kappel's (1985) samples, 50–66% were less than 10, and only a quarter were older than 20 years of age. Incarcerated juvenile offenders, who are typically older than a nonincarcerated group (Groth, 1977; Longo, 1982; Van Ness, 1984), had older victims, but these victims were still usually younger than the offenders themselves. The only exception to this general rule seems to be where noncontact offenses such as exhibitionism and obscene telephone calls are involved; in these instances peers and adults were more frequent targets (Fehrenbach et al., 1986). In studies where adolescent child molesters are defined on the basis of being 4–5 years older than the victim, the majority of these victims are even younger than this age-defined discrepancy. Indeed, the victims are typically only 6–9 years of age, with male victims younger than female victims (Awad & Saunders, 1989; Becker, Cunningham-Rathner, & Kaplan, 1986; Pierce & Pierce, 1987).

The majority (69–84%) of the victims of sexual assaults by juveniles are female (Awad et al., 1984; Groth, 1977; Fehrenbach et al., 1986; Longo, 1982; Van Ness, 1984; Wasserman & Kappel, 1985), and this is especially true in noncontact offenses (Fehrenbach et al., 1986). However, as the age of the victim decreases, the victim is more likely to be male, since 45–63% of the child victims of adolescent offenders are male (Awad & Saunders, 1989; Shoor et al., 1966; Van Ness, 1984).

Most of the victims of juveniles are known to the offender and are usually friends or relatives. Relatives constitute between 6% and 40% of victims (Groth, 1977; Fehrenbach et al., 1986; Wasserman & Kappel, 1985), while friends were victims in 41–51% of cases reported (Groth, 1977; Fehrenbach et al., 1986). Strangers were victims in 17%–48% of cases (Groth, 1977; Fehrenbach et al., 1986; Van Ness, 1984). There is an increasing tendency toward victimizing strangers in rape compared with child molestation. For example, in a sample of adolescent rapists, Vinogradov et al., (1988) found that only one-third knew their victims before the rape took place. In contrast, almost all of Awad and Saunders's (1989) child molesters knew their victims, either as relatives, children of friends of the parents, or children the offenders had been babysitting.

CONCLUSION

Sexual assault is an important and serious problem in society today because of the numbers of victims, the frequency of assaults, and the consequences of victimization in the short and long term. The most direct way of preventing sexual assault is to identify, control, and treat offenders who commit such offenses. Both adult and juvenile sex offenders share many of the same characteristics. Further research is required, focusing specifically on the juvenile, to elucidate the differences between juvenile and adult offenders.

REFERENCES

Abel, G. G., Becker, J. V., Cunningham-Rathner, J., Rouleau, J., Kaplan, M., & Reich, J. (1984). *Treatment manual: The treatment of child molesters.* Tuscaloosa, AL: Emory University Clinic, Department of Psychiatry.

Abel, G. G., Blanchard, E. B., & Jackson, M. (1974). The role of fantasy in the treatment of sexual deviation. *Archives of General Psychiatry, 30,* 467–475.

Abel, G. G., Mittleman, M. S., & Becker, J. V. (1985). Sex offenders: Results of assessment and recommendations for treatment. In M. H. Ben-Aron, S. J. Hucker, & C. D. Webster (Eds.), *Clinical criminology: The assessment and treatment of criminal behavior* (pp. 207–220). Toronto: M & M Graphics.

Ageton, S. (1983). *Sexual assault among adolescents.* Lexington, MA: Lexington Books.

American Psychiatric Association. (1987). *Diagnostic and statistical manual of mental disorders* (3rd ed., rev.). Washington, DC: Author.

Amir, M. (1971). *Patterns of forcible rape.* Chicago: University of Chicago Press.

Anderson, S. C., Bach, C. M., & Griffith, S. (1981, April). *Psychosocial sequelae in intrafamilial victims of sexual assault and abuse.* Paper presented at the Third International Conference on Child Abuse and Neglect, Amsterdam, The Netherlands.

Atcheson, J. D., & Williams, D. C. (1954). A study of juvenile sex offenders. *American Journal of Psychiatry, 111,* 366–370.

Awad, G. A., & Saunders, E. (1989). Adolescent child molesters: Clinical observations. *Child Psychiatry and Human Development, 19,* 195–206.

Awad, G. A., Saunders, E., & Levene, J. (1984). A clinical study of male adolescent sex offenders. *International Journal of Offender Therapy and Comparative Criminology, 28,* 105–116.

Bagley, C., & Ramsay, R. (1985). Psychosocial correlates of suicidal behaviors in an urban population. *Crisis, 6,* 63–77.

Barbaree, H. E., & Marshall, W. L. (1988). Deviant sexual arousal, offense history, and demographic variables as predictors of reoffense among child molesters. *Behavioral Sciences and the Law, 6,* 267–280.

Barbaree, H. E., & Marshall, W. L. (1989). Erectile responses among heterosexual child molesters, father–daughter incest offenders, and matched non-offenders: Five distinct age preference profiles. *Canadian Journal of Behavioral Science, 21,* 70–82.

Barbaree, H. E., & Serin, R. C. (1993). Role of male sexual arousal during rape in various rapist subtypes. In G. C. Nagayama Hall, R. Hirschman, J. R. Graham, & M. S. Zaragoza (Eds.), *Sexual aggression: Issues in etiology, assessment, and treatment.* Washington, D.C.: Taylor and Francis.

Bard, L. A., Carter, D. L., Cerce, D. D., Knight, R. A., Rosenberg, R., & Schneider, B. (1987). A descriptive study of rapists and child molesters: Developmental, clinical, and criminal characteristics. *Behavioral Sciences and the Law, 5,* 203–220.

Baxter, D. J., Marshall, W. L., Barbaree, H. E., Davidson, P. R., & Malcolm, P. B. (1984). Deviant sexual behavior: Differentiating sex offenders by criminal and personal history, psychometric measures, and sexual response. *Criminal Justice and Behavior, 11,* 477–501.

Becker, J. V. (1988). Adolescent sex offenders. *Behavior Therapist, 11,* 185–187.

Becker, J. V., & Abel, G. G. (1985). Methodological and ethical issues in evaluating and treating adolescent sexual offenders. In E. M. Otey & G. D. Ryan (Eds.), *Adolescent sex offenders: Issues in research and treatment* (pp. 109–129). Rockville, MD: Department of Health and Human Services.

Becker, J. V., Cunningham-Rathner, J., & Kaplan, M. S. (1986). Adolescent sexual offenders: Demographics, criminal and sexual histories, and recommendations for reducing future offenses. Special Issue: The prediction and control of violent behavior: II. *Journal of Interpersonal Violence, 1,* 431–445.

Becker, J. V., Kaplan, M. S., Cunningham-Rathner, J., & Kavoussi, R. J. (1986). Characteristics of adolescent incest sexual perpetrators: Preliminary findings. *Journal of Family Violence, 1,* 85–97.

Blaske, D. M., Borduin, C. M., Hengeler, S. W., & Mann, B. J. (1989). Individual, family, and peer characteristics of adolescent sex offenders and assaultive offenders. *Developmental Psychology, 25,* 846–855.

Brancale, R., Ellis, A., & Doorbar, R. R. (1952). Psychiatric and psychological investigations of convicted sex offenders: A summary report. *American Journal of Psychiatry, 109,* 17–19.

Briere, J. (1984, April). *The effects of childhood sexual abuse on later psychological functioning: Defining a "post-sexual-abuse syndrome."* Paper presented at the Third National Conference on Sexual Victimization of Children, Washington, DC.

Briere, J., & Runtz, M. (1989). University males' sexual interest in children: Predicting potential indices of "pedophilia" in a nonforensic sample. *Child Abuse and Neglect, 13,* 65–75.

Brittain, R. P. (1970). The sadistic murderer. *Medicine, Science, and the Law, 10,* 198–207.

Brown, E. J., Flanagan, T. J., & McLeod, M. (Eds.). (1984). *Sourcebook of criminal justice statistics—1983.* Washington, DC: Bureau of Justice Statistics.

Browne, A., & Finkelhor, D. (1986). The impact of child sexual abuse: A review of the research. *Psychological Bulletin, 99,* 66–77.

Chatz, T. L. (1972). Recognizing and treating dangerous sexual offenders. *International Journal of Offender Therapy and Comparative Criminology, 16,* 109–115.

Christie, M. M., Marshall, W. L., & Lanthier, R. D. (1979). A descriptive study of incarcerated rapists and pedophiles. *Report to the Solicitor General of Canada.*

Cohen, L. J., & Roth, S. (1987). The psychological aftermath of rape: Long-term effects and individual differences in recovery. *Journal of Social and Clinical Psychology*, 5, 525–534.

Cohen, M. L., Garafalo, R. F., Boucher, R. J., & Seghorn, T. K. (1971). The psychology of rapists. *Seminars in Psychiatry, 3*, 307–327.

Cook, E. B. (1934). Cultural marginality in sexual delinquency. *American Journal of Sociology, 39*, 493–500.

Courtois, C. A. (1979). The incest experience and its aftermath. *Victimology: An International Journal, 4*, 337–347.

Davis, G. E., & Leitenberg, H. (1987). Adolescent sex offenders. *Psychological Bulletin, 101*, 417–427.

DeFrancis, V. (1969). *Protecting the child victim of sex crimes committed by adults*. Denver, CO: American Humane Association.

Deisher, R. W., Wenet, G. A., Paperny, D. M., Clark, T. F., & Fehrenbach, P. A. (1982). Adolescent sexual offense behavior: The role of the physician. *Journal of Adolescent Health Care, 2*, 279–286.

DeYoung, M. (1982). *The sexual victimization of children*. Jefferson, NC: McFarland.

Doshay, L. (1943). *The boy sex offender and his later career*. New York: Grove & Stratton.

Federal Bureau of Investigation. (1987). *Uniform Crime Report*. Washington, DC.

Fehrenbach, P. A., & Monastersky, C. (1988). Characteristics of female adolescent sexual offenders. *American Journal of Orthopsychiatry, 58*, 148–151.

Fehrenbach, P. A., Smith, W., Monastersky, C., & Deisher, R. W. (1986). Adolescent sexual offenders: Offender and offense characteristics. *American Journal of Orthopsychiatry, 56*, 225–233.

Finkelhor, D. (1979). What's wrong with sex between adults and children? Ethics and the problem of sexual abuse. *American Journal of Orthopsychiatry, 49*, 692–697.

Finkelhor, D. (1990). Early and long-term effects of child sexual abuse: An update. *Professional Psychology Research and Practice, 21*, 325–330.

Finkelhor, D., Hotaling, G., Lewis, I., & Smith, C. (1989). Sexual abuse and its relationship to later sexual satisfaction, marital status, religion and attitudes. *Journal of Interpersonal Violence, 4*, 379–399.

Freund, K. (1967). Erotic preference in pedophilia. *Behavior Research and Therapy, 5*, 339–348.

Friedrich, W. N., & Luecke, W. J. (1988). Young school-age sexually aggressive children. *Professional Psychology Research and Practice, 19*, 155–164.

Fromuth, M. (1983). *The long term psychological impact of childhood sexual abuse*. Unpublished doctoral dissertation, Auburn University, Auburn, AL.

Gagnon, J. H. (1965). Female child victims of sex offenders. *Social Problems, 13*, 176–192.

Gavey, N. (1991). Sexual victimization prevalence among New Zealand university students. *Journal of Consulting and Clinical Psychology, 59*, 464–466.

Gebhard, P., Gagnon, J., Pomeroy, W., & Christenson, C. (1965). *Sex offenders*. New York: Harper & Row.

Green, D. (1987). Adolescent exhibitionists: Theory and therapy. *Journal of Adolescence, 10*, 45–56.

Groth, A., Longo, R. E., & McFadin, J. (1982). Undetected recidivism among rapists and child molesters. *Crime and Delinquency, 28*, 450–458.

Groth, A. N. (1977). The adolescent sexual offender and his prey. *International Journal of Offender Therapy and Comparative Criminology, 21*, 249–254.

Groth, A. N. (1979). *Men who rape: The psychology of the offender.* New York: Plenum Press

Hall, G. C. N., Maiuro, R. D., Vitaliano, P. P., & Proctor, W. C. (1986). The utility of the MMPI with men who have sexually assaulted children. *Journal of Consulting and Clinical Psychology, 54,* 493–496.

Hare, R. D. (1980). A research scale for the assessment of psychopathy in criminal populations. *Personality and Individual Differences, 1,* 111–119.

Hare, R. D. (1985). Comparison of procedures for the assessment of psychopathy. *Journal of Consulting and Clinical Psychology, 53,* 7–16.

Herman, J. (1981). *Father-daughter incest.* Cambridge, MA: Harvard University Press.

Howell, L. M. (1972). Clinical and research impressions regarding murder and sexually perverse crimes. *Psychotherapy and Psychosomatics, 21,* 156–159.

James, J., & Meyerding, J. (1977). Early sexual experience and prostitution. *American Journal of Psychiatry, 134,* 1381–1385.

Johnson, T. C. (1988). Child perpetrators: Children who molest other children: Preliminary findings. *Child Abuse and Neglect, 12,* 219–229.

Johnson, S. D., Gibson, L., & Linden, R. (1978). Alcohol and rape in Winnipeg, 1966–1975. *Journal of Studies on Alcohol, 39,* 1887–1894.

Johnson, T. C., & Berry, C. (1989). Children who molest: A treatment program. *Journal of Interpersonal Violence, 4,* 185–203.

Kavoussi, R. J., Kaplan, M., & Becker, J. V. (1988). Psychiatric diagnoses in adolescent sex offenders. *Journal of the American Academy of Child and Adolescent Psychiatry, 27,* 241–243.

Knight, R. A., & Prentky, R. A. (1990). Classifying sexual offenders: The development and corroboration of taxonomic models. In W. L. Marshall, D. R. Laws, & H. E. Barbaree (Eds.), *Handbook of sexual assault: Issues, theories, and treatment of the offender* (pp. 23–52). New York: Plenum Press.

Knight, R. A., Rosenberg, R., & Schneider, B. A. (1985). Classification of sexual offenders: Perspectives, methods, and validation. In A. W. Burgess (Ed.), *Rape and sexual assault* (pp. 222–293). New York: Garland.

Knopp, F. H. (1982). *Remedial intervention in adolescent sex offenses: Nine program descriptions.* Syracuse, NY: Safer Society Press.

Knopp, F. H. (Ed.). (1984). *Retraining adult sex offenders: Methods and models.* Syracuse, NY: Safer Society Press.

Koss, M. P., & Dinero, T. E. (1988). Predictors of sexual aggression among a national sample of male college students. In R. A. Prentky & V. L. Quinsey (Eds.), *Human sexual aggression: Current perspectives* (pp. 133–147). New York: New York Academy of Sciences.

Koss, M. P., Gidycz, C. A., & Wisniewski, N. (1987). The scope of rape: Incidence and prevalence of sexual aggression and victimization in a national sample of higher education students. *Journal of Consulting and Clinical Psychology, 55,* 162–170.

Langevin, R. (1983). *Sexual strands: Understanding and treating sexual anomalies in men.* London: Erlbaum.

Langmade, C. J. (1983). The impact of pre- and postpubertal onset of incest experiences in adult women as measured by sex anxiety, sex guilt, sexual satisfaction and sexual behavior. *Dissertation Abstracts International, 44,* 917B. (University Microfilms No. 3592).

Laws, D. R. (1981). Personal communication cited in. In F. H. Knopp (Ed.), *Retraining adult sex offenders: Methods and models.* Syracuse, NY: Safer Society Press.

Lewis, D. O., Shankok, S. S., & Pincus, J. H. (1979). Juvenile male sexual assaulters. *American Journal of Psychiatry, 136,* 1194–1196.

Longo, R. E. (1982). Sexual learning and experience among adolescent sexual offenders. *International Journal of Offender Therapy and Comparative Criminology, 26,* 235–241.

Longo, R. E., & Groth, A. N. (1983). Juvenile sexual offenses in the histories of adult rapists and child molesters. *International Journal of Offender Therapy and Comparative Criminology, 27,* 150–155.

Longo, R. E., & McFadin, B. (1981). Sexually inappropriate behavior: Development of the sexual offender. *Law and Order, 29,* 21–23.

McCarty, L. M. (1986). Mother–child incest: Characteristics of the offender. *Child Welfare, 65,* 447–458.

McConaghy, N., Blaszczynski, A. P., Armstrong, M. S., & Kidson, W. (1989). Resistance to treatment of adolescent sex offenders. Archives of Sexual Behavior, 18, 97–107.

McDermott, M. J., & Hindelang, M. J. (1981). Juvenile criminal behavior in the United States: Its trends and patterns. (Analysis of National Crime Victimization Survey Data to Study Serious Delinquent Behavior, Monograph No. 1). Washington, DC: Office of Juvenile Justice and Delinquency Prevention.

Maclay, D. T. (1960). Boys who commit sexual misdemeanours. *British Medical Journal, 11,* 186–190.

Malamuth, N. M. (1986). Predictors of naturalistic sexual aggression. *Journal of Personality and Social Psychology, 50,* 953–962.

Malamuth, N. M. (1988). A multidimensional approach to sexual aggression: Combining measures of past behavior and present likelihood. In R. A. Prentky & V. L. Quinsey (Eds.), *Human sexual aggression: Current perspectives* (pp. 123–132). New York: New York Academy of Sciences.

Malamuth, N. M., Sockloskie, R. J., Koss, M. P., & Tonaka, J. S. (1991). Characteristics of aggressors against women: Testing a model using a national sample of college students. *Journal of Consulting and Clinical Psychology, 59,* 670–681.

Markey, O. B. (1950). A study of aggressive sex misbehavior in adolescents brought to juvenile court. *American Journal of Orthopsychiatry, 20,* 719–731.

Marshall, W. L. (1989). Intimacy, loneliness, and sexual offenders. *Behaviour Research and Therapy, 27,* 491–503.

Marshall, W. L., Barbaree, H. E., & Butt, J. (1988). Sexual offenders against male children: Sexual preferences for gender, age of victim, and type of behavior. *Behaviour Research and Therapy, 26,* 383–391.

Marshall, W. L., Barbaree, H. E., & Christophe, D. (1986). Sexual offenders against female children: Sexual preferences for age of victims and type of behavior. *Canadian Journal of Behavioural Science, 18,* 424–439.

Marshall, W. L., & Christie, M. M. (1981). Pedophilia and aggression. *Criminal Justice and Behavior, 8,* 145–158.

Megargee, E. I. (1984). Aggression and violence. In H. E. Adams & P. B. Sutker (Eds.), *Comprehensive handbook of psychopathology* (pp. 523–545). New York: Plenum Press.

Meiselman, K. C. (1978). *Incest.* San Francisco: Jossey-Bass.

Mohr, J. W., Turner, R. E., & Jerry, M. B. (1964). *Pedophilia and exhibitionism: A handbook.* Toronto: University of Toronto Press.

National Adolescent Perpetrator Network. (1988). Preliminary report from the National Task Force on Juvenile Sexual Offending. *Juvenile and Family Court Journal, 39,* 1–67.

Panton, J. H. (1979). MMPI profile configurations associated with incestuous and non-incestuous child molesting. *Psychological Reports, 45,* 335–338.

Peters, J. J. (1976). Children who are victims of sexual assault and the psychology of offenders. *American Journal of Psychotherapy, 30,* 398–421.

Pierce, L. H., & Pierce, R. L. (1987). Incestuous victimization by juvenile sex offenders. *Journal of Family Violence, 2,* 351–364.

Prentky, R. A., & Knight, R. A. (1986). Impulsivity in the lifestyle and criminal behavior of sexual offenders. *Criminal Justice and Behavior, 13,* 141–164.

Prentky, R. A., & Knight, R. A. (1991). Identifying critical dimensions for discriminating among rapists. *Journal of Consulting and Clinical Psychology, 59,* 643–661.

Quinsey, V. L. (1984). Sexual aggression: Studies of offenders against women. In D. Weisstub (Ed.), *Law and mental health: International perspectives* (Vol. 1, pp. 84–122). New York: Pergamon Press.

Quinsey, V. L. (1986). Men who have sex with children. In D. N. Weisstub (Ed.), *Law and mental health: International perspectives* (Vol. 2, pp. 140–172). New York: Pergamon Press.

Reiss, A. J. (1960). Sex offenses: The marginal status of the adolescent. *Law and Contemporary Problems, 25,* 309–330.

Revitch, E. (1965). Sex murder and the potential sex murderer. *Diseases of the Nervous System, 26,* 626–640.

Roberts, R. E., Abrams, L., & Finch, J. R. (1973). Delinquent sexual behavior among adolescents. *Medical Aspects of Human Sexuality, 7,* 162–183.

Roberts, R. E., McBee, G. W., & Bettis, M. C. (1969). Youthful sex offenders: An epidemiologic comparison of types. *Journal of Sex Research, 5,* 29–40.

Robertson, J. M. (1990). Group counselling and the high risk offender. *Federal Probation, 54,* 48–51.

Roth, S., & Lebowitz, L. (1988). The experience of sexual trauma. *Journal of Traumatic Stress, 1,* 79–107.

Ryan, G., Lane, S., Davis, J., & Isaac, C. (1987). Juvenile sex offenders: Development and correction. *Child Abuse and Neglect, 11,* 385–395.

Saunders, E. B., Awad, G. A., & White, G. (1986). Male adolescent sexual offenders: The offender and the offense. *Canadian Journal of Psychiatry, 31,* 542–549.

Scully, D., & Marolla, J. (1984). Convicted rapists' vocabulary of motive: Excuses and justifications. *Social Problems, 31,* 530–544.

Sedney, M. A., & Brooks, B. (1984). Factors associated with a history of childhood sexual experience in a nonclinical female population. *Journal of the American Academy of Child Psychiatry, 23,* 215–218.

Segal, Z. V., & Marshall, W. L. (1985a). Self-report and behavioral assertion in two groups of sexual offenders. *Journal of Behavior Therapy and Experimental Psychiatry, 16,* 223–229.

Segal, Z. V., & Marshall, W. L. (1985b). Heterosexual social skills in a population of rapists and child molesters. *Journal of Consulting and Clinical Psychology, 53,* 55–63.

Seghorn, T. K., Boucher, R. J., & Prentky, R. A. (1987). Childhood sexual abuse in the

24   THE JUVENILE SEX OFFENDER

lives of sexually aggressive offenders. *Journal of the American Academy of Child and Adolescent Psychiatry, 26,* 262–267.

Serin, R. C., Malcolm P. B., Khanna, A., & Barbaree, H. E. (in press). Psychopathy and deviant sexual arousal in incarcerated sexual offenders. *Journal of Interpersonal Violence.*

Shoor, M., Speed, M. H., & Bartelt, C. (1966). Syndrome of the adolescent child molester. *American Journal of Psychiatry, 122,* 783–789.

Smets, A. C., & Cebula, C. M. (1987). A group treatment program for adolescent sex offenders: Five steps toward resolution. *Child Abuse and Neglect, 11,* 247–254.

Smith, W. R. (1988). Delinquency and abuse among juvenile sexual offenders. *Journal of Interpersonal Violence, 3,* 400–413.

Smith, W. R., & Monastersky, C. (1986). Assessing juvenile sexual offenders' risk for reoffending. *Criminal Justice and Behavior, 13,* 115–140.

Smith, W. R., Monastersky, C., & Deisher, R. M. (1987). MMPI-based personality types among juvenile sexual offenders. *Journal of Clinical Psychology, 43,* 422–430.

Stenson, P., & Anderson, C. (1987). Treating juvenile sex offenders and preventing the cycle of abuse. *Journal of Child Care, 3,* 91–102.

Stermac, L. E., & Quinsey, V. L. (1986). Social competence among rapists. *Behavioral Assessment, 8,* 171–185.

Swigert, V. L., Farrell, R. A., & Yoels, W. C. (1976). Sexual homicide: Social, psychological and legal aspects. *Archives of Sexual Behavior, 5,* 391–401.

Tarter, R. E., Hegedus, A. M., Alterman, A. I., & Katz-Garris, L. (1983). Cognitive capacities of juvenile, violent, nonviolent, and sexual offenders. *Journal of Nervous and Mental Disease, 171,* 564–567.

Thornton, W. E., & Pray, B. J. (1975). The portrait of a murderer. *Diseases of the Nervous System,* 176–178.

Tufts' New England Medical Center, Division of Child Psychiatry (1984). *Sexually exploited children: Service and research project.* Final report for the Office of Juvenile Justice and Delinquency Prevention. Washington, DC: U.S. Department of Justice.

Van Ness, S. R. (1984). Rape as instrumental violence: A study of youth offenders. Special Issue: Gender issues, sex offenses, and criminal justice: Current trends. *Journal of Offender Counselling, Services and Rehabilitation, 9,* 161–170.

Vinogradov, S., Dishotsky, N. I., Doty, A. K., & Tinklenberg, J. R. (1988). Patterns of behavior in adolescent rape. *American Journal of Orthopsychiatry, 58,* 179–187.

Waggoner, R., & Boyd, D. (1941). Juvenile aberrant sexual behavior. *American Journal of Orthopsychiatry, 11,* 275–291.

Wasserman, J., & Kappel, S. (1985). *Adolescent sex offenders in Vermont.* Burlington: Vermont Department of Health.

Weiner, B. A. (1985). Legal issues raised in treating sex offenders. *Behavioural Sciences and the Law, 3,* 325–340.

Williams, A. H. (1964). The psychopathology and treatment of sexual murderers. In I. Rosen (Ed.), *The pathology and treatment of sexual deviation: A methodological approach* London: Oxford University Press.

Wormith, J. (1983). A survey of incarcerated sexual offenders. *Canadian Journal of Criminology, 25,* 379–390.

CHAPTER 2

Legal Responses to the Juvenile Sex Offender

Nicholas Bala
Ira Schwartz

Since the beginning of the 20th century, every jurisdiction in North America has had a juvenile justice system to deal with children and adolescents who violate the criminal law. It is separate from the adult system and deals with juveniles in a distinctive fashion. The system is based on the notion that juveniles are more likely to be amenable to rehabilitation than adult offenders, and that juveniles are likely to be detrimentally affected if they are incarcerated along with older offenders. There is also a recognition that because of their limited intellectual and moral capacities, juveniles who violate the criminal law should generally not be held as fully accountable as adults who commit the same acts. It also seems that the behavior of juveniles is less likely than adults to be influenced by the prospect of criminal sanctions. That is, the court system has a limited deterrent effect on adolescent criminal conduct and hence principles applicable in adult court may have to be modified in the juvenile court.

As originally established, the juvenile courts were relatively informal. Trials were conducted without a jury and in the absence of the public. Lawyers rarely appeared, and judges often lacked formal legal training.

The juvenile justice system gave very significant discretionary authority to judges, probation officers, and correctional officials in order to permit them to do what they considered to be in the "best interests" of the delinquent. The system was, at least in theory, based on attempts to ascertain the causes of delinquent behavior, followed by the provision of appropriate assistance or treatment. This marked a move away from the sentencing process in adult court, where the primary focus was, and is, upon punishment for an offense, rather than the needs of the offender. The system was geared toward a rapid response to the problems posed by juvenile offenders, and by those whose conduct or circumstances indicted that they were in danger of becoming delinquents. The past quarter century has witnessed great change in this system.

In its landmark decision *In re* Gault (1967), the U.S. Supreme Court established that juveniles were constitutionally entitled to "due process," including the right to be represented by a lawyer and to have a fair trial before any conviction and possible sentencing. The Supreme Court later established that a delinquency must be proven on the criminal standard of proof, "proof beyond a reasonable doubt" (*In re* Winship, 1970). These decisions were at least in part based on a recognition that the juvenile justice system often failed to meet its rehabilitative ideals. Before juveniles are to be subjected to intrusive and sometimes ineffective treatment at the hands of the state, they are entitled to a fair legal procedure.

At the same time as the courts were beginning to impose requirements of due process on the juvenile justice system, legislatures were beginning to question the effectiveness of the system for protecting society, and moved towards increasing sanctions for juvenile offenders and facilitating transfer into the adult system for those considered unsuitable for the more lenient treatment afforded in the juvenile system (Feld, 1987). Similar trends in Canada resulted in the Young Offenders Act in 1984, a statute placing greater emphasis on both the legal rights of young offenders and the protection of society, with concomitant notions of accountability.

While there is significant variation between different jurisdictions in North America in the way they deal with juvenile offenders, and indeed there is substantial variation within jurisdictions, there are also certain distinctive and shared characteristics of juvenile justice systems. This chapter describes the fundamental nature of the juvenile justice process, with specific reference to juvenile sex offenders, and attempts to capture some of the diversity as well as some of the commonalities. It must, however, be appreciated that each American state has its own juvenile offender legislation, with specific and distinctive features. Canada has federal legislation, the Young Offenders Act, but there is also significant variation in the way this statute is interpreted and applied in different provinces. Practitioners are cautioned of the need to be familiar with the specific laws and policies of their own jurisdiction.

JUVENILE COURT JURISDICTION: AGE AND OFFENSES

The minimum age of juvenile court jurisdiction varies from 6 to 12, with many states setting 10 as the lowest age of criminal responsibility; Canada has a minimum age of 12. In some states there is no statutory minimum, and it must be established in each case that the juvenile in question displayed sufficient intellectual and emotional maturity to justify a criminal conviction. In a number of states there are absolute age-based minimums, such as 7, and for youths between certain ages, such as 7 to 13, there is a discretionary jurisdiction; in this age range a youth may rely on the "immaturity defense" if it cannot be proven that he had sufficient mental capacity to appreciate the consequences of the act charged.

Where a child below the age of juvenile court jurisdiction commits what would otherwise be a criminal act, it may be possible to invoke child protection laws to allow intervention to assist the child and family; in cases where parents are shown to be unwilling or unable to provide appropriate care or treatment for their child, it may be possible to obtain a court order under such legislation, removing the child from their care.

Depending upon the state or province, the maximum age of juvenile court jurisdiction runs from 15 to 17. In Canada and most American states, adulthood begins for criminal law purposes at the 18th birthday, with the reference date being the date of the commission of the alleged offense. Adult court jurisdiction commences at age 17 in Georgia, Illinois, Louisiana, Massachusetts, Michigan, Missouri, South Carolina, and Texas, and at 16 in Connecticut, New York, and North Carolina (Schwartz, 1989).

Juveniles charged with more serious offenses, including many types of sexual offenses, may in certain circumstances be subject to "transfer" (or "certification" or "waiver") into the adult system for trial; if convicted there, they may face more severe adult sentences and can be incarcerated in adult correctional facilities.

The legal definition of what constitutes a sexual offense varies from one statute to another. Those seeking to invoke the criminal law in their work with adolescent offenders should be aware of the specific definitions in their jurisdictions and avoid relying on clinical or moralistic notions of what constitutes appropriate or inappropriate behavior.

In every jurisdiction, touching the genitalia of another person for a sexual purpose, whether or not this involves intercourse, is a criminal offense unless the other person freely consents. This would encompass such offenses as rape, sexual assault, and aggravated sexual assault. In some jurisdictions, there is a statutory minimum age for certain types of sexual offenses, such that a youth below a specified age, such as 14, is regarded as legally incapable of committing such an offense. In other jurisdictions, it may be possible for juveniles to raise an immaturity defense, based on their lack of appreciation of the sexual quality of their acts.

In New Jersey, a state that has no statutory minimum age, two boys, aged 6 and 9, were charged with aggravated sexual assault as a result of the insertion of their fingers into the vagina of a 6-year-old girl. The court accepted psychiatric evidence that the boys were "emotionally immature" and "quite un-informed" on sexual matters, and dismissed the charges due to lack of capacity (*State in Interest of C.P. & R.D.*, 1986).

Every jurisdiction in North America has legislation that protects children and adolescents from sexual involvement with those who are legally regarded as being in a position to exploit the youthfulness of the "victim." This legislation renders what would otherwise be consensual sexual relations a criminal offense, at least for the "exploitative" party. There is substantial variation in how such "statutory rape" provisions are drafted, and some jurisdictions criminalize what other jurisdictions regard as legally acceptable adolescent sexual activity. For example, it is an offense for a 15-year-old to be involved in a consensual sexual relationship with a 13-year-old in New York, but not in Canada. However, in Canada it is a criminal offense for a 16-year-old to be sexually involved with a 13-year-old.

In some jurisdictions it is an offense for a male, regardless of his age, to be involved in consensual sexual relations with a female under a specific age, such as 18; it is a criminal offense, even if the male is of the same age or younger. However, it may not be an offense for a female over age 18 to engage in sexual relations with a male under that age (*Michael M. v. Superior Court*, 1981).

There are also certain specific types of sexual conduct that may be pro-scribed. In particular, in several American states, individuals who engage in private consensual homosexual acts are guilty of an offense (*Bowers v. Hardwick*, 1985). In Canada, individuals under the age of 18 who have consensual anal intercourse are guilty of an offense, although if both parties are adults, no offense is committed.[1]

Each jurisdiction has a range of other types of sexual offenses prohibiting such acts as exhibitionism, engaging the services of a juvenile prostitute, and distributing obscene material. Some of these may be relevant to specific types of adolescent sexual behavior.

THE JUVENILE JUSTICE PROCESS

Reporting

It is known that virtually all youths commit some criminal offenses at some point during their adolescence, although typically these offenses are of a rela-tively minor nature and involve theft or damage to property, or are a "victim-

[1] A trial judge has ruled that Canada's Charter of Rights requires that the age of consent for anal intercourse should be the same as for any other sexual act, namely 14 (*R. v. C.M.*, 1992).

less" offense like drinking under age. Offenses become an issue for the juvenile justice system only if they are reported to the police or some other state agency, and legal proceedings are commenced.

To some extent, it is a matter of chance whether the police become involved. In many cases the victim or person who discovers the offense may want to deal with the matter informally, not involving the authorities. The police are likely to be contacted if the offense is more serious, although in the case of sexual offenses, even ones involving violence, many victims feel too embarrassed, upset, or guilty to report the offense to the authorities.

In general, adult victims are not obligated to report the offense to the police, nor are professionals obligated to report situations they believe involved an offense. Indeed, there may be situations in which it is a violation of professional standards, or confidentiality laws, for a person such as a physician or therapist to report to the police that a patient has disclosed the commission of an offense in the course of treatment.

However, in situations involving suspected child abuse there is an important exception to the general rules about confidentiality and the lack of an obligation to report offenses. In every jurisdiction in North America there are laws that impose an obligation to report situations of suspected child abuse or neglect to the child welfare authorities or police. In some jurisdictions the obligation is only placed on professionals, like doctors and teachers, while in others they apply to everyone. These laws are intended to protect children who may be the victims of abuse, and override the laws governing professional confidentiality. Those who report offenses are generally immune from civil liability for slander or malicious prosecution, even if the report is ultimately proven unfounded, as long as they are not acting maliciously or without reasonable grounds.

It is clear that professionals, and others, have an obligation to report situations where parents are suspected of abusing their children. There is, however, less clarity about whether there is a legal obligation to report situations in which a juvenile is believed to have sexually abused another minor. Legislation in different jurisdictions varies on this issue; in some it is quite ambiguous.

This lack of clarity may cause some difficulty for professionals who are working with children who disclose that they have been victims of abuse perpetrated by adolescents, but request that this not be revealed to the authorities. There may be even greater difficulty for professionals who work with adolescents who disclose that they have abused other children. Depending on the exact wording of the legislation, the failure to report abuse that should be reported could be an offense, but the reporting of abuse which need not be reported could result in sanction for violation of laws about professional confidentiality.

Professionals who work with adolescents must be familiar with the details of the child abuse reporting legislation in their own jurisdiction.

Investigation

If a suspected offense is reported to the police, they will conduct an investigation whose nature will vary with the complexity and circumstances of the offense. In sexual offense cases, physicians, child welfare staff, and other experts may be consulted by the police to help establish whether an offense has occurred or to help establish the identity of the perpetrator. An interview with the victim is a standard part of most investigations, but may not be possible if the victim is an infant or deceased.

Because of the lack of sophistication of most juvenile offenders, investigations of offenses committed by adolescents are typically a little easier for the authorities to resolve than those involving adults, who may do a better job of escaping detection. However, it must be appreciated that there are many crimes committed by juveniles that the police are unable to resolve, even after careful investigation.

When the police or other authorities responsible for the investigation of an offense have sufficient evidence to establish the identity of a suspect, a decision will be made regarding criminal prosecution; in the case of a juvenile, this will usually be conducted in the juvenile court. There is a degree of variability, depending on the jurisdiction and the nature of the case, as to who decides to commence a prosecution; it may involve police, a lawyer in the prosecutor's office, or, in appropriate cases, child welfare workers.

Arrest and Questioning the Youth

Where the police believe an adolescent has committed a sexual offense, they will typically arrest the youth and question him about the suspected offenses. If appropriate procedures are followed, any statement made by the youth to the police will be admissible in proceedings against the youth. Such statements, or "confessions," often form a crucial part of the prosecution's case. If appropriate procedures are not followed, however, the statement may be ruled inadmissible at a subsequent trial, and the youth may be acquitted despite his acknowledgment of guilt. The strict approach to ensuring that appropriate steps are followed is intended to ensure that a youth's legal rights are protected.

In both Canada and the United States there are rules requiring the police to advise the youth of constitutionally recognized rights, including the right to remain silent and the right to have the advice of a lawyer. In some jurisdictions, there are additional legal requirements that a youth must be advised specifically of the right to have a parent or other adult present during police questioning. There is significant evidence that many youths will, after a police warning, waive their rights and make a statement, often without truly appreciating the consequences of doing so (Grisso, 1980).

If the police are involved in investigating an offense, it is generally best for other professionals involved in the case to leave the initial questioning of the suspect about the alleged offense to the police. The police are trained in investigative interviewing, and have the responsibility for ensuring that the youth receives an appropriate legal caution before making a statement. There have been cases in which social workers have become involved in questioning a youth who has been arrested by the police and have failed to appropriately caution the youth, resulting in the statement given by the youth being ruled inadmissible (*Cates v. Texas*, 1989).

Pretrial Detention

When the police arrest a youth for a relatively serious charge, such as a sexual offense, especially one involving allegations of violence, it may be felt that the youth should be detained pending a trial. If such pretrial detention is sought, the youth must be brought before a judge within a relatively short period of time (in most jurisdictions 24 to 72 hours) to determine whether the youth should be released. While the criteria for pretrial detention vary from one jurisdiction to another, certain factors are important in most jurisdictions, including (1) a well-founded concern that the youth may not appear at trial; (2) the seriousness of the charge, although detention is never automatic; (3) the likelihood of the youth committing an offense before the trial; and (4) whether or not a responsible adult, such as a parent, is willing to take responsibility for the youth pending trial (*Schall v. Martin*, 1984; and *R. v. Ashford and Eddie*, 1985).

Pretrial detention is an intrusive step, particularly since the youth has not yet been convicted of any offense, and detention is often in a maximum security-type of facility. At least in theory, a youth should not be detained prior to trial as a form of punishment, nor should an alleged juvenile offender be detained solely because professionals or police may feel that the youth's home is unsuitable, nor indeed because the youth may not have a residence. In practice, however, these may be factors, at least in some localities.

In some jurisdictions, the decision to seek pretrial detention is made by the police and prosecutor, but in some localities juvenile correctional officials may also have a role in assessing whether such detention is appropriate. The ultimate decision about detention must always be made by a judge, although in many jurisdictions the issue of pretrial detention need not be dealt with by a juvenile court judge.

Youths who are detained pending trial must normally be confined in facilities separate from adults (*D.B. v. Tewksbury*, 1982). Pretrial detention with adults can occur only in exceptional circumstances and is judicially controlled. However, it is usual for youths awaiting trial to be placed in facilities with youths who have already been convicted of offenses. Indeed, in many localities, juveniles pending trial may be placed in facilities with adolescents who have been found to be children in need of protection, or who have been found to have committed such "status offenses" as "unmanageability." This may pose special challenges for staff, as those charged with committing a sexual offense may be placed in the same facilities as children who have been victims of sexual abuse, typically as a result of the acts of their parents.

Diversion

In some cases, especially those involving juveniles without a prior juvenile criminal record, a decision may be made not to invoke a formal legal response to a situation where an offense is believed to have occurred. For example, in a case involving a relatively minor theft, the police may decide to resolve the matter by warning the youth not to get in trouble again, and may speak to the youth's parents or make a referral to a social agency. In cases where adolescents have engaged in consensual sexual activities that may technically violate the criminal law, a decision might be made that it is not appropriate to invoke a criminal sanction.

Many of these "diversion" or "alternative measures" programs are directed toward relatively minor offenses and involve such responses as an apology or restitution for a victim. Such programs are generally inappropriate for those charged with sex offenses. However, in some localities there are diversion programs specifically aimed at juvenile sex offenders. These programs are designed to encourage a therapeutic response, without having the youth suffer the potential trauma of a more formal, punitive response.

Davidson (1987) reports on a court diversion program in Sacramento, California, that requires a juvenile to sign a diversion "contract" with the prosecutor's office, agreeing to enter the treatment program for a minimum of 2 years. The agreement provides that the youth can be referred back for prosecution for (1) a refusal to participate in an assessment or education; (2) a determination of nontreatability due to severe psychiatric illness; (3) commission of new offenses; or (4) a determination that the juvenile is too high a risk to be permitted to continue in a community-based, nonsecure treatment program.

Davidson observes that "with any diversion arrangement, it is essential that the youth's progress be as closely supervised as it would be under formal probation or parole" (p. 18). It is also important that the youth's participation in the program not jeopardize the youth's legal rights, either by being used as a vehicle to gather incriminatory evidence or by coercing a youth who denies wrongdoing into participating in diversion rather than having a trial.

There may also be situations in which the police or investigators believe that an adolescent has committed a sexual offense but recognize that the

available evidence would not meet the relatively high standard of proof necessary for a juvenile prosecution. In these cases it is useful to consider an appropriate child welfare or mental health response.

In many jurisdictions there are status offenses, such as unmanageability,
that may result in an adolescent being removed from his home. These types of
responses may involve a court hearing, but the hearing is not focused on proving
that an offense occurred. The scope of inquiry in such civil proceedings is
broader and the evidentiary rules not as strict, with the focus of inquiry on the
ability of the state to meet the youth's needs through coercive intervention,
rather than on offending behavior.

The Role of the Juvenile's Lawyer

Historically very few lawyers appeared in juvenile court, but it is now accepted
that juveniles have the same rights to legal representation as adults facing
criminal charges and may need special protection, since they may have less
understanding of their position than adults.

The U.S. Supreme Court has recognized that juveniles have a constitutionally guaranteed right to legal representation, and if their parents are unwilling or unable to afford a lawyer, at least in theory, counsel must be provided
by the state (*In re Gault*, 1965). However, American studies have shown that
in practice fewer than half of juveniles appearing in juvenile court for delinquency charges are actually receiving the assistance of counsel to which they are
constitutionally entitled. Feld (1987) writes:

> Despite *Gault*'s promise of the right to counsel, most juveniles face potentially
> coercive state action without seeing a lawyer, waive their right to counsel without
> consulting with an attorney or appreciating the legal consequences, and, thereby,
> face the prosecutorial power of the state alone and unaided. Although waiver of
> the right to counsel is the most common explanation, the variations in rates of
> representation within a state suggest that nonrepresentation reflects judicial po-
> licies, especially juvenile court judges' continuing hostility towards lawyers, rather
> than any systematic differences in youthful competence. (p. 532)

While in general it seems that youths facing more serious charges are more
likely to be legally represented, there are disturbing indications that American
youths frequently face sanction without legal assistance.

In Canada, Section 11 of the Young Offenders Act creates the right of
legal representation that in practice is substantially broader than that afforded
youths in the United States. Parental financial resources are not even considered when assessing eligibility for a government-paid lawyer (*R. v. Ronald H.*,
1984), and it is apparent that most Canadian youths have legal representation
when appearing in court. In a serious case, such as one involving a sexual

offense, a youth will invariably have a lawyer, usually paid for by the government.

There is some controversy within the legal profession about the appropriate role for lawyers representing a juvenile. Some lawyers argue that they should have a concern about the "best interests" of their clients; these lawyers may feel that they should not attempt to "beat the rap" on a technicality, for example by having an improper but true confession excluded from the evidence (Bogden, 1980). However, a more common view within the legal profession is that a lawyer acting for a juvenile is in the same position as one representing an adult; in particular, in the absence of the client wishing to plead guilty, there should not be a conviction for a serious offense unless the prosecution can strictly prove its case (Law Society of Upper Canada, 1981).

Treatment personnel, parents, victims, and others must be prepared to accept that the young person's lawyer may raise every legal defense and may vigorously pursue cross-examination of prosecution witnesses, including victims, although the reality of juvenile court is that most cases are ultimately resolved by means of a guilty plea. Sometimes the youth feels a genuine sense of remorse and wishes to have the case resolved quickly, and hence pleads guilty. Not infrequently this is the result of a "plea bargain" between the prosecutor and the lawyer for the juvenile. There may, for example, be an agreement that the youth will plead guilty to a charge for one offense if other charges are dropped. In some jurisdictions there may be an agreement to plead guilty in return for the prosecution supporting the youth's request for a particular sentence; although technically judges are not bound by such agreements, they generally adopt them as the basis of their sentences.

The representation of juveniles is often a difficult task for a lawyer. Many juveniles involved in the legal system do not communicate well with adult authority figures, including their lawyers. Parents generally have to be consulted and informed by a juvenile's lawyer, but they should also be made to realize that the lawyer is taking instructions from their child and not from them.

There are substantial concerns about the quality of legal representation that some lawyers provide to juveniles. While many knowledgeable and sensitive lawyers engage in this type of work, too often the lawyers who represent juveniles seem to lack the necessary knowledge, experience, and sensitivity. In particular, at the sentencing stage, which for many juveniles is the most critical part of the process, some lawyers seem to feel that their job is done and they remain silent (Hanscom, 1988; Knitzer & Sobie, 1984).

The Juvenile Court Trial

If a juvenile decides to plead not guilty, there must be a trial. In most jurisdictions, trials in juvenile court are conducted by a judge sitting alone, although in the United States some states specifically grant juveniles the option of trial by jury.

Legislation generally requires that parents of a juvenile are to be notified of proceedings and have a right to attend. In some jurisdictions, the proceedings are open to the public, although a judge has the discretion to close them; in other jurisdictions, the proceedings are closed to the public. In all jurisdictions there are restrictions on the publication of information that would serve to identify youths involved in juvenile court, although there are limited situations in which this type of information can be publicized (*In re J.S.*, 1981; *Smith v. Daily Mail Publishing*, 1979).

The onus is on the prosecution to prove its case on the criminal standard of proof, proof beyond a reasonable doubt. The same strict rules of evidence that apply to adult criminal trials apply in juvenile court; evidence that is obtained in violation of a juvenile's constitutional rights may be excluded. A juvenile who is charged with an offense is not obligated to testify, or to adduce any evidence tending to disprove guilt, although there is a right to adduce this type of evidence and to cross-examine all witnesses for the prosecution.

A youth's lack of mental capacity, due to retardation or mental illness, may be an issue in some cases. In such situations, assessments by one or more mental health professionals may provide crucial evidence.

In most jurisdictions, a youth can be subjected to juvenile (or adult) court sanction only if he has the capacity to understand the fundamental nature of the proceedings and instruct a lawyer. Usually, a juvenile who lacks the capacity to stand trial will be subject to some form of indeterminate committal under appropriate criminal or civil legislation, although in some jurisdictions a juvenile who lacks the capacity to stand trial may in some circumstances simply be released (*In re W.A.F.*, 1990).

A youth who has the capacity to stand trial may still be found not guilty by reason of insanity, if the court finds that at the time of the alleged offense he lacked the capacity to appreciate the criminality of his conduct or to conform to the law. Generally, a finding of "not guilty by reason of insanity" will result in indefinite committal to a mental health facility, with release when a cure has been effected or there is no longer a significant danger to society.

In some states, like Michigan, legislation prevents juveniles from resorting to an insanity defense (*Matter of Ricks*, 1988). This legislation is based on the notion that the juvenile justice system focuses on treatment and rehabilitation, and youths who lack mental capacity should not, on this ground, be denied access to juvenile justice services. Most jurisdictions, however, recognize that juvenile justice laws are basically criminal legislation and that juveniles should be afforded similar legal rights to adults.

In a case involving an alleged sexual offense, it is generally necessary for the victim to testify and to be available for cross-examination. There have, however, been recent legislative innovations that have made it easier for child victims to give evidence (Bala, 1992a). For example, in many jurisdictions, in a sexual abuse case a child may testify from behind a screen or via closed-circuit television from another room, so that the alleged abuser will not again confront the victim. In some jurisdictions there is also legislation allowing courts to receive videotapes of an interview with a child or to hear about statements that a child made out of court to another person, such as a parent. Recently courts have demonstrated more flexibility in permitting mental health experts, who may have examined the alleged victim, to testify about their opinions as to whether or not the child was abused, although there are limits to the admissibility of this type of evidence.

The general thrust of these developments has been to make it easier to prosecute child sexual abuse cases and to reduce the trauma of court experience for young victims. While these innovations have more frequently been applied in cases involving the prosecution of adults, they are also applicable in cases where a juvenile is alleged to have sexually abused a child (R. v. G.B. et al., 1990).

Sentencing

If a juvenile pleads guilty, or is convicted after a trial, the proceeding moves from an "adjudicative stage" to a "dispositional stage"; that is, the judge must determine what sentence to impose.

While it is possible for a juvenile to be sentenced immediately following adjudication, in more serious cases, such as those involving sexual offenses, the case is usually adjourned to a later date for sentencing. This allows for the preparation of reports for use by the court for sentencing, as well as allowing the lawyers to summon witnesses who may have testimony relevant to this issue.

In serious cases, it is usual to have a presentence report (also known as a predisposition report or social history) prepared by a probation officer. This report typically includes a narrative of the child's social history, previous juvenile court record, comments regarding available sentencing alternatives, and a recommendation about an appropriate sentence.

In some jurisdictions, it is also possible to have a psychiatric or psychological assessment report prepared in more serious cases, like those involving a sexual assault. Such reports may contain a description of the youth's mental history and makeup, a diagnosis and a prognosis, and in some jurisdictions a recommendation about an appropriate sentence. The recommendations in these reports are not binding on the juvenile court, and parties are entitled to challenge their contents and recommendations or to call their own witnesses. However, in practice, these reports are generally very quite influential on the sentencing judge.

Juvenile court judges generally have more discretion in determining an appropriate sentence than do judges in adult court because rehabilitation is an important concern. However, judges are bound by the juvenile sentencing principles articulated by their legislature and appellate courts. Historically, juvenile courts were, at least in theory, expected to focus exclusively on the rehabilitation or best interests of the juvenile offender, but in the past quarter century there has been increasing emphasis on balancing rehabilitative concerns with concerns about accountability and deterrence. The move toward accountability is probably clearest in Washington State, which in 1977 adopted "juvenile disposition standards," with ranges of sentencing established, using a grid system, based on the nature of the offense and the youth's prior record (Becker, 1979). This shift toward accountability is also apparent in Canada's Young Offenders Act, which came into force in 1984 and which also moved away from a welfare-oriented approach to one explicitly recognizing the need to protect society, albeit also recognizing the special needs of young offenders (Bala & Kirvan, 1990).

It also came to be accepted that the juvenile courts should provide for the rehabilitation of the juvenile offender but in the least intrusive fashion possible.

Juvenile courts generally have a fairly broad range of sentencing options, including the possibility of ordering restitution to a victim or performance of community service work. However, with a sex offense, the court will usually be considering two basic options: probation or custody.

Probation generally keeps juveniles living with their families in the community, subject to certain conditions, usually including the supervision of a probation officer. Of particular importance for sex offenders, it may be a condition of probation that a youth undertake treatment. In some American states, parents may be required to pay for this treatment if they have the means or appropriate insurance. However, in many places their are no suitable community-based treatment programs for juvenile sexual offenders who are on probation.

In most jurisdictions, a judge may require a youth on probation to live somewhere other than his home, for example, with a relative, although this is not usually done. There are also jurisdictions that allow juvenile offenders to be placed in treatment or mental health facilities. For example, in Canada a young offender can be "detained for treatment" in a hospital or other setting, instead of being placed in a youth custody facility, but only if the youth and the treatment facility both agree (Bala & Kirvan, 1990).

The juvenile courts can require that a youth attend counseling or therapy sessions, whether as a condition of probation or otherwise, and can serve as a lever to induce a youth to accept treatment. However, offenders cannot be forced to respond in treatment; this requires a degree of willingness. The courts may sanction an individual who refuses to attend a judicially mandated therapy session, but they will be very reluctant to punish an individual whose therapist is dissatisfied with the offender's progress or degree of cooperation.

For juvenile offenders who have committed more serious sex offenses, or who have a history of offending, it is likely that the juvenile court will order them removed from parental care and placed under the care of juvenile correctional authorities. In the original juvenile court model, the committal to care

was for an indefinite period, since its purpose was rehabilitative and it was
impossible to predict how long this would take. Some states retain a model of
indeterminate committal, with the stay in custody ending when the correctional
authorities consider it appropriate, but prior to a stipulated age, generally 21.
A number of American states and Canada have adopted determinate judicial
sentencing for juvenile offenders.

There is a range of facilities in which juvenile offenders can be placed in,
including wilderness camps, group homes, and custodial institutions. While
traditionally juvenile custodial institutions have been quite large, some Canadian provinces and a few states, including Massachusetts, Utah, Missouri, and
more recently Florida, are also using small high-security facilities to provide
treatment of violent and chronic young offenders. In most jurisdictions the
court commits the youth to the custody of juvenile correctional authorities; it
is the responsibility of the authorities to determine the specific facility in which
an offender will be placed. In some jurisdictions, juvenile court judges have a
limited role in deciding where a youth will be placed; for example, in Canada
the sentencing judge must specify whether an offender who receives a custodial
sentence will be placed in "open" or "secure" custody.

Youths in custody should have access to educational and rehabilitative
services. Indeed, in the United States it has been held that juveniles in training
school have a constitutional "right to treatment" (*Nelson v. Heyne*, 1974), that
is, to have access to therapeutic services while in custody. However, forcing
juveniles in custody to receive any treatment to modify their behavior may
constitute "cruel and unusual" punishment or violate other constitutional
rights. This suggests that juvenile sex offenders should not be administered
antiandrogens like Depo-Provera, without their informed consent, appropriate
medical supervision, and the involvement of parents or guardians. Indeed, any
kind of intrusive therapeutic interventions or aversive conditioning should be
undertaken only after ensuring that legal and ethical requirements are satisfied,
especially with offenders in custody.

In every jurisdiction there is some process to review the progress of juvenile
offenders in the care of the state, although the models of review vary. In Canada
and some of the American states, the juvenile court has the authority to review
a case and release a youth prior to the completion of the original sentence. In
other states, correctional or parole officials have this responsibility. Inevitably
the views of treatment professionals who work in the correctional system
concerning the youth's progress and the likelihood of reoffending will be
significant in any review.

Transfer to the Adult System

The most serious consequence for a juvenile who is charged with an offense is
transfer to the adult system (also called "waiver" of jurisdiction, or "certi-

fication" as an adult). Transfer must occur prior to any adjudication of guilt or innocence. Juveniles who are transferred will face a trial in adult court, with its attendant likelihood of publicity, and in many jurisdictions can result in pretrial detention with adults.

Juveniles convicted in adult court typically face the possibility of more severe sanctions than what youths receive in juvenile court. In sentencing a youth, adult court may take into account the age of the offender as a mitigating factor, and in some jurisdictions the court even has the option of imposing the same type of sentence as a juvenile court. There is some indication from some American states that many youths are being transferred for offenses that do not involve violence and may be receiving sentences that are, on average, no longer than those which would be imposed on those youths in the juvenile courts (Feld, 1987, p. 501). However, it is apparent that in many jurisdictions, youths are receiving longer sentences, especially those transferred for offenses involving violence or sexual assault. Further, transferred youths typically serve their sentences in adult correctional institutions, which usually have less suitable educational and rehabilitative resources and a more hostile environment.

At least some judges have recognized the potential damage to juveniles from being in adult correctional facilities and have accordingly demonstrated reluctance to transfer cases. In a case in which the Ontario Court of Appeal refused to transfer a number of youths charged with the forcible confinement and sexual assault on a 14-year-old girl, the court remarked:

> The punishment in an [adult] penitentiary is much harsher than in an institution in which it is intended that youthful offenders would be incarcerated . . . particularly its effect on youthful or young sex offenders. This include[s] the fact that there [is] a real risk of physical danger, a risk of becoming involved in involuntary homosexual activities, and the likelihood of the young person having to accept or adopt the codes of behavior in living in such a place. (R. v. W.S., 1989, p. 171)

Legislative provisions governing transfer vary considerably from one jurisdiction to another. There are also very substantial differences in judicial and prosecutorial attitudes to transfer, and transfer rates for the same offense vary markedly from locale to locale. On the whole, transfer appears to be considerably more common in the United States than in Canada. Feld (1987) observed:

> Idiosyncratic differences in judicial philosophies and the locale of a waiver hearing are far more significant for the adulthood decision than is any inherent quality of the criminal act or characteristic of the offending youth. The inconsistency in the interpretation and application of waiver statutes is hardly surprising in view of the subjectivity of the dispositional issue, the lack of effective guidelines to structure the decision, and the latent as well as manifest functions that the process serves. (p. 494)

In some jurisdictions it is quite unlikely that a juvenile facing a sexual offense charge will be transferred (R. v. W.S., 1989). In other places, a juvenile facing a sexual offense charge, especially one involving use of force or a weapon, is quite likely to be transferred. In several American states there is a presumption that juveniles above a certain age and charged with rape and other specified offenses should be dealt with as adults.

The most widely employed method for determining whether a juvenile should be dealt with as an adult is the juvenile court hearing. At this hearing, the juvenile court will receive evidence from the prosecution about why the youth should be transferred; the youth is not obliged to present evidence, but has the right to do so. The rules of evidence are less strict at a transfer hearing than in a trial. The prosecution is not obliged to prove beyond a reasonable doubt that the offense occurred, but rather focuses on the appropriate forum for the trial and the types of sentencing alternatives that should be available.

A number of factors are important in deciding whether to transfer a youth, including the seriousness and circumstances of the alleged offense; the injury suffered by the alleged victim; the record and previous history of the juvenile, including a consideration of the sophistication and maturity of the youth; the amenability of the juvenile to rehabilitation within the juvenile system; and the prospects for the adequate protection of the public if the juvenile is not transferred (R. v. Shawn R., 1990).

Testimony of mental health experts who have worked with the juvenile, or conducted an assessment for the purposes of the transfer hearing, are likely to be very important at a transfer hearing, especially on the issues of the etiology of the juvenile's behavior and his prognosis in the juvenile correctional system.

In a number of American states, juveniles above a certain age and charged with a stipulated offense, including some serious sexual offenses, will initially appear in adult court. The adult court may then decide that the youth should be "transferred down," but the onus may be upon the youth to justify this decision.

In a few states, including Florida, Nebraska, Georgia, and Wyoming, the prosecutor has the discretion for certain offenses to decide whether to proceed in adult court (Krisberg, 1989). A few jurisdictions, including Washington, D.C., have specified in legislation that for certain types of charges, including rape, a juvenile shall automatically be dealt with in adult court.

It should be noted that in recent years, in both Canada and the United States, with increased public concern about violent offenses committed by juveniles, there have been moves to facilitate the transfer of youths charged with violent offenses into the adult system (Bala, 1992b; Feld, 1987), as well as to increase the severity of juvenile court sanctions. Schwartz (1989) summarized some of the changes:

> These statutory changes fall into three categories: (1) making it easier to prosecute juvenile offenders in adult courts (California and Florida), (2) lowering the age of judicial waiver (Tennessee, Kentucky, and South Carolina), and (3) excluding

certain offenses from juvenile court jurisdictions (Illinois, Indiana, Oklahoma, and Louisiana). In addition, a number of states have attempted to stiffen juvenile court penalties for serious juvenile offenders through (1) mandating minimum terms of incarceration (Colorado, New York, and Idaho), or (2) enacting a comprehensive system of sentencing guidelines (Washington). (p. 7)

ASSESSING THE IMPACT OF LEGAL INTERVENTION

It is apparent that North American society is increasingly utilizing a criminal justice response to deal with sexual offenders. The women's movement has heightened awareness of the inadequacy of traditional legal responses to, and legislation concerning, the sexual assault of women and children, and police charging practices have changed. There has been a significant increase in the number of sex offenders who have been prosecuted for rape, sexual assault, and child sexual abuse. Almost all of these offenders are male, and the majority are adults, but a very significant number, roughly one-quarter, are adolescents.

In the past there was a tendency to view certain kinds of juvenile sexual offending as relatively harmless experimentation, especially if the victims were children. This attitude is changing as the damage to victims of child sexual abuse is increasingly recognized. It is also becoming apparent that most adult sex offenders begin their pattern of behavior as adolescents, and earlier social intervention is desirable. However, it is important to appreciate that there are both positive and negative aspects to a legal response to the juvenile sex offender. This may affect how professionals or parents deal with individual cases, as well as how society responds to these types of offenders.

The prosecution of a juvenile sexual offender can serve the purpose of accountability, clearly informing him that his conduct is socially unacceptable and will be sanctioned. The prosecution may serve a deterrent function, though there is some controversy about the deterrent effect of prosecution of juvenile offenders in situations where they do not receive appropriate treatment as a result of prosecution (Schneider & Ervin, 1988).

Prosecution of the offender may also serve an important psychological function for victims, providing vindication and tending to assuage feelings of guilt and inadequacy. Victims of sexual offenses may also seek financial compensation. While a civil suit against a juvenile sex offender is unlikely to be of much value, since few juveniles have the resources to satisfy a judgment, some jurisdictions, including all Canadian provinces, have government-funded programs to provide some financial compensation to victims of violent crime.

Sexual offenders have a tendency to deny the nature of their problem, and rarely voluntarily seek out help; those who do often fail to complete their treatment. Prosecution can serve the vitally important function of confronting the offender with his conduct. The legal system and the threat of further sanctions can be crucial levers for keeping the offender in therapy, although it must be recognized that ultimately it is impossible to force a truly unwilling individual to engage in a meaningful therapeutic relationship.

Those who use the juvenile court system to respond to a sexual offense must be aware of its limitations. One is that a youth who is charged, and is in fact guilty, may nevertheless be acquitted because of the difficulty of proving a case according to the rigorous standards of proof demanded by criminal law. If this occurs, the youth will clearly receive an inappropriate message, namely, that with luck or a good lawyer he can get away with continued offending. Where the legally admissible evidence appears weak, it may be appropriate to consider some alternative to a juvenile court prosecution, such as a child welfare or status offense response.

Also, those who hope that the juvenile court system will respond with an appropriate therapeutic response may be disappointed. Once a prosecution is commenced, concerns for the protection of society or accountability may result in the case being transferred to adult court, where rehabilitation of the offender may be less likely than in the juvenile system. Even if the youth remains in the juvenile system, there may not be adequate rehabilitative resources provided to the youth; the experience may simply provide sanctions and no therapy.

Further, even with the best therapeutic services, not all sexual offenders will be amenable to treatment; some may reoffend after release, even if they have received treatment. At least prosecution offers protection to society while an offender is in custody. Prosecution may also serve an important function of social identification, so that if there is a repetition of offending, a custodial sentence commensurate with the protection of society can be imposed. However, many jurisdictions have some restrictions on access to juvenile court records, and there may be situations in which a prior juvenile court conviction cannot be taken into account in sentencing at a later adult proceeding.

The efficacy of the juvenile justice system for dealing with an adolescent sex offender is in significant measure a reflection of the adequacy of the applicable legislation and of the resources and facilities available. Recent reports in both Canada (Rogers, 1990) and the United States (National Task Force on Adolescent Sexual Offending, 1988) have documented many of the inadequacies of present responses and have charted pathways for reform. It is to be hoped that professionals and politicians ensure that society takes the necessary measures to deal effectively with adolescent sexual offenders, as well as taking more fundamental preventive steps to reduce the incidence of sex offending.

ACKNOWLEDGMENT

The authors wish to acknowledge the research assistance of Ian McCowan (LL.B., 1991—Queen's University), whose services were made available under a grant of the Law Foundation of Ontario to the Faculty of Law at Queen's University.

CASES CITED

Bowers v. Hardwick, 478 U.S. 186 (1985).
Cates v. Texas, 776 S.W.2d 170 (Tex. Ct. App. 1989).
D.B. v. Tewksbury, 545 F. Supp. 896 (U.S.D.C., Ore. 1982).
In re Gault, 387 U.S. 1 (1967).
In re J.S., 438 A.2d 1125 (Vt. 1981).
Michael M. v. Superior Court, 450 U.S. 464 (1981).
Nelson v. Heyne, 491 F.2d 352 (7 Cir. 1974), cert. denied 417 U.S. 976.
R. v. Ashford and Eddie (1985, Ont. H.C.), Y.O.S. 86-010 (Ont. H.C. 1985).
R. v. G.B. et al., 56 C.C.C. (3d) 200 (S.C.C. 1990).
R. v. C.M., 75 C.C.C. (3d) 556 (Ont. Gen. Div. 1992).
R. v. Ronald H., 12 W.C.B. 334, Y.O.S. 84-025 (Alta. Prov. Ct. 1984).
R. v. Shawn R., 73 O.R. (2d) 355 (Ont. H.C. 1990), aff'd. 1 O.R. (3d) 785 (Ont. C.A. 1991).
R. v. W.S., 69 C.R. (3d) 168 (Ont. C.A. 1989).
Matter of Ricks, 421 N.W.2d 667 (Mich. App. 1988).
Schall v. Martin, 194 S.Ct. 2403 (1984).
Smith v. Daily Mail Publishing, 443 U.S. 97 (1979).
State in Interest of C.P. & R.D., 514 A.2d 850 (N.J. Super. Ct. 1986).
In re W.A.F., 573 A.2d 1264 (D.C. Ct. App. 1990).
In re Winship, 397 U.S. 358 (1970).

REFERENCES

Bala, N. (1992a). Child sexual abuse in Canada: A measure of progress. *Annals of Health Law, 1*, 177–195.
Bala, N. (1992b). The Young Offenders Act: The legal structure. In R. Corrado, N. Bala, R. Linden, & M. Le Blanc (Eds.), *Juvenile justice in Canada* (pp. 21–73). Toronto: Butterworths.
Bala, N., & Kirvan, M. (1990). The statute: Its principles and provisions and their interpretation by the courts. In A. W. Leschied, P. C. Jaffe, & W. Willis (Eds.), *The Young Offenders Act Revolution: Changing the face of Canadian juvenile justice* (pp. 71–114). Toronto: University of Toronto Press.
Becker, M. K. (1979). Washington State's new juvenile code: An introduction. *Gonzage Law Review, 14*, 289–312.
Bogden, E. (1980). Beating the rap in Juvenile Court. *Juvenile and Family Court Journal, 31*, 19–22.
Davidson, H. A. (1987). Improving the legal response to juvenile sex offenders. *Children's Legal Rights Journal, 8*, 15–20.
Feld, B. C. (1987). The Juvenile Court meets the principle of the offence: Legislative changes in juvenile waiver statutes. *Journal of Criminal Law and Criminology, 78*, 471–533.
Grisso, T. (1980). Juvenile's capacities to waive Miranda rights: An empirical analysis. *California Law Review, 68*, 1134–1166.

Hanscom, D. K. (1988). *The Dynamics of disposition in Youth Court.* Unpublished LL.M. thesis, University of Toronto, Toronto.

Knitzer, J., & Sobie, M. (1984). *Law guardians in New York State: A study of legal representation of children.* New York: New York State Bar Association.

Krisberg, B. (1989). *Juvenile justice: A critical examination.* San Francisco CA: National Council on Crime and Delinquency.

Law Society of Upper Canada. (1981). *Report of the subcommittee on the legal representation of children.* Toronto: Author.

National Task Force on Juvenile Sexual Offending. (1988). Preliminary report 1988. *Juvenile & Family Court Journal, 39,* 1–67.

Rogers, R. (1990). *Reaching for solutions: The report of the special advisor to the Minister of National Health and Welfare on child sexual abuse in Canada.* Ottawa: Health & Welfare Canada.

Schneider, A. L., & Ervin, L. (1988). *Deterrence and juvenile crime: Expanding the behavioural assumptions of public policy.* Paper presented to the 1988 annual meeting of the American Society of Criminology, Chicago.

Schwartz, I. (1989). *Justice for juveniles: Rethinking the best interests of the child.* Lexington, MA: Lexington Books.

CHAPTER 3

Exploring Characteristics for Classifying Juvenile Sex Offenders

Raymond A. Knight
Robert A. Prentky

The heterogeneity of adult sex offenders has been well documented (Knight, Rosenberg, & Schneider, 1985), and concerted efforts are under way to identify more homogeneous subgroups for the purposes of elucidating etiology, improving prediction, and enhancing dispositional accuracy (Knight & Prentky, 1990; Knight, 1992). No comparable taxonomic program has, however, been undertaken for juvenile sex offenders. The purpose of this chapter is to assess the need for such a program for juvenile offenders and to examine what dimensions and taxonomic structures might serve as reasonable points of departure in the systematic exploration for viable typologies for young offenders.

THE HETEROGENEITY OF JUVENILE SEX OFFENDERS

Three arguments support the contention that juvenile sex offenders are at least as heterogeneous as sexually coercive adults. First, data indicating that a significant portion of adult rapists and child molesters have engaged in sexually coercive behavior as juveniles suggest that the heterogeneity found among adult offenders may also exist among juvenile offenders. Second, the apparently low recidivism rates reported for juvenile offenders indicate that there may be a substantial subgroup of these offenders whose deviant sexual behavior does not persist into adulthood. It is reasonable to hypothesize that offenders whose sexually coercive behavior desists may differ in substantive ways from those who continue to assault as adults. Third, juvenile offender samples typically comprise both rapist and child molester subgroups. Among adults, particular victim-age-preference subgroups have been shown to differ on a number of critical characteristics. It is plausible to speculate that these differences generalize to adolescent offenders. We will discuss each of these arguments in turn.

When adult sex offenders are assured that their responses are either anonymous or held in strict confidence, as many as 50% of them report that their first sexual assault occurred during adolescence (e.g., Abel, Mittelman, & Becker, 1985; Becker & Abel, 1985; Groth, Longo, & McFadin, 1982; Smith, 1984). This indicates that a large subsample of adult sex offenders were also juvenile offenders. Consequently, prima facie evidence for the heterogeneity of juvenile sex offenders would be provided, if it could be shown that adult sex offenders with histories of sexual assaults as adolescents (juvenile sex offenders [JSOs]) did not differ from adult sex offenders who had no juvenile sex offense histories (Not-JSOs) in the distribution of their typological assignments to taxonomic systems devised to reduce the heterogeneity among the adult offenders. To examine this issue we compared the typological assignments of JSOs and Not-JSOs sampled from the Massachusetts Treatment Center (MTC).

Although, as we have just indicated, there are juvenile sex offenders who continue their deviant sexual behavior into adulthood, the overall recidivism rates of juvenile offenders are reportedly substantially lower than those of adult offenders (Atcheson & Williams, 1954; Furby, Weinrott, & Blackshaw, 1989; Smith, 1984; Smith & Monastersky, 1986). Even though these recidivism data are highly problematic and do not permit cross-study comparisons, they nonetheless suggest that some juvenile sex offenders may desist from assaultive sexual behavior and would not be considered sex offenders as adults. The JSO group in our MTC sample obviously only includes those males whose sexually coercive behavior has persisted into adulthood. Thus, we will not be able to test directly whether males who continue to be sexually aggressive can be discriminated from those who do not. If, however, consistent characteristics of the JSOs in our sample could be identified, these would certainly constitute a set of variables worthy of further study as vulnerability markers for recidivism in juvenile offender samples.

Because of the greater difficulty differentiating between age-appropriate and age-inappropriate sexual preferences for offenders who commit sexual assaults as adolescents, generic juvenile offender samples are, with rare exceptions (Groth, 1977), heterogeneous with respect to their victim-age preferences. Although there may be notable overlaps on certain dimensions between adult rapists and child molesters (Rosenberg & Knight, 1988), there are also critical differences between these general groups (Bard et al.,1987). Moreover, there appear to be subgroups in each that are sufficiently different to constitute exclusive victim-age subgroups (Rosenberg & Knight, 1988). In Groth's (1977) analysis of adult offenders who committed juvenile offenses, he divided the offenders into three groups by the relative age of the victims in their juvenile crimes. His results suggest that victim-age-preference differences may be as important among juvenile offenders as they are among adult offenders. Our examination of the assignments of the JSOs to both rapist and child molester adult typologies will allow us not only to assess the prevalence within juvenile offenders of the various rapist and child molester types, but also to determine whether the more exclusive age-preference types are represented among JSOs.

In addition to justifying the taxonomic study of juvenile sex offenders, these three arguments also suggest that studying the differences between adult offenders with a history of juvenile sexual aggression and those without may provide a strategy for exploring what dimensions and structures may be good candidates for discriminating among juvenile offenders. By studying adult offenders on whom a substantial amount of both life history and typological information were available, we were able to identify those who had been convicted or charged with juvenile sexual offenses (i.e., were identified as JSOs as adolescents) and those for whom there is no evidence of juvenile sexual aggression in their juvenile criminal records (Not-JSOs). Then, by comparing the distributions of rapist and child molester type assignments for these two groups and by examining the differences between these groups on selected critical variables, we were able to determine which of the taxonomic structures found to be important for discriminating among adults were potentially important for discriminating among juvenile offenders. For a subset of the MTC sample we also had self-report data on their juvenile sex offending. Using these data, we were able to divide the Not-JSO group into two subgroups: (1) a "hidden" group of juvenile offenders, who reported that they had been sexually aggressive as adolescents, but who had not been caught and charged (Hidden-JSO), and (2) a group of offenders who neither reported nor were charged with juvenile sex offenses (No Ev-JSO). Contrasting Hidden-JSO groups with the charged juvenile offenders allowed us to separate those dimensions related simply to being apprehended as a juvenile from those that were specifically related to early sexual aggression. Thus, comparisons among these three groups (JSO, Hidden-JSO, and No Ev-JSO) could suggest dimensions that are particularly important for a typology of juvenile sex offenders. Moreover, discriminating characteristics should provide potential markers for separating those juvenile sex offenders who are at risk to continue their deviant sexual aggression into adulthood from those whose sexual aggression is confined to adolescence.

Generating and Evaluating Typologies for Juvenile Sex Offenders

As we have discussed elsewhere (Knight, 1992; Knight & Prentky, 1990; Knight et al., 1985) a methodology for generating and assessing typological systems has been developed and applied to adult offenders with some success. This programmatic approach to taxonomy building, which provides general procedural guidelines for creating juvenile offender taxonomics, calls for the application of both inductive/empirical and deductive/rational research strategies simultaneously. The two strategies differ in their points of departure.

In the inductive strategy one focuses initially on identifying and operationalizing the dimensions that are purported critical for discriminating among offenders. Various clustering algorithms can then be applied to these dimensions to generate various typological models. The validity of these models is then tested by determining, for instance, whether the types differ in their developmental histories, whether they vary on critical hypothesized dimensions in consistent ways, and whether they have distinguishable outcomes. The inductive strategy is not, of course, devoid of theory. The initial dimension-selection process and the choice of clustering techniques must be guided by some theoretical considerations (Popper, 1972). Indeed, this strategy inevitably fails when theoretical speculations are absent, insufficient, or wrong (Blashfield, 1980; Meehl, 1979).

When applying the deductive strategy, theoretical speculations of taxonomic structure are more critical than in the inductive method. Here one operationalizes a putative theoretical taxonomic model, adjusts classification criteria until adequate reliability is attained, classifies offenders according to these criteria, and assesses the validity of the system in the same way that the typological models generated by the inductive strategy are evaluated. The simultaneous application of both strategies to the same sample allows a cross-fertilization of results, and can ultimately lead to an integrative bootstrapping of a new, hopefully more valid model (see Knight & Prentky, 1990).

The emphasis in both of these strategies on the importance of some theoretical guidance in choosing potential dimensions and structures as starting points for building typologies is central to the focus of this chapter. To the degree that we choose the most appropriate dimensions and structures as starting points for our taxonomic program on juvenile sex offenders, we increase the probability of success. Thus, our choice of preliminary dimensions and structures must be informed both by the extant empirical data gathered on these offenders and by the relevant taxonomic speculations on juvenile offenders in the clinical literature. Indeed, in implementing our dimension-identification strategy of studying adult sex offenders who began their sexual coercion as juveniles, we should consider not only the taxonomic structures that have proven successful with adults, but also the dimensions that have emerged in the empirical and theoretical literatures as discriminating characteristics of juvenile sex offenders. Consequently, we reviewed the empirical studies on juvenile offenders, focusing on discerning the dimensions that appear to be either critical discriminators among these offenders or differentiators of these offenders from other related groups. We also examined the taxonomic systems proposed for juvenile offenders to determine which of the proposed types in the literature appear to be viable candidates for operationalization and testing. We then assessed the ability of these dimensions and structures to discriminate the JSOs and Hidden-JSOs from the No Ev-JSOs in our study.

Empirical Studies of Possible Discriminating Dimensions

Unfortunately, most of the empirical studies on juvenile sex offenders are limited to simple tallies of the frequencies of particular descriptive characteristics of these offenders and their offenses, such as their ages, the history of their previous sex and nonsex offending, the types of sexual crimes they have committed, and the ages and sexes of their victims (see Davis & Leitenberg, 1987, for a review). Only a handful of studies have actually compared juvenile sex offenders to delinquent or normal controls, and the few studies that have assessed the discriminatory power of variables among juvenile sex offenders have been only minimally informative for taxonomic purposes. Thus, the empirical literature provides only weak speculations about the importance of particular dimensions. We will review the most important of these dimensions.

Family environment. It has frequently been hypothesized that being physically abused or observing family violence may contribute to the development of sexual violence in adolescence (Fehrenbach, Smith, Monastersky, & Deisher, 1986; Gomes-Schwartz, 1984; Boone-Hamilton, 1991). In accord with these speculations, Van Ness (1984) found that whereas only 15% of a matched sample of delinquents indicated that they had been physically abused or neglected, 41% of adolescent sex offenders reported such abuse. Likewise, Lewis, Shanok, and Pincus (1981) found that whereas 75% of their violent adolescent sex offenders had been physically abused, only 29% of other delinquents had experienced such abuse. Physical abuse was not, however, unique to sex offenders. An equal percentage of violent nonsex offenders had also been physically abused. Physical abuse must be distinguished from punitive disciplinary practices, however, because nonincarcerated adolescent sex offenders were not found to differ from controls on such parental practices (McCord, McCord, & Venden, 1962).

Sexual history and adjustment. It has been hypothesized that the sexual aggression of juveniles may be due in part to the recapitulation of their own sexual victimization (Rogers & Terry, 1984). Support for this contention has been found in the relatively high proportion of adolescents in samples of sexual aggressors who were themselves the victims of sexual abuse (Becker, Kaplan, Cunningham-Rathner, & Kavoussi, 1986 [23%]; Fehrenbach et al., 1986 [19%]; Friedrich & Luecke, 1988 [81%]; Longo, 1982 [47%]). These incidences exceed estimates of sexual abuse in the general male population (Finkelhor, 1979), and they are higher than the incidences of such abuse among

juvenile offenders who have been accused of noncontact sexual offenses (Fehrenbach et al., 1986). Moreover, Becker (1988) argued that the rates reported
by juvenile sex offenders may actually underestimate the prevalence of sexual
victimization in these samples, because the reporting of sexual abuse often
emerges only after the adolescent has been in therapy. Although there is some
evidence that there is a high frequency of sexual deviation in the homes of
juvenile sex offenders (38%) (Awad, Saunders, & Levene, 1984), this proportion has not been found to differ from the frequency evident in the homes of
non-sex delinquents.

Among college students and adults deviant sexual arousal patterns have
been identified as one of the most consistent discriminators of the propensity
to engage in sexually coercive behavior (see Prentky & Knight, 1991). Unfortunately, controlled studies of the patterns of sexual arousal and of sexual
fantasies of adolescent sex offenders have thus far been neglected. A distinction has been proposed in the clinical, taxonomic literature (Becker, 1988)
between juvenile offenders with deviant recurrent fantasies and a preference
for deviant activity and those for whom sexual aggression is simply a part of
their impulsive behavior. One would expect the former to be likely to manifest
a higher rape index (i.e, a higher phallometrically assessed arousal response to
sexually coercive stimuli than to consensual sexual stimuli). The majority of
adolescent sex offenders report that they have had prior consenting genital
sexual experience (Becker et al., 1986; Groth, 1977) or consenting intercourse
(Longo, 1982), and there is some evidence that they may have had significantly more heterosexual experience than nonoffending controls (McCord et
al., 1962). Also, there is evidence that a majority of them (Longo, 1982) might
also have experienced some prior sexual dysfunction, most often impotence or
premature ejaculation.

Social competence. Despite the fact that social competence has been
found to be a poor discriminator between adult sex offenders as a general group
and criminal controls (Prentky & Knight, 1991), it still apparently plays an
important role as a differentiator among subtypes of sex offenders (Knight,
1992; Knight & Prentky, 1990). Although no studies have been conducted that
have compared juvenile sex offenders to delinquent controls on social skills
measures, social deficits have been among the most common characteristics
attributed to adolescent sex offenders. Fehrenbach et al. (1986) found evidence
of serious social isolation in 65% of the adolescent sex offenders evaluated in
their program. Becker and Abel (1985) hypothesized that juvenile sex offenders
may become isolated from their peers because of poor social skills, particularly
assertiveness. Groth (1977) argued that juvenile sex offenders were deficient in
their ability to create and maintain close friendships, and Shoor, Speed, and
Bartelt (1966) reported that a large portion of adolescents in their sample who
had molested younger children were socially isolated. In addition, Awad et al.

(1984) found that significantly more sex offenders (46%) than juvenile delinquent controls (17%) were loners.

Behavioral problems. A number of studies have found that adolescent sex offenders frequently have histories of other criminal activity. Shoor et al. (1966) found that 63% of the juvenile offenders in their sample reported previous delinquent activity and one-third had juvenile records. In Amir's (1971) sample 41% of the adolescent rapists had earlier arrest records. In Van Ness's (1984) incarcerated sample, 86% of the sex offenders had engaged in four or more previous aggressive behaviors, and 44% of the adolescent sex offenders in Fehrenbach et al.'s (1986) sample had committed at least one earlier nonsexual offense. In addition, 50% of the adolescents in Becker et al.'s (1986) sample had prior nonsexual offense records, and 55% were diagnosed as having character disorders. Consistent with these findings 50% of Awad et al.'s (1984) adolescent sex offenders had histories of previous court appearances and/or police contacts, but a greater proportion of their delinquent controls (75%) had such histories.

Neurological and cognitive problems. Consistent with earlier studies (Atcheson & Williams, 1954; Sauceda, 1978), Awad et al. (1984) found that their sample of adolescent sex offenders had significantly lower IQs than delinquent controls. In contrast, Tarter, Hegedus, Alterman, and Katz-Garris (1983) found no apparent differences between adolescent sex offenders and nonsex juvenile delinquents on a comprehensive cognitive and neuropsychological battery. Lewis et al. (1981) have found considerable soft neurological and cognitive differences between violent juvenile sex offenders and delinquents, but no differences on these dimensions between the sex offenders and violent, non–sex juvenile offenders. Their results suggest that the cognitive and organic impairments may be more associated with violence in general rather than with sexual violence in particular. Indeed, Lewis et al.'s (1981) hypothesis that juvenile sex offenders are characterized by a cluster of symptoms consisting of signs of organic impairment, an IQ below 80, and increased incidence of aggressive behavior, both sexual and nonsexual, may only be true of more violent sex offenders. The discrepancies across various studies in the IQ comparisons between juvenile sex offenders and delinquent controls might be accounted for by variations in the frequency of violent sex offenders in different samples.

School achievement. Although the data on IQ and cognitive abilities are somewhat inconsistent, there is relatively consistent evidence that juvenile sex offenders have some problems in school. In Fehrenbach et al.'s (1986) adolescent sex-offender sample, only 57% had attained their appropriate or superior grade placement. Over 80% of the sex offenders in Awad et al.'s (1984) sample had experienced learning and/or behavioral difficulties during some part of their school career. Indeed, 71% of the sex offenders, compared to 46% of the delinquent controls, had had remedial education.

Level of force and physical injury to victims. A study using the Nation Crime Victimization Survey Data (McDermott & Hindelang, 1981) compared adolescents, young adults, and adults in the level of coercion employed in sexual assaults against victims who were 12 years old or older. The authors concluded that adolescents were less likely than young adults or adults to use weapons or to injure their victims physically in their sexual assaults. Even though adolescents may inflict less overall injury on their victims than adults may, a wide range of coercion and violence has been reported in the sexual assaults committed by juveniles, ranging from no intimidation or threat, through threat, physical force, and extreme violence (Fehrenbach et al., 1986; Groth, 1977; Lewis et al., 1981; Wasserman & Kappel, 1985). This variation suggests that violence may play the same taxonomic role in juvenile offenses as it does in adult offenses (Knight & Prentky, 1990; Prentky & Knight, 1991). It is difficult to predict whether JSOs will differ from Not-JSOs in the violence in their offenses, because it may be that the less violent adolescents are those whose sexual aggression does not persist into adulthood. Alternatively, less violent offenders may be less likely to be caught.

Race. Among juvenile sex offenders blacks appear to be overrepresented, and this is especially true in forcible rape (Brown, Flanagan, & McLeod, 1984). Of course, arrest rates are biased against blacks. The female head-of-household that predominates in lower-class black families has been used to account for this higher prevalence of blacks in juvenile sex offender samples (Davis & Leitenberg, 1987), but it does not seem to be an adequate explanation. Rosen (1969) found that father-absent homes were not overrepresented in adolescents who offended against people, which included adolescents accused of rape. The comparison in our analyses between charged (JSO) and unapprehended juvenile offenders (Hidden-JSO) will provide a test of whether this race discrepancy is due to apprehension.

Thus, these studies identify a constellation of variables that appear to characterize sizable subgroups of juvenile sex offenders. Although these variables do not consistently differentiate sex offenders from generic delinquents, these studies do suggest dimensions that might be useful for creating more homogeneous subtypes of juvenile sex offenders. It is noteworthy that some of these dimensions (e.g., social competence, lifestyle impulsivity, and sexualization) are part of the typologies we will be examining, and other variables (e.g., neurological and cognitive deficits and sexual victimization) have been found to be related to our child molester typology in consistent ways (e.g., Knight, 1992). Consequently, by studying the distribution of types in JSOs and Not-JSOs, and by determining the prevalence of these variables among JSOs and comparing the JSOs and Not-JSOs on these dimensions, we will be able to evaluate the potential of these dimensions as taxonomic discriminators for juvenile sex offenders.

Taxonomic Speculations about Juvenile Sex Offenders

Taxonomic speculation about juvenile offenders is quite meager. Although several researchers have speculated about possible subgroups (e.g., Becker, 1988; Groth, 1977), we know of only one taxonomic system that has been proposed specifically for juvenile offenders (O'Brien & Bera, 1986). Unfortunately, no concrete criteria have been provided for this system. Because this typology has apparently not yet been implemented, neither reliability estimates, nor evidence of group homogeneity, nor validity assessments exist. Of the seven types proposed in this typology, two, the Naive Experimenter and the Group-Influenced, appear to be situationally determined cases with hypothetically good prognosis. In one of the more serious types, the Disturbed Impulsive, the sexual aggression is hypothesized to be secondary to severe psychopathology or substance abuse. Of the four types in which the sexual aggression seems to be primary, one type is characterized by its low social competence, a second by early childhood abuse (sexual, physical, or emotional), a third by its impulsive lifestyle, and the fourth by sexual preoccupation and compulsivity. Thus, there is considerable overlap between the dimensions we have identified in our review of the empirical literature and the key discriminating dimensions proposed in this speculative typological system.

Becker (1988) made a distinction between juvenile offenders who have deviant recurrent sexual fantasies and a preference for deviant sexual activity and another group whose sexual aggression is simply a part of its delinquent or conduct-disordered behavior. These two types bear some descriptive similarity to O'Brien and Bera's (1986) Sexual Compulsive and Sexual Aggression types, respectively. Groth (1977) has suggested that the dynamics of juvenile offenders parallel those of adult offenders. Therefore, he has hypothesized that in juvenile offender samples there should be power and anger rapist subtypes, as well as a passive, fixated child molester type. Because these types or their equivalents have not been found to be optimal subdivisions in adult offender samples (e.g., Knight, 1989, 1992; Knight & Prentky, 1987, 1990; Prentky, Knight, & Rosenberg, 1988), they are not likely to tap major taxonomic boundaries in juvenile offender samples. Thus, although taxonomic speculations about juvenile sex offenders have focused on dimensions similar to those that the empirical literature has identified as prevalent in juvenile samples, no compelling, reliable, validated system has emerged. Consequently, we have chosen to examine the utility of two reliable, reasonably valid typologies that we have generated—one for child molesters (Knight, Carter, & Prentky, 1989) and one for rapists (Knight & Prentky, 1990)—as preliminary models for exploring the taxonomic structures of juveniles.

METHOD

Subjects

The subjects in this study were 564 male sex offenders who had been committed as sexually dangerous to the Massachusetts Treatment Center in Bridgewater, Massachusetts. The center was established in 1959 under special legislation for the purpose of evaluating and treating individuals convicted of repetitive and/or aggressive sexual offenses. The legislation provided for a civil, day-to-life commitment for those deemed to be "sexually dangerous." The present sample includes all of those offenders who were committed to MTC since 1959. The subsamples of offenders who were administered the Developmental Interview ($n = 150$) and the Multidimensional Assessment of Sex and Aggression (MASA) ($n = 127$) were drawn from the currently committed offenders on a voluntary basis. In the present study, the term *rapist* refers to an adult male whose sexual offenses were committed against adult women (i.e., age > 16). The term *child molester* refers to an adult male whose sexual offenses were committed against victims under the age of 16. A sexual offense was defined as any sexually motivated assault involving physical contact with the victim. In this sample 254 offenders were classified as rapists, and 207 were classified as child molesters. The remaining 103 either could not be classified exclusively as either rapists or child molesters because they had victims who were both above and below 16, or there was insufficient information to assign an offender to a specific type.

Subjects in the entire sample were divided into two groups—those (JSOs) whose criminal records indicated that they had been charged with or convicted of a serious sexual crime (i.e., a crime involving physical contact with a victim) prior to their 19th birthday, and those (Not-JSOs) who had not been charged or convicted of a serious sexual crime until after their 19th birthday. For the subsample of these offenders who had been administered the Developmental Interview, we were able to identify a third group (Hidden-JSOs), offenders who reported engaging in sexually coercive behavior as adolescents, but were never apprehended for their activities.

Procedures

Clinical File Coding and Abstraction

The primary data source for subtyping subjects and for coding variables was an offender's extensive clinical file, which included all information gathered during the man's evaluation and commitment periods at the treatment center. Information collected during the man's observation period included, in addition to reports of diagnostic and psychometric assessments and clinical interviews conducted as part of the evaluation itself, data from multiple sources external to the treatment center, such as past institutionalization records, school and employment reports, police reports, court testimony, parole summaries, probation records, and social service notes. These reports not only originated from different agencies, but were also written at different points in the subject's life to describe events as they were occurring at that time. In almost all cases (90% or higher), social service and school reports were available that predated the subject's first arrest for a sexual offense. Access to these original reports helped to counteract the retrospective biases inherent in file research based largely on summary reports of a subject's life written after events of particular importance have already taken place (in the case of this study, after the onset of criminal activity). Postcommitment information routinely available included such treatment center records as treatment reports, behavioral observation reports, work reports, and summaries of program participation.

The files were rated using a set of rationally scaled variables that were created after we had reviewed the literature (see Knight et al., 1985) and closely examined the clinical files that were the data source for the ratings. Levels on all scales were criterion based and tailored to the information available in the files. The content and structure of the individual scales are described in the tables in which they appear.

Two trained research assistants independently coded and rated each file and then met to reach a consensus agreement regarding their ratings, if discrepancies existed. Interrater reliabilities were calculated on the independent, preconsensus ratings. Because consensus ratings were used in all subsequent analyses, the reliability estimates are the Spearman–Brown transformations of the preconsensus ratings, reflecting the increased reliability gained by averaging judgments (see Roff, 1981). Reliabilities ranged from .80 to .98.

During the coding process a research assistant created for each offender a case-history abstract that contained all essential life-history and criminal data. These abstracts were used for classification purposes.

Classification Procedure

The abstracts created by the above procedure were read by two of a group of six clinicians or research assistants trained in the use of the MTC Rapist Typology, Version 3 (MTC:R3) or the MTC Child Molester Typology, Version 3 (MTC:CM3). Each rater independently assigned each offender either to an MTC:R3 type or to the Axis I and Axis II types of MTC:CM3. When two raters disagreed on a type assignment, they met to resolve their discrepancy and reach consensus. In the rare instances in which they could not reach a mutually satisfactory type classification, a third rater made an independent rating, and this rating was used to resolve the discrepancy. All of the distribution analyses presented in this study were computed on the consensus ratings.

Assigning rapists to types. The classification system for rapists (MTC:R3; see Figure 3.1) is a prototypical model whose structure was generated by juxtaposing types according to their proximity on cluster dentrograms and the similarities of their profiles on critical variables (e.g., lifestyle impulsivity/ antisocial behavior, social competence, aggression in their sexual assaults, expressive aggression, and sexualization) (see Knight & Prentky, 1990). Assignment to types in this typology is achieved by an offender meeting a specific set of criteria for each type. For the Opportunistic types (Types 1 and 2) the sexual assaults appear to be impulsive, predatory acts, controlled more by situational and contextual factors than by sexual fantasy or explicit anger at women. The primary motivation for the Pervasively Angry type (Type 3) is hypothesized to be global and undifferentiated anger (i.e., these offenders are equally likely to express their unmanageable aggression at men and women). There are four types whose motivation is hypothesized to be "sexual" (i.e., marked by the presence of protracted sexual or sadistic fantasies that influence as well as sustain the rapes). These offenders (Types 4, 5, 6, and 7 in Figure 3.1) have in common some form of enduring sexual preoccupation. This preoccupation may be distorted by the fusion of sexual and aggressive feelings (Types 4 and 5) or be characterized by dominance needs and/or acute feelings of inadequacy (Types 6 and 7). The final hypothesized motivation involves misogynistic anger. It is hypothesized that for the two Vindictive offender types (8 and 9) women are a central and exclusive focus of their anger. The sexual assaults of these men are distinguished by behaviors that are explicitly intended to harm the woman physically, as well as to degrade and humiliate her. MTC:R3 has recently been

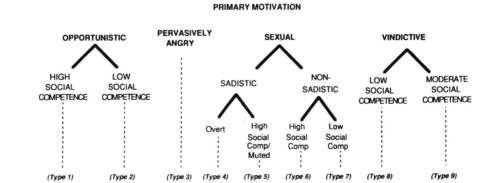

FIGURE 3.1. Relative similarity positioning and hierarchical organization of the polythetic types in MTC:R3.

used to classify 254 offenders. Preliminary analyses on the reliability and concurrent validity of this revised model are encouraging. The kappa for the primary subtype assignment for the 254 offenders was .68, which by Cicchetti and Sparrow's (1981) criteria is good. In cases where the victim selection appeared to be indiscriminate (i.e., victims were both under and over the age of 16 with no primary target age), the case was excluded from classification. In addition, when the clinical file of an offender contained insufficient information for making a reliable classification the case was excluded.

Assigning child molesters to types. The classification system for child molesters (MTC:CM3) consists of two independent axes (see Figure 3.2). Axis I consists of two dichotomous, crossed constructs—fixation and social competence—yielding four types. The fixation variable (Decision 1 on Axis I) is coded "high" if there is unequivocal, direct evidence that children have been a central focus of the offender's sexual and interpersonal thoughts and fantasies for a protracted period (at least 6 months). Behavioral evidence of high fixation includes three or more sexual contacts with children over a period greater than 6 months, enduring relationships with children, and contact with children in numerous situations over the lifetime. The social competence variable (Decision 2 on Axis I) is coded "high" if the subject has demonstrated two or more of the following: (a) a single job lasting 3 years or longer; (b) marriage or cohabitation with an adult (over age 16) for 1 year or longer; (c) raising a child for 1 year or longer; (d) active membership in an adult-oriented organization for 1 year or longer (organizations such as the Cub Scouts/Boy Scouts are excluded); (e) friendship with a peer, not involving marriage or cohabitation, lasting 1 year or longer.

Axis II of MTC:CM3 consists of a hierarchical series of decisions beginning with Amount of Contact with children. A basic distinction is made between the amount of time an individual spends in close proximity with children (e.g., as a camp counselor, school teacher, bus driver, etc.) over a protracted period of time (Decision 1 on Axis II) and the strength of an individual's pedophilic interest (i.e., the extent to which children are a major focus of the individual's thought and attention), as captured by the degree of fixation (Decision 1 on Axis I). An individual is coded as "high contact" if there is clear evidence that he spends time with children in multiple contexts, both sexual and nonsexual. Such contexts may be vocational (e.g., school teacher) or avocational (e.g., little league coach). In addition, repeated (three or more) sexual encounters with the same child are considered evidence for high contact.

For high-contact offenders a subsequent distinction (Decision 2 on Axis II) is made between those molesters who seek to establish interpersonal relationships with children (Type II-1) and those whose high contact is exclusively sexually motivated (Type II-2). For low-contact offenders subsequent dichotomous discriminations on the degree of physical injury inflicted on the child

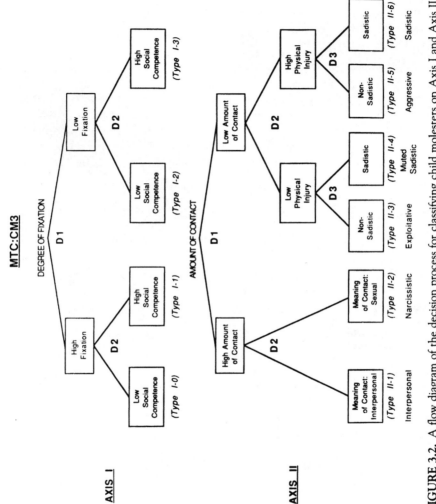

FIGURE 3.2. A flow diagram of the decision process for classifying child molesters on Axis I and Axis II of MTC:CM3. D1 = Decision 1; D2 = Decision 2; D3 = Decision 3.

(Decision 2) and on the absence or presence of sadism (Decision 3) yield the four low-contact groups (Types II-3 to II-6) depicted at the bottom of the figure. The complete classification criteria are presented in Knight et al. (1989).

MTC:CM3 already has demonstrated reasonable reliability. Based on a sample of 177 offenders, the kappas for dimensions discussed in this paper are good: Fixation (.67), Social Competence (.84), Amount of Contact with Children (.70), Physical Injury (.76), and Sadism (.60) (Knight et al., 1989). In addition, MTC:CM3 has evidenced ties to antecedent life events (Prentky, Knight, Rosenberg, & Lee, 1989), recidivism, and symptom domains (Knight, 1992).

Developmental Interview

The Developmental Interview, which was compiled by our research team, consists of 541 questions and statements regarding the subject's family, developmental experiences, school experiences, peer relations through childhood, and numerous events that may or may not have occurred (e.g., serious illness, death of a family member, divorce or separation, institutionalization, etc.). There is also a lengthy section containing self-descriptive statements. Items were selected on a rational basis after reviewing several interview schedules that explored developmental histories, most notably the Minnesota–Briggs History Record (Briggs, 1955), the developmental interviews used in Project Competence at the University of Minnesota (Garmezy, available on request from the author), and the interview schedule designed by Finkelhor (1979) for his study of childhood sexual victimization. In addition to covering areas of conventional developmental psychopathology, items were also selected for their hypothetical relevance in defining the various dimensions found to antecede aggressive and/or antisocial behavior. Although most of the items had a multiple-choice response format, a small proportion of the items required a simple dichotomous (i.e., yes/no) response.

The interview was programmed for computer administration using AVID, a software package from Advanced Interactive Systems. AVID permitted considerable flexibility in formatting and presenting questions, allowing response-based branching so that interview efficiency could be maximized and follow-up questions could gather more detailed information about specific responses. For example, if a subject indicated that he had no siblings, those sections dealing with siblings were skipped. If he indicated that one of his siblings had trouble with the law, the details of this specific sibling's difficulties were questioned.

The interview was administered by a DEC PRO 350-D System Unit to 150 of the sex offenders committed to MTC. The keyboard was masked so that only the keys required for responding were available to the subject. Instructions on how to use the computer terminal to answer interview questions were given individually. Although each subject had privacy during the interview, a research assistant was available to answer questions. Prior to the administration of the interview a very brief life history was taken by the research assistant to determine those individuals who had played a significant role during the subject's formative years. For the majority of offenders these individuals included grandparents, stepparents, foster parents, and aunts or uncles. Additional questions pertaining to these individuals were included only if the subject or the research assistant felt that the individual had impacted significantly on the life of the subject. In such cases, "secondary caregiver" sections that duplicated the questions in the mother or father sections were administered. The headings and references in these secondary caregiver sections were changed to the name of the designated caregiver.

Each interview lasted between 2 to 3 hours, depending on the number of subroutines administered to a given individual. When a subject indicated that he was fatigued or he was observed to be fatigued or anxious, the interview was terminated and one or two additional, shorter sessions were scheduled.

Multidimensional Assessment of Sex and Aggression

We designed an inventory to complement our clinical file data sources and to gather information on areas critical for classifying rapists by MTC:R3 criteria. We focused especially on areas like sexual fantasies that were inadequately represented in our archival database. The items in the inventory were generated by a five-step process. First, we surveyed all extant, appropriate self-report inventories (e.g., Chambless & Lifshitz, 1984; Eysenck, 1973; Langevin, Handy, Paitich & Russon, 1985; Minnesota Multiphasic Personality Inventory (MMPI); Mosher & Anderson, 1986; Nichols & Molinder, 1984; Singer & Antrobus, 1972; Thorne, 1966) for examples of items that appeared relevant to all domains of MTC:R3. Second, four clinicians who were very familiar with MTC:R3 scales and rating criteria judged the appropriateness of each item in the preliminary pool for assessing each of the a priori specified constructs. Third, a subset of items was selected when three or four of the raters agreed. In a few instances in which there were too few items in a particular domain, additional items on which two of the four raters agreed were added. Fourth, we adapted the final item sets both in content and in format to fit the assessment requirements of MTC:R3. Fifth, we evaluated the final item sets and created new items to cover critical areas for which no items had been identified.

The interview consists of five separate sections and can be administered in two sessions, each lasting 1 to 1½ hours. The five sections assess the major components of MTC:R3—social competence, juvenile and adult unsocialized behavior, pervasive anger, expressive aggression, sexualization, sadism, and offense planning.

We administered this inventory to 127 of the sex offenders currently committed to MTC and repeated administration after a 6-month interval for a subsample of 35 of those offenders. The test–retest reliabilities of rationally derived, empirically validated Likert scales were reasonably good, with 84% of the scales equaling or exceeding .70, and 58.3% equaling or exceeding .80. It is noteworthy that 91.7% of the scales equaled or exceeded the test–retest reliability of the MMPI K scale, which is a widely used scale in criminal populations (Gearing, 1979). Moreover, the Likert scales proved to have high internal consistency. The alphas of all scales exceeded .60, and 94% of the scales achieved alphas greater than .70. We focused on the sexualization scales in the present study.

RESULTS

Demographics

Demographic characteristics for rapists and child molesters are presented separately in Table 3.1. For each sample the variables are partitioned by the presence (JSOs) or absence (Not-JSOs) of juvenile sex offense history. JSO rapists had significantly less education, were much more likely to have had juvenile penal records, were less likely to have been married, had achieved a lower skill level in their employment, and were less likely to be Caucasian than their Not-JSO counterparts. Moreover, because they were significantly younger when first incarcerated as adults, they also had less opportunity for employment than Not-JSOs. Likewise, JSO child molesters were also much more likely to have had juvenile penal records and less likely to have married than Not-JSO child molesters. In addition, they had a lower achieved skill level, were incarcerated at an earlier age, and had substantially less opportunity for employment. Both JSO and Not-JSO child molesters, unlike the rapists, were almost entirely Caucasian and did not differ in the amount of formal education they had had. The two samples were, otherwise, quite similar.

Taxonomic Comparisons

Table 3.2 presents the frequencies of the MTC:R3 classifications of JSO and Not-JSO rapists. Offenders in these two groups differed significantly in the distribution of their MTC:R3 type assignments. The biggest frequency differences were that whereas Type 2 offenders were overrepresented in the JSOs, Type 9 offenders were overrepresented in the Not-JSOs. Moreover, classification was less widely distributed among types in the JSOs than in the Not-JSOs. Whereas only four JSO types (2, 3, 8, and 7) achieved a 10% or greater representation, seven Not-JSO types (8, 9, 3, 7, 2, 6, and 4) achieved this level of representation.

As can be seen in Table 3.3, the JSO offenders were significantly more likely to be classified in types that are judged low in social competence (see

TABLE 3.1. Social and Demographic Characteristics

		Rapists			Child molesters		
		JSO[a] (n = 61)	Not-JSO (n = 216)		JSO[a] (n = 55)	Not-JSO (n = 184)	
				χ^2			χ^2
Race	% Caucasian	76.60	90.20	8.75*	92.50	95.30	0.69
Marriage	% Never	76.10	48.30	20.11**	68.80	48.80	7.90*
Juvenile penal record	% Present	60.60	24.50	32.79**	47.40	19.80	17.34**
				F			F
IQ	$\bar{x}$	99.46	101.50	1.11	94.53	97.26	1.37
	SD	13.45	13.59		15.11	15.73	
	Range	61–142	69–138		65–132	57–128	
Education (last grade completed)	$\bar{x}$	8.82	9.71	12.29**	8.52	9.02	1.50
	SD	1.95	2.03		1.79	2.96	
	Range	4–16	4–15		4–13	2–16	
Achieved skill level[b]	$\bar{x}$	1.04	1.68	13.67**	0.58	1.71	33.24**
	SD	1.23	1.29		0.80	1.53	
	Range	0–5	0–5		0–4	0–5	
Years employable	$\bar{x}$	3.12	7.17	59.65**	5.44	14.75	63.90**
	SD	2.92	4.48		4.80	9.26	
	Range	0–13.30	0.30–25.10		0–20.3	1.9–43.6	
Age at first adult imprisonment	$\bar{x}$	18.49	22.44	61.49**	21.03	25.87	19.23**
	SD	3.01	4.40		4.96	8.17	
	Range	15–33	16–39		16–39	16–50	

[a]Presence or absence of charges for victim-involved sex offenses during adolescence.
[b]7-point scale: 0 = unskilled; 6 = high level professional.
*$p < .005$.
**$p < .001$.

Figure 3.1). The Sexualization Scale scores of the two groups, also presented in Table 3.3, were equivalent. Finally, there was no difference between the percentage of JSOs and Not-JSOs that were classified as high in expressive aggression (Types 3, 4, 8, and 9), 51.9% and 57.9%, respectively.

Tables 3.4 and 3.5 report MTC:CM3 subtype assignments for the JSO and Not-JSO child molesters. The overall subtype distributions on both Axis I and II for the two subgroups were significantly different (see Table 3.4). About 85% of the JSO child molesters were classified as Low Social Competence/High Fixation types on Axis I, compared with approximately half of the Not-JSO child molesters. These group differences were produced predominantly by differences in Social Competence. As is evident in Table 3.5, whereas there were no differences between the two groups in the distribution of High and Low-

TABLE 3.2. Classification of Rapists with and without Juvenile Sex Offense Histories[a]

JSO			Not-JSO		
MTC:R3 types	N	%	MTC:R3 types	N	%
2	25	24%	8	25	17.9%
3	25	24%	9	21	15.0%
8	15	14.4%	3	21	15.0%
7	12	11.5%	7	17	12.1%
4	9	8.7%	2	16	11.4%
1	7	6.7%	6	15	10.7%
6	6	5.8%	4	14	10.0%
9	5	4.8%	1	7	5.0%
5	0	0	5	4	2.9%
		$\chi^2_{(8)} = 19.59, p < .02.$			

[a]Presence or absence of charges for victim-involved sex offenses during adolescence.

Fixation Types, proportionately seven and a half times as many Not-JSOs as JSOs were classified as high in Social Competence.

The major difference that emerged on Axis II was that those types that have been found empirically to have the highest levels of lifestyle impulsivity (Types 4, 5, and 6) (see Knight, 1992) were overrepresented in the JSOs (43.9% vs. 22.8% for Not-JSOs). JSOs did not differ from Not-JSO offenders on the

TABLE 3.3. Classification of Rapists with and without Juvenile Sex Offense Histories[a]

Dimensional classifications using MTC:R3	JSO n (%)	Not-JSO n (%)
Social competence		
High (types 1, 5, 6 and 9)	18 (25.7)	47 (44.8)
Low (types 2, 7 and 8)	52 (74.3)	58 (55.2)
	$\chi^2_{(1)} = 6.53, p = .01$	
Sexualization Scale[b]		
0	55 (53.4)	68 (48.9)
1	28 (27.2)	41 (29.5)
2	17 (16.5)	23 (16.5)
3	3 (2.9)	7 (5.0)
	$\chi^2_{(3)} = 0.99$, n.s.	

[a]Presence or absence of charges for victim-involved sex offenses during adolescence.
[b]Scale consists of three dichotomous variables (sexual preoccupation, sexual deviance, and sexual assaults reported to be compulsive).

TABLE 3.4. Classification of Child Molesters with and without Juvenile Sex Offense Histories[a]

MTC:CM3 types		JSO n (%)	Not-JSO n (%)
Axis I			
Low social competence/high fixation	(0)	68 (85.0)	64 (50.4)
High social competence/high fixation	(1)	4 (5.0)	40 (31.5)
Low social competence/low fixation	(2)	8 (10.0)	15 (11.8)
High social competence/low fixation	(3)	0 (0)	8 (6.3)
		$\chi^2_{(5)} = 30.61, p < .001$	
Axis II			
Interpersonal	(1)	7 (8.8)	15 (11.8)
Narcissistic	(2)	24 (30.0)	45 (35.4)
Exploitative	(3)	14 (17.5)	38 (29.9)
Muted Sadistic	(4)	13 (16.3)	7 (5.5)
Non-sadistic Aggressive	(5)	15 (18.8)	14 (11.0)
Sadistic	(6)	7 (8.8)	8 (6.3)
		$\chi^2_{(5)} = 12.24, p < .05$	

[a]Presence or absence of charges for victim-involved sex offenses during adolescence.

TABLE 3.5. Classification of Child Molesters with and without Juvenile Sex Offense Histories[a]

Dimensional Classifications Using MTC:CM3	JSO n (%)	Not-JSO n (%)
Axis I		
Fixation		
High (0 + 1)	72 (90.0)	104 (81.9)
Low (2 + 3)	8 (10.0)	23 (18.1)
	$\chi^2_{(1)} = 2.54, p < .15$	
Social competence		
High (1 + 3)	4 (5.0)	48 (37.8)
Low (0 + 2)	76 (95.0)	79 (62.2)
	$\chi^2_{(1)} = 28.06, p < .001$	
Axis II		
Amount of contact with children		
High (1 + 2)	31 (38.8)	60 (47.2)
Low (3 − 6)	49 (61.3)	67 (52.8)
	$\chi^2_{(1)} = 1.44$	

[a]Presence or absence of charges for victim-involved sex offenses during adolescence.

proportion of offenders assigned to types having high contact with children (Types 1 and 2), 38.8% vs. 47.2%, respectively (see Table 3.5). Overall, slightly more JSOs than Not-JSOs were classified as high-injury types (Types 5 and 6), 27.6% versus 17.3%, respectively.

Critical Domain Comparisons

We next examined the differences between JSOs and Not-JSOs in the eight domains that from our review of the literature we had identified as potentially important taxonomic discriminators for juvenile sex offenders. We compared JSOs and Not-JSOs separately for rapists and child molesters. We found some evidence for the hypothesis that physical abuse and neglect would be more frequently found among juvenile offenders. Whereas JSO rapists were more likely to have experienced emotional neglect than Not-JSO rapists, JSO child molesters were more likely to have been physically abused than Not-JSO child molesters (see Table 3.6).

The hypothesis that JSO offenders would be more likely to have been sexually abused than Not-JSO offenders was only partially supported. Although the JSO and Not-JSO offenders in both samples did not differ with respect to intrafamilial sexual abuse of the offender, JSO child molesters, but not JSO rapists, had more frequently experienced sexual abuse as children than Not-JSOs (see Table 3.6). JSO rapists did tend, however, to come more frequently than the Not-JSO rapists from families in which sexually deviant or abusive behavior was directed at other family members. As we saw in Table 3.3, no

TABLE 3.6. Presence of Childhood Abuse among Rapists and Child Molesters with and without Juvenile Sex Offense Histories

File coded variables[a]	Rapists			Child molesters		
	JSO	Not-JSO	χ^2	JSO	Not-JSO	χ^2
Physical abuse	53.0	40.0	3.10	46.9	32.0	3.70*
Neglect	51.6	34.0	4.83**	53.6	47.1	0.57
Sexual abuse of subject by family members	13.3	8.0	1.71	21.9	14.5	1.65
Sexual abuse within family *not* involving subject	22.8	14.2	2.73	22.0	19.1	0.21
Sexual abuse *ever*	30.4	21.9	2.07	65.6	44.4	7.00***

[a]All variables are dichotomous; *df* for all χ^2 values = 1
*p = .05.
**p < .05.
***p < .01.

differences emerged between JSO and Not-JSO rapists in ratings of sexual preoccupation and deviance (i.e., sexualization). Consistent with this, neither rapist nor child molester JSOs were noted to have had a greater prevalence of paraphilias than their associated Not-JSO groups (see Table 3.7).

As can be seen in Table 3.7, the hypotheses that JSOs would be lower in social competence and higher in antisocial behavior received strong support. JSO offenders in both rapist and child molester samples were much lower in social competence on a life management scale, further supporting the results of our taxonomic analyses (see Tables 3.3 and 3.5). JSO offenders in both rapist and child molester samples were much higher on two scales reflecting impulsive, antisocial behavior during adolescence (see Table 3.7). The JSOs were not, however, higher in their adult antisocial activity, but this might simply reflect

TABLE 3.7. Behavioral Differences among Rapists and Child Molesters Who Did, or Did Not, Have Juvenile Sex Offenses[a]

File coded variables	Rapists			Child molesters		
	JSO	Not-JSO	F	JSO	Not-JSO	F
	(Mean/SD)			(Mean/SD)		
Life Management[b]	−.31/.57	.11/.56	34.14**	−.32/.55	.12/.54	31.13**
Paraphilias[c]	−.17/.52	−.13/.56	0.28	.26/.70	.22/.74	0.17
Juvenile unsocial behavior[d]	.64/.33	.34/.37	44.39**	.46/.38	.24/.35	18.08**
Delinquency and antisocial behavior[e]	.39/.62	.04/.53	24.45**	.00/.65	−.28/.52	11.59**
Adult unsocial behavior[f]	.53/.29	.46/.28	3.71	.33/.30	.30/.26	0.69
Neurocognitive deficits[g]	.01/.58	−.13/.47	4.53*	.42/.82	.04/.56	14.87**
Level of sexual aggression[h]	2.29/.84	2.46/.93	2.19	1.39/1.01	1.30/1.03	0.39

[a]Presence or absence of charges for victim-involved sex offenses during adolescence.
[b]Standardized scale consisted of five Guttman-scaled items: achieved skill level and consistency of skill level in employment, degree of independent living in community, and two assessments of degree of involvement in relationships.
[c]Standardized scale consisted of six dichotomously scored items: fetishism, voyeurism, transvestism, exhibitionism, promiscuity, compulsive masturbation.
[d]Standardized mean of six dichotomous items on MTC:R3 Juvenile. Unsocialized Behavior Scale.
[e]Standardized scale consisted of 18 dichotomously scored items, including stealing, truant, rebellious, physical aggression, impulsive, running away, temper tantrums, destructive, and homicide.
[f]Standardized mean of eight dichotomous items on MTC:R3 Adult Unsocialized Behavior Scale.
[g]Standardized scale consisted of seven dichotomously scored items: attention, learning, speech, motor coordination problems, late maturing, retardation, and learning disabilities.
[h]Five-point Guttman scale, ranging from 0 (no evidence of sexual aggression) to 4 (extreme amount of aggression).
*$p < .05$.
**$p < .001$.

their earlier incarceration and consequent reduction in time outside of prison as adults to indulge their impulsivity.

Both the neurological deficit and school achievement hypotheses received moderate corroboration. Both rapist and child molester JSOs scored higher on the developmental cognitive deficits factor (see Table 3.7), and the JSO rapists, but not the JSO child molesters, attended fewer years of school than Not-JSOs (see Table 3.1). As we saw earlier (see Table 3.1), however, neither group of JSOs differed from the Not-JSOs in IQ level. Although juvenile offenses have been found less violent than adult offenders (McDermott & Hindelang, 1981), no differences between JSOs and Not-JSOs emerged in the amount of injury they inflicted on their victims during their offenses (see Level of Sexual Aggression in Table 3.7). Finally, although our sample was predominantly Caucasian, nonwhites were somewhat overrepresented in the JSO rapists relative to the Not-JSO rapists, but no race differences were found among child molesters (see Table 3.1).

Using self-report information derived from the computerized developmental interview, we examined the relation between the self-report of juvenile sexual offenses and evidence for such offenses in the criminal records. Approximately one-third (27 out of 83, or 33%) of those adult sex offenders with no official charges for juvenile sexual offenses reported that they had in fact engaged in sexually coercive behaviors as adolescents (see Table 3.8). Only 5.7% ($n = 8$) of the offenders who took the interview did not report that they had engaged in sexually coercive activity as adolescents, when the criminal records indicated that they had been charged with a sexual assault as a juvenile. Of these eight cases six were rapists and four admitted coercive sexual activity at or before age 21, but not before age 19. The remaining four reported that they been sexually coercive only after age 21. In all subsequent analyses we tested our a priori hypotheses using three groups: JSOs, those who were charged with and reported juvenile sexual offenses; Hidden-JSOs, juvenile sex offenders, who were never charged with, but who reported, coercive sexual activity as juveniles; and No Ev-JSOs, those with no evidence of juvenile sexual offenses, who

TABLE 3.8. Comparison of Two Reports of Juvenile Sex Offenses

	Not-JSO	JSO[a]
Juvenile Sexual Coercion History[b]		
Absent	56	8
Present	27	50

[a]Record of one or more official charges for a juvenile sex offense in the institutional file
[b]Offender's report of whether or not he committed a sex offense as a juvenile

were neither charged with, nor reported, sexually coercive behaviors as juveniles.

Table 3.9 presents the comparisons among the three JSO groups on archival scales that assessed physical abuse and neglect. As noted in the table, the three-group analyses of physical abuse and neglect did not reach significance.. A perusal of the data for the rapists and child molesters separately (not presented in the table) indicated, however, that the pattern found earlier in the larger sample also held in this subsample. Whereas both the Hidden-JSO and JSO child molesters tended to experience more physical abuse than the No Ev-JSO child molesters, Hidden-JSO and JSO rapists tended to experience more neglect. These results approached, but did not reach significance because of the small number of subjects in these smaller samples. Both of these types of child abuse covaried with the offenders' reports of their sexually coercive behavior as adolescents, rather than with the fact that these offenders had been apprehended and charged with a sexual assault.

The three-group analyses corroborated the a priori hypothesis that sexually coercive juveniles would be more likely than offenders with no such histories to have been sexually assaulted themselves during childhood. Table 3.9 presents the offenders' self-reports about whether they were sexually abused as children, about the level of such abuse (i.e., fondling through intercourse), about the coercion employed in these sexual assaults, and about the age at which they were abused. The pattern of results in these comparisons was

TABLE 3.9. Childhood Abuse History

	JSO	Not-JSO		χ^2/F
		Hidden-JSO	No Ev-JSO	
Physical abuse[a]	67.6	78.9	52.4	4.45
Neglect[a]	56.8	52.9	41.2	1.79
Family sexual deviation *not* involving subject[a]	31.6	23.1	29.2	0.56
Childhood sexual assault[b]	$0.74_a/0.44$	$0.78_a/0.42$	$0.50_b/0.50$	4.84**
Level of sexual abuse[c]	$2.68_a/2.00$	$2.78_a/2.12$	$1.63_b/1.99$	4.60*
Coercion in sexual assault[d]	1.36/1.17	1.40/1.19	1.04/1.26	1.42
Age at first sexual assault[e]	$1.30_a/1.04$	$1.41_a/0.97$	$0.84_b/1.01$	4.05*

[a]File-coded dichotomous variable: 0 = no, 1 = yes.
[b]Self-report of the presence or absence of childhood sexual abuse.
[c]Self-report 6-level variable: 0 = no assault; 5 = penetration.
[d]Self-report 4-level variable: 0 = no assault; 3 = physical force.
[e]Self-report 4-level variable: 0 = no assault; 1 = 9–12; 2 = 6–8; 3 = < 6.
Means with different subscripts differ significantly at $p < .05$ (Duncan Multiple Range Test).
*$p < .05$.
**$p < .01$.

consistent across all four self-report scales, and three of the four comparisons reached significance. Both the Hidden-JSOs and JSOs indicated that they were more likely than No Ev-JSOs to have been sexually abused as children. Moreover, the level of their sexual abuse was higher and the abuse occurred at an earlier age. Thus, in this sample early sexual victimization was related to early involvement of the offender in sexually coercive behavior, rather than to the offender's apprehension for a sexual assault as a juvenile.

The hypothesis that men with juvenile sexual offense histories would report more problems with sexuality, more preoccupation with sexual fantasies, or more sexually deviant conduct was not supported (see Table 3.10). In fact, for the first five self-report variables examined, the JSO group had the lowest mean. Overall, there was little evidence for a differentially higher prevalence of deviant sexual fantasies and behavior among the three groups. From the apparently high level of sexualization reported in the entire sample, this would suggest that all groups were high, but this conclusion can be made only after we have assessed a matched group of normals.

We found that the JSOs were lower than the Not-JSOs in their social and vocational competence in the previous set of analyses. The three-group analyses presented in Table 3.11 indicate that the Hidden-JSOs occupied a middle ground between the JSOs and No Ev-JSOs on these variables. Whereas the Hidden-JSOs were closer to the JSOs on measures that assessed social and interpersonal competence (e.g., marriage), they were more like the No Ev-JSOs on variables that reflected their vocational competence and employment history (i.e., independence, achieved skill level, and years employable). On the Life Management factor, which combined both kinds of competence, they were

TABLE 3.10. Sexual Fantasy and Behavior

	JSO	Not-JSO		F
		Hidden-JSO	No Ev-JSO	
		(Mean/SD)		
MASA Inventory scales[a]				
Sexual Preoccupation	−.05/.63	.08/.62	.19/.54	0.93
Sexual Compulsivity	−.19/.57	.09/.54	.16/.65	2.44
Masculine Sexual Identity	−.13/.58	.14/.61	.06/.61	1.14
Sexual Inadequacy	−.18/.45	.11/.51	−.02/.44	2.12
Sexual Guilt	−.12/.50	.22/.49	.16/.70	1.94
Pornography Use	.20/.66	.21/.70	−.01/.50	0.85
Offense Planning	.11/.86	.15/.98	−.04/.74	0.30
Paraphilias[b]	.06/.74	.21/.74	.02/.73	0.60

[a]All scales are standardized z score composites derive from the MASA self-report inventory.
[b]Standardized (z score) composites of six dichotomous variables.

TABLE 3.11. Social/Vocational Competence and Race

	JSO	Not-JSO		χ^2/F
		Hidden-JSO	No Ev-JSO	
Marriage: % never	74.0	66.7	44.6	10.10**
Independence[a]	$1.33_a/1.55$	$2.32_b/1.70$	$2.82_b/1.52$	11.95***
Life management[b]	$-.28_a/0.51$	$-0.03_b/0.58$	$.23_c/0.53$	12.05***
Education (last grade completed)	$8.79_a/1.56$	$10.00_b/2.65$	$10.35_b/2.22$	7.25***
Achieved skill level[c]	$.91_a/1.17$	$1.93_b/1.52$	$2.05_b/1.43$	9.69***
Neurocognitive deficits[d]	$.24_a/0.72$	$-0.01_{a,b}/0.59$	$-0.08_b/0.52$	3.68*
Years employable	$3.47_a/2.98$	$9.50_b/6.10$	$10.21_b/6.33$	22.74***
Age at first adult imprisonment	$18.61_a/2.70$	$24.29_b/6.58$	$24.52_b/5.45$	20.24***
Race: % Caucasian	86.0	96.3	91.1	2.19

[a]Five-point Guttman Scale (0 = subject has never maintained himself in the community; 4 = maintained independently for at least 2 years).
[b]Standardized scale comprised five Guttman-scaled items: achieved skill level, consistency of skill level in employment, degree of independent living in community, and two assessments of degree of involvement in relationships.
[c]Seven-point scale: 0=unskilled; 6=high level professional.
[d]Standardized scale consisted of seven dichotomously scored items: attention, learning, speech, motor coordination problems, late maturing, retardation, and learning disabilities.
Means with different subscripts differ significantly at $p < .05$ (Duncan Multiple Range Test).
*$p < .05$.
**$p < .01$.
***$p < .001$.

solidly in the middle, differing significantly from both groups. Consistent with and offering a possible explanation for the poor employment record of the JSOs was their significantly earlier first penal incarceration than the other two groups.

The hypothesis that juvenile sex offenders would be higher in lifestyle impulsivity and general antisocial behavior was strongly corroborated by the three-group analyses (see Table 3.12). For most of the variables examined, the scores of the Hidden-JSOs fell between the means for the JSOs and No Ev-JSOs. In some instances they were more like the No Ev-JSOs, and differed significantly from the JSOs (e.g., in the Delinquency and Antisocial Behavior factor, in their aggressive response to frustration, and in their childhood and juvenile vandalism). In their verbal and physical assaults on peers in school the Hidden-JSOs were more like the JSOs and differed significantly from the No Ev-JSOs. Finally, on several other measures (the subjective experience of acting on impulse, verbal and physical assault on teachers, childhood and juvenile fighting, and nonsexual aggression in adulthood) the JSOs and No Ev-JSOs differed significantly from each other, but the Hidden JSOs did not differ significantly from either group.

In the three-group analyses of the final four domains, neurological/cognitive deficits, school achievement (education), and race, reported in Table

3.11, and level of sexual coercion, reported in Table 3.12, only education and the Neurocognitive Deficits factor reached significance. The JSOs completed fewer years of school than either of the other groups and scored significantly higher than the No Ev-JSOs, but not than the Hidden JSOs, on the Neurocognitive Deficits factor. It is noteworthy in the three-group analysis of race, even though it did not reach significance, only in the JSOs was there any evidence that nonwhites were overrepresented. This suggests that the overrepresentation of nonwhites among the rapist JSOs in the previous analysis was due more to an increased probability of nonwhites being apprehended, than to a higher prevalence of sexual coercion among nonwhite juveniles.

TABLE 3.12. Delinquency, Lifestyle Impulsivity, and Level of Sexual Aggression

	JSO	Not-JSO Hidden-JSO (Mean/SD)	No Ev-JSO	F
Delinquency and antisocial behavior[a]	.44$_a$/.64	−.04$_b$/.56	−.12$_b$/.52	13.52****
Aggressive response to frustration[b]	.85$_a$/.36	.52$_b$/.51	.44$_b$/.50	9.24****
Subjective experience of acting on impulse[b]	.68$_a$/.47	.43$_{a,b}$/.51	.36$_b$/.49	4.08*
Disruptiveness in school: Verbal or physical asssault on peers[c]	.76$_a$/.43	.61$_a$/.50	.32$_b$/.47	10.13****
Disruptiveness in school: Verbal or physical assault on teachers[c]	.57$_a$/.50	.43$_{a,b}$/.51	.22$_b$/.42	5.88***
Vandalism[c]	.56$_a$/.50	.30$_b$/.47	.26$_b$/.44	4.94**
Fighting[c]	.70$_a$/.46	.57$_{a,b}$/.51	.38$_b$/.49	5.13**
Assaultive offenses[c]	.45/.50	.48/.51	.29/.46	1.89
Nonsexual victimless offenses[d]	5.72/3.72	5.36/4.39	5.13/4.18	0.23
Degree of nonsexual aggression in adulthood[e]	3.08$_a$/1.33	2.50$_{a,b}$/1.82	2.00$_b$/1.54	6.52***
Adult unsocial behavior[f]	.52$_a$/.29	.49/.35	.39$_b$/.30	2.63
Degree of sexual aggression[g]	1.96/1.00	1.62/1.08	1.99/1.09	1.25

[a]Standardized scale consisted of 18 dichotomously scored items, including stealing, truant, rebellious, physical aggression, impulsive, running away, temper tantrums, destructive, and homicide.
[b]Dichotomous variables: 0 = absent; 1 = present.
[c]Dichotomous variables: 0 = absent; 1 = present (coded prior to age 16).
[d]Number of such offenses.
[e]Seven-point scale: 0 = no aggression; 6 = extreme (coding excludes sex-related aggression).
[f]Standardized mean of 8 dichotomous items on MTC:R3 Adult Unsocialized Behavior Scale.
[g]Five-point Guttman scale, ranging from 0 (no evidence of sexual aggression) to 4 (extreme amount of aggression).
Means with different subscripts differ significantly at $p < .05$ (Duncan Multiple Range Test).
*$p < .05$.
**$p < .01$.
***$p < .005$.
***$p < .001$.

DISCUSSION

The comparisons between sex offenders who had been charged with sexual offenses as juveniles and those for whom no such charges were recorded yielded consistent group differences for both rapists and child molesters. These differences narrowed the distribution of types that were represented among juvenile sex offenders. Three of the four types that accounted for 74% of the juvenile rapist classifications were defined in part by low social competence (the Low Social Competence Opportunistic type [2], the Low Social Competence Nonsadistic, Sexual type [7], and the Low Social Competence Vindictive type [8], see Figure 3.1). The fourth, the Pervasively Angry type [3], although not specifically defined as low in social competence, nonetheless typically included offenders who were judged low in social competence (i.e., individuals with poor employment records who do not maintain lasting interpersonal relationships). Similarly, the JSOs who were classified in our child molester typology were, in contrast to the Not-JSOs, predominantly assigned to types with low social competence. These differences in type assignment were consistent with the comparisons between JSOs and Not-JSOs on the Life Management factor scale. Rapist and child molester JSOs were also disproportionately assigned to types that are characterized by higher lifestyle impulsivity and criminal activity. Consistent with this, JSOs were found higher on dimensions assessing juvenile antisocial and criminal behavior. The failure to find differences between these JSOs and Not-JSOs on adult antisocial activity is likely due to their reduced opportunity for such activity because of early incarceration (see Table 3.1).

In addition to the lower social competence and higher juvenile antisocial behavior of the JSOs, differences emerged on a number of other dimensions. Consistent with what might be expected from the empirical literature on juvenile sex offenders that we reviewed earlier, JSOs had experienced either more physical abuse (child molesters) or neglect (rapists) in their families than Not-JSOs. The hypothesis that sexual abuse would be more prevalent among JSOs was not as clear. This hypothesis maintains that sexual aggression in adolescence may be either a recapitulation for sexual victimization or be modeled from observations of sexual abuse in the family. Some support was found for the hypothesis that those who had been charged with sexually coercive behavior in adolescence (JSOs) and who subsequently became child molesters, were more likely to have been sexually abused as children. In contrast, subsequent rapists, who had been charged with a sexual assault as juveniles, had a tendency ($p < .10$) to have observed more sexually abusive behavior toward others in their families. Neither JSO rapists nor JSO child molesters, however, engaged in more paraphilias as adults, and the JSO rapists were not rated as evidencing more sexual preoccupation or deviance as adults on the MTC:R3 Sexualization Scale than the Not-JSOs. Moreover, the JSO rapists had no more evidence of sexual preoccupation or deviance as adults than the Not-JSOs. In the intellectual domain, although both rapists and child molester JSO groups' IQs were equivalent to those of the Not-JSOs, the JSO rapists dropped out of school earlier and both JSO groups manifested more soft neurological signs and minor cognitive deficiencies than Not-JSOs.

In summary, the taxonomic results and the analyses of group differences suggest that only a subset of the types found in adult sexually aggressive samples may be appropriate for juvenile samples. More specifically, for both the rapist and child molester typologies, the low social competence, high antisocial types appeared to be the most prevalent among juvenile sex offenders.

The percentage of the present sample who were charged with at least one juvenile sexual offense (approximately 38%) is somewhat below the percentage of adult sex offenders who have admitted to such coercive behavior in their adolescence, when they have been assured that their responses were either anonymous or strictly confidential (e.g., Abel et al., 1985; Becker & Abel, 1985; Groth et al., 1982; Smith, 1984). This suggests that there was a subgroup in the present sample who were sexually coercive as adolescents, but whose aggressive behavior was never officially detected, and thus they were included among the Not-JSOs in the previous analyses. Consequently, the differences we have just described between the JSOs and Not-JSOs do not allow the unequivocal attribution of lower social competence, higher antisocial behavior, sexual deviance in the family of origin, neurological/cognitive deficits, and more problems in school to those whose sexually coercive behavior has an early onset. Nor can one discount the contribution of the early experience of sexual victimization or of the presence of sexual preoccupation or sexual deviance to the juvenile onset of sexual aggression. The correlates of juvenile offending in the comparisons described above may be related only to being apprehended rather than to engaging in early sexual coercion.

Fortunately, on a subgroup of our MTC sample we had responses to a confidential computerized interview in which subjects had been asked about the age at which they had first sexually coerced someone. In this interview 55% of the sample admitted that they had sexually coerced someone during their adolescence. These responses allowed us to identify a hidden group of juvenile offenders who had not been detected in the official criminal records. By comparing these hidden juvenile offenders (Hidden-JSOs) to their charged counterparts (JSOs) and to offenders whose sexual aggression began in adulthood (No Ev-JSO), we were able to assess which behavioral domains were related to being apprehended as an adolescent and which to early involvement in sexual coercion.

These comparisons suggest that specific dimensions were related more exclusively to having engaged in sexually coercive behavior as a juvenile (the combined JSOs and Hidden-JSOs) rather than to having been apprehended for and charged with a sexual assault as an adolescent (only the JSOs). These dimensions included whether the offender had been the victim of a sexual assault as a child, how young he was when the assault occurred, and whether the assault involved penetration. Also related to early sexually coercive activity were tendencies for more frequent physical abuse in the families of origin of subsequent child molesters and for more physical neglect in the families of origin of subsequent rapists. Compared to juveniles who had no evidence of sexual coercion in adolescence, sexually coercive juveniles were more frequently involved in verbal and physical assaults on their peers in school, and as adults they married less frequently and appeared to have more problems in their adult social relationships. These results are consistent with studies that suggest that early sexual abuse of children is related to sexual maladjustment in childhood and later problems in maintaining healthy close relationships (Browne & Finklehor, 1986; Conte, 1988), and are consistent with the hypothesis that early sexual abuse may play a significant role in leading to early sexually coercive behavior.

The factors that covaried with being apprehended for an early sexual assault (JSO), as opposed to having been sexually coercive as an adolescent, comprised a wide range of antisocial behaviors, including delinquency and antisocial acting out, proneness to aggression when frustrated, and impulsivity. Apprehended juveniles also evidenced more soft neurological signs and minor cognitive deficits, and the subgroup of juvenile sex offenders who were subsequently classified as rapists dropped out of school earlier and had a disproportionate number of nonwhites. Not surprisingly, the apprehended juvenile sex offenders were incarcerated earlier, had fewer years in which they were available for employment, were less able to support themselves independently, and achieved a lower job skill level than both Hidden-JSOs and No EV-JSOs.

Certain factors appeared to be related to both having been sexually coercive as a juvenile and to being apprehended for a sexual offense. The apprehended group manifested the highest levels of aggression against teachers in school, of vandalism as an adolescent, and of unsocialized aggression in both adolescence and adulthood. The unapprehended, sexually coercive adolescents occupied a middle ground on these variables between the apprehended group and those who evidenced no sexually coercive behavior as adolescents, differing significantly from neither.

These data supplement and change our interpretation of the taxonomic analyses discussed earlier. They suggest that whereas being sexually coercive as an adolescent covaries with being the victim of early sexual abuse and coming from a dysfunctional family, being apprehended for such coercion is more likely when the offender is impulsive and engages in other antisocial behavior. They also indicate that the limitations in taxonomic distributions of the JSOs in the MTC:R3 and MTC:CM3 typologies were more likely attributable to the criminal status of the JSOs than to the presence of sexual coercion in their adolescent histories. Although the sample of offenders who took our computerized interview was not sufficiently large to allow taxonomic analyses, a cursory perusal of the type distribution of the Hidden-JSOs was consistent with the hypothesis that they expanded the number of types represented in the JSOs. When the Hidden-JSOs joined the charged JSOs to define the sexually coercive juvenile group, offenders with higher social competence, especially with better employment histories, and lower impulsivity and antisocial behavior were added. Because it was these two dimensions that were primarily responsible for the restriction in the original JSO type representation, types that were found to be underrepresented among the JSOs were more frequent among the combined JSOs and Hidden-JSOs. These data suggest that with appropriate modifications of MTC:R3 and MTC:CM3, so that they can easily be applied to adolescent samples, these typologies could serve as viable points of departure for studying the taxonomic structure of sexually coercive juveniles.

It is noteworthy that even though the JSOs and Hidden-JSOs differed on a number of dimensions from those offenders whose sexual aggression began in adulthood (No Ev-JSOs), no differences among any of these groups emerged on either sexualization or on the level of aggression in sexual offenses. The lack of evidence for differences on numerous measures of sexualization, derived both from the offender's archival records and from a self-report inventory, is consistent with the hypothesis that sex offenders share some problems in their sexual adaptation that are unrelated to when their sexual aggression begins. These data also suggest that taxonomic differences in sexualization may be as important for juvenile offenders as they are for adult offenders (Prentky & Knight, 1991). The lack of a relation between the level of aggression and the age of onset of sexual aggression, and the equal representation of sadistic types in the JSOs and Not-JSOs, suggests that, although most sadists may report an early onset of their sexual/aggressive fantasies (Burgess, Hartman, Ressler, Douglas, & McCormack, 1986), either the acting out of the sexual component of these fantasies can be delayed until adulthood, or some sadists may develop their fantasies at a later age. Because a wide range of injury to victims was found in the present sample, it is possible that the level of violence in the sexual crimes of juveniles could play a taxonomic role for these offenders that is similar to its role among adult offenders (Prentky & Knight, 1991).

An important methodological consideration is illustrated in the variation between the results when only the JSO group was considered and when the Hidden-JSO group was introduced. Whereas the former group relied exclusively on official criminal records for the determination of sexual coercion in adolescence, the latter measure depended on the self-report of the offenders under conditions of strict confidentiality. Not only was there a discrepancy in the estimated frequency of juvenile sexual coercion using these two assessment procedures (38% versus 55%), but a different pattern of covariates emerged for the two measures. The pattern of covariates suggests that it was not simply that the self-report measure was encompassing a broader sampling from the same population, but that a different set of selection criteria were operating in the criminal records. That is, being apprehended for sexual coercion entailed a number of characteristics that were different from the correlates of only engaging in sexual coercion. Clearly, such data indicate that when data only from criminal record sources are available, extreme caution must be exerted in interpreting the correlates of specific crimes or in predicting criminal outcome.

The larger amount of physical and sexual abuse and neglect that characterized the families of the offenders who either began their sexually coercive behavior as adolescents or were apprehended as sexually aggressive adolescents suggests that dysfunctional families play an important role in producing and maintaining such deviant behavior. Viewed from a transactional developmental perspective (Salzinger, Feldman, Hammer, & Rosario, 1991), it is not difficult to imagine how such dysfunctional families could disrupt the child's negotiation of key early cognitive, emotional, and social tasks, and how consequent deficiencies could impact on subsequent learning and adaptation. Moreover, the negative behaviors that the child acquires in such a family could affect his environment, especially his social environment, causing it to change as well, and contributing to an escalation of the child's negative reactions.

There is a remarkable correspondence between the behavioral domains that have been identified as problematic in studies of children from abusive families and those that have differentiated the sexually coercive juveniles in our sample. Other samples of abused, maltreated children show the same low social competence manifested in our JSOs and Hidden-JSOs (e.g., Coster, Gersten, Beeghly, & Cicchetti, 1989; Howes, 1984; Howes & Eldredge, 1985; Salzinger, Kaplan, Pelcovitz, Samit, & Krieger, 1984). The literature on delinquency shows a strong relation between early abuse and the same kinds of aggressive, antisocial behavior that we found characteristic of our sample of juvenile offenders (e.g., Garbarino & Platz, 1984; Gray, 1988; Lewis, Mallouh, & Webb, 1989; McCord, 1983). The relation between abuse and the victim's aggression is found across the life span from early childhood through young adulthood (Dodge, Bates, & Pettit, 1990; Graybill, MacKie, & House, 1985; Kinard, 1980; Main & Goldwyn, 1984; Pollock et al., 1990). Moreover, Williamson, Borduin, and Howe (1991) found that neglected, sexually abused, and physically abused adolescents, but particularly the physically abused juveniles, differed from non-maltreated controls in their level of conduct disorder, and that both the neglected and physically abused adolescents differed from controls in the amount of socialized aggression reported. The relation between physical abuse and the presence of neurocognitive deficits has also been established (Frank, Zimmerman, & Leeds, 1985; Lynch & Roberts, 1982; Martin, 1976), and Williamson et al. (1991) found that all three kinds of abuse (neglect, sexual, and physical) covaried with significantly more attention problems. The deficits found in abused children in learning situations (e.g., Aber, Allen, Carlson, & Cicchetti, 1989) are also consistent with the JSOs' lower school achievement.

In addition to behavioral domains for which the sexually aggressive juveniles have demonstrated substantial overlap with abused children, there are also some characteristics of abused children that have not been studied in juvenile sex offenders that might be important for understanding the behavior of juvenile offenders and for developing intervention strategies. For instance, abused children show less empathy than nonabused children (Miller & Eisenberg, 1988); they are have more difficulty recognizing appropriate emotions in others and in taking the perspective of another (Barahal, Waterman, & Martin, 1981); and they are less concerned with the distress of their peers (Main & George, 1985).

The data we have presented in this chapter suggest that sexual and physical abuse and neglect are intertwined in complex patterns in the developmental histories of sexually aggressive juveniles. The interaction among these abuses and other antecedents can only be disentangled by integrating converging lines of evidence from cross-sectional and longitudinal studies of both the consequences of specific patterns of childhood abuse with similar studies of juvenile sex offenders and their families. A transactional, developmental perspective offers an overarching framework to guide such an integration and to suggest potentially fruitful domains that should be assessed. In addition, the data in this chapter corroborate the hypothesis that juvenile sex offenders are heterogeneous and suggest that two typologies developed for adult sex offenders (MTC:R3 and MTC:CM3; see Knight & Prentky, 1990) have some promise for reducing the heterogeneity of these offenders. Indeed, such taxonomic differentiation might prove useful in differentiating etiologic components and helping to unravel the complex interaction among the developmental antecedents of sexual aggression.

Given the marked heterogeneity of these offenders, it is surprising that there has not been a greater concern for taxonomic specification among these offenders. Perhaps the lack of concern with taxonomics is simply a consequence of the mistaken view, described by Groth (1977), that adolescents commit few sexual offenses of serious consequence. It may also reflect the general reluctance of clinicians to apply deviant labels, especially sexually deviant labels, to children (Longo & Groth, 1983). The documentation of the seriousness and prevalence of adolescent sexual aggression (e.g., Davis & Leitenberg, 1987) has clearly dispelled the first barrier to taxonomic inquiry. The second concern has some merit because clinical labels can have some negative consequences (e.g., Mosher, 1978; Sarbin, 1967). If, however, we refrain from "applying labels" because of fears about the possible negative consequences of the misapplication of such labels, we would also forfeit our chances of discerning causes, of designing intervention programs that address the more specific needs of subgroups, of identifying vulnerable individuals who might profit from primary prevention programs, and of improving our dispositional decisions about specific subgroups of offenders. Categorization is a necessary prerequisite and sustainer of all scientific inquiry (Hempel, 1965). Our ability to improve our

understanding of and decisions about these offenders rests firmly on the reliability and the validity of the categorical structures we generate and apply. Thus,
categorization yields multiple advantages, and must be pursued. We must also
remain cognizant of the limits of our taxonomic models and continually challenge our constructs and scrutinize the empirical validity of the measures and
types we generate. In essence, we must apply the taxonomic research program
we described earlier. The data described in this chapter offer a viable starting
place for implementing such a program.

ACKNOWLEDGMENTS

Preparation of this chapter was supported by the National Institute of Mental Health
(MH 32309), the National Institute of Justice (82-IJ-CX-0058), and the Common-
wealth of Massachusetts. We wish to thank Judith Sims-Knight for her helpful comments on an earlier version of this chapter.

REFERENCES

Abel, G. G., Mittelman, M. S., & Becker, J. V. (1985). Sexual offenders: Results of
    assessment and recommendations for treatment. In H. H. Ben-Aron, S. I.
    Hucker, & C. D. Webster (Eds.), Clinical criminology (pp. 191–205). Toronto:
    MM Graphics.
Aber, J. L., Allen, J. P., Carlson, V., & Cicchetti, D. (1989). The effects of maltreatment
    on development during early childhood: Recent studies and their theoretical,
    clinical, and policy implications. In D. Cicchetti & V. Carlson (Eds.), Child
    maltreatment (pp. 579–619). Cambridge, Eng.: Cambridge University Press.
Amir, M. (1971). Patterns in forcible rape. Chicago: University of Chicago Press.
Atcheson, J. D., & Williams, D. C. (1954). A study of juvenile sexual offenders.
    American Journal of Psychiatry, 111, 366–370.
Awad, G. A., Saunders, E., & Levene, J. (1984). A clinical study of male adolescent
    sexual offenders. International Journal of Offender Therapy and Comparative Crim-
    inology, 28, 105–115.
Barahal, R. M., Waterman, J., & Martin, H. P. (1981). The social cognitive development
    of abused children. Journal of Consulting and Clinical Psychology, 49, 508–516.
Bard, L. A., Carter, D. L., Cerce, D. D., Knight, R. A., Rosenberg, R., & Schneider, B.
    (1987). A descriptive study of rapists and child molesters: Developmental,
    clinical and criminal characteristics. Behavioral Sciences and the Law, 5, 203–
    220.
Becker, J. V. (1988). The effects of child sexual abuse on adolescent sexual offenders.
    In G. E. Wyatt & G. J. Powell (Eds.), Lasting effects of child sexual abuse. Newbury
    Park, CA: Sage Publications.
Becker, J. V., & Abel, G. G. (1985). Adolescent sexual offenders. In E. M. Otey & G.
    D. Ryan (Eds.), Issues in research and treatment (pp. 109–129). (Research Mono-

graph from NCPCR. DHHS Publication No. 85–1396). Washington, DC: U.S. Department Health & Human Services.

Becker, J.V., Kaplan, M.S., Cunningham-Rathner, J., & Kavoussi, R. (1986). Characteristics of adolescent incest sexual perpetrators: Preliminary findings. *Journal of Family Violence, 1*, 85–97.

Blashfield, R. K. (1980). Propositions regarding the use of cluster analysis in clinical research. *Journal of Consulting and Clinical Psychology, 48*, 456–459.

Boone-Hamilton, B. (1991, April). *A family psychosocial assessment tool: Implications for treatment of the adolescent sex offender and the family.* Paper presented at the 62nd annual meeting of the Eastern Psychological Association, New York.

Briggs, P. F. (1955). *Preliminary validation of a standard personal history for psychiatric diagnosis.* Unpublished doctoral dissertation, University of Minnesota.

Brown, E. J., Flanagan, T. J., & McLeod, M. (Eds.). (1984). *Sourcebook of criminal justice statistics—1983.* Washington, DC: Bureau of Justice Statistics.

Browne, A., & Finkelhor, D. (1986). Impact of child sexual abuse: A review of the research. *Psychological Bulletin, 99*, 66–77.

Burgess, A. W., Hartman, C. R., Ressler, R. K., Douglas, J. E., & McCormack, A. (1986). Sexual homocide: A motivational model. *Journal of Interpersonal Violence, 1*, 251–272.

Chambless, D., & Lifshitz, J. L. (1984). Self-reported sexual anxiety and arousal: The expanded Sexual Arousability Inventory. *Journal of Sex Research, 20*, 241–254.

Cicchetti, D. V., & Sparrow, S. S. (1981). Developing criteria for establishing interrater reliablity of specific items: Applications of assessment of adaptive behavior. *American Journal of Mental Deficiency, 86*, 127–137.

Conte, J. R. (1988). The effects of sexual abuse of children: Results of a research project. In R. A. Prentky & V. Quinsey (Eds.), *Human sexual aggression: Current perspectives* (Vol. 528, pp. 310–326). New York: Annals of the New York Academy of Sciences.

Coster, W., Gersten, M., Beeghly, M., & Cicchetti, D. (1989). Communication functioning in maltreated toddlers. *Developmental Psychology, 25*, 1020–1029.

Davis, G. E., & Leitenberg, H. (1987). Adolescent sexual offenders. *Psychological Bulletin, 101*, 417–427.

Dodge, K. A., Bates, J. E., & Pettit, G. S. (1990). Mechanisms in the cycle of violence. *Science, 250*, 1678–1683.

Eysenck, H. J. (1973). Personality and attitudes to sex in criminals. *Journal of Sex Research, 9*, 295–306.

Fehrenbach, P. A., Smith, W., Monastersky, C., & Deisher, R. W. (1986). Adolescent sexual offenders: Offender and offense characteristics. *American Journal of Orthopsychiatry, 56*, 225–233.

Finkelhor, D. (1979). *Sexually victimized children.* New York: Free Press.

Frank, Y., Zimmerman, R., & Leeds, M. D. (1985). Neurological manifestations in abused children who have been shaken. *Developmental Medicine and Child Neurology, 27*, 312–316.

Friedrich, W., & Luecke, W. (1988). Young school age sexually aggressive children. *Professional Psychology: Research and Practice, 19*, 155–164.

Furby, L., Weinrott, M. R., & Blackshaw, L. (1989). Sex offender recidivism: A review. *Psychological Bulletin, 105*, 3–30.

Garbarino, J., & Platz, M. (1984). Child abuse and juvenile delinquency: What are the links? In E. Gray (Ed.), *Child abuse: Prelude to delinquency?* Final Report. Chicago: National Committee for Prevention of Child Abuse.

Gearing, M. L. (1979). MMPI as a primary differentiator and predictor of behavior in prison: A methodological critique and review of the recent literature. *Psychological Bulletin, 86,* 929–963.

Gomes-Schwartz, B. (1984). Juvenile sexual offenders. In *Sexually exploited children: Service and research project* (pp. 245–260). Washington, DC: U.S. Department of Justice.

Gray, E. (1988). The link between child abuse and juvenile delinquency: What we know and recommendations for policy and research. In G. Hotaling, D. Finkelhor, J. T. Kirkpatrick, & M. A. Straus (Eds.), *Family abuse and its consequences* (pp. 109–123). Newbury Park, CA: Sage.

Graybill, D., MacKie, D., & House, A. (1985). Aggression in college students who were abused as children. *Journal of College Student Personnel, 26,* 492–495.

Groth, A. N. (1977). The adolescent sexual offender and his prey. *International Journal of Offender Therapy and Comparative Criminology, 21,* 249–254.

Groth, A. N., Longo, R. E., & McFadin, J. B. (1982). Undetected recidivism among rapists and child molesters. *Crime and Delinquency, 28,* 450–458.

Hempel, C. G. (1965). *Aspects of scientific explanation.* New York: Free Press.

Howes, C. (1984). Social interactions in patterns of friendships in normal and emotionally disturbed children. In T. Field, J. Roopnarine, & M. Segal (Eds.), *Friendships in normal and handicapped children* (pp. 163–185). Norwood, NJ: Ablex.

Howes, C., & Eldredge, R. (1985). Responses of abused, neglected, and non-maltreated children to the behaviors of their peers. *Journal of Applied Developmental Psychology, 6,* 261–270.

Kinard, M. (1980). Emotional development of physically abused children. *American Journal of Orthopsychiatry, 50,* 686–696.

Knight, R., Rosenberg, R., & Schneider, B. (1985). Classification of sexual offenders: Perspectives, methods and validation. In A. Burgess (Ed.), *Rape and sexual assault: A research handbook* (pp. 222–293). New York: Garland.

Knight, R. A. (1989). An assessment of concurrent validity of a child molester typology. *Journal of Interpersonal Violence, 4,* 131–150.

Knight, R. A. (1992). The generation and corroboration of a taxonomic model for child molesters. In W. O'Donohue & J. H. Geer (Eds.), *The sexual abuse of children: Theory, research, and therapy* (pp. 24–70). Hillsdale, NJ: Erlbaum.

Knight, R. A., Carter, D. L., & Prentky, R. A. (1989). A system for the classification of child molesters: Reliability and application. *Journal of Interpersonal Violence, 4,* 3–23.

Knight, R. A., & Prentky, R. A. (1987). The developmental antecedents and adult adaptations of rapist subtypes. *Criminal Justice and Behavior, 14,* 403–426.

Knight, R. A., & Prentky, R. A. (1990). Classifying sexual offenders: The development and corroboration of taxonomic models. In W. L. Marshall, D. R. Laws & H. E. Barbaree (Eds.), *The handbook of sexual assault: Issues, theories, and treatment of the offender* (pp. 27–52). New York: Plenum Press.

Langevin, R., Handy, L., Paitich, D., & Russon, A. (1985). Appendix A: A new version of the Clarke Sex History Questionnaire for males. In R. Langevin (Ed.), *Erotic preference, gender identity and aggression in men* (pp. 287–305). Hillsdale, NJ: Erlbaum.

Lewis, D. O., Mallouh, C., & Webb, V. (1989). Child abuse, delinquency, and violent criminality. In D. Cicchetti & V. Carlson (Eds.), *Child maltreatment* (pp. 707–721). Cambridge, England: Cambridge University Press.

Lewis, D. O., Shanok, S. S., & Pincus, J. H. (1981). Juvenile male sexual assaulters: Psychiatric, neurological, psychoeducational, and abuse factors. In D. O. Lewis (Ed.), *Vulnerabilities to delinquency* (pp. 89–105). New York: SP Medical & Scientific Books.

Longo, R. E. (1982). Sexual learning and experience among adolescent sexual offenders. *International Journal of Offender Therapy and Comparative Criminology, 26,* 235–241.

Longo, R. E., & Groth, A. N. (1983). Juvenile sexual offenses in the histories of adult rapists and child molesters. *International Journal of Offender Therapy and Comparative Criminology, 27,* 150–155.

Lynch, M. A., & Roberts, J. (1982). *Consequences of child abuse.* New York: Academic Press.

McCord, J. (1983). A forty year perspective on effects of child abuse and neglect. *Child Abuse and Neglect, 7,* 265–270.

McCord, W., McCord, J., & Venden, P. (1962). Family relationships and sexual deviance in lower-class adolescents. *International Journal of Social Psychiatry, 8,* 165–179.

McDermott, M. J., & Hindelang, M. J. (1981). *Juvenile criminal behavior in the United States: Its trends and patterns.* (Analysis of National Crime Victimization Survey Data to Study Serious Delinquent Behavior Monograph No. 1). Washington, DC: Office of Juvenile Justice and Delinquency Prevention.

Main, M., & George, C. (1985). Responses of abused and disadvantaged toddlers to distress in agemates: A study in the day care setting. *Developmental Psychology, 21,* 407–412.

Main, M., & Goldwyn, R. (1984). Predicting rejection of her infant from mother's representation of her own experience: Implications for the abused-abusing intergenerational cycle. *Child Abuse and Neglect, 8,* 203–217.

Martin, H. P. (1976). *The abused child: A multidisciplinary approach to developmental issues and treatment.* Cambridge, MA: Ballinger.

Meehl, P. E. (1979). A funny thing happened on the way to the latent entities. *Journal of Personality Assessment, 43,* 564–581.

Miller, P. A., & Eisenberg, N. (1988). The relation of empathy to aggressive and externalizing/antisocial behavior. *Psychological Bulletin, 103,* 324–344.

Mosher, D. L., & Anderson, R. D. (1986). Macho personality, sexual aggression, and reactions to guided imagery of realistic rape. *Journal of Research in Personality, 20,* 77–94.

Mosher, L. R. (1978). Can diagnosis be nonpejorative? In L. C. Wynne, R. L. Cromwell, & S. Matthysse (Eds.), *The nature of schizophrenia: New approaches to research and treatment* (pp. 690–695). New York: Wiley.

Nichols, H. R., & Molinder, I. (1984). *Multiphasic Sex Inventory Manual: A test to assess the psychosexual characteristics of the sexual offender* (Research Edition Form A). Tacoma, WA: Nichols & Molinder.

O'Brien, M., & Bera, W. (1986). Adolescent sexual offenders: A descriptive typology. *A News Letter of the National Family Life Education Network, 1*, 1–5.

Pollock, V. E., Briere, J., Schneider, L., Knop, J., Mednick, S. A. & Goodwin, D. W. (1990). Childhood antecedents of antisocial behavior: Parental alcoholism and physical abusiveness. *American Journal of Psychiatry, 147*, 1290–1293.

Popper, K. R. (1972). *The logic of scientific discovery.* London: Hutchinson.

Prentky, R. A., & Knight, R. A. (1991). Dimensional and categorical discrimination among rapists. *Journal of Consulting and Clinical Psychology, 59*, 643–661.

Prentky, R. A., Knight, R. A., & Rosenberg, R. (1988). Validation analyses on the MTC Taxonomy for Rapists: Disconfirmation and reconceptualization. In R. A. Prentky & V. Quinsey (Eds.), *Human sexual aggression: Current perspectives* (Vol. 528) (pp. 21–40). New York: Annals of the New York Academy of Sciences.

Prentky, R. A., Knight, R. A., Rosenberg, R., & Lee, A. (1989). A path analytic approach to the validation of a taxonomic system for classifying child molesters. *Journal of Quantitative Criminology, 5*, 231–257.

Roff, J. D. (1981). Reminder: Reliability of global judgments. *Perceptual and Motor Skills, 52*, 315–318.

Rogers, C. M., & Terry, T. (1984). Clinical interventions with boy victims of sexual abuse. In I. Stuart & J. Greer (Eds.), *Victims of sexual aggression* (pp. 91–104). New York: Van Nostrand Reinhold.

Rosen, L. (1969). Matriarchy and lower class Negro male delinquency. *Social Problems, 17*, 175–189.

Rosenberg, R., & Knight, R. A. (1988). Determining male sex offender subtypes using cluster analysis. *Journal of Quantitative Criminology, 4*, 383–410.

Salzinger, S., Feldman, R. S., Hammer, M., & Rosario, M. (1991). Risk for physical child abuse and the personal consequences for its victims. *Criminal Justice and Behavior, 18*, 64–81.

Salzinger, S., Kaplan, S., Pelcovitz, D., Samit, C., & Krieger, R. (1984). Parent and teacher assessment of children's behavior in child maltreating families. *Journal of the American Academy of Child Psychiatry, 23*, 458–464.

Sarbin, T. R. (1967). On the futility of the proposition that some people be labeled "mentally ill." *Journal of Consulting Psychology, 31*, 447–453.

Sauceda, J. M. (1978). *Juvenile sexual assaulters: A comparative study. Unpublished manuscript.* (As cited in Awad, Saunders, & Levene, 1984)

Shoor, M., Speed, M. H., & Bartelt, C. (1966). Syndrome of the adolescent child molester. *American Journal of Psychiatry, 122*, 783–789.

Singer, J. L., & Antrobus, J. S. (1972). Daydreaming, imaginal processes, and personality: A normative study. In P. Sheehan (Ed.), *The function and nature of imagery* (pp. 175–202). New York: Academic Press.

Smith, W. R. (1984). *Patterns of re-offending among juvenile sexual offenders.* Unpublished manuscript, University of Washington, Juvenile Sexual Offender Program, Seattle. (As cited in Davis & Leitenberg, 1987)

Smith, W. R., & Monastersky, C. (1986). Assessing juvenile sexual offenders' risk for reoffending. *Criminal Justice and Behavior, 13*, 115–140.

Tarter, R. E., Hegedus, A. M., Alterman, A. I., & Katz-Garris, L. (1983). Cognitive capacities of juvenile violent, nonviolent, and sexual offenders. *Journal of Nervous and Mental Disease, 171*, 564–567.

Thorne, F. C. (1966). The sex inventory. *Journal of Clinical Psychology, 22*, 367–374.

Van Ness, S. R. (1984). Rape as instrumental violence: A study of youth offenders. *Journal of Offender Counseling, Services, and Rehabilitation, 9*, 161–170.

Wasserman, J., & Kappel, S. (1985). *Adolescent sex offenders in Vermont.* Burlington: Vermont Department of Health.

Williamson, J. M., Borduin, C. M., & Howe, B. A. (1991). The ecology of adolescent maltreatment: A multilevel examination of adolescent physical abuse, sexual abuse, and neglect. *Journal of Consulting and Clinical Psychology, 59*, 449–457.

CHAPTER 4

Where Does Sexuality Come From?: Normative Sexuality from a Developmental Perspective

William M. Bukowski
Lorrie Sippola
William Brender

T he establishment of a satisfying and coherent sexuality during adolescence and young adulthood is one of the most important and challenging tasks of the life cycle. The centrality of this facet of development to the experience of young persons is readily apparent in lives of young persons depicted in literature, drama, and music. Indeed, in Salinger's *Catcher in the Rye*, Nabokov's *Lolita*, Joyce's *Portrait of an Artist*, Shakespeare's *Romeo and Juliet*, Bernstein's *West Side Story*, Tolstoy's *Cossaks* and *Happy Ever After*, Schoenberg's *Verklarte Nacht*, and Anderson's *Winesburg Ohio*, we find adolescents and young adults struggling with issues of sex, love, identity, and personal commitment. Moreover, adolescent pop culture is replete with themes of sexuality and love in interpersonal relations. Surprisingly, however, current work in the area of social and personality development are bereft of both theory and research on sexuality. Although there are exceptions to this gap in the psychological literature (e.g., Goldman & Goldman, 1982, 1988), psychologists have devoted remarkably little attention to the factors and processes related to sexual development.

In this chapter, we bring together ideas and issues from three domains related to sexuality, namely, the biological, social/personal, and cognitive. For each of these areas, we consider current concepts and findings to account for the developmental transition from the relative asexuality of the school-age years to the emergence of a more pronounced sense of sexuality in adolescence. Our discussion of these domains is focused also on how these phenomena are related to individual differences in the development of sexuality.

This chapter is organized into four sections. In the first section, we provide a framework in which the concept of sexual development can be understood. Here, we offer a conceptualization of sexuality as a multidimensional form of development that consists of several integrative processes. A basic premise of this discussion is that sexual development cannot be separated from the development of interpersonal relations. In the second section, we show how sexuality is a feature of development. That is, we indicate how sexual themes, in their various manifestations, are apparent across the childhood years. The major point of this section is that sexuality begins to unfold during the preschool and school-age years, and that individual differences in experiences during these developmental periods will affect sexual development during adolescence. In the third section, we discuss the factors related to individual differences in the transitions or emergence of sexuality during adolescence. Consistent with the points of our first section, we show that many interdependent processes underlie the changes in sexuality during adolescence. In our concluding section, we use the conceptual framework of developmental psychopathology to speculate about the pathways by which some individuals become juvenile sex offenders. Specifically, we discuss issues from the literature on normal sexual development that can be used as a means of understanding "abnormal" sexuality.

SEXUALITY, SYNTHESIS, AND DEVELOPMENT: WHAT IS SEXUAL DEVELOPMENT?

When we use the term "sexuality" we refer to several interrelated experiences. It has been noted already (e.g., Efron, 1985; Goldman & Goldman, 1988; Roberts, 1980) that sexual development is frequently conceptualized in a very narrow manner, namely, as either the physical changes or behavioral/interpersonal changes that are related to puberty and adolescence. According to this perspective, sexuality essentially begins at puberty and is largely a physical or behavioral construct. Alternatively, we propose that sexuality and sexual development are processes that begin at birth and continue across the life span. Moreover, we see sexuality as being embedded within the broader context of interpersonal relations.

Clearly, a basic premise of our approach to the understanding of the emergence of sexuality is that it is a multidimensional form of development. We argue in particular that sexual development is the result of the integration of many phenomena and processes. The integration of these processes presents a challenge because some of the component processes that need to be integrated can be contradictory to each other (e.g., sexual urges and moral proscriptions). Accordingly, we propose that in order to explain sexual development, one must recognize that it largely consists of a "synthetic" process. By synthetic we mean that sexual development derives from the individual's synthesis, or integration, of many dimensions of experience, including feelings of sexual desire and interpersonal attraction, one's sense of morality, social convention, interpersonal security, and one's view of others as sexual beings who have their own needs, desires, and rights.

Because sexual development consists of a process of synthesis, it is ultimately up to the individual to make sense out of the various factors related to sexuality, regardless of the inconsistencies among them. Roberts (1980) has commented already on this multifaceted nature of sexuality when she wrote that sexuality and sexual development consist of not only becoming "aware of the body's shape, size, functions, and capacities for pleasure" (p. 3) but also of many other phenomena regarding personal and interpersonal functioning and the "rules" and rituals of the broader societal context. We propose that for children, the development of a healthy sense of sexuality includes (1) learning about intimacy through interaction with peers; (2) developing an understanding of personal roles and relationships, both within and outside of the family; (3) revising or adapting one's body schema to changes in physical size, shape, and capabilities, especially during early adolescence; (4) adjusting to erotic feelings and experiences and integrating them into one's life; (5) learning about societal standards and practices regarding sexual expression; and (6) developing an understanding and appreciation of reproductive processes. Indeed, considering that sexuality is such a multifaceted construct, it is no wonder that the term *chaos* first appeared within the context of sex (Feldman, 1971).

It should be recognized that we have conceptualized the processes underlying sexual development as a "trialectic" of self, other, and society. That is, we see sexual development as a process that requires an integration of self and other (i.e., personal and interpersonal) within a societal context. It is a process in which individuals acquire a sense of their own desires and integrate them into their relations with others. In this respect, sexual development is dependent upon both personal and interpersonal understanding within the demands and forces of a particular societal context.

A clear corollary of our perspective is that because sexual development is embedded within interpersonal and societal processes, phenomena that affect interpersonal relations and experiences are also likely to affect sexuality and sexual development. Accordingly, the processes by which persons regulate interpersonal experiences and the way that persons ascribe meaning to relationships will affect their sexual experiences. Thus, the themes that an individual uses to ascribe meaning to relationships will become the themes of the individual's sexuality. For example, if power and dominance (or non-assertiveness and submission) in relationships are important for a person, these will also become important themes of the person's sexuality. This pattern has clear repercussions for the understanding of sexuality for males and females. Because males and females are known to ascribe different types of meaning to their interpersonal relationships and emphasize different themes in their relationships (Hinde, 1984), it is likely that the development of sexuality will be a different experience for boys and girls.

What Is "Healthy" Sexual Development?

In many areas of development, the end point or goal of development is clear. Two goals or end points of language development, for example, are the acquisition of syntax and conversational competence. Although these two goals are abstract, they nevertheless have very clear "concrete" manifestations, such as the ability to use proper verb endings or by the ability to sustain a dialogue with a peer. The goals, or end points, of sexual development, however, are less clear. Attempts to identify the goal of sexual development have generally relied heavily on abstraction, thus giving little guidance as to what necessarily constitutes healthy, or unhealthy, sexual development. Because sexuality consists of factors that are largely subjective, interpersonal, and socially embedded, and that may vary considerably as a function of age, cultural context, and gender, specifying the numerous goals of healthy sexual development presents a formidable task.

Such a pluralistic conceptualization of sexuality presents an obvious problem to the study of sex. Specifically, because sexuality is a phenomenon that is nearly impossible to define operationally or to be represented by simple variables that can be generalized across age, cultural groups, and gender, the study of sexuality is necessarily a multidimensional endeavor. Moreover, a further corollary of the difficulty in operationally defining sexuality according to observable patterns of behavior is that a large portion of the study of an individual's sexuality must focus on the person's subjective experiences. This is not to say that there may be no universal characteristic of a healthy sexuality. We mean only that the manifestations of these features may vary according to several conditions and may depend upon several subjective experiences.

In summary, we propose that sexual development involves the integration of one's sense of sexuality into one's interpersonal relations, and that this integration is influenced by the demands or standards of the cultural context. Consequently, healthy sexuality would be defined as a person's ability to combine the sexual and the interpersonal. Just as the successful resolution of the self/other dialect would consist of an individual's synthesis of her or his needs, goals, rights, and perspectives and those of others, healthy sexual development would consist of the individual's integration of sexuality into an interpersonal context so that the sexual and personal needs, goals, and rights of both the self and the other are compatible. Consistent with the arguments of Sullivan (1953) and others (e.g., Foucault, 1970), this conceptualization of healthy sexuality implies that the personal and the interpersonal cannot be disentangled from each other. Moreover, because this integration occurs within a particular cultural context, the extent to which a person can achieve this integration depends upon the social context. For example, in societies in which patterns of sexual desire or behavior are rigidly prescribed (or proscribed), or interpersonal roles are strictly defined, the complete integration of personal and interpersonal goals may be exceedingly difficult.

SEXUALITY IN CHILDHOOD

There is abundant evidence that sexuality, broadly defined, is a theme of childhood. Although its manifestations differ considerably from the appearance of sexuality at other ages, sexuality in childhood can be seen in children's behaviors and in their questions and curiosities. Jersilo (1954) stated this quite clearly in his essay on emotional development in the second edition of the *Manual of Child Psychology*: "Freud's theory that sex is not something that is visited upon the child at about the time of puberty but is a development that goes back to early infancy can be confirmed by everyday observation" (p. 906).

What evidence is there to suggest that sexuality or sexual learning is a feature of development? Jersilo pointed to a variety of evidence—for example, that preschool children show a curiosity about parts of their bodies; that children, especially preschool boys, would touch their genitals; and that children of this age regularly ask questions about the functions of the genitals. These same points, and others, have been raised more recently by several writers. Efron (1985) has argued, for instance, that sexuality is manifested in childhood as children begin to develop a sense of comfort with their own bodies and achieve a sense of comfort in their interactions with others. The comfort that he describes is more than just physical. He points out that it has a large emotional component in the sense that children develop attitudes regarding the body and its functions and an orientation toward others in regard to their needs for affection. Efron proposes that these attitudes are likely to derive from a child's experiences of being touched and handled tenderly (i.e., "somatosensory affectional contact", p. 119 [c.f., Prescott, 1979]) by others and from the child's recognition that his or her body and its functions are treated with respect by others.

Rosen and Hall (1984) have proposed that there may be early developmental differences between infant boys and girls in their experiences with touch. Specifically, they refer to research (Clarke-Stewart & Hevey, 1981) indicting that mothers are more likely to touch their 12-month-old sons than their similarly aged daughters but that by age 18 months this pattern is reversed. These differences in the extent to which boys and girls are touched by parents during the early years of life may contribute to gender differences in the patterns of sexual development.

Goldman and Goldman (1982, 1988), in a very large and multidimensional inquiry into sexuality during childhood, showed that in many ways there are themes related to sexuality in childhood. These themes are apparent in children's thoughts about sexual matters and in their behavior. Children's thinking about sexuality is apparent in several domains. First, as Serbin and Sprafkin (1987) have shown, there is a clear developmental trajectory in children's thinking about the differences between boys and girls and between men and women. Typically, children from a relatively young age identify with their own gender and develop a belief system regarding the behaviors that are consistent with being a girl or boy or a woman or man. It has been argued (Kohlberg, 1966) that as children develop a concept of what it means to be a girl or boy, they begin to shape their behaviors to achieve consistency between their behavior and the behavior they believe is appropriate for their gender.

Second, Goldman and Goldman (1982, 1988) showed also that children are curious about "where babies come from," sometimes going so far as developing their own theories about reproduction. Children ask questions about how the baby gets inside of a mother's belly and who determines when or under what conditions a woman can have a child. Mendelson (1990) has noted that for an older child, the news that a younger sibling is on the way provides a strong stimulus for a child's curiosity about reproduction. Goldman and Goldman (1982, 1988) reported that although children of all ages show a fascination for the processes of reproduction, it is not until they are in the early adolescent years that they have a full understanding of the mechanisms that result in procreation. Even then, many teenagers show a very crude understanding of the menstrual cycle and reproduction (Zelnick & Kantner, 1973).

In regard to a third aspect of sexuality, children eventually acquire an understanding of sexual intercourse. There are clear cultural differences in the age at which children learn about sexual intercourse and begin to understand how it fits into an individual's interpersonal relations. Goldman and Goldman report that sexual intercourse is a complete mystery for most young children but that by preadolescence, however, most children know that babies are conceived in sexual intercourse and that intercourse is a very pleasurable experience. Consistent with our view that sexual development is a process of synthesis, Goldman and Goldman show that young adolescents struggle to conceptualize intercourse as a multifaceted phenomenon—that is, as a means of procreation, as a uniquely pleasurable experience, as an expression of love, and as a "natural" form of desire. Of all the areas of sexuality they studied, the understanding of sexual intercourse as a personal and interpersonal event, and as an emotional and biological phenomenon, appeared to be one of the most challenging features of sexual development.

A fourth feature of children's thinking about sexuality concerns their understanding of the concepts of privacy and personal boundaries. In nearly all societies persons wear clothing, or at least cover their genitals. Concerns about nakedness, however, emerge with age. Goldman and Goldman (1982, 1988) indicate that whereas young children may show little concern with being seen naked by others, this same experience is likely to be profoundly embarrassing for early adolescents. Clearly, one feature of development is the acquisition of the sense that the body is private. Although young children may believe that persons wear clothes for legal reasons, by preadolescence, boys and girls report that wearing clothes and regarding some features of the body as "personal" are social conventions. Some older children and early adolescents recognize that there may be no rational reason for wearing clothes, but that it is a personal decision that results from an individual's self-consciousness or desire for privacy.

A fifth feature of children's thinking that is related to sexuality is children's understanding of relationships. There is now a large literature about children's understanding of the properties of relationships and of the processes underlying interpersonal interaction (Selman & Schultz, 1990). If sexuality, as we have defined it, consists largely of interpersonal issues, then children's understandings of relationships should play a central role in the way an individual integrates sexual themes into personal relationships. By the time children reach adolescence, they recognize that relationships consist not only of shared activities and mutual liking, but also of interpersonal commitments and emotional closeness (Berndt, 1982; Bukowski, Newcomb, & Hoza, 1987). It is apparent also that during adolescence girls are more likely than boys to see intimacy as a feature of their friendships with other-sex peers (Sharabany, Gershoni, & Hofman, 1981). Accordingly, we should not be surprised that girls may be more likely than boys to conceptualize their initial sexual experiences in terms of intimacy and emotional closeness (Miller & Simon, 1980).

Finally, it is difficult, if not impossible, to shelter children from sexual issues in Western society. In the pictures and images of advertising and popular culture, in the songs broadcast on the radio, in discussions about AIDS, and in many of societies' most basic rituals (e.g., that persons use toilet facilities in private) and "institutions" (e.g., heterosexual marriage), sexual themes are at least implicit and frequently much more so. As a result it is not surprising that children are curious and ask questions about sexuality. Goldman and Goldman (1982, 1988) report that children make inquiries about individual differences in sexuality (e.g., what is homosexuality), about the meaning of various sex-related terms or expressions (e.g., contraception), and about the processes underlying particular events related to sexual development (e.g., why women have breasts). Just as children are curious about many of the phenomena they observe in other domains of their experience, they are curious about phenomena related to sex and its various manifestations.

In addition to evidence that sexuality is apparent in children's thinking, there is evidence also that sexuality may be a component of children's behavior also. To be sure, between the sexual "behavior" of children and that of adults there are very large differences in motivation, intensity, and meaning. Nevertheless, there are some behaviors of childhood that are at least analogs of some adult sexual activity.

Perhaps the clearest and most universal manifestation of sexuality in childhood is the child's responsiveness to physical touch. Children respond when they are touched by adults (see Efron, 1985). Being held by an adult can be a soothing and comforting experience for young children. Moreover, children learn behavioral means of giving comfort to others (e.g., hugging a sibling when she or he is distressed). Although the responsiveness to touch may not be an explicitly sexual experience, touch is certainly a component of many sexual behaviors. Indeed, Efron (1985) has argued that physical touch is the most direct means by which parents can begin to shape a healthy sense of intimacy and sexuality in their children.

There is also evidence that many children "touch themselves" or engage in "play" with friends that involves the genitals. Goldman and Goldman (1982) reported that nearly two-thirds of children claim to have had some sort of sexual experience with peers prior to age 12. Much of this "play" consists of young children showing their genitals to each other, and it happens most frequently among close friends or relatives (e.g., cousins). Goldman and Goldman point out that this form of interaction is nearly always based on "play" or curiosity. They reported also these instances are only rarely based on one child's desire for sexual pleasure, and that these events usually occur when there is a large age gap between the children involved.

As alluded to above, one important question regarding these "sexual" behaviors of childhood is whether they have the same meaning as sexual behaviors in adulthood or whether, in spite of the appearance of continuity, these behaviors have a very different significance. For example, is the self-stimulation of infancy and childhood a form of masturbation in the same way that such behavior is in adolescence and adulthood? Several authors (Goldman & Goldman, 1982, 1988; Masters, Johnson, & Kolodny, 1985) have concluded that these behaviors of childhood have some of the features of adult experiences (e.g., there are reports that even infants and young children derive pleasure from genital self-stimulation) but that these behaviors are at best a precursor to the actual sexual experiences of adulthood. For example, like sexual behavior in adulthood, the sex play of childhood frequently happens within a particular interpersonal context (e.g., between close friends), but it clearly lacks the intense feelings of pleasure and eroticism associated with adult sexual behavior.

Sexual themes are apparent in children's behavior, in children's jokes, and in their play rituals. Preschoolers frequently act out themes of heterosexual relation in their dramatic play, as they assume the roles of mother and father, either as a couple or as the caretakers of a baby. During the school-age years children tell jokes that involve the mention of private body parts of personal articles or clothing. In the preadolescent years, the same-sex peer group often provides a context, for both boys and girls, for the discussion of the "other-sex" (Fine, 1981).

In summary, prior to adolescence, children think about sexual issues, show a curiosity about issues related to sexuality, and display behaviors that are analogous to forms of adolescent and adult sexuality. Nevertheless, in spite of the similarity between some "sexual" behaviors of childhood and adulthood, it is clear that sexuality in childhood is very different from the manifestations of sexuality in adolescence and adulthood. In the next section we consider the changes in sexuality during adolescence and the processes that underlie these changes.

SEXUALITY IN ADOLESCENCE: WHAT CHANGES?

A quick perusal of the content of music videos aimed at the teenage audience and an inspection of the summertime movies shown at shopping mall cinemas will reveal that sexuality is linked closely with adolescence. Indeed, many people regard adolescence as the time of life when sexuality emerges in an overflowing abundance. Adolescence is, of course, a time of many changes, as children take a big step toward adulthood in nearly every phase of their lives and experience. Adolescence is characterized by fundamental changes in the way a person looks, thinks, and behaves in society. Indeed, adolescence is frequently defined as a time of transition in which changes occur in thinking and achievement and in adolescents' feelings of identity, autonomy, and independence. During adolescence there are also changes in legal and social status, and in relations within the family and with peers. In short, it is a time when adolescents begin to think about themselves and about others in very different ways while at the same time the manner in which they are perceived by others also changes—they are no longer perceived as children, but instead as persons who are acquiring the properties of adulthood.

Clearly, however, among the most pronounced transitions of adolescence are changes in the body and changes in sexuality. During adolescence, there are marked changes in the size, shape, and functioning of the body, and it is during adolescence that many individuals have their initial interpersonal sexual experiences. To a large extent, many of the physical changes of adolescence are the result of hormonal processes. Indeed, one of the oldest perspectives on adolescence (Hall, 1904) is that it is simply a turmoil-filled, hormone-driven blip on the growth curve of life. Nevertheless, because of its multidimensional nature, sexuality cannot be explained solely according to hormonal influences.

Our goal is to show that sexual development in adolescence consists of a constellation of phenomena that ultimately fits within an individual's personal matrix of experience and meaning. Consistent with our basic premises that (1) sexual development is a process in which the individual plays an active role as a "synthesizer" and (2) that sexuality is ultimately a very subjective phenomena, we propose that it is easy to recognize that sexuality is the result of many processes but that it is difficult to show how any one of them has a particular impact on any specific component of sexuality. We start our discussion with a description of the physical aspects of sexual maturation in adolescence. We then use the physical domain as a point of departure for a discussion of how other components of sexuality emerge in adolescent girls and boys. Specifically, we show that the physical changes of adolescence are interwoven into other transitions of adolescence. Accordingly, these changes affect the way adolescents think about themselves as individuals and in relation to others, and they influence the way that the maturing adolescent is perceived by others.

Physical Changes

For heuristic purposes, it is possible to conceptualize the physical changes of adolescence according to two rough dichotomies: one dichotomy being whether the changes are associated with either reproduction or physical maturation, and the other being whether the changes are structural or physiological. We recognize that these are ultimately false dichotomies—after all the development of the penis and vagina, for example, is part of physical maturation, and physiological changes and structural changes emerge together via interdependent processes. Nevertheless, the use of these dichotomies points out that changes in sexuality involve many components of experience. As shown in Table 4.1, the changes related to reproduction that are structural consist of changes in the

TABLE 4.1. Physical Changes of Adolescence

	Changes related to reproduction	Changes related to physical maturation
Physiological	Onset of menarche Production of seminal fluid	Maturation of the hypothalamic–pituitary system Changes in pulmonary and circulatory systems
Structural	Changes in genitalia; growth of penis and testes; lengthening of vagina	Growth spurt; muscle and skeletal growth; fat deposits; weight gain

size of the vagina and penis and in the levels of various hormones in the blood. The physiological changes include, in males, the onset of the production of sperm in the testes, and, in females, changes in the functioning of the ovaries, which result in the onset of menses. Changes that are primarily part of physical development, and less directly related to reproduction, include structural changes as seen in skeletal growth and the development of musculature, and changes in physiology, such as in the activity of parts of the endocrine system and in the capacity of the circulatory and pulmonary systems.

For both boys and girls, there is a consistent pattern in which the events of puberty occur (Masters et al., 1985). In females, breast development is the first pubertal event to occur followed by the appearance of pubic hair. Menarche, a particularly salient point in female development, as it is often perceived as the "hallmark" of "womanhood," occurs as breast development is completed and after the peak growth spurt. Physical changes in young boys generally begin 1 to 2 years later than girls. These changes include growth of the testes and scrotum and the appearance of pubic hair. A growth spurt in height is accompanied by growth of the penis and further development of darker, coarser pubic hair. In addition to the growth spurt, the more obvious changes that happen in the later stages of the pubertal cycle are the appearance of facial hair and a deepening of the voice due to a growth in the larynx. Although boys do not experience anything like menarche that so clearly demarcates the transition to "manhood," Masters et al. (1985) have suggested that the appearance of nocturnal emissions ("wet dreams") and the ejaculatory capacity in masturbation can often be as much of a concern for the unprepared, sexually naive adolescent boy.

Although these events of puberty are uniquely tied to adolescence, and although they happen in nearly the same sequence for all individuals, there are wide individual differences in the timing and rate at which they occur (see Grumbach, 1980). Development of secondary sex characteristics in girls begins between ages 8 and 13 (mean age = 11) and can take anywhere from 1½ years to 6 years to complete. The figures for boys are between nine and 14 years of age for onset of pubertal development (mean age = 11.6) which can take between 2 to 4½ years to complete.

It has been widely documented that the pubertal changes outlined above are largely the result of the endocrine system. Specifically, these changes happen as levels of various hormones in the blood increase in response to the maturation of the hypothalamic-pituitary system. In response to a decreased sensitivity of the hypothalamus to sex hormones, which occurs at puberty, the pituitary gland stimulates several other glands to increase secretion of their hormones with the result that the physical changes of adolescence emerge. Changes in the levels of growth hormone released from the thyroid and of corticosteroids from the adrenal cortex account for changes in physical maturation, whereas changes in the levels of androgens secreted by the adrenal gland, as well as testosterone released by the testes and estrogen released by the ovaries, account for changes in the reproductive systems and for some aspects of physical growth (Grumbach, 1980). In this respect, one can conclude that the physical changes related to sexual development in adolescence are linked to hormonal mechanisms. However, in addition to the physical transitions of adolescence, there are also changes that involve an emerging awareness of sexual desire, in the way adolescents' think about themselves and others in regard to sexual themes, the appearance of new behaviors or new interpersonal experiences, and changes in the self-concept as a result of a changing body image. Although it is possible to categorize these changes into separate sets of transitions, these changes are, for the most part, inextricably related to each other and cannot be attributed solely to changes in hormonal levels.

Changes in Self-Concept

The physical metamorphoses of puberty are among the most salient transitions of adolescence and can be a source of concern, anxiety, and preoccupation for many youngsters. Because these concerns may be accentuated by the changing perceptions of others toward the adolescent, there may also be a transformation of the self-concept in response to the internal and external reactions to their changing physical appearance. Many of these responses reflect an increasing awareness, by the adolescent and by others, of the individual's sexuality.

The wide range in the time of onset and rate of pubertal change has been shown to influence the adolescent's perception of his or her body. Specifically, self-concept may be related to any deviation from the "norms" for onset and rate of pubertal development. Furthermore, gender differences have been shown in body image and suggest different experiences of pubertal development for boys and girls (Tobin-Richards, Boxer, & Petersen, 1983).

The relationship between pubertal development and body image in adolescent females tends to be curvilinear (Tobin-Richards et al., 1983). That is, early-maturing girls view their bodies more negatively than either on-time or late maturers, and late-maturing girls view their bodies more negatively than girls whose maturation rate falls within the norm. These responses may be influenced by the social context in which development occurs. For example, Blythe, Simmon, and Zakin (1985) have shown that adolescent girls view their bodies more positively if they approximate the cultural ideal of thinness (resulting in an advantage for late maturers) and if they are not experiencing school transitions (e.g., from elementary to high school) at the same time that pubertal changes are occurring (advantage to early maturers).

In addition to the timing and rate of pubertal changes, the type of physical change (i.e., onset of menarche vs. breast development) experienced may have differential effects on the young girls' self-image and self-esteem. Postmenarcheal girls experience themselves as "more womanly" and begin to reflect upon their future reproductive roles (Koff, 1983). Rierdan and Koff (1980) suggest that onset of menarche has an integrative impact on adolescent girls in that postmenarcheal girls demonstrate greater sexual differentiation and clarity of sexual identity than premenarcheal girls. However, some women have reported feeling a loss of self-esteem at onset of menarche and have perceived boys as gaining in power at this time (Grief & Ulman, 1982). These reactions may be the result of the negative attitudes toward menarche that tend to pervade North American culture. Menarche is often viewed as a hygienic crisis (i.e., the "curse"; Delaney, Lupton, & Toth, 1988) by many young girls who begin to express concern about inopportune moments of onset and the restrictions on their freedom to participate in certain activities.

Puberty is a collection of changes, which vary in terms of when they occur in the pubertal cycle, how noticeable they are to others, what meaning they have to the individual and to others, and what impact they may have on an adolescent girl's daily functioning. Typically, responses to menarche have been studied as a means of examining the psychological impact of puberty. Brooks-Gunn and Warren (1988) have pointed out, however, other events (e.g., the pubertal growth spurt and breast development) occur prior to menarche, and the impact of these aspects of puberty may differ from the impact of menarche. For example, breast development has been found to be related to higher scores on measures of adjustment, positive peer relationships, and positive body images (Brooks-Gunn & Warren, 1988). Nevertheless, it is possible that the changes that occur during the later parts of the pubertal cycle are most likely to be experienced negatively because these changes are most directly related to sexuality and reproduction. Indeed, as an adolescent girl's sexual maturity becomes more apparent, her emerging sexuality may become a source of concern for parents who may respond by placing new restrictions (either implicit or explicit) on her behavior, especially for early-maturing girls (Danza, 1983; Savin-Williams & Small, 1986).

For boys, the consequences of physical maturation on the self-concept appear to be generally positive, perhaps due to the more positive societal attitude toward masculine characteristics. However, timing of pubertal developments also affects boys' self-concept, although the pattern of influence is unlike that observed in girls. Specifically, early-maturing boys perceive their body images more positively than either on-time or late-maturing boys (Tobin-Richards et al., 1983).

In general, much less is known about the psychological effects of pubertal development on boys beyond the apparent physical changes that occur. However, first ejaculation ("spermarche"; Gaddis & Brooks-Gunn, 1985) may be a significant point of development in puberty, although the psychological effects of this event have rarely been studied. One study that examined this development (Gaddis & Brooks-Gunn, 1985) found that most of the 13 boys studied associated positive feelings with spermarche: 55% felt "very grown up," 73% were very excited, and 36% felt very happy and proud; few boys had strong negative feelings toward the experience. The most common reaction was curiosity and surprise. These findings contrast with the ambivalent reaction to menarche reported in adolescent girls (Ruble & Brooks-Gunn, 1982). Obviously, these differences may be attributed to an accompanying sense of discomfort associated with menarche; however, one cannot ignore the different social values implicit in the experiences of males and females.

A potential contributing factor to the more positive self-concept in boys is the response of others to their development. In contrast to girls, parents of adolescent boys react to their sons' development with increased tolerance for independence, decreased tolerance for emotional displays, less protectiveness, and subtle encouragement of sexual activity (Tobin-Richards, et al., 1983).

In summary, internal and external responses to changes in the adolescent's body structure, size, and functioning may contribute to changes in self-concept. As adolescents change physically they acquire increased awareness of gender roles and sexuality, and their identity with their gender may be enhanced. It is apparent, however, that the impact of puberty differs for the various components of puberty and according to whether the individual is an early, on-time, or late maturer.

Sexual Behavior

As adolescents change physically, and as their identities and self-concepts include a clearer emphasis on sexuality, their sexual behavior changes and takes on new meaning to themselves and to others. A substantial amount of information is available regarding the sequence of sexual experiences and behaviors that typically unfold during adolescence (see Simon & Gagnon, 1969; Gagnon, 1972). In spite of some variability across individuals and rather clear sex and racial differences (e.g., boys report engaging in the various sexual behaviors at earlier ages than girls), a set of discrete "developmental" steps in sexual experiences can be observed. For most teenagers, males and females alike, there is a progression from having sexual desires and urges, to feeling a sexual attraction to other persons, followed by going on dates, holding hands, kissing, touching or fondling another person, to eventually engaging in sexual intercourse (Schofield, 1965). In most North American white teens this process unfolds over a period of a year or two or more during adolescence and young adulthood and is quite predictable. However, among black teenagers the process tends to be shorter and may not follow exactly the same pattern (Smith, 1989).

The factors that underlie the emergence of these behaviors during adolescence is not entirely clear. Udry and his colleagues (Billy & Udry, 1985a, 1985b; Newcomer & Udry, 1987; Smith, Udry, & Morris, 1985; Thornton, 1990; Udry & Billy, 1987; Udry, Billy, Morris, Groff, & Raj, 1985; Udry, Talbert, & Morris, 1986), in a set of ground-breaking studies, have shown that individual differences in sexual behavior in adolescence can be traced to both hormonal and social processes. In regard to hormonal processes Udry's research has revealed that adolescent sexual behavior is related to levels of androgens among girls (Udry et al., 1986) and testosterone among boys (Udry et al., 1985). The effect of social factors has been demonstrated also. Specifically, Billy and Udry (1985a, 1985b), Newcomer and Udry (1987), and Udry and Billy (1987) reported that social indicators, such as the sexual behavior of peers, predict sexual activity among adolescents, especially adolescent girls. Thornton (1990) has suggested also that as a teenager's relationship moves through the transition from dating to courtship to commitment (e.g., dating someone who would be considered a marriage partner), sexual experience develops rapidly. That is, the more committed the relationship is, the more likely intercourse is likely to become a part of it. Thornton suggests that as the level of commitment in a relationship develops so does the range of sexual experience that is acceptable in the relationship. In other words, as adolescents "gain experience at one level of involvement, they become prepared for more intensive sexual involvement" (p. 270).

As Smith et al. (1985) point out, however, it is not simply the independent contribution of hormonal and social factors that leads to sexual behavior, but instead these factors interact to facilitate sexual behavior. Physical maturity may be related not only to an adolescent's level of sexual urges, but also to how sexually attractive the adolescent is and how physically mature one's friends are. Alone, none of these factors may be adequate to facilitate sexual behavior; together, however, they may interact to increase the likelihood that an adolescent may engage in sexual behavior.

Adolescent Sexuality: Summary

Consistent with our perspective that sexuality is more than just behavior, it is important to consider the many sides of sexuality in adolescence. As a multifaceted construct that is embedded in a matrix of causes and effects, adolescents' sense of sexuality results from biological, social, and psychological factors. As a synthetic construct, it appears that sexuality results from the individual's integration of previous experience, expectations, and the subjective meaning attributed to sociosexual behavior. Gagnon (1972), in his conceptualization of sexuality as a script, has argued that adolescents combine physical, emotional, social, and personal motives and concerns to form a new mode of experience. From this perspective, the sequence of these behaviors is a very important component of the developmental process because it provides a context in which the synthesis and integration of the various facets of sexuality take place. In this respect, the sequence is not just an index of development, but it is the context in which development occurs. Moreover, the social and cultural context in which these changes occur affects the adolescent's concept of the self according to dimensions related to sexuality. Indeed, as seen in Lerner, Lerner, and Tubman's (1989) "developmental contextual" model of adolescent development, biological "events" or changes in the individual influence, and are influenced by, the psychosocial context within which they are expressed. This view not only implies an interaction between the environment and the organism but, rather, suggests that the individual may act as a stimulus in eliciting reactions from others, a processor of information about his or her development, and, finally, as an agent, selector and shaper of his or her developmental contexts.

SUMMARY AND CONCLUSION

In this chapter we have tried to describe sexuality as a uniquely developmental phenomenon. As a process of synthesis, individuals actively participate in sexual development as they integrate the various facets of experience and context that are related to sex. In this process, individuals experience a transformation in their concept of self, in their behavior, and in their relations with others. Studying the processes that underlie normal sexual development helps us understand how this aspect of human experience happens in the "normal" or "typical" person. It is conceivable also that by understanding the "normal" processes of sexual development we can gain considerable insight into the origins of atypical or socially deviant development.

According to a current perspective known as developmental psychopathology, knowing about normal developmental processes is a prerequisite for understanding atypical development. Specifically, Sroufe and Rutter (1984) argue that from the perspective of developmental psychopathology, many "abnormal" behaviors should be understood not as distortions derived from abnormal processes, but instead as the result of normal processes that were distorted by atypical circumstances or experiences. Sroufe and Rutter's conceptualization of developmental psychopathology is heavily steeped in systems theory (see Sameroff, 1983), and consequently they emphasize the importance of considering the interdependence of developmental processes.

The concepts underlying the perspective of developmental psychopathology have important implications for the understanding of the development of juvenile sex offenders. First, in light of our conceptualization of sexuality as a synthesis of factors in which the individual plays a central integrative role, theory about juvenile sex offenders should be oriented toward understanding how these individuals were unable to synthesize the trialectic of self, other, and society. Whereas it may be that one of these components may be to "blame" for making such a synthesis impossible, the focus of theory about juvenile sex offenders should be on the process of synthesis itself, rather than on any individual component.

Second, in light of our conceptualization of sexuality as something that exists across the childhood years, it is important to recognize the developmental experiences or trajectory that underlies the manifestation of "atypical" (or unacceptable) behavior in adolescence. Benedict (1934) conceptualized childhood and adolescence as a process of adaptation to adult roles, responsibilities, and privileges. She proposed that as part of development, some modes of experience were reversed completely, as children move away from the dependency and submissive roles of childhood into independence and the dominant roles of adulthood. She argued that a further major transition of childhood and adolescent years is the transition in sexuality. Benedict argued that the key component to the successful negotiation of transitions in adolescence is the continuity of experience across the childhood years. Indeed, individuals who have had experiences that combine personal and interpersonal goals and desires into their social relations, with both same-sex and other-sex peers, across the childhood years are probably most likely to make the transition to an adolescent sexuality in the most "healthy" manner. Individuals whose experiences in these regards are the most discontinuous are most likely to have the most difficulty.

At the outset, we described sexuality as a most challenging aspect of development. Accordingly, the understanding of the factors underlying sexual development and individual differences in sexuality presents a challenge to persons who study both typical and atypical patterns of experience and behavior during adolescence. By indicating how these processes are embedded within physical, social, and cognitive developmental processes, we have tried to provide a point of departure for subsequent work on sexual development during childhood and adolescence.

ACKNOWLEDGMENT

The first author's work on this paper was supported by the W. T. Grant Foundation's Faculty Scholars Program.

REFERENCES

Benedict, R. (1934). *Patterns of culture.* Boston: Houghton Mifflin.
Berndt, T. J. (1982). The features and effects of friendship in early adolescence. *Child Development, 53,* 1447–1460.
Billy, J. O., & Udry, J. (1985a). The influence of male and female best friends on adolescent sexual behavior. *Adolescence, 20,* 21–32.
Billy, J. O., & Udry, J. (1985b). Patterns of adolescent friendship and effects on sexual behavior. *Social Psychology Quarterly, 48,* 27–41.
Blythe, D., Simmon, R., & Zakin, D. (1985). Satisfaction with body image for early adolescent females: The impact of pubertal timing within different school environments. *Journal of Youth and Adolescence, 14,* 207–225.

Brooks-Gunn, J., & Warren, M. P. (1988). The psychological significance of secondary sexual characteristics in nine- to eleven-year-old girls. *Child Development, 59,* 1061–1069.

Bukowski W. M., Newcomb, A. F., & Hoza, B. (1987). *Friendship, popularity and the "self" during early adolescence.* Unpublished manuscript.

Clarke-Stewart, A., & Hevey, C. M. (1981). Longitudinal relations in repeated observations of mother–child interaction from 1.5 to 2 years. *Developmental Psychology, 17,* 127–145.

Danza, R. (1983). Menarche: Its effects on mother–daughter and father–daughter interactions. In S. Golub (Ed.), *Menarche* (pp. 99–105). Lexington, MA: Heath.

Delaney, J., Lupton, M., & Toth, E. (1988). *The curse: A cultural history of menstruation.* Urbana: University of Illinois Press.

Efron, A. (1985). The sexual body: An interdisciplinary perspective. *Journal of Mind and Behavior, 6,* 1–314.

Feldman, T. P. (1971). Personification and structure in Hesiod's theogony. *Symbolae Osloenses, 46,* 7–41.

Fine, G. A. (1981) Friends, impression management, and preadolescent behavior. In S. R. Asher & J. M. Gottman (Eds.), *The development of children's friendships* (pp. 29–52). New York: Cambridge University Press.

Foucault, M. (1970). *The order of things.* New York: Pantheon Books.

Gaddis, A., & Brooks-Gunn, J. (1985). The male experience of pubertal change. *Journal of Youth and Adolescence, 14,* 61–69.

Gagnon, J. H. (1972). The creation of the sexual in early adolescence. In J. Kagan & R. Coles (Eds.), *Twelve to sixteen: Early adolescence* (pp. 231–257). New York: Norton.

Goldman, R., & Goldman, J. (1982). *Children's sexual thinking.* London: Routledge & Keegan Paul.

Goldman, R., & Goldman, J. (1988). *Show me yours: Understanding children's sexuality.* New York: Penguin.

Grief, E. B., & Ulman, K. J. (1982). The psychological impact of menarche on early adolescent females: A review of the literature. *Child Development, 53,* 1413–1430.

Grumbach, M. M. (1980). The neuroendocrinology of puberty. In D. Krieger & J. Hughes (Eds.), *Neuroendocrinology: The interrelationships of the body's two major integrative systems-in normal physiology and in clinical disease* (pp. 249–258). New York: HP Publishing.

Hall, G. S. (1904). *Adolescence.* New York: Appleton.

Hinde, R. A. (1984). Why do the sexes behave differently in human relationships? *Journal of Social and Personal Relationships, 1,* 471–502.

Jersilo, A. T. (1954). Emotional development. In L. Carmichael (Ed.), *Manual of child psychology* (pp. 833–917). New York: Wiley.

Koff, E. (1983). Through the looking glass of menarche: What the adolescent girl sees. In S. Golub (Ed.), *Menarche* (pp. 77–86). Lexington, MA: Heath.

Kohlberg, L. (1966). A cognitive-developmental analysis of children's sex-role concepts and attitudes. In E. E. Maccoby (Ed.), *The development of sex differences* (pp. 82–173). Stanford: Stanford University Press.

Lerner, R. M., Lerner, J. V., & Tubman, J. (1989). Organismic and contextual bases of development in adolescence: A developmental contextual view. In G. R. Adams, R. Montemayor, & T. P. Gullotta (Eds.), *Biology of adolescent behavior and development* (pp. 11–37). Newbury Park, CA: Sage.

Masters, W., Johnson, V. E., & Kolodny, R. C. (1985). *Human sexuality*. Boston: Little, Brown.

Mendelson, M. (1990). *Becoming a brother*. Cambridge, MA: MIT Press.

Miller, P., & Simon, W. (1980) The development of sexuality in adolescence. In L. Adelson (Ed.), *Handbook of adolescent psychology* (pp. 367–398). New York: Wiley.

Newcomer, S., & Udry, J. (1987). Parental marital status effects on adolescent sexual behavior. *Journal of Marriage and the Family, 49*, 235–240.

Prescott, J. W. (1979). Deprivation of physical affection as a primary process in the development of physical violence: A comparative and cross-cultural perspective. In D. Gil (Ed.), *Child abuse and violence* (pp. 66–137). New York: AMS Press.

Rierdan, J., & Koff, E. (1980). The psychological impact of menarche: Integrative versus disruptive changes. *Journal of Youth and Adolescence, 9*, 49–58.

Roberts, E. J. (1980). Dimensions of sexual learning in childhood. In E. J. Roberts (Ed.), *Childhood sexual learning* (pp. 1–15). Cambridge, MA: Ballinger.

Rosen, R., & Hall, E. (1984). *Sexuality*. New York: Random House.

Ruble, D. N., & Brooks-Gunn, J. (1982). The experience of menarche. *Child Development, 53*, 1557–1566.

Sameroff, A. J. (1983). Developmental systems: Contexts and evolution. In P. H. Mussen (Series Ed.) & W. Kessen (Vol. ed.), *Handbook of child psychology: Vol. 1. History, theories and method* (pp. 237–294). New York: Wiley.

Savin–Williams, R. C., & Small, S. A. (1986). The timing of puberty and its relationship to adolescent and parent perceptions of family interactions. *Developmental Psychology, 22*, 342–347.

Schofield, M. (1965). *The sexual behaviour of young people*. Boston: Little, Brown.

Selman, R., & Schultz, L. H. (1990). *Making a friend in youth*. Chicago: University of Chicago Press.

Serbin, L. A., & Sprafkin, C. (1987). A developmental approach: Sexuality from infancy through adolescence. In J. Geer & W. O'Donohue (Eds.), *Theories of human sexuality* (pp. 163–196). Hillsdale, NJ: Erlbaum.

Sharabany, R., Gershoni, R., & Hofman, J. (1981). Girlfriend, boyfriend: Age and sex differences in intimate friendship. *Developmental Psychology, 17*, 800–808.

Simon, W., & Gagnon, J. H. (1969). On psychosexual development. In D. Goslin (Ed.), *Handbook of socialization theory and research* (pp. 733–752). New York: Rand McNally.

Smith, E. A. (1989). A biosocial model of adolescent sexual behavior. In G. R. Adams, R. Montemayor, & T. P. Gullotta (Eds.), *Biology of adolescent behavior and development* (pp. 143–167). Newbury Park, CA: Sage.

Smith, E. A., Udry, J., & Morris, N. M. (1985). Pubertal development and friends: A biosocial explanation of adolescent sexual behavior. *Journal of Health and Social Behavior, 26*, 183–192.

Sroufe, L., & Rutter, M. (1984). The domain of developmental psychopathology. *Child Development, 55*, 17–29.

Sullivan, H. S. (1953). *The interpersonal theory of psychiatry*. New York: Norton.

Thornton, A. (1990). The courtship process and adolescent sexuality. *Journal of Family Issues, 11*, 239–273.

Tobin-Richards, M. H., Boxer, A. M., & Petersen, A. C. (1983). The psychological significance of pubertal changes: Sex differences in perceptions of self during early adolescence. In J. Brooks-Gunn & A. Petersen (Eds.), *Girls at puberty* (pp. 127–177). New York: Plenum Press.

Udry, J. R., & Billy, J. O. (1987). Initiation of coitus in early adolescence. *American Sociological Review, 52*, 841–855.

Udry, J. R., Billy, J. O., Morris, N. M., Groff, T. R., & Raj, M. H. (1985). Serum androgenic hormones motivate sexual behavior in adolescent boys. *Fertility and Sterility, 43*, 90–94.

Udry, J. R., Talbert, L. M., & Morris, N. M. (1986). Biosocial foundations for adolescent female sexuality. *Demography, 23*, 217–227.

Zelnick, M., & Kantner, J. (1973). Sex and contraception among unmarried teenagers. In C. Westoff et al. (Eds.), *Toward the end of growth: Population in America* (pp. 7–18). Englewood Cliffs, NJ: Prentice Hall.

CHAPTER 5

Sexual Assault through the Life Span: Adult Offenders with Juvenile Histories

Gene G. Abel
Candice A. Osborn
Deborah A. Twigg

Adult sexual aggression can result from a variety of etiological sources. Adults may become sexually aggressive as a result of impaired judgment resulting from drug or alcohol abuse; a lack of acquisition of the cultural prohibitions regarding sexual aggression; organic brain disease (e.g., temporal lobe lesion); antisocial personality characteristics; culturally defined gender roles (e.g., males are stereotypically expected to be dominant, while females are reinforced for passivity); or as a result of repetitive, obsessive sexual arousal to the fantasies and cognitions of deviant sex acts. It is this last group of individuals with sustained, deviant sexual preference, the so called paraphilias, on which this chapter focuses.

Paraphilias are of special concern because they have been identified by psychiatry and psychology as a distinctive category of sexual aggression that has a strong psychological etiology. The third revised edition of the *Diagnostic and Statistical Manual of Mental Disorders* (DSM III-R) (American Psychiatric Association, 1987) has classified such individuals as having recurrent, intense sexual urges and sexually arousing fantasies involving either (1) nonhuman objects (i.e., fetishism), (2) the suffering or humiliation of one or one's partner (i.e., sadism or masochism), or (3) children or other nonconsenting persons (i.e., pedophilia or exhibitionism). The severity of the paraphilias is rated as either mild (a paraphiliac is markedly distressed by recurrent paraphilic urges but has never acted on them), moderate (the paraphiliac has occasionally acted on the deviant urges), or severe (the person has repeatedly acted on paraphilic urges). The paraphilias will be focused on because individuals with this condition commit very high numbers of sex crimes, usually beginning in adolescence, and have consistently been seen as having psychiatric/psychological causes for their behavior.

SEXUAL DEVELOPMENT

Adolescence may be a very traumatic period for children. During this time, the individual is attempting to establish an identity of his or her own, as well as adjusting to the physiological and biochemical changes that are occurring within the body. Physiologically, females reach puberty between 9 and 14 years of age. This development is due to the increased amount of estrogen within the system and is marked by the appearance of secondary sex characteristics and menstruation. Males enter puberty between the ages of 10 and 17. There is an increase in the production of androgens within the male system, primarily testosterone, as well as the development of secondary sex characteristics and the maturing of the genitalia (Birren, Kinney, Schaie, & Woodruff, 1981).

These physiological and biological developments are accompanied by an increase in sexual drive, with a concomitant increase in sexual interaction and experimentation. Although both males and females reach puberty during adolescence, males tend to show a more rapid increase in sexual activity. This is partially attributed to the higher level of testosterone in adolescent males (Birren et al., 1981). The increase of activity and interest in sexual behaviors are normal processes of the adolescent stage of human development.

ETIOLOGY OF SEXUAL DEVIANCE

Most individuals seek out interactions that will permit a fulfillment of their sex drive, while others, for religious or other various reasons, try to inhibit their sexual drive. The majority of individuals pursue peers of the opposite sex, some peers of the same sex, while still others seek sexual relations with children of a much younger age and/or participate in sexual behaviors that are considered sexually deviant (i.e., exhibitionism, voyeurism, etc.).

Several theories have been advanced in an attempt to explain why an individual pursues deviant, rather than appropriate, sexual behaviors to satisfy their sex drive. One theory, proposed by Malmquist (1972), suggests that sexual deviancy results from "the persistence beyond childhood of earlier forms of sexuality as preferred expressions." Malmquist attributes this preference to an individual who is dominated by his or her id and suffering from a malfunctioning superego. There is a sense of security as these individuals continue in their familiar expressions of childhood, as opposed to the fear of expressing one's sexual desires in an unknown realm (with peers or adults). Deviant sexual behavior is viewed as an alternative to neurotic development, with the difference being attributed to ego acceptance of particular unrepressed infantile sexual fantasies. According to this theory, the paraphilic adolescent is viewed as developmentally impaired.

A second theoretical model of sexually deviant behaviors is the cognitive model. This model suggests that individuals engage in sexually assaultive behaviors due to cognitive distortions. These distortions, or thinking errors, provide a rationale for the justification of such behaviors, allowing the perpetrator to continue in his inappropriate sexual behavior. Some of these distortions include: "If I expose my penis to a woman, she will want to have sex with me"; "Sex between a child and an adult causes the child no emotional problems"; "Watching a woman through a window as she undresses does not cause her any harm"; "No woman can be raped unless she really wants to be"; and so on. In addition to these cognitive distortions, a number of characteristics have been found to be common among sex offenders. These include low self-esteem; objectification of females; hostility or rage; feelings of powerlessness and/or emptiness; poor impulse control; gender identity confusion; a fear of intimacy; and poor coping and problem-solving skills (Davis & Leitenberg, 1987; Groth, 1977; Hains, Herrman, Baker, & Graber, 1986). Together, the cognitive distortions and the common offender characteristics enable the offender to continue in his sexually assaultive behaviors with minimal regard for his victim.

A third theoretical model of deviant sexual behavior is the conditioning and social learning model (Laws & Marshall, 1990). This model suggests that individuals learn deviant sexual arousal/behaviors in the same manner in which other behaviors are learned—through observational learning or modeling and through the pairing and association of deviant thoughts or behaviors with a positive reinforcer (orgasm). Sexually deviant arousal/behaviors are subject to schedules of reinforcement, as are any learned behaviors. Such behaviors fall under the intermittent, variable-ratio schedule of reinforcement—the most difficult schedule to extinguish.

Marshall and Barbaree (1990) contend that most researchers seem to take a rather narrow perspective concerning factors that play a role in the etiology of sex offending and its maintenance. They purport an integration of the role of learning experiences, sociocultural factors, and biological processes to account for sex offending.

DO SOME ADOLESCENTS HAVE PARAPHILIAS?

During the late 1970s, Groth and his associates (Groth, 1977; Groth, Longo, & McFadin, 1982; Longo, 1983; Longo & Groth, 1983) began to emphasize the necessity of addressing sexual misconduct in adolescents as more than simply part of the normal maturational process. A number of studies followed and verified the existence of sexual pathology in adolescents. Lewis, Shankok, and Pincus (1978) evaluated 17 juvenile offenders convicted of sexual assault and found the average age at which deviance was first documented was 6 years. Other studies of juvenile offenders found that age of onset of sexual deviance ranged from 13 to 15.5 years (Awad, Saunders, & Levene, 1979; Becker, Cunningham-Rathner, & Kaplan, 1986; Smets & Cebula, 1987). Studies of adolescent offenders conducted by Deisher, Wenet, Paperny, Clark, & Fehrenbach (1982) and Smith & Monastersky (1986) indicated that adolescents commit a wide variety of paraphilic behaviors including rape, child molestation, voyeurism, exhibitionism, obscene phone calls, transvestism, and fetishism, beginning as early as 10 years of age.

Research conducted with adult offenders also supports the existence of deviant sexual behavior in adolescents. Groth et al. (1982) interviewed 137 felons convicted of either rape or child molestation at two penal institutions. The modal age at the time of first offense for both groups of offenders in the combined sample was 16 years. Abel, Mittelman, and Becker (1985) evaluated 411 adult sex offenders seen voluntarily at an outpatient clinic. Of this sample, 58.4% reported the onset of their deviant sexual arousal prior to the age of 18.

Most of these studies also attempted to determine the extent of the deviant sexual behavior committed by adolescents. Groth (1977) found, in almost three-fourths of his sample, the juvenile offender was likely to have committed a previous sexual assault. Lewis et al. (1978) found that 10 of the 17 boys they evaluated had committed two or more sexual assaults. Fifty-seven percent of all categories of offenders had committed multiple offenses in the study by Deisher et al. (1982). Smith and Monastersky (1986) discovered that 62.5% of the juveniles in their study had committed at least one sexual offense before the offense for which they were referred.

Becker et al. (1986) found that 79.1% of their sample reported being arrested once for a prior sexual offense, 7.5% twice, and 3%, three or more times. The 67 adolescents in their sample had committed a total of 313 sexual offenses and attempted 25 more. Eighty-two percent had engaged in non-deviant, nongenital sexual behavior, and 58% had engaged in nondeviant, genital sexual behaviors. Thus, for the majority, deviant behavior did not constitute their first or only sexual contact.

THE AGE OF ONSET OF PARAPHILIAS

The above studies support Groth's (1977) supposition that adolescents who engage in deviant sexual behaviors are not merely experimenting, but may be developing patterns of deviant sexual interest similar to those found in adult offenders. However, the majority of studies reviewed were based on relatively small sample sizes, involved only juveniles, and were conducted with incarcerated offenders, primarily rapists and child molesters.

Age of onset of various paraphilic interests was determined by a review of data from males seen for evaluation by the first author at outpatient clinics in Memphis, New York City, and Atlanta. Detailed clinical interviews documented the age of onset of paraphilic interest by identifying major life events surrounding the onset of the paraphilia(s). Histories of 1,025 paraphiliacs revealed that 446 (42.3%) reported the onset of paraphilias prior to age 18. Figure 5.1 shows the average age of onset of various paraphilias from this population. Transvestism had the earliest age of onset of all the paraphilias, averaging 13.6 years of age, followed by fetishism, bestiality, voyeurism, and the other common paraphilias. As expected, pedophilia involving female incest victims (identified as Pedophilia F Incest in the figure) and pedophilia involving male incest victims (identified as Pedophilia M Incest in the figure) had the latest average age of onset of 23.5 and 27.1 years of age, respectively. These two groups of paraphilias included not only adolescents involved in incestuous relationships with siblings, but also adults who had fathered children that they eventually molested, or who were of an age that they lived with a sexual partner in the father role and molested their partner's children.

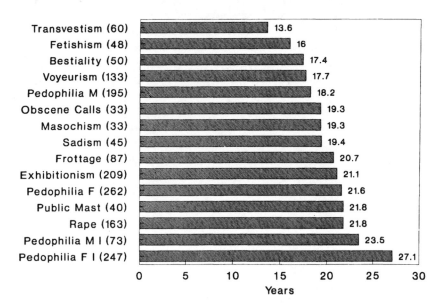

FIGURE 5.1. Average age of onset of various paraphilias.

Figure 5.2 shows the percentage of individuals by specific diagnosis who demonstrated paraphilic interest by age 17. The percentages varied from a high of 81.7% for transvestites to a low of 27.5% for public masturbators. As can be seen in Figure 5.2, irrespective of the paraphilia, a high percentage of individuals reported the onset of their paraphilic interest by age 17.

Further evidence supporting paraphilic interest in adolescents is seen by comparing the frequency of specific paraphilias in adolescents with frequency of specific paraphilias in adults. Table 5.1 shows the various paraphilic diagnoses in adolescents versus adults seen in our clinic. Although there are some slight differences seen in the relative occurrences of different paraphilias, the percentages are surprisingly similar. This suggests that the same process leading to paraphilic diagnoses in adulthood is operating in adolescents, and subsequently producing identical frequencies of paraphilic diagnoses.

PARAPHILIACS WHO WERE ADOLESCENTS WHEN EVALUATED

Although paraphilic interests are present at an early age, this does not necessarily imply that paraphilic behavior begins at an early age. The following data

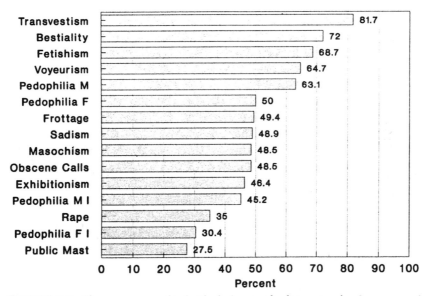

FIGURE 5.2. The percentage of individuals, by specific diagnosis, who demonstrated paraphilic interest by age 17.

TABLE 5.1. Comparison of Frequency of Specific Paraphilias in
Adolescents and Adults

Paraphilic category	Adolescents	Adults
Pedophilia	62.5%	59.1%
Rape	13.9	7.3
Exhibitionism	13.9	13.6
Voyeurism	13.9	12.9
Frottage	5.6	3.8
Public masturbation	1.4	6.3
Transsexualism	0.0	0.7
Transvestism	9.7	4.9
Fetishism	8.3	4.9
Sadism	4.2	2.4
Masochism	2.8	3.1
Obscene phone calls	5.6	3.5
Bestiality	8.3	8.0
Other	1.4	2.1

from the authors' adolescent paraphiliacs, in order to reflect a more con-
servative approach to this issue, include information gathered only from adolescents who admit to paraphilic interest that meet the criteria of DSM III-R for
paraphilia. Adolescents whose arrest records were highly suggestive of paraphilia, or whose behavior when observed by others strongly supports paraphilic
interest, were excluded unless the adolescent admitted to repetitive urges and
fantasies that meet the DSM-III-R criteria. Participants included 119 males
under the age of 18 undergoing evaluation or treatment for paraphilia at the
clinics previously mentioned. Their average age was 15.5 years (SD 1.4), and
they ranged in age from 11 to 17 with a modal age of 17.

Table 5.2 presents the range and average number of victims for various
paraphilias by the ages at which the paraphilic adolescent was evaluated. Some
individuals reported more than one paraphilic interest and are thus represented
in multiple categories. Excluded from this table are categories of paraphilia
without victims, such as transvestism or fetishism. These data reflect that even
at these early ages there are a fair number of victims, especially in cases of
obscene phone callers, voyeurs, and frotteurs.

What Happens to Untreated Adolescent Paraphiliacs?

The above studies document that adolescents do indeed exhibit sexual paraphilias and that they have a significant number of victims. However, very little
research has been published that evaluates the behavior of such adolescents
once they reach adulthood. Predicting the consequences of not treating adolescent paraphiliacs is difficult.

TABLE 5.2. Frequency of Adolescent Paraphiliacs by Age at Time when They Were Evaluated and Mean Number and Range of Victims per Paraphilia

Diagnosis	Age when evaluated					Total n = 119	Mean no. of victims	Range for each diagnosis[a]
	≤13	14	15	16	17			
Voyeurism	0	3	2	6	6	17	75.94	1–730
Pedophilia M	6	4	7	3	9	29	4.93	1–50
Pedophilia F	4	4	6	7	10	31	1.35	0–5
Frottage	0	0	1	3	4	8	30.86	1–180
Sadism	0	2	0	1	1	4	0.25	0–1
Masochism	0	1	0	2	0	3	0.00	—
Obscene phone calls	0	0	0	1	0	1	100.00	—
Exhibitionism	0	1	4	7	6	18	6.50	1–36
Pedophilia M I	2	2	2	5	4	15	1.20	1–2
Pedophilia F I	2	4	8	6	7	27	1.30	1–2
Rape	0	5	3	4	9	21	1.29	0–4
Public masturbation	0	0	0	1	0	1	5.00	0–5
Total frequencies	14	26	33	46	56			

[a]Includes individuals who met diagnostic criteria due to recurrent urges but who may not have actually carried out the behavior.

Some adolescent paraphiliacs may simply lose their deviant interests prior to adulthood; others may stop their paraphilic behavior due to realization of either the inappropriateness of their sexual interests or of the legal consequences of their sexual behavior; or, for many adolescents, their inappropriate sexual behavior may not come to the attention of psychological or legal services and they may continue to engage in the same types of behaviors or progress to more serious offenses. Unfortunately we know nothing about the frequency with which these various outcomes occur. It is unethical to conduct longitudinal studies on adolescent offenders without attempting treatment, so the best possible assessment of consequences of nonintervention with juvenile offenders is through the study of adult offenders who admit that their deviant sexual interests began during adolescence.

Two studies document the progression by adolescent offenders to more serious sexual offenses as adults. Longo and McFadin (1981), in a study of 84 adult rapists and child molesters, found that many of the offenders had participated in noncontact offenses such as exhibitionism and voyeurism while juveniles. Longo and Groth (1983) interviewed 231 adults convicted of sexual assault regarding their sexual development, experiences, and behavior. Thirty-two percent of the combined sample exhibited compulsive masturbatory activity as juveniles. Twenty-four percent of the sample sexually exposed themselves repetitively as juveniles, and 54% had persistently engaged in voyeuristic activities. They concluded that a significant number of offenders (at least one in three) show some evidence of progression from nonviolent sexual offenses in adolescence to violent sexual offenses as adults.

ADULT PARAPHILIACS REPORTING THE ONSET OF PARAPHILIC INTEREST PRIOR TO AGE 18

Relying on data from 446 paraphiliacs who had reported the onset of paraphilias prior to age 18 as described above, the authors tabulated the number of victims resulting from the various paraphilic acts. As one might expect, in some categories there was a tremendous variation in the number of victims. Particularly problematic were those individuals in various paraphilic categories whose huge numbers of victims skewed the group mean. Generally these individuals were involved in frottage, exhibitionism, obscene phone calls, voyeurism, and/or public masturbation. Including data from these individuals in the average number of victims, by the age when the paraphiliac was first evaluated, tended to greatly inflate the average number of victims. As a compromise the median number of victims was tabulated, not only to minimize the effect of high-frequency paraphiliacs, but also to more accurately represent categories with small sample sizes.

The cumulative median number of victims was subsequently plotted (see Figures 5.3, 5.4, and 5.5) for those paraphilic categories with adequate sample sizes per category. The cumulative median number of victims from paraphiliacs, ages ≤ 13 through 47, when evaluated, was graphed. Each age represented on the graph (15, 20, 25, 30, 35, 40, 45) is the blocked data for the 5 years surrounding these ages (e.g., age 15 reflects the median between the ages of 13 and 17 when evaluated). Subjects over the age of 47 were excluded for two reasons: (1) number of victims did not significantly increase beyond this age, and (2) n's for older age groups were too small and thus produced skewed data. The cumulative medians of 181 individuals involved in four categories of pedophilic behavior with children 13 years of age or younger are shown in Figure 5.3. The cumulative median number of victims of these pedophiles who had committed acts against girls outside of the home (Pedophilia F), against girls within the home (Pedophilia F I), against boys outside of the home (Pedophilia M), and against boys within the home (Pedophilia M I) is plotted. A steady increase in the cumulative median number of victims per pedophile indicates these pedophiles continue molesting children. It is also apparent that pedophiles who molest boys outside the home have the highest number of victims, and there is a dramatic increase in the number of victims from age block 35 to age block 40.

Figure 5.4 shows the cumulative median number of victims for those paraphiliacs perpetrating frottage, exhibitionism, public masturbation, obscene

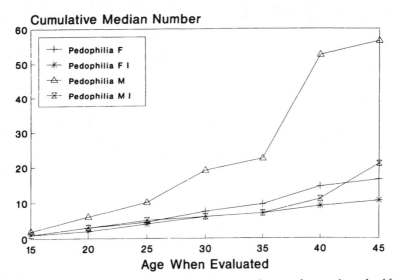

FIGURE 5.3. Cumulative median number of victims, by age when evaluated, of four categories of pedophilic behavior with children below the age of 14.

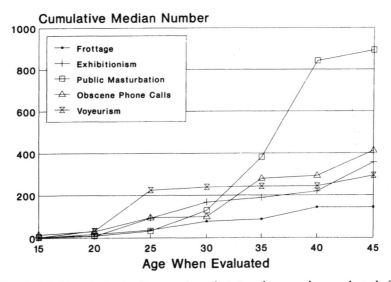

FIGURE 5.4. Cumulative median number of victims, by age when evaluated, for paraphiliacs perpetrating frottage, exhibitionism, public masturbation, obscene phone calls, and voyeurism.

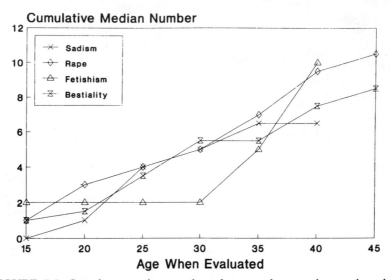

FIGURE 5.5. Cumulative median number of victims, by age when evaluated, for paraphiliacs perpetrating sadism, rape, fetishism, and bestiality.

phone calls, and voyeurism. Data from these individuals show a steady rise in the median number of victims, indicating continued involvement in the para-philic behavior as the age of the paraphiliac increases from 15 to 45. One exception appears to be voyeurs whose deviant behavior appears to plateau at age 25. Of great concern should be the tremendous number of victims in this group of paraphiliacs. This is especially obvious in the cumulative median number of victims of public masturbators, with a cumulative median of 900 victims by age 45.

Figure 5.5 reflects the cumulative median number of victims of a group of paraphiliacs with comparatively small numbers of victims. This includes para-philiacs involved in sadism, rape, fetishism, and bestiality (fetishism was only included if the individual's fetish arousal involved specific body parts of a victim). Bestiality, of course, included no human victims, only animals.

In each of these paraphilias we see a surprisingly low median number of victims relative to the paraphilias in Figures 5.3 and 5.4.

SUMMARY AND CONCLUSION

Figures 5.3, 5.4, and 5.5 reflect the anticipated number of victims of paraphiliacs if treatment interventions are not initiated or if they fail to curtail the offender's inappropriate sexual behavior. As can be seen from these figures, the potential number of victims, as adolescent perpetrators mature into adult offenders, is astronomical. Groth and his associates (Groth, 1977; Groth & Loredo, 1981; Groth et al., 1982; Longo, 1983; Longo & Groth, 1983) have emphasized the importance of concentrating on juvenile offenders in order to detect this problem early and prevent or reduce later victimization. They point out that, by the time juveniles are referred to a clinician, it is often the result of persistent behavior rather than a first occurrence, and, therefore, an in-depth assessment should be conducted. The all-too-frequent diagnosis of adolescent adjustment reaction often results in the adolescent's deviant sexual behavior going unrecognized and thus untreated. This diagnosis is preferred by the legal system so as not to "inappropriately" stigmatize the adolescent as a sex offender for behaviors that may have been experimental in nature.

Regardless of how one develops arousal toward deviant sexual behaviors, there is a need for intervention as early as possible. If an individual begins to engage in such behaviors and is not subject to intervention and/or negative consequences for such actions, he will be reinforced by the innate positive reinforcers of the sexual act. These inherent positive reinforcers include, but are not limited to, the pleasure of orgasm, the pleasure of stress reduction, and the feeling of power the individual may feel over another person (Twigg, 1990). Ryan, Lane, Davis, and Isaac (1987) contend that early intervention is indicated both for prevention of multiple victimization and to interrupt the reinforcing nature of the deviant sexual behaviors.

Costs to Society of Nonintervention

Societal costs are extensive once one considers the total costs resulting from child molestation, rape, exhibitionism, and so on. Victimization leads to costs for counseling services of these victims and their families. It is clear that the consequences of a public health problem impacting on a sizable portion of our culture cannot be dealt with by treatment of only the victims of child molestation, rape, and the other paraphilias. The number of victims alone surpasses society's ability to provide therapy to them.

The financial costs of dealing with a paraphiliac through the criminal justice system are also astounding. Litigation costs can be enormous. Incarceration of the offender, with the paraphiliac's loss of income and the increased expense of public support of his family, adds considerably to the financial and emotional burden society must pay as a consequence of continued paraphilic behavior. The only successful means of dealing with public health problems to date has been to focus on the causative agent of that problem, in this case, the paraphiliac himself. Since paraphilic interest frequently begins in adolescence, it seems only practical to bring assessment and treatment to bear on the adolescent paraphiliac if we are to significantly reduce this public health problem.

REFERENCES

Abel, G. G., Mittelman, M. S., & Becker, J. V. (1985). Sex offenders: Results of assessment and recommendations for treatment. In M. H. Ben-Aron, S. J. Hucker, & C. D. Webster (Eds.), Clinical criminology: The assessment and treatment of criminal behavior (pp. 207–220). Toronto: M & M Graphics.

American Psychiatric Association. (1987). Diagnostic and statistical manual of mental disorders (3rd ed., rev.). Washington, DC: Author.

Awad, G. A., Saunders, E., & Levene, J. (1979). A clinical study of male adolescent sex offenders. International Journal of Offender Therapy and Comparative Criminology, 28, 105–116.

Becker, J. V., Cunningham-Rathner, J., & Kaplan, M. S. (1986). Adolescent sexual offenders: Demographics, criminal and sexual histories, and recommendations for reducing future offenses. Journal of Interpersonal Violence, 1, 431–445.

Birren, J. E., Kinney, D. K., Schaie, K. W., & Woodruff, D. S. (1981). Developmental psychology: A lifespan approach. Boston: Houghton Mifflin.

Davis, G. E., & Leitenberg, H. (1987). Adolescent sex offenders. Psychological Bulletin, 101, 417–427.

Deisher, R. W., Wenet, G. A., Paperny, D. M., Clark, T. F., & Fehrenbach, P. A. (1982). Adolescent sexual offense behavior: The role of the physician. Journal of Adolescent Health Care, 2, 279–286.

Groth, A. N. (1977). The adolescent sexual offender and his prey. International Journal of Offender Therapy and Comparative Criminology, 21, 249–254.

Groth, A., Longo, R. E., & McFadin, B. (1982). Undetected recidivism among rapists and child molesters. Crime and Delinquency, 28, 450–458.

Groth, A. N., & Loredo, C. M. (1981). Juvenile sex offenders: Guidelines for assessment. International Journal of Offender Therapy and Comparative Criminology, 25, 31–39.

Hains, A. A., Herrman, L. P., Baker, K. L., & Graber, S. (1986). The development of a psycho-educational group program for adolescent sex offenders. Journal of Offender Counseling, Services and Rehabilitation, 11, 63–76.

Laws, D. R., & Marshall, W. L. (1990). A conditioning theory of the etiology and maintenance of deviant sexual preference and behavior. In W. L. Marshall, D. R. Laws, & H. E. Barbaree (Eds.), Handbook of sexual assault: Issues, theories, and treatment of the offender (pp. 209–229). New York: Plenum Press.

Lewis, D. O., Shankok, S. S., & Pincus, J. H. (1978). Juvenile male sexual assaulters. American Journal of Psychiatry, 136, 1194–1196.

Longo, R. E. (1983). Sexual learning and experience among adolescent sexual offenders. International Journal of Offender Therapy and Comparative Criminology, 26, 235–241.

Longo, R. E., & Groth, A. N. (1983). Juvenile sexual offenses in the histories of adult rapists and child molesters. International Journal of Offender Therapy and Comparative Criminology, 27, 150–155.

Longo, R. E., & McFadin, B. (1981). Sexually inappropriate behavior: Development of the sexual offender. Law and Order, 29, 21–23.

Malmquist, C. P. (1972). Juvenile sex offenders. In H. L. Resnik & M. E. Wolfgang

(Eds.), *Sexual behaviors: Social, clinical and legal aspects* (pp. 76–77). Boston: Little, Brown.

Marshall, W. L., & Barbaree, H. E. (1990). An integrated theory of the etiology of sexual offending. In W. L. Marshall, D. R. Laws, & H. E. Barbaree (Eds.), *Handbook of sexual assault: Issues, theories, and treatment of the offender* (pp. 257–275). New York: Plenum Press.

Ryan, G., Lane, S., Davis, J., & Isaac, C. (1987). Juvenile sex offenders: Development and correction. *Child Abuse and Neglect, 11*, 385–395.

Smets, A. C., & Cebula, C. M. (1987). A group treatment program for adolescent sex offenders: Five steps toward resolution. *Child Abuse and Neglect, 11*, 247–254.

Smith, W. R., & Monastersky, C. (1986). Assessing juvenile sexual offenders' risk for reoffending. *Criminal Justice and Behavior, 13*, 115–140.

Twigg, D. A. (1990). *The effects of treatment on sex offenders: A literature review.* Unpublished manuscript.

CHAPTER 6

Pavlovian Conditioning Processes in Adolescent Sex Offenders

William L. Marshall
Anthony Eccles

Numerous authors over many years have proposed that human sexual behavior involves at least some learned components. Some have suggested that humans inherit no more than a nonspecific sexual drive, the particular expression of which is learned (Kinsey, Pomeroy, Martin, & Gebhard, 1953). Others however, specifically propose that deviations from so-called normative sexual behaviors are learned (Jaspers, 1963; McGuire, Carlisle, & Young, 1965). The learning mechanism that is thought to mediate the acquisition of sexual deviations is some form of conditioning. This idea is so well entrenched in those who espouse cognitive-behavioral approaches to the assessment and treatment of these men, that it is typically simply accepted or advanced with little in the way of evidence offered in support of the actual occurrence of conditioning processes.

There are at least three reasons for considering the value of conditioning theories of the acquisition of deviant sexuality. In the first place, an evaluation of the supporting literature will contribute to our understanding of the relevance of such theories, and this, in itself, seems worth the effort given the prominent role that conditioning notions have played, and continue to play, in explanations of human sexual behavior. Second, many behavioral interventions aimed at modifying sexual preferences are derived from a conditioning account of the maintenance, if not the acquisition, of such preferences. And, finally, a consideration of the implications of conditioning theories should generate hypotheses that may lead to empirical studies whose outcome will expand our knowledge whether or not they offer support for conditioning theories.

THE NATURE OF CONDITIONING THEORIES

Conditioning theories of human behavior were originally derived from research on animal learning, and certainly there has been a widespread belief among animal researchers that sexual behavior is conditionable (Bermant & Davidson, 1974). However, the actual evidence for Pavlovian processes in shaping the sexual behavior of animals is quite limited. Farris (1967) observed marginal effects on copulatory behavior in rats as a result of manipulating Pavlovian contingencies, and both Graham and Desjardins (1980) and Kamel, Mock, Wright, and Frankel (1975) showed that an olfactory-conditioned stimulus paired with the presentation of a receptive female came to be as effective as the female's presence in eliciting sex steroid changes in male rats. More recently, Zamble and his colleagues (Cutmore & Zamble, 1988; Zamble, Hadad, Mitchell, & Cutmore, 1985; Zamble, Mitchell, & Findlay, 1986) have shown limited control over copulation as a result of Pavlovian conditioning. Obviously, there is evidence that conditioning contingencies can influence sexual behavior in nonhuman animals, but this evidence is not extensive and reveals effects only on the rate or intensity of copulation with a sexually receptive female rather than a shift in sexual expression toward the conditional stimulus itself.

This observation reveals an important difference between what limited findings there are of conditioning the sexual behavior of animals and the proposals offered by conditioning theorists of human behavior, so it seems appropriate at this time to describe in more detail just what it is these latter theorists propose. It is not enough to simply say, in support of conditioning theories of human sexual behavior, that conditioning processes have been demonstrated to modify animal behavior; we must show a reasonably close match if we are to rely at all on the evidence from animal learning.

McGuire et al. (1965) were the first to clearly articulate a conditioning account of sexual deviations in humans. On the basis of the self-reported case histories of sexual deviants, McGuire et al. concluded that the pairing of deviant fantasies with masturbatory-induced arousal provided the conditioning basis for the development of patients' unusual sexual proclivities. These authors appear to offer two quite different origins of these deviant fantasies. In what appears to be the primary cause in their explanation, McGuire et al. claim that deviant fantasies arise as a result of an initial seduction or other direct experience with a deviant act. Because this is seen as "the first *real* sexual experience as opposed to stories" (p. 186, italics in original), it is said to have greater salience than fantasies of consenting heterosexual intercourse with a peer-aged partner, since up to this time the individual has not actually experienced heterosexual relations. Also, McGuire et al. claim that there is a predisposition in these patients that makes it less likely that they will look to normal sexual relations for their fantasies. Men who develop deviant interests are said to have had "early aversive heterosexual experiences or feelings of physical or social inadequacy" (p. 186) that made them believe that a normal sex life was not possible for them. Obviously for this to have affected their attraction to the deviant fantasies, these feelings or aversive experiences must have preceded the actual deviant act that came to serve as the basis for their masturbatory fantasies. It is difficult to see exactly how these men are able to have both a prior early aversive experience with an appropriate heterosexual partner and at the same time have, as their first sexual experience, a deviant act. However, it is possible to modify the hypothetical sequence so that the overall argument makes sense; that is, so long as both of these experiences (i.e., the deviant act and the aversive heterosexual contact) occurred either in close temporal relations or without other intervening direct sexual contacts, the theory remains sound.

A second feature claimed by McGuire et al. to have relevance for the development of deviance concerns the processes by which masturbatory fantasies are said to get modified. Over time, recall may distort fantasies and this, along with the accidental focus on particular cues, is said to initiate a feedback loop that will gradually move the content of masturbatory fantasies in a progressively more deviant direction. Deviant cues become more and more dominant because when they are the focus of fantasies they are associated with sexual arousal and so become more sexually stimulating. This means they will probably arise in future masturbatory thoughts and be further endowed with sexual provocativeness, and so on ad infinitum. At the same time, other (more appropriate) sexual stimuli will be subject to extinction, since they will be progressively less frequently associated with sexual arousal.

Abel and Blanchard (1974) have also endorsed a Pavlovian view of the acquisition and maintenance of sexual deviation along the lines of that espoused by McGuire et al. (1965). In their review of studies that address the role of fantasy in deviant sexual behavior, Abel and Blanchard conclude that deviant fantasizing is the pivotal process that results in sexual offending. Laws and Marshall (1990), on the other hand, see Pavlovian processes as one small part of the acquisition of sexual preferences to deviant themes. Laws and Marshall, like Quinn, Harbison, and McAllister (1970) before them, see an important role for operant conditioning and social learning in developing and conserving deviant interests. Since we are here interested only in Pavlovian processes our focus will be on the theories advanced by McGuire et al. (1965), and Abel and Blanchard (1974).

The general notion involved in these learning accounts of the acquisition of sexual interests is that Pavlovian conditioning processes are the basis for acquired preferences that are expressed in overt behavior. Traditional accounts of Pavlovian (or classical) conditioning processes are quite simple: When a previously neutral stimulus (conditional stimulus [CS]) consistently predicts the occurrence of another stimulus (unconditioned stimulus [UCS]) which has the power to automatically evoke a biologically important response (unconditioned response [UCR]), the previously neutral stimulus will, over time, come to evoke at least some portion of this biological response (conditioned response [CR]). Thus, when a CS is consistently paired with a UCS (e.g., tactile stimulation of the genitals) that automatically evokes sexual arousal, then this CS may eventually come to evoke arousal independently of the occurrence of the UCS. In terms of sexual behavior, although the CS may seemingly take many forms, the range of stimuli to which human males sexually respond is actually quite limited, and it would seem likely that some stimuli may be easily conditioned to elicit a sexual response while others may never acquire the power to evoke arousal. This modification to the conditioning paradigm is derived from Seligman's (1970) general argument concerning the effects of evolutionary history on the "preparedness" of certain stimuli to function readily as conditional stimuli in Pavlovian processes and is not contained in the traditional behavioral accounts of the acquisition of sexual deviance. We simply note it here for completeness.

Until recently in the behavior therapy literature, classical conditioning has been understood to operate on physiological response systems that are under relatively limited voluntary control or at least the acquisition mechanisms are thought to be beyond conscious control even if the fantasized CS is deliberately generated. This view derives from traditional Pavlovian notions but does not agree with current animal learning models that invoke cognitive processes as essential to conditioning (cf. Mackintosh, 1974). Indeed, Zinbarg (1990) has argued that current thinking in behavioral or cognitive-behavioral therapy regarding conditioning is antiquated and should be revised in terms of modern animal learning analyses. We will give more consideration to Zinbarg's position later when we develop our own account, but for the moment we will focus on the more strictly Pavlovian model, since that has been the basis of theorizing about human sexual behavior to this point.

There appear to be two ways in which Pavlovian conditioning processes could be initiated: (1) by pairing a CS with tactile-induced sexual arousal or (2) by pairing a CS with a nontactile stimulus known to elicit sexual arousal. In the former case the UCS (i.e., tactile stimulation of the genitals) is said to be a primary unlearned elicitor of sexual arousal, whereas in the latter case the UCS (i.e., a nontactile stimulus) is said to be a second-order elicitor of sexual arousal. Second-order UCSs are stimuli that have acquired, by prior Pavlovian processes, the power to evoke arousal; that is, they were at one time CSs paired with a primary UCS, but they have acquired such automatic eliciting power that they are able to function as UCSs in a subsequent Pavlovian process. With respect to human subjects, both these paradigms (i.e., CS-tactile UCS, and CS-nontactile UCS) have been explored, although neither has been examined extensively.

EVIDENCE FOR CONDITIONING

Studies Using Nontactile UCSs

Rachman (1966) and Rachman and Hodgson (1968) claimed to have successfully conditioned sexual responding to a previously neutral stimulus. They presented either nondeviant males with a colored slide of a pair of black, knee-length woman's boots (CS) that was followed 1 second later by the presentation of a colored slide of an attractive nude or scantily clad female (UCS). Erectile responses were measured by a mercury-in-rubber strain gauge. There were, of course, marked variations in the number of pairings (CS-UCS) necessary for each subject to reach the criterion of five successive trials on which arousal occurred to the CS, but all reached criterion. Consistent with conditioning principles, generalization was demonstrated to similar stimuli, as was extinction of the conditioned response due to repeated, unpaired presentations of the CS. Also, backward conditioning (i.e., UCS-CS pairings) did not produce any changes in response to the CS; only forward conditioning (i.e., CS-UCS pairings) produced the expected results. Again, these observations were consistent with expectations from Pavlovian conditioning theory as it was understood at that time. A somewhat limiting problem with Rachman's reports concerns the fact that he did not clearly describe the magnitude of arousal displayed in response to the CS. If it was simply just above base line, then the findings are not as compelling as they have been taken to be.

In a similar study, McConaghy (1970) demonstrated that penile volume responses could be conditioned to a previously neutral stimulus. Rachman's CS (women's boots) represents a class of stimuli that are known to have acquired erotic properties in some males (i.e., fetishists), and given that they were articles of female clothing and might be expected to lie at some point in a sexually provocative generalization gradient for avowed heterosexual males, we would anticipate a distinct possibility that such stimuli may readily serve as effective CSs in a conditioning paradigm. McConaghy, however, used stimuli (red circles and green triangles), which might be expected, from a preparedness perspective (Seligman, 1970), to fail to serve as effective CSs. Nevertheless, he found clear

evidence of conditioned arousal to the CS in 10 heterosexual and 15 homo-
sexual males. McConaghy's results do not suffer from the defect observed in
Rachman's report, as the group data revealed reasonably substantial arousal to
the CS after only ten trials where the CS preceded the UCS (unfortunately the
CS-UCS interval was not specified). However, over trials the response to the
CS was consistently lower than the response to the UCS.

These two series of studies provide evidence that when an externally
presented CS consistently precedes a stimulus (in these two studies, remember,
the UCS was also an externally presented stimulus) that evokes sexual arousal
(UCR), the CS will eventually come to elicit conditioned sexual arousal (CR).
Results from these studies provided the basis for a series of attempts to enhance
arousal to appropriate stimuli in sexual deviants using similar procedures, and
the findings of these interventions are, of course, relevant to conditioning
theories.

Beech, Watts, and Poole (1971) successfully shifted the sexual preferences
of a young male who was aroused by simply observing prepubescent girls.
Pretreatment erectile measures and self-reported interests revealed strong sexual arousal to photographs of young girls but no arousal at all to adult females.
Pictures of naked females were grouped according to age into four categories
ranging from prepubertal girls (Group 1) to adult, sexually mature women
(Group 4). Initially Group 1 pictures served as the UCS, while Group 2 pictures
served as the CS. Once a consistent CR was evident to the Group 2 pictures,
they served as the UCS for Group 3 pictures, and then Group 3 served as the
UCS for Group 4. Nine CS-UCS pairings occurred at each stage with the CS
presented for 5 seconds, while the UCS was presented until an erectile response
occurred. Not only were penile responses conditioned to all the stimuli presented, the young man reported that outside the treatment setting he was
aroused by adult females and his interest in young girls had markedly declined.
While these data are consistent with the idea that the laboratory procedures
produced the beneficial changes in this young man, treatment extended over a
3-month period and many other things went on both in the young man's life
outside therapy and between the therapists and the patient, which may have
contributed to these changes.

In any case, two subsequent studies were not as successful. In an attempt
to shift the sexual preferences of three homosexual males, Herman, Barlow, and
Agras (1974) found some limited value for this conditioning procedure. The CS
was a 1-minute presentation of a colored slide of a nude adult female and the
UCS was a 1-minute segment of a film of homosexual content. For the first
subject (a 26-year-old male), backward conditioning, as expected, failed to
produce any changes, while forward conditioning had the desired effects:
Arousal to females increased and the patient began masturbating to fantasies
involving women. A second subject (a 16-year-old male) failed to show any
changes as a result of the usual Pavlovian procedures (i.e., where the CS

precedes the UCS) but enhanced arousal to females occurred when the CS and the UCS were presented simultaneously. When Herman et al. inspected the data from the classical conditioning phase with this adolescent male, they observed that erectile responses to the homosexual film did not occur until 15 seconds after onset of the UCS. They took this to mean that the contingency between the CS and the UCR was more critical than the contingency between the CS and the UCS, although they offer no reason for supposing this to be true. Indeed, contrary to Herman et al.'s notion, it has been observed in animal research that the optimal delay between the CS and the UCS (in this case a receptive female) is quite long. Zamble et al. (1986), for instance, found little or no evidence of conditioned sexual responding when the CS-UCS interval was less than 8 minutes or more than 16 minutes. In any event, when Herman et al. projected the CS and the UCS on adjoining screens, they observed increases over trials in arousal to females. Their final subject (a 22-year-old male) failed to show the hoped-for changes under any conditions despite being exposed to 45 forward and 45 simultaneous pairings of the CS-UCS.

Despite these rather disappointing results, Herman et al. discuss their findings as clear evidence that Pavlovian procedures can alter sexual preferences. Marshall (1974), on the other hand, found no evidence of conditioned changes in sexual responses with four sexual offenders. Base-line assessment revealed little or no arousal in these men to appropriate sexual stimuli and very strong arousal to their preferred deviant stimuli. Following Beech et al.'s (1971) procedures, Marshall presented subjects with a CS (one of a series of colored slides of nude adult females) for 30 seconds immediately prior to presenting the UCS (one of a series of colored slides that matched their deviant category and elicited strong arousal during base-line assessment) for a further 30 seconds. The CS-UCS pairing was presented 324 times to each subject over a 3-week period, and yet the minimal changes that did occur were inconsistent and so small as to be clinically insignificant.

The evidence, then, in support of the possibility that sexual preferences can be changed by pairing an externally presented CS and UCS, seems at best to be weak and inconsistent. It seems unlikely, then, that such contingencies play an important role in the acquisition of deviant behavior. In terms of using such a procedure as a treatment intervention, the data suggest that this would result in few subjects showing positive changes.

Studies Using Tactile UCSs

One of the very interesting, but neglected observations of Herman et al.'s (1974) report is the fact that in the two subjects who showed evidence of change, these benefits were readily reversed by switching the contingencies. This suggests that the effects of the conditioning procedures were not at all resilient and that in the absence of engaging in some additional behavior (e.g., masturbating to appropriate fantasies) outside the laboratory setting, the conditioned changes would extinguish rapidly. From their remarks, it seems likely that Herman et al.'s patients did engage in extratherapeutic masturbation while imagining females, and Beech et al.'s (1971) patient seems to have done the same thing. Remember also that Herman et al. could not produce changes in arousal in Subject 2 unless they paired the CS with the UCR. These observations suggest that appropriate conditioning procedures require the CS to be paired with a UCS that immediately induces the UCR; direct tactile stimulation (in a nonsatiated subject) typically guarantees this. Thus, procedures that pair a CS with masturbatory-generated arousal would seem to be optimal, and in any case this more closely matches the implications of conditioning theories.

Various procedures, involving pairing a stimulus with masturbation, have been employed to initiate or enhance sexual responsiveness to normative sexual stimuli. Typically in these cases the client displays, at laboratory assessment, strong arousal to a deviant stimulus (or at least arousal to a stimulus that he finds unacceptable—e.g., egodystonic homosexuality) and little or no arousal to consenting sex with an adult partner (or an egosystonic partner). One goal for such clients, then, is to increase arousal to acceptable sexual stimuli. Laws and Marshall (1991) have reviewed this literature, and, unfortunately, they could find little in the way of support for the value of these procedures.

Marquis (1970) described one variation of a procedure that is variously called "orgasmic reconditioning" or "thematic shift." In this procedure the client is instructed to masturbate while attempting to insert thoughts of appropriate sexual acts (or partners) into his otherwise deviant fantasies. The rationale is that repeated pairings of appropriate images with masturbatory-induced arousal or orgasm will gradually, by way of Pavlovian processes, endow thoughts of appropriate sex with erotic properties such that these thoughts will come to replace deviant images as the most preferred fantasies. Such changed preferences are then expected to be expressed in overt behaviors. The only controlled examination of the power of this procedure failed to demonstrate the expected changes in sexual preferences (Conrad & Wincze, 1976).

Another approach, first described by Abel, Blanchard, Barlow, and Flanagan (1975), has the client alternate blocks of trials during which the client imagines only deviant or nondeviant fantasies. Several reasonably well controlled single-case studies have evaluated this "fantasy alternation" procedure. Again, however, Laws and Marshall (1991) could find little in the way of support for this so-called conditioning procedure.

"Directed masturbation," described most clearly by Maletzky (1985), requires the deviant client to masturbate exclusively to appropriate images. Most of the descriptions of the use of this procedure reveal the concurrent employment of various other procedures, although one controlled single-case study (Kremsdorf, Holmen, & Laws, 1980) did provide direct support for this approach.

In fact, the only conditioning procedure employing masturbation to change sexual preferences that has generated consistent (albeit limited) empirical support is "satiation" (Marshall & Lippens, 1977). Satiation describes a procedure, the goal of which is to facilitate the extinction of arousal to deviant themes. This is done by having the client generate fantasies of deviant acts when he is in a postorgasm-induced, relative refractory state. Obviously the demonstration of the extinction of sexual preferences is no less supportive of a conditioning theory than is evidence of the conditioned acquisition of a preference. While several controlled case studies (Alford, Morin, Atkins, & Schoen, 1987; Laws, Osborn, Avery-Clark, O'Neil, & Crawford, 1987; Marshall, 1979) have shown the expected changes in various deviants, the evidence for the effectiveness of satiation is not extensive.

Overall, then, it cannot be said that there are strong supportive data for the notion that pairing previously neutral sexual stimuli with masturbatory-induced sexual arousal will initiate conditioning processes resulting in a change in sexual preferences. We have already seen that the externally presented pairing of a CS and a UCS does not reliably induce conditioning processes leading to changes in sexual interests. Support from these sources for a conditioning theory of the acquisition of sexual preferences, then, is not at all strong. However, there are other direct implications of a conditioning theory that may offer more support.

Evidence from Patients' Histories

Some classical conditioning theorists appear to suggest that in all cases of sexual deviation, it is conditioning that began the process that eventually led to the unacceptable overt behavior. Other theorists appear to allow that Pavlovian conditioning may play a part in some but not necessarily all cases. Laws and Marshall (1990) took the latter position. It is our interpretation of McGuire et al.'s (1965) account, and that proposed by Abel and Blanchard (1974), that these theorists are making the strong claim that all sexual deviants have a history of masturbatory-induced classical conditioning. Now it is necessary to be very clear about what is being claimed here. We need to identify the initial event that is said to have triggered the conditioning process, we need to know at what age this is said to most likely occur, whether it preceded or followed the initial deviant act, whether those who are affected by the initial event in this way (i.e., who subsequently masturbate to images of it rather than to normal sexual images) have particular vulnerable features, and whether this apparent ease of conditioning is likely to lead to the generation of multiple deviances.

In one version of their theory, which they claim describes the principal means by which deviance is entrenched, McGuire et al. (1965) claim that the triggering event occurs in a sexually naive male and involves either an actual deviant act or an act with deviant components. Thus, an exhibitionist should report a predeviant accidental experience of exposing, a child molester should say that his first sexual experience was either with a child or with a rather youthful partner, and a rapist should remember forceful or noncompliant elements to his first sexual experience. These experiences are said to supply the raw material for subsequent masturbatory fantasies, and they become sexually preferred by being repeatedly paired with arousal and by becoming progressively more focused upon during masturbation. The only evidence we know of in support of this comes from McGuire et al.'s description of their 7 patients who were selected from 45 patients to best illustrate their theory; this hardly constitutes strong supportive evidence, although clearly it is illustrative.

Both Abel and Blanchard (1974) and McGuire et al. (1965) put the most probable point of origin at around puberty, since they argue that the initial deviant experience will be the one most likely to induce conditioning processes (i.e., become the exclusive focus of masturbatory fantasies) if it occurs in a sexually naive male. Furthermore, it is very clear that these theorists claim that however, or whenever, deviant fantasies are developed, they precede and serve to activate, overt deviant acts.

Self-reports of early experiences have provided the only evidence to date concerning the temporal origins of deviant sexual preferences. Abel et al. (1987) adopted stringent procedures to protect the identity of their patients so that they would feel confident in reporting to the interviewers all aspects of their deviant sexual histories. Fifty-eight percent of their mixed group of offenders reported having experienced sexual arousal to deviant fantasies prior to age 18, and these fantasies, they said, preceded their deviant acts. Of the men who molested young boys, 50% developed their interests prior to age 18, as did 40% of those who molested young girls. Even among father–daughter incest offenders, 25% claimed to have had a sexual interest in female children prior to age 18. In our study (Marshall, Barbaree, & Eccles, 1991), however, only 29.5% of the total sample of child molesters recalled having deviant fantasies about children before they were 20 years of age, and only 21.7% of the total sample said that deviant sexual fantasies preceded their molestation of children. Among incestuous fathers only 10.5% remembered using fantasies of children for sexual purposes before age 20. Perhaps not surprisingly, we found that only 7.9% of the incest offenders had molested a child before they were 20 years old, although slightly more than 45% of nonfamilial child molesters had offended prior to this age.

Abel's data and ours are in obvious disagreement, and on the possibility that his patient population was more deviant than ours (i.e., had higher arousal to deviant acts, had more extensive offense histories, or both), we extracted, in several ways, the most deviant of our offenders. However, even though the numbers of early deviants increased accordingly, they never approached anything like Abel's percentage of an early onset of deviance.

Considering that many young males experience early contacts with deviant sexuality, McGuire et al. (1965) recognize the need to expand their strictly Pavlovian view to account for why it is that some develop deviant tendencies as a result of such experiences while others do not. We have already noted one aspect of their response to this: that the initiation of deviant fantasizing during masturbation is thought to be more likely when the actual deviant experience occurs in a sexually naive male. This, of course, is more likely when the initial contact occurs in adolescence. In our clinical work over the past 20 years, we have certainly seen many patients whose first deviant act occurred in adulthood after a long history of appropriate sexual behavior. Although we have not conducted the type of thorough study needed to estimate the percentage of all cases that these contradictions to McGuire et al.'s theory represent, they seem likely to constitute sufficient numbers to be problematic for this theory.

McGuire et al., however, also propose an alternative that suggests a vulnerability in some males to respond to deviant experiences by finding them attractive. They suggest that such individuals have come to believe, as a result of feelings of inadequacy or aversive heterosexual experiences, that a normal sex life is not possible for them. Other, more broad-based theories (e.g., Finkelhor, 1984; Marshall, 1989b; Marshall & Barbaree, 1990a) have similarly claimed that sex offenders respond in an antisocial way to a variety of experiences as a result of a developmentally produced vulnerability. Support for this view, that potential sex offenders have a vulnerability to respond in a negative way to experiences that might otherwise be ignored, is indirect but reasonably substantial, and Finkelhor (1984), and Marshall and Barbaree (1990a) have reviewed this literature. However, evidence for this vulnerability could be, and has been, interpreted as support for a variety of nonconditioning accounts of the origins of deviant sexuality (Russell, 1984).

Finally, McGuire et al. (1965) specifically predict that "A deviant who masturbates to fantasies as his main sexual outlet should be liable to develop other deviations" (p. 187). Abel and his colleagues echo these sentiments by suggesting that most sex offenders have more than one paraphilia. According to Abel and Rouleau (1990), the initial deviant interest develops before the age of 18, and they argue that frequently this fades and is replaced by another deviant interest. Abel and Rouleau note that "some sex offenders have as many as ten categories of paraphilic interest throughout their lifetime" (p. 14). Thus, we should find among sexual deviants, the presence of multiple paraphilias, and such polymorphous perversity should be related to higher frequencies of masturbatory practices.

Again the data on this issue rely on self-reports, although once again Abel and his colleagues (Abel, Becker, Cunningham-Rathner, Mittelman, & Rouleau, 1988) used their procedures to protect the identity of their clients so as to increase the likelihood of obtaining accurate reports. They found very high rates of multiple paraphilias among sex offenders, and so did Freund (1990). For example, more than 80% of Abel et al.'s (1988) nonfamilial child molesters, and more than 70% of their incest offenders, reported having more than one paraphilia. Even more surprisingly, 17.8% of the men who molested girls and 17.6% of those who molested boys reported having six or more different paraphilias. We, however, found far lower frequencies of multiple deviances (Marshall, Barbaree, & Eccles, 1991). Only 14% of those who had molested girls, 11.8% of those who molested boys, and 7.9% of the incest offenders reported more than one paraphilia.

Obviously the evidence on this issue is inconsistent, and it is unclear why these disparate observations were made. Perhaps it depends on how the subjects interpreted the instructions. For instance, if a young man brought up on a farm recalled having once thought of or even once acted upon thoughts of having sex with an animal, would this count as evidence of bestiality; not according to the third revised edition of the *Diagnostic and Statistical Manual of Mental Disorders* (DSM-III-R) (American Psychiatric Association, 1987), but perhaps it is possibly so in the minds of the subjects in these studies.

Evidence of Deviant Sexual Preferences

Perhaps the most compelling and direct implication of classical conditioning theories is that sexual deviants, at least those who are most persistent, should demonstrate deviant sexual preferences at laboratory assessment. Indeed, if conditioning provides the basis for the development of deviant sexual preferences, which precede and cause the male to overtly engage in deviant sexual behavior, then all sex offenders should display deviant preferences. In a recent review of the relevant literature, we could find little evidence supporting the idea that even most sex offenders are characterized by deviant sexual preferences (Marshall & Eccles, 1991).

Although early, small-scale studies of rapists suggested that they differed from nonrapists in their erectile responses to forced sex (Abel, Barlow, Blanchard, & Guild, 1977; Barbaree, Marshall, & Lanthier, 1979; Quinsey & Chaplin, 1982), more recent analyses, involving larger numbers of subjects, have failed to find clear differences between rapists and nonrapists (Baxter, Marshall, Barbaree, Davidson, & Malcolm, 1984; Baxter, Barbaree, & Marshall, 1986; Langevin et al., 1985; Marshall, Barbaree, Laws, & Baxter, 1986; Murphy, Krisak, Stalgaitis, & Anderson, 1984). Even the data from the early studies do not clearly support the conditioning hypothesis. According to this hypothesis, rapists should have a history of masturbating to fantasies of forced sex which thereby entrenched a sexual preference for such acts. Rapists, accordingly, should show greater arousal to forced sex, than to consenting sex; all studies, except for one (Quinsey, Chaplin, & Upfold, 1984), have failed to demonstrate this. For example, in both the Abel et al. (1977) study and that of Barbaree et al. (1979), the rapists did not display a preference for forced sex, but rather they showed little difference in responding to forced and consenting sex.

When we consider the erectile preferences of child molesters, the published data offer somewhat greater, although limited support for conditioning theories. Numerous studies (Freund, 1987; Marshall, Barbaree, & Butt, 1988; Marshall, Barbaree, & Christophe, 1986; Murphy, Haynes, Stalgaitis, & Flanagan, 1986; Quinsey, Chaplin, & Carrigan, 1979; Quinsey, Steinman, Bergerson, & Holmes, 1975) have demonstrated group differences in sexual responses to children between nonfamilial child molesters and matched nonoffenders. However, a more detailed analysis of our own data (Barbaree & Marshall, 1989) revealed that only 27% of the men who had molested other people's daughters displayed clear preferences for children. In fact, 30% showed normal preferences (i.e., they preferred adult female partners), while 21% responded equally to adults and children; 22% failed to display sufficient arousal to allow for valid interpretations of their data.

Exhibitionists offer even less support for conditioning theories. Only Maletzky (1980) has found high arousal among exhibitionists to scenes of exposing. Murphy, Abel, and Becker (1980) claimed that "By definition, exhibitionists display excessive sexual arousal to inappropriate interactions with the sexual object (i.e., the act of exposing)" (p. 348), but provided group data that revealed greater arousal to nondeviant themes in their exhibitionists. Similarly, despite Freund's (1990) claim that exhibitionists suffer from a courtship disorder that causes them to display greater arousal to exposing than to consensual intercourse, his own data clearly contradict that claim (Freund, Scher, & Hucker, 1984). We (Marshall, Payne, Barbaree, & Eccles, 1991) found that fewer than 10% of exhibitionists showed equivalent or greater arousal to exposing than to consenting sex. In fact, the majority of our exhibitionists declared that their masturbatory fantasies, and even their thoughts when they were exposing, were of having intercourse with their victims rather than exposing to them.

McConaghy (1989) quite rightly points out that the two different technologies used to assess erectile preferences (volumetric vs. circumferential measures of changes in the penis) may reveal quite different patterns of responding. Essentially, he claims that the volumetric device picks up far clearer differences between sex offenders and nonoffenders than do the circumferential measures. He may be correct for some offender groups, although this has not yet been demonstrated satisfactorily, but McConaghy is certainly not correct with respect to exhibitionists. As we have seen, Freund (Freund et al., 1984) failed to demonstrate greater arousal to exposing than to intercourse among exhibitionists, and yet he employed the volumetric approach. We do not believe that any approach to the assessment of erectile responding will reveal clear preferences for deviant acts among more than a limited number of sex offenders, but, in any case, the responsibility for contradicting this belief lies with those who argue that sex offenders have deviant preferences. Indeed, for conditioning theories, at least those articulated by Abel and Blanchard (1974) and McGuire et al. (1965), it must be shown that all, or nearly all, sex offenders have clear deviant sexual preferences. This has not yet been demonstrated, and the available evidence is not supportive.

However, an alternative account of the etiology of sex offending could allow for conditioning processes to gradually entrench deviant preferences as a result of repeated deviant practices. It is to the elaboration of such a theory that we now turn.

A MULTIFACETED THEORY OF ADOLESCENT SEX OFFENDING

We will not reprise all the details of our theorizing about sex offenders, as this is available elsewhere (Marshall, 1989b; Marshall & Barbaree, 1984, 1990a), but simply point to two aspects that are relevant to the present issue. The evidence we have considered in our various papers has persuaded us that sex offenders have a developmental history that makes them vulnerable to a variety of influences and to situational events that would otherwise go unrecognized or at least be ignored by males who are not so vulnerable. This vulnerability, we believe, arises most particularly by the failure during their infancy and childhood, of the parents of sex offenders to ensure that secure attachment bonds are formed between them and their children (Marshall, 1989a; Marshall, Hudson, & Hodkinson, Chapter 8, this volume). Secure attachments provide the growing child with a view of others that is affectionate and empathic and that instills a desire for, and the skills and confidence necessary to achieve, intimacy with peers.

The shift in attachments at puberty from parents to peers, is a particularly difficult transition that may be hindered by parents who either care little about the child or who are possessively jealous of the child's other relationships. Of course, such parents are very unlikely to have formed secure attachments with their child, and, consequently, the boy will be further limited in developing extrafamilial relations by his lack of self-confidence, his self-interested disposition, and his lack of skills at forming peer relations. In particular, such a boy will have difficulties relating to peer-aged females, and consequently he will find appealing those media messages (in pornography and advertising, as well as in regular fare on television and movies, and in books and magazines) that express attitudes toward women and children that objectify and demean them. Pubescing boys experience a dramatic fourfold increase in circulating testosterone levels over the 2-year period at the beginning of adolescence (Sizonenko, 1978). Consequently, the expression of the concomitant marked increase in sexual matters presents further problems for these vulnerable boys in developing relationships with peer-aged females. Since these boys lack confidence, are unskilled interpersonally, and may fear intimacy given their history of insecure attachments, they are likely to find appealing those sexual scripts that make no demands on their confidence or skills and that do not involve intimacy. Raping a peer, molesting a child, exposing their genitals to an uncooperative female, making obscene telephone calls, and peeping in windows are all sexual scripts that meet these requirements. Consequently insecure adolescent boys may use fantasies of these scripts in their masturbatory practices and, thereby, initiate conditioning processes. Unlike the proposals of McGuire et al. (1965), in this scenario the conditioning processes are initiated independently of an actual overt deviant act. In our view, early experience with overt deviance is but one route by which adolescents may develop deviant sexual interests and, indeed, is a less likely route than is fantasy-generated deviance. One implication of our view is that sex offenders should have a disproportionate history of early exposure to pornography. At least two studies (Goldstein, Kant, & Hartman, 1973; Walker, 1970) found that far more sex offenders (e.g., 30% of rapists) reported having viewed explicit pornography before age 10 than did non-offender controls (only 2% of whom reported such early exposure).

Clearly, exposure to deviant sex or pornography at an early age can account for some adolescents developing deviant sexual interests. However, it has yet to be explained why it is essentially only male adolescents who develop such interests. Any theory of sexually assaultive behavior has to account for this most basic characteristic of sex offenders (i.e., their gender), and it is especially difficult for traditional Pavlovian accounts to do so. In fact, if, as McGuire et al. (1965) argue, the determining factor in the development of deviant interests is the precipitating incident that is the first "real" sexual experience, then we would expect more females to develop deviant interests, since they constitute the majority of sexual assault victims (Badgley Report, 1984). McGuire et al. (1965) attempted to explain the lack of female deviancy by suggesting that females fail to condition deviancy because according to Kinsey et al. (1953) they masturbate less often than males and begin such practices at a later age. However, more recent evidence suggests that gender differences in masturbation onset and frequency are small (e.g., Arafat & Cotton, 1974; Hite, 1976) and are unlikely to explain why it is all but exclusively men who develop deviancy and become sex offenders. A possible resolution to this question may come from more modern, cognitive accounts of Pavlovian conditioning.

One reason that may account for why Pavlovian explanations of sexual deviance have little support empirically is that behavior therapists have been applying an outdated concept of the conditioning process. Zinbarg (1990) notes that historically there was an early departure between the applied and the experimental behavioral movements with each developing independent literature. As a consequence, most behaviorists working in applied settings lost track of developments in conditioning theory, such that "there are some behavior therapists who still view conditioning in the way it was viewed by learning theorists 20 years ago, as a primitive form of learning with minimal cognitive mediation" (Zinbarg, 1990, p. 171).

In his review, Zinbarg demonstrates that the central tenets of traditional Pavlovian conditioning (that temporal *contiguity* between a CS and UCS results in conditioning and that this in turn results in stimulus-response connections) have been shown to be fundamentally unsound. As a consequence, modern learning theorists (e.g., Mackintosh, 1983; Rescorla, 1988) have been developing more cognitive models of Pavlovian conditioning. Rescorla (1988) argues that "Pavlovian conditioning is not a stupid process by which the organism willy-nilly forms associations between any two stimuli that happen to co-occur. Rather, the organism is better seen as an information seeker using logical and perceptual relations among events, along with its own preconceptions, to form a sophisticated representation of its world" (p. 154). Indeed, based on Rescorla's earlier work, Reiss (1980) in applying these concepts to phobias concluded that "associative learning alone cannot explain the initial acquisition of all, or even most, phobias" (p. 388). Reiss went on to develop an Expectancy Model of phobias, which maintains that "what is learned in Pavlovian conditioning is an expectation regarding the occurrence, or non-occurrence, of a UCS onset or a change in UCS magnitude or duration. Expectations are considered to be mediating responses with covert stimulus properties that can become elicitors of a number of anticipatory responses" (Reiss, 1980, p. 387).

If, as Reiss argues, these expectations result from cognitive learning, associative learning, covert conditioning, and observation of models, then we must look at the context within which adolescent offenders live (e.g., the family and culture as a whole) to understand the expectations that result and the form of the sexual fantasies to which they contribute. A number of studies support the view that the values and stereotypes adopted and maintained by Western culture produce adolescent males who have an extremely sexualized view of the world. Furthermore, they tend to perceive predatory and even aggressive sexual behavior to be acceptable and even expected (e.g., Burt, 1980; Clark & Lewis, 1977; Goodchilds & Zellman, 1984; Muehlenhard, Friedman, & Thomas, 1985). In a survey of the attitudes of 432 adolescents, for instance, Goodchilds and Zellman (1984) describe as "sobering" their data, which clearly indicate "that adolescents view sexual aggression by the man against women as an ever-present and sometimes acceptable possibility in the context of intimate cross-gender encounters" (p. 243). These messages may be particularly attractive to young adolescent males, lacking in self-confidence and social skills, and for whom intimacy in a relationship is foreign and discomforting. Once these messages are accepted, then the content of sexual fantasies would be expected to change accordingly. Repeated sexual fantasizing of forcing a woman to have sex, or brutalizing females during sex, would enhance expectancies that females desire or will accept this type of behavior, thereby reducing whatever inhibitions may have been present to prevent the expression of sexual assault. Similar processes could be expected in the other sexual offenses.

Cognitive models of Pavlovian conditioning have not, as far as we are aware, been previously applied to deviant sexual fantasies. We have attempted to illustrate above one way in which this might be done. Although we believe that a reformulated, cognitive view of Pavlovian conditioning may play a role in the development of sexual deviancy, it is still apparent that, the issue of the development of deviant fantasies aside, most adolescent offenders *do not* have such fantasies. Many of our patients (adolescents and adults) have emphatically declared that they could not recall ever having thought about offending prior to their initial offense. Indeed, many of them claim to have been repulsed by sex offenses before they themselves offended and to have felt strongly antagonistic toward offenders. Their own first offense accordingly distressed them, although in most cases their distress dissipated over time, particularly with repeated subsequent offending.

In our individual analyses of the preference profiles of child molesters (Barbaree & Marshall, 1989) we examined a variety of related features in their history. Our particular concern here was to see if we could make sense of those men who had offended but whose preferences were clearly nondeviant. Our examination revealed that the classic pedophiles had far more victims and used far more forcefulness in their most recent offense than was true of any of the offenders displaying other age-preference profiles (Barbaree & Marshall, 1989). Since their earlier offenses also involved less sexually intrusive behavior, we are inclined to conclude that experience with offending tends to increase the sexual and aggressive nature of offending. We think it is equally reasonable on the basis of the above data to conclude that increased practice with actual offending is what entrenches deviant sexual preferences.

In a similar detailed analysis of the data from another study (Marshall, 1988), we have observed that those child molesters who reported usually or always using deviant sexual fantasies during masturbation had a higher number of victims than did those who reported rarely or never engaging in deviant fantasizing. The men who reported using deviant images when masturbating also appeared more deviant at laboratory assessment of their preferences. While these observations with nonfamilial child molesters provide some support for a conditioning account, they tend to deny the claims by McGuire et al. (1965) and Abel and Blanchard (1974) that it is fantasizing sex with children that instills the deviant attraction. A substantial proportion of these child molesters (over 70%) said that they either did not entertain sexual fantasies of children at all, or that, if they did, these fantasies followed rather than preceded their first assault, which in over 50% of the cases did not occur until they were adults. Even in those whose first offense took place prior to age 20 (approximately 46% of the sample), only 14% said that fantasies of sex with children preceded their initial deviant act. What is perhaps even more relevant here is that among both those who had commenced offending as teenagers and those who began after attaining adulthood, the majority confidently declared that it was only after repeated offending that they began to masturbate to fantasies of children.

From these data we are persuaded that conditioning of some kind plays a role in the development of deviant tendencies in some nonfamilial child molesters, but we are also persuaded that such processes operate quite differently from what is claimed by other conditioning theorists. It seems to us that for some of these men (i.e., those who display a pedophilic profile at assessment) the development of deviant fantasies, and their use during masturbation, follows rather than precedes overt deviant acts. Indeed, we are more inclined to believe that it is the repeated enactment of child molestation that represents the conditioning trials rather than pairings of fantasies with masturbatory-induced arousal. Each time the offender has sex with a child, he obviously pairs heightened sexual arousal with vivid, realistic visions of children and the proprioceptive stimuli produced by his own actions. These contacts provide powerful conditioning trials and, if repeated often enough, should entrench a growing attraction to sex with children even in the absence of masturbating to children. Likewise, such experiences should change the offender's beliefs or expectancies regarding the nature and acceptability of sex with children, as well as his view of the role of children in sex with adults. That sex offenders do hold such views is now well accepted (Murphy, 1990; Segal & Stermac, 1990), and the present analysis suggests how these distorted cognitions come to be acquired.

Since nonfamilial offenders who have many victims obviously experience arousal while acting sexually with a range of different children, we would expect these offenders, by virtue of these repeated overt acts alone, to display a generalized response to all children of the same gender. Incest offenders, on the other hand, who have repeated experiences with only one child, would not be expected to display generalized arousal to all children but ought to show arousal to the child they molested. Since assessment involves the presentation of previously unseen children, far more nonfamilial offenders than incest offenders, would be expected to display arousal to children, and this is what has been observed. However, if we were to present images of their own child to those incest offenders who had repeatedly assaulted the child, then we should, if our conditioning view is correct, see deviant arousal in these men. If conditioning results entirely from masturbatory practices, and if images in masturbation are constantly undergoing modifications as McGuire et al. suggest, then repetitive incestuous relations should produce a generalized response to all children, and yet this is very rarely observed.

When we subjected Marshall's (1988) data on rapists to the same sort of analysis we applied to the child molesters, we found far less support for a conditioning theory. In the first place fewer of the rapists characteristically used deviant sexual fantasies when masturbating and among those who did, there was only a trend toward greater arousal at assessment to these deviant images. Similarly, in our study of exhibitionists (Marshall, Payne, et al. 1991) not only did very few of them display deviant arousal at assessment, by far the majority reported that their masturbatory fantasies were not of exposing but rather of having intercourse with one of their victims. Thus, for rapists and exhibitionists, a conditioning theory of any kind seems poorly suited to an understanding of their deviant behavior.

CONCLUSION

In summary, then, we do not believe the evidence supports a theory, based strictly on traditional concepts of conditioning, of the etiology and maintenance of rape, exhibitionism, or incestuous offending. While conditioning processes appear to play some role in nonfamilial child molestation, we see such processes as but one small component in the overall complex of factors that lead to the acquisition and maintenance of such behaviors. Furthermore, we believe that when conditioning does play a part, it is by direct experience that these processes are induced, and they result in changed expectancies rather than in physiologically based changes.

Our view is that some males, as a result of their developmental history, are made vulnerable such that particular sexual scripts (i.e., deviant ones) will appeal to them. These scripts may be communicated to them through various media, through conversations with peers, or even through self-generated ideas. When this happens at a young age, the boy may incorporate these deviant images into his masturbatory fantasies and pairing these thoughts with self-induced sexual arousal will initiate conditioning processes that may finally lead to attitudinal changes, deviant preferences, and possibly deviant acts. Alternatively, and it seems to us more likely, this vulnerability may make the developing male (or for that matter the still vulnerable adult) eagerly responsive to circumstantial opportunities to engage in deviant acts, and this may lead to repeated offending, which will, in itself, provide conditioning trials sufficient to entrench deviant sex as a preferential pattern. However, the absence of deviant sexual preferences in many sex offenders (e.g., in most rapists, incest offenders and exhibitionists, and a substantial proportion of nonfamilial child molesters) strongly suggests that conditioning trials have been insufficient to entrench a deviant preferential pattern and cannot, therefore, be invoked to explain the offensive behavior in these cases.

As for the treatment implications of this review, clearly we should attend to attitudinal and motivational features of the offender other than simply signs of deviant sexuality. In fact, such an alternative view is desperately needed with rapists, since our reviews of the treatment literature indicate that we are far less effective with these men than we are with child molesters (Marshall &

Barbaree, 1990b; Marshall & Eccles, 1991; Marshall, Jones, Ward, Johnston, & Barbaree, 1991; Marshall, Ward, Jones, Johnston, & Barbaree, 1991). In a similar vein, when we shifted our emphasis in treatment of exhibitionists from a focus on the role of deviant sexuality to an emphasis on interpersonal functioning, we obtained far better long-term outcome (Marshall, Eccles, & Barbaree, 1991).

We believe that a comprehensive theory of sex offending is probably not possible. We need to develop specific theories for each type of offense that emphasize different processes. In all these theories, conditioning that stresses actual experiences rather than fantasies will likely play a small role in some but not all offenders. Even here we must account for why it is that some males see particular circumstances as opportunities to engage in deviant sex in the first place. Whether such initial acts are followed by processes that entrench an acquired deviant tendency seems less interesting than why it is that some males respond sexually to circumstances that others would either not notice or would ignore.

REFERENCES

Abel, G. G., Barlow, D. H., Blanchard, E. B., & Guild, D. (1977). The components of rapists' sexual arousal. *Archives of General Psychiatry, 34,* 895–903.

Abel, G. G., Becker, J. V., Cunningham-Rathner, J., Mittleman, M. S., & Rouleau, J. L. (1988). Multiple paraphilic diagnoses among sex offenders. *Bulletin of the American Academy of Psychiatry and the Law, 16,* 153–168.

Abel, G. G., Becker, J. V., Mittelman, M. S., Cunningham-Rathner, J., Rouleau, J. L., & Murphy, W. D. (1987). Self-reported sex crimes of nonincarcerated paraphiliacs. *Journal of Interpersonal Violence, 2,* 3–25.

Abel, G. G., & Blanchard, E. B. (1974). The role of fantasy in the treatment of sexual deviation. *Archives of General Psychiatry, 30,* 467–475.

Abel, G. G., Blanchard, E. B., Barlow, D. H., & Flanagan, B. (1975, December). *A case report of the behavioral treatment of a sadistic rapist.* Paper presented at the 9th Annual Convention of the Association for the Advancement of Behavior Therapy, San Francisco, CA.

Abel, G. G., & Rouleau, J. L. (1990). The nature and extent of sexual assault. In W. L. Marshall, D. R. Laws, & H. E. Barbaree (Eds.), *Handbook of sexual assault: Issues, theories, and treatment of the offender* (pp. 9–21). New York: Plenum Press.

Alford, G. S., Morin, C., Atkins, M., & Schoen, L. (1987). Masturbatory extinction of deviant sexual arousal: A case study. *Behavior Therapy, 18,* 265–271.

American Psychiatric Association. (1987). *Diagnostic and statistical manual of mental disorders* (3rd ed., rev.). Washington, DC: Author.

Arafat, I. S., & Cotton, W. L. (1974). Masturbation practices of males and females. *Journal of Sex Research, 10,* 293–307.

Badgley Report. (1984). *The report of the committee on sexual offenses against children and youths.* Ottawa: Supply and Services Canada.

Barbaree, H. E., & Marshall, W. L. (1989). Erectile responses among heterosexual child molesters, father–daughter incest offenders, and matched nonoffenders: Five distinct age preference profiles. *Canadian Journal of Behavioral Sciences, 21*, 70–82.

Barbaree, H. E., Marshall, W. L., & Lanthier, R. D. (1979). Deviant sexual arousal in rapists. *Behaviour Research and Therapy, 17*, 215–222.

Baxter, D. J., Barbaree, H. E., & Marshall, W. L., (1986). Sexual responses to consenting and forced sex in a large sample of rapists and nonrapists. *Behaviour Research and Therapy, 24*, 513–520.

Baxter, D. J., Marshall, W. L., Barbaree, H. E., Davidson, P. R., & Malcolm, P. B. (1984). Deviant sexual behavior: Differentiating sex offenders by criminal and personal history, psychometric measures and sexual responses. *Criminal Justice and Behavior, 11*, 477–501.

Beech, H. R., Watts, F., & Poole, A. P. (1971). Classical conditioning of a sexual deviation: A preliminary note. *Behavior Therapy, 2*, 400–402.

Bermant, G., & Davidson, J. M. (1974). *Biological bases of sexual behavior.* New York: Harper & Row.

Burt, M. R. (1980). Cultural myths and supports for rape. *Journal of Personality and Social Psychology, 38*, 217–230.

Clark, L., & Lewis, D. (1977). *Rape: The price of coercive sexuality.* Toronto: Women's Press.

Conrad, S. R., & Wincze, J. P. (1976). Orgasmic reconditioning: A controlled study of its effects upon the sexual arousal and behavior of adult male homosexuals. *Behavior Therapy, 7*, 155–166.

Cutmore, T. R. H., & Zamble, E. (1988). A Pavlovian procedure for improving sexual performance of noncopulating male rats. *Archives of Sexual Behavior, 17*, 371–380.

Farris, H. E. (1967). Classical conditioning of courting behavior in the Japanese quail. (*Coturnix coturnix japonica*). *Journal of the Experimental Analysis of Behavior, 10*, 213–217.

Finklehor, D. (1984). *Child sexual abuse: New theory and research.* New York: Free Press.

Freund, K. (1987). Erotic preference in paedophilia. *Behaviour Research and Therapy, 5*, 339–348.

Freund, K. (1990). Courtship disorder. In W. L. Marshall, D. R. Laws, & H. E. Barbaree (Eds.), *Handbook of sexual assault: Issues, theories, and treatment of the offender* (pp. 195–208). New York: Plenum Press.

Freund, K., Scher, H., & Hucker, S. (1984). The courtship disorders: A further investigation. *Archives of Sexual Behavior, 13*, 133–139.

Goldstein, M. J., Kant, H. S., & Hartman, J. J. (1973). *Pornography and sexual deviance.* Berkeley: University of California Press.

Goodchilds, J. D., & Zellman, G. L. (1984). Sexual signalling and sexual aggression in adolescent relationships. In N. M. Malamuth & E. Donnerstein (Eds.), *Pornography and sexual aggression* (pp. 233–243). Orlando, FL: Academic Press.

Graham, J. M., & Desjardins, C. (1980). Classical conditioning: Induction of lutenizing hormone and testosterone secretion in anticipation of sexual activity. *Science, 210*, 1039–1041.

Herman, S. H., Barlow, D. H., & Agras, W. S. (1974). An experimental analysis of classical conditioning as a method of increasing heterosexual arousal in homosexuals. *Behavior Therapy, 5,* 33–47.

Hite, S. (1976). *The Hite report.* New York: Dell.

Jaspers, K. (1963). *General psychopathology.* Manchester: Manchester University Press.

Kamel, F., Mock, E. J., Wright, W. W., & Frankel, A. I. (1975). Alterations in plasma concentrations of testosterone, LH, and prolactin associated with mating in the male rat. *Hormones and Behavior, 6,* 277–288.

Kinsey, A. C., Pomeroy, W. B., Martin, G. E., & Gebhard, P. H. (1953). *Sexual behaviour in the human female.* Philadelphia: Saunders.

Kremsdorf, R. B., Holmen, M. L., & Laws, D. R. (1980). Orgasmic reconditioning without deviant imagery: A case report with a pedophile. *Behaviour Research and Therapy, 18,* 203–207.

Langevin, R., Ben-Aron, M. H., Coulthard, R., Heasman, R., Purins, J. E., Handy, L., Hucker, S. J., Russon, A. R., Day, D., Roper, V., Bain, J., Wortzman, G., & Webster, C. D., (1985). Sexual aggression: Constructing a predictive equation: A controlled pilot study. In R. Langevin (Ed.), *Erotic preference, gender identity, and aggression in men: New research studies* (pp. 39–76). Hillsdale, NJ: Erlbaum.

Laws, D. R., & Marshall, W. L. (1990). A conditioning theory of the etiology and maintenance of deviant sexual preference and behavior. In W. L. Marshall, D. R. Laws, & H. E. Barbaree (Eds.), *Handbook of sexual assault: Issues, theories and treatment of the offender* (pp. 209–229). New York: Plenum Press.

Laws, D. R., & Marshall, W. L. (1991). Masturbatory reconditioning with sexual deviates: An evaluative review. *Advances in Behaviour Research and Therapy, 13,* 13–25.

Laws, D. R., Osborn, C. A., Avery-Clark, C., O'Neil, J. A., & Crawford, D. A. (1987). *Masturbatory satiation with sexual deviates.* Unpublished manuscript, University of South Florida, Florida Mental Health Institute, Tampa.

McConaghy, N. (1970). Penile response conditioning and its relationship to aversion therapy in homosexuals. *Behavior Therapy, 1,* 213–221.

McConaghy, N. (1989). Validity and ethics of penile circumference measures of sexual arousal: A critical review. *Archives of Sexual Behavior, 18,* 357–369.

McGuire, R. J., Carlisle, J. M., & Young, B. G. (1965). Sexual deviations as conditioned behaviour: A hypothesis. *Behaviour Research and Therapy, 2,* 185–190.

Mackintosh, N. (1974) *The psychology of animal learning.* New York: Academic Press.

Mackintosh, N. (1983). *Conditioning and associative learning.* London: Academic Press.

Maletzky, B. M. (1980). Assisted covert sensitization. In D. J. Cox & R. J. Daitzman (Eds.) *Exhibitionism: Description, assessment, and treatment* (pp. 187–252). New York: Garland STPM Press.

Maletzky, B. M. (1985). Orgasmic reconditioning. In A. S. Bellack & M. Hersen (Eds.), *Dictionary of behavior therapy techniques* (pp. 157–158). New York: Pergamon Press.

Marquis, J. (1970). Orgasmic reconditioning: Changing sexual object choice through controlling masturbation fantasies. *Journal of Behavior Therapy and Experimental Psychiatry, 1,* 263–271.

Marshall, W. L. (1974). The classical conditioning of sexual attractiveness: A report of four therapeutic failures. *Behavior Therapy, 5,* 298–299.

Marshall, W. L. (1979). Satiation therapy: A procedure for reducing deviant sexual arousal. *Journal of Applied Behavior Analysis*, 12, 10–22.

Marshall, W. L. (1988). The use of sexually explicit stimuli by rapists, child molesters and nonoffenders. *Journal of Sex Research*, 25, 267–288.

Marshall, W. L. (1989a). Intimacy, loneliness and sexual offenders. *Behaviour Research and Therapy*, 27, 491–503.

Marshall, W. L. (1989b). Pornography and sex offenders. In D. Zillman & J. Bryant (Eds.), *Pornography: Recent research, interpretations, and policy considerations*. (pp. 185–214). Hillsdale, NJ: Erlbaum.

Marshall, W. L., & Barbaree, H. E. (1984). A behavioural view of rape. *International Journal of Law and Psychiatry*, 7, 51–77.

Marshall, W. L., & Barbaree, H. E. (1990a). An integrated theory of the etiology of sexual offending. In W. L. Marshall, D. R. Laws, & H. E. Barbaree (Eds.), *Handbook of sexual assault: Issues, theories and treatment of the offender* (pp. 257–275). New York: Plenum Press.

Marshall, W. L., & Barbaree, H. E. (1990b). Outcome of comprehensive cognitive-behavioral treatment programs. In W. L. Marshall, D. R. Laws, & H. E. Barbaree (Eds.), *Handbook of sexual assault: Issues, theories, and treatment of the offender* (pp. 363–385). New York: Plenum Press.

Marshall, W. L., Barbaree, H. E., & Butt, J. (1988). Sexual offenders against male children: Sexual preferences. *Behaviour Research and Therapy*, 26, 383–391.

Marshall, W. L., Barbaree, H. E., & Christophe, D. (1986). Sexual offenders against female children: Sexual preferences for age of victims and type of behavior. *Canadian Journal of Behavioral Science*, 18, 424–439.

Marshall, W. L., Barbaree, H. E., & Eccles, A. (1991). Early onset and deviant sexuality in child molesters. *Journal of Interpersonal Violence*, 6, 323–336.

Marshall, W. L., Barbaree, H. E., Laws, D. R., & Baxter, D. (1986, September) *Rapists do not have deviant sexual preferences: Large scale studies from Canada and California*. Paper presented at the 12th Annual Meeting of the International Academy of Sex Research, Amsterdam.

Marshall, W. L. & Eccles, A. (1991). Issues in clinical practice with sex offenders. *Journal of Interpersonal Violence*, 6, 68–93.

Marshall, W. L., Eccles, A., & Barbaree, H. E. (1991). Treatment of exhibitionists: A focus on sexual deviance versus cognitive and relationship features. *Behaviour Research and Therapy*, 29, 129–135.

Marshall, W. L., Jones, R., Ward, T., Johnston, P., & Barbaree, H. E. (1991). Treatment outcome with sex offenders. *Clinical Psychology Review*, 11, 465–485.

Marshall, W. L., & Lippens, K. (1977). The clinical value of boredom: A procedure for reducing inappropriate sexual interests. *Journal of Nervous and Mental Diseases*, 165, 283–287.

Marshall, W. L., Payne, K., Barbaree, H. E., & Eccles, A. (1991). Exhibitionists: Sexual preferences for exposing. *Behaviour Research and Therapy*, 29, 37–40.

Marshall, W. L., Ward, T., Jones, R., Johnston, P. & Barbaree, H. E. (1991). An optimistic evaluation of treatment outcome with sex offenders. *Violence Update*, March, 1–8.

Muehlenhard, C. L., Friedman, D. E., & Thomas, C. M. (1985). Is date rape justifiable?

The effects of dating activity, who initiated, who paid, and men's attitudes towards women. *Psychology of Woman Quarterly, 9,* 297–310.

Murphy, W. D. (1990). Assessment and modification of cognitive distortions in sex offenders. In W. L. Marshall, D. R. Laws, & H. E. Barbaree (Eds.), *Handbook of sexual assault: Issues, theories and treatment of the offender* (pp. 331–342). New York: Plenum Press.

Murphy, W. D., Abel, G. G., & Becker, J. V. (1980). Future research issues. In D. J. Cox & R. J. Daitzman (Eds.), *Exhibitionism: Description, assessment, and treatment* (pp. 339–392). New York: Garland STPM Press.

Murphy, W. D., Haynes, M. R., Stalgaitis, S. J., & Flanagan, B. (1986). Differential sexual responding among four groups of sexual offenders against children. *Journal of Psychopathology and Behavioral Assessment, 8,* 339–353.

Murphy, W. D., Krisak, J., Stalgaitis, S., & Anderson, K. (1984). The use of penile tumescence measures with incarcerated rapists: Further validity issues. *Archives of Sexual Behavior, 13,* 545–554.

Quinn, J. T., Harbison, J., & McAllister, H. (1970). An attempt to shape human penile responses. *Behaviour Research and Therapy, 8,* 27–28.

Quinsey, V. L., & Chaplin, T. C. (1982). Penile responses to nonsexual violence among rapists. *Criminal Justice and Behavior, 9,* 372–384.

Quinsey, V. L., Chaplin, T. C., & Carrigan, W. F. (1979). Sexual preferences among incestuous and nonincestuous child molesters. *Behavior Therapy, 10,* 562–565.

Quinsey, V. L., Chaplin, T. C., & Upfold, D. (1984). Sexual arousal to nonsexual violence and sadomasochistic themes among rapists and non-sex offenders. *Journal of Consulting and Clinical Psychology, 52,* 651–657.

Quinsey, V. L., Steinman, C. M., Bergersen, S. G., & Holmes, T. F. (1975). Penile circumference, skin conductance and ranking responses of child molesters and "normals" to sexual and nonsexual visual stimuli. *Behavior Therapy, 6,* 213–219.

Rachman, S. (1966). Sexual fetishisms: An experimental analogue. *Psychological Record, 16,* 293–296.

Rachman, S., & Hodgson, R. J. (1968). Experimentally induced "sexual fetishism": Replication and development. *Psychological Record, 18,* 25–27.

Reiss, S. (1980). Pavlovian conditioning and human fear: An expectancy model. *Behavior Therapy, 15,* 131–136.

Rescorla, R. (1988). Pavlovian conditioning: It's not what you think it is. *American Psychologist, 43,* 151–160.

Russell, D. E. H. (1984). *Sexual exploitation: Rape, child sexual abuse and workplace harassment.* Beverly Hills, CA: Sage.

Segal, Z. V., & Stermac, L. E. (1990). The role of cognition in sexual assault. In W. L. Marshall, D. R. Laws, & H. E. Barbaree (Eds.), *Handbook of sexual assault: Issues, theories and treatment of the offender* (pp. 161–174). New York: Plenum Press.

Seligman, M. E. P. (1970). On the generality of the laws of learning. *Psychological Review, 77,* 406–418.

Sizonenko, P. C. (1978). Endocrinology in preadolescents and adolescents. *American Journal of Diseases of Children, 132,* 704–712.

Walker, C. E. (1970). Erotic stimuli and the aggressive sexual offender. In *Technical* reports of the Commission on Obscenity and Pornography (Vol. 7). Washington, DC: U.S. Government Printing Office.

Zamble, E., Hadad, M., Mitchell, J. B., & Cutmore, T. R. H. (1985). Pavlovian conditioning of sexual arousal: First and second order effects. Journal of Experimental Psychology: Animal Behavior Processes, 11, 598–610.

Zamble, E., Mitchell, J. B., and Findlay, H. (1986). Pavlovian conditioning of sexual arousal: Parametric and background manipulations. Journal of Experimental Psychology: Animal Behavior Processes, 12, 403–411.

Zinbarg, R. E. (1990). Animal research and behavior therapy: Part 1. Behavior therapy is not what you think it is. Behavior Therapist, 13, 171–175.

CHAPTER 7

The Phylogenetic and Ontogenetic Development of Sexual Age Preferences in Males: Conceptual and Measurement Issues

Vernon L. Quinsey
Marnie E. Rice
Grant T. Harris
Kelly S. Reid

A central theoretical problem in human sexology is the variation in sexual preference among adult males. Sexual preference is a psychological construct indexed by self-report of images used in sexual or masturbatory fantasies, psychometric judgments of the sexual attractiveness of various persons or activities, phallometric assessments that record penile tumescence changes in response to various stimuli, and history of sexual partner and activity choices. The theoretical distinction between overt sexual behaviors and sexual preferences is important in part because sexual preferences cannot always be inferred from overt sexual behaviors. Actual sexual behaviors are constrained by opportunity, societal norms, and a variety of other factors. For example, because of these constraints, a man who prefers children as sexual partners may nevertheless engage in sexual activity with adult females most of the time.

The best documented variations in male sexual preference are for different sexes (referred to in this literature as gender preferences) and different ages of sexual partners (e.g., Freund & Blanchard, 1989; Freund & Costell, 1970; Freund, Watson, & Rienzo, 1989; Quinsey & Chaplin, 1988a; Quinsey, Chaplin, & Carrigan, 1979; Quinsey, Steinman, Bergersen, & Holmes, 1975). In addition to their theoretical centrality, inappropriate sexual age preferences are among the most important single treatment targets for intervention among extrafamilial child molesters (Quinsey & Earls, 1990; Quinsey, Chaplin, Maguire, & Upfold, 1987). Although such treatment is reactive, almost always occurring after one or more children have been victimized, there is good evidence that various paraphilias, including pedophilia, are often manifest by early adolescence (Becker, Cunningham-Rathner, & Kaplan, 1986). Preventive interventions aimed at children who might be at risk for the development of inappropriate sexual age preferences are at present difficult to develop because very little is known about the developmental course of either normative or abnormal sexual age preferences (Quinsey, 1986).

Although there has been considerable theoretical effort to explain homosexual preferences (e.g., Bell, Weinberg, & Hammersmith, 1981; Ellis & Ames, 1987), no one has attempted to provide a theory to account for the development of different sexual age preferences because no systematic studies of children's sexual age preferences have been attempted. There are theories that invoke conditioning and social learning processes in combination with concepts such as preparedness, societal or cultural phenomena, and hormonal variables that can explain in principle adult sexual preferences (e.g., Laws & Marshall, 1990; Marshall & Barbaree, 1990), but these theories cannot be applied to the ontogenetic development of sexual age preferences, because nothing is really known about this development. It is unknown whether adult males' typical preference for adult females results from the developmental inhibition of interest in other categories of person, the specific creation of an interest in adult females at birth or later, the culmination of a process of preferring opposite-sex age peers, or whatever. Simply stated, there are no theories to account for the development of sexual age preferences, because their developmental course is almost completely unknown. We know from retrospective studies that erotic *gender* preferences appear prepubertally (Bell et al., 1981), but children have simply not been asked questions about relative sexual age or gender preferences (Goldman & Goldman, 1982).

The most obvious hindrance to the investigation of the development of sexual preferences is the difficulty in finding measures that can be used with large, representative samples of children. Children, and especially adolescents, are notoriously shy about talking to adults about sexual matters and are likely to be very concerned that their sexual interests appear "normal." What is needed, then, is a set of unobtrusive and ethically sound indices of sexual interest grounded in relevant theory and data. Various measures of sexual preference will be examined below to determine what they show about male sexual preferences and which might be most suitable for studying the development of sexual age preferences.

A further hindrance to the development of a theory of sexual age preferences is the lack of a theoretical framework. A powerful theory would be able to account for normative and abnormal sexual preferences in both males and females. A potential framework for understanding normative sexual preferences is provided by evolutionary theory. Evolutionary theory could explain why some stimuli appear to be easier to connect to sexual arousal than others. For example, selection pressure could be responsible for the striking restriction of male sexual preferences to variations of normal human courtship patterns (toucheurism, voyeurism, and so on, Freund, 1990), dominance and submission, and stimuli associated with adult females (Quinsey, 1984, 1986). It is, for example, unheard of for someone to develop a strong sexual interest in beds, despite the amount of sexual activity that has occurred in them.

This chapter examines sexual preferences within the framework of evolutionary theory, assesses various measures of sexual preference within this framework as candidates for studying the ontological development of males' sexual interests, and presents some preliminary experimental work that compares different methods of measuring sexual preference.

EVOLUTIONARY EXPLANATIONS OF
SEXUAL PREFERENCE

In the context of evolutionary theory, sexual preferences are much more than a matter of aesthetics or pathology; they are directly related to reproductive success. Males who do not sexually prefer reproductively viable females are at an evolutionary disadvantage compared to men who do (Bateson, 1983). Despite criticisms of evolutionary theory, or at least naive applications of it, it is very plausible that such preferences have inevitable evolutionary consequences (Symons, 1989). However, because evolutionary accounts of male sexual preference deal with ultimate causation (the history of natural selection), they say nothing about the neural, social, or conditioning mechanisms responsible for such preferences; in addition, they do not speak to the development of sexual preferences within individuals.

Symons (1979) has argued on evolutionary grounds that human male sexual arousal should be based on visual cues and be proportional to a female's perceived reproductive value. Reproductive value refers to the expected number of a woman's future offspring and is maximal shortly after puberty. In this view, exclusive homosexual preferences are likely to have been selected against and would more likely be interpreted as pathology as opposed to an adaptation. There is some evidence that exclusive homosexual preferences among men are related to the failure of testosterone-induced prenatal masculinization of the brain (Ellis & Ames, 1987); homosexual males, then, might be expected to have the sexual preferences of females. It is unlikely, however, that a similar mechanism could be used to account for pedophilic preferences.

Symons (1979) has reviewed evidence suggesting that visual stimuli are a more potent source of sexual arousal for men than they are for women, and has argued that natural selection has favored a basic tendency for males to become sexually aroused by the sight of females and that the strength of the arousal should be proportional to their perceived reproductive value. Because of females' substantially greater investment in childbearing, their best reproductive strategy would be seriously undermined if they were to be sexually aroused by the sight of males. Symons further argued that heterosexual men universally assess women in terms of physical attractiveness and universally desire attractive women, and that these assessments and desires promote males' reproductive success. Some physical features, such as a good complexion, are universally considered attractive, Symons asserts, because they are indicators of good physical health and, therefore, higher reproductive value.

The way in which female age affects females' sexual attractiveness to males is not exactly known, but there is little doubt that females' sexual attractiveness to males declines after early adulthood (see below). Symons argues that, cross-culturally, men should be most strongly attracted to women between the ages of approximately 17 to 28, because these are the ages of fertility onset to the end of the best ages for conception, pregnancy, and childbirth. If males have been designed by natural selection to assess women's attractiveness as wives, as opposed to single-time sexual partners, the ages from 17 to 22 should be most preferred, because a male who marries a woman of this age maximizes his chances of monopolizing her entire reproductive career. On the other hand, Symons speculated, men should be most attracted to women aged 23 to 28 if selection pressures have led men to evaluate females primarily as a one-time partner for sexual intercourse. Because the age of menarche (and presumably nubility and maturity) has been declining for females in modern Western societies, he hypothesized that Western males should actually prefer women of slightly younger ages.

In the section that follows, we examine different measures of sexual interest to determine their suitability for use in studies of the development of sexual preference and the amount of evidence they provide for an evolutionary account of sexual preference.

MEASURES OF SEXUAL INTEREST

Ratings of Physical Attractiveness

Physical attractiveness is known to play an extremely important role in our social lives and is one of the principal determinants of dating and marital partner choice (Berscheid, 1981; Patzer, 1985). Despite the significance of physical attractiveness, little has been known about the development of physical appearance preferences until recently (Adams, 1977). Cavior and Lombardi (1973) had children aged 5 to 8 rate the physical attractiveness of photographs of 11- to 17-year-olds, and found that by age 7 or 8 children could make reliable ratings. Moreover, the ratings by the 7- and 8-year-olds showed close agreement with ratings made by 11- and 17-year-olds. Dion (1973) found that children as young as 3 could reliably rate the physical attractiveness of facial photos of age peers and that their ratings closely matched those of adults.

There have been a few studies in which subjects have been asked to rate the physical attractiveness of stimulus persons of different or apparently different ages. Korthase and Trenholme (1982) found that, among their adolescent and adult raters, perceived age of the stimulus person (stimuli were facial photographs of young, middle-aged, and older adults) was very strongly negatively correlated with judgments of physical attractiveness. Other studies using photographs of male and female adults as stimuli have found that younger-looking faces and faces with "babylike" features are generally judged to be more physically attractive than others, whether the raters are males or females (Berry & McArthur, 1985; Cash & Horton, 1983; Cunningham, 1986).

Cross and Cross (1971) asked male and female subjects aged 7, 12, 17, and adult (mean age 36) to rate the physical attractiveness of facial photos of males and females in one of three approximate age categories: ages 7, 17, or adult. Although male and female judges differed somewhat in their ratings, there was no overall effect for age of judge. For all categories of judges, the 17-year-old female stimuli were rated as most beautiful. Adult women were the second most preferred stimuli for the adult male judges, but the 17-year-old males were preferred by all other groups of male judges. Adult women were rated third by the 12- and 17-year-old raters, while 7-year-old girls were rated third by the 7-year-old males. Thus, although evidence was found for consistency across age of judge, there was also a tendency toward a preference for age peers. Judges of both sexes showed a preference for female stimuli.

Cross and Cross chose their stimuli by selecting six examples that they considered to be representative of the range of facial types in a random selection of photographs they were able to collect for each age and sex category. The photographs of the grade-school children were taken from class pictures, the high school students from yearbooks, and the adults from pictures of personnel rosters of various businesses. Unfortunately, it was neither ensured that the pools from which they selected their stimuli were equally representative of the range of physical attractiveness for persons of that age, nor that stimulus persons selected from the different age pools were of equal physical attractiveness relative to their age peers. The issue of equality or representativeness of stimulus persons from different age-gender categories raises the very real possibility of confounding physical attractiveness with age-gender category.

Langlois and Roggman (1990) have reviewed recent studies reporting high levels of interrater, cross-cultural agreement in judgments of the attractiveness of ethnically diverse faces, and literature that indicates that 3- to 6-month-old infants spend more time looking at adult-judged attractive than adult-judged unattractive faces. These recent cross-cultural and infant findings suggest innate or very early acquired universal attractiveness criteria. Langlois and Roggman hypothesized on both cognitive and evolutionary grounds that average or typical faces should be those judged to be the most attractive. From a cognitive point of view, prototypical faces are those most easily judged as faces by infants. From an evolutionary standpoint, extreme population characteristics are those most commonly selected against; those individuals farthest from the population average are those most likely to carry harmful genes.

To test these hypotheses, Langlois and Roggman digitized and averaged different numbers of faces of college students; the attractiveness of the resulting composites (of either male or female faces) were then rated by other students. In firm support of the predictions, a strong linear trend showed that the composites were judged to be more attractive the greater the number of faces they were based upon.

In summary, there is evidence that physical attractiveness is perceived in infancy, can be reliably rated as early as age 3 years and that, within gender and relatively narrow age stimulus categories, judges of different ages, sexes, and cultures show agreement on physical attractiveness ratings. In addition, there is evidence that physical attractiveness declines with apparent age from late adolescence onward, regardless of age or sex of rater or sex of stimulus person. Averaged faces are seen as most attractive within a narrow age range.

A further series of studies have examined preference for body shapes. Fallon and Rozin (1985) had college males and females rate their current weight, their own ideal weight, and their preferred weight for members of the opposite sex along a scale that ranged from well below average to well above average for each sex. Males' average ideal weight for women was below the average weight for adult women (how that weight was determined was not specified), but was not especially thin and was higher than the average ideal weights reported by women. Cohn, Adler, Irwin, Millstein, Kegeles, and Stone (1987) replicated Fallon and Rozin's study with a sample of sixth, seventh, and eighth graders. It appears (though it was not possible to compare the results of the studies directly) that the adolescent boys' average preferred weight for women was somewhat heavier than college males' preferred weight for women, suggesting that there might be age differences in male preferences for female body shapes. In addition, in this study, the authors had subjects rate their own level of pubertal development on Tanner's scales (Marshall & Tanner, 1969, 1970; Tanner, 1962, 1971). They did not, unfortunately, assess whether or not a boy's pubertal status affected his perception of the ideal figure for females.

There are few other studies that have examined adult males' preferences for different female figures. Horvath (1981) had college males rate line drawings of females with one of three different breast sizes, and one of four degrees of torso curvedness. Apparent weight and faces were held constant across all figures. He found that males' judgments of attractiveness of the stimuli were not influenced by breast size, and that high levels of curvedness were judged as unattractive. In another study, he found that female hip and waist widths were negatively correlated with attractiveness, while slenderness was positively corre-lated (Horvath, 1979). In contrast, Meuser, Grau, Sussman, and Rosen (1984) reported data indicating that breast size is an important determinant of the physical attractiveness of *Playboy* models to college men. In a study of male college students' ratings of whole body silhouettes of adult females, Wiggins, Wiggins, and Conger (1968) found that, in general, an average figure was preferred, with large figures particularly disliked. The figure with slightly larger than average breasts, but average in terms of other characteristics, was the most preferred figure.

Although there are other references to the relationship between sexually dimorphic traits and sexual attractiveness (Nakdimen, 1984), there is, in fact, little evidence bearing on this issue. Generally, the characteristics of female bodies that are attractive to adult males appear to be those associated with young, sexually mature females of average weight.

Physical attractiveness has been measured primarily by simple ratings of the physical attractiveness of stimulus persons on a Likert scale (e.g., Berry & McArthur, 1985; Cunningham, 1986; Horvath, 1981; Mueser et al. 1984). Other methods have been to ask subjects to rank order the stimuli according to the amount of "beauty" they see in each stimulus (Cross & Cross, 1971), or to have subjects rank order a set of stimuli according to physical attractiveness (Cavior & Lombardi, 1973; Korthase & Trenholme, 1982). In some cases, subjects were told to rate according to their own personal standards rather than according to popular norms, while in others they were not. Although there have been no studies comparing different methods of measuring physical attractive-ness, the results of studies using different methods have been essentially the same.

Stimuli used for rating have most often been slides or photos of faces only (Berry & McArthur, 1985; Cross & Cross, 1971; Cunningham, 1986; Dion, 1973; Dion, Berscheid, & Walster, 1972; Korthase & Trenholme, 1982; Lang-lois & Roggman, 1990). More rarely, researchers have used ratings of full body photos (Cavior & Lombardi, 1973; Mueser et al., 1984), in vivo ratings of the physical attractiveness of stimulus persons (Berscheid, Dion, Walster, & Walster, 1971), or drawings of full bodies (Horvath, 1979, 1981; Wiggins et al., 1968). Berscheid and Walster (1974) concluded that the results obtained were generally similar, regardless of whether faces only or full bodies were used. Mueser et al. (1984) compared the relative importance of facial versus body features on male college students' ratings of overall physical attractiveness of photos of college females and found that both bodily and facial appearance contributed to overall attractiveness ratings, but that facial appearance contributed more.

Ratings of physical attractiveness, although valuable indicators of sexual preference, are necessarily somewhat ambiguous. First, as with any self-report measure concerning subjects' sexual or quasi-sexual interests, they can be influenced by strong demand characteristics, but more importantly, depending upon the nature of the instructions given to raters, they can represent the respondents' understanding of cultural standards of beauty, their personal preferences, or some combination of both. This methodological issue clouds the relationships among cultural standards of attractiveness, personal standards of attractiveness, and sexual interest. Moreover, it is clear that there is no straightforward correspondence between ratings of physical and sexual attractiveness: Males and females have no difficulty in appraising the physical attractiveness of persons of their sexually preferred or nonpreferred gender and agree with each other in their ratings (e.g., Morse, Grusen, & Reis, 1976).

Ratings of Sexual Attractiveness

As discussed above and in support of Symons's theory, there is considerable evidence for a strong relationship between female physical and sexual attractiveness as perceived by heterosexual males. Adams (1977) reviewed research on physical attractiveness and cited evidence to show that physical attractiveness is related to sex appeal, and to sensations of love and emotional arousal. Berscheid (1981) reviewed evidence of the extremely potent effect physical attractiveness has on dating choice, especially for males' choices. As an example of this relationship, Cash and Horton (1983) had facial photographs of women rated on a number of dimensions before and after they had received plastic surgery. Raters rated the women as significantly more physically attractive following surgery, as well as more sexually warm and responsive, more likely to marry men of their choice, and more competent as marriage partners.

In another study, Dion et al. (1972) found that physically attractive young men and women (head and shoulder photos) were rated as more exciting and sexually warm than less attractive persons. Morse, Grusen, and Reis (1976) found that males (in contrast to females) rated both sex appeal and physical attractiveness as the most important considerations in assessing the opposite sex. Snyder, Tanke, and Berscheid (1977) arranged for men and women to meet over the telephone. Some of the men (unbeknownst to the women) were led to believe that the woman they were to talk to was physically attractive, while others were led to believe the woman was unattractive. Their conversations were recorded and later rated by judges. Male subjects who talked to women whom they believed were more attractive were judged, on the basis of their conversations, to be more sexually warm, bold, and sexually permissive than men who were led to believe they were talking to unattractive women. Further evidence of a strong relationship between physical attractiveness and sexual attractiveness comes from a study in which college males gave higher ratings of the physical attractiveness of a "pretty blonde coed" when they were sexually aroused before making the rating, compared to when they were not aroused (Stephan, Berscheid, & Walster, 1971).

Cunningham (1986) found very high positive correlations for male college students between a woman's physical attractiveness and her desirability as a dating partner, a sexual partner, and as a mother for their children. He also found, using a stimulus set consisting of facial photos of high school seniors and beauty queen contestants, that male undergraduates primarily preferred females with "baby-face" features (cf. Sternglanz, Gray, & Murakami, 1977) but that they also preferred women with some "mature" features. Cunningham speculated that the combination of mature and babylike features was judged to be attractive because it signaled that the female was at an optimal age for mating. Nevertheless, he commented that he could not explain why some "mature" features (such as cheekbone width) were consistently rated as attractive, while others (such as small eyes or large nose) were not. Nakdimen (1984) has argued that high cheekbones are quite different in males and females. The cheekbone in males is the zygomatic arch itself, whereas in females it is the soft tissue overlying the bone and extending to the nasolabial fold. This sexually dimorphic trait, Nakdimen asserts, makes women appear as if they are smiling. Taken together with Langlois and Roggman's (1990) work reviewed above, these data appear to indicate that males prefer regular or average faces of older adolescent or young adult females that exhibit certain sexually dimorphic and youthful traits.

Thus, an evolutionary account asserts that for heterosexual male subjects rating female stimuli, physical and sexual attractiveness are equivalent. Such an account suggests that the two are not necessarily equivalent for female subjects. Available data, with the exception of one methodologically confounded study (Cross & Cross, 1971), are consistent with such an evolutionary view. If sexual and physical attractiveness are equivalent, at least for heterosexual males' ratings of postpubertal females, then one would expect that female body characteristics that indicate physical maturity would be important contributors to males' overall judgments of physical attractiveness. In support of this notion, and in support of Symons's contention regarding the importance of visual stimuli for men, Barclay (1973) studied male and female sexual fantasies and found that males much more frequently mentioned visual aspects of their fantasies, often reporting details about the appearance of female sexual characteristics such as pubic hair and breast size. This attention to visual aspects should be especially true when judging the sexual attractiveness of younger postpubertal females because it is difficult for a male to judge a female's maturity from facial stimuli alone. Furthermore, male pubertal status might be expected to influence their choices of physically (and, hence, sexually) attractive females. Among prepubertal boys, there is presumably little evolutionary advantage to male preference for the most reproductively viable females, and evolutionary theory is silent about their sexual preferences.

In sum, there is evidence that the characteristics that contribute to physical attractiveness, most particularly in the case of postpubertal heterosexual males' appraisals of females, are precisely those that would be expected to relate to sexual maturity and fertility by an evolutionary account that asserts that physical and sexual attraction are isomorphic. It should be noted, however, that evolutionary theory says nothing about the relationship between appraisals of sexual and physical attractiveness concerning persons of the nonpreferred gender.

Phallometric Assessment

Phallometric assessment has become the most scientifically accepted method of measuring specifically sexual interests among males, although it is not without problems of its own, such as dissimulation (Quinsey & Chaplin, 1988b). In this technique, changes in penile tumescence are measured as a function of different stimuli presented to the subject. Adult heterosexual males show the greatest penile response to slides of adult women, and progressively less response to other nude female slides, the younger the depicted person; responses to male stimuli are below those of the youngest females. For homosexuals, the results concerning age are the same as for heterosexuals, but the role of the sex of the stimulus person is reversed (Freund, Langevin, Cibiri, & Zajac, 1973). Phallometric data consistently discriminate persons with histories of extrafamilial child molestation from other persons (e.g., Freund, 1967; Freund & Blanchard, 1989; Quinsey & Chaplin, 1988a; Quinsey et al., 1975). Although not all child molesters have inappropriate sexual age preferences (i.e., are pedophiles), the likelihood increases the younger the victim(s), and with male victim choice (because most adult males are not particularly interested in very young or male sexual partners), increasing numbers of victims (because the likelihood that situational factors can explain a given offender's sexual activities with children diminish the greater the number of his victims). Child molesters' sexual preferences, as determined phallometrically, generally correspond to their sexual histories, although it is not uncommon for child molesters to show sexual interest in both adults and children. The proportion of child molesters with interest in children of both sexes is very high (Quinsey, 1986).

Sexual Partner Choice

Choice of sexual partner is used as the most important criterion for evaluating various measures of sexual preference. Some relation between measures of physical attractiveness, sexual attractiveness, phallometric data, and sexual history is both required and expected. As mentioned earlier, these various predictors are linked to the concept of sexual preference used in a theory to explain actual sexual behaviors. There is a variety of circumstances that can create a disparity between sexual preferences and sexual history; most importantly, societal disapproval of a person's sexual interactions with his or her preferred type of sexual partner.

In a large cross-cultural study, Buss (1989) found strong evidence that adult males preferred potential marital partners to be younger than themselves and in their mid-20s (i.e., in line with Symons's [1979] speculation concerning selection pressure on men to prefer single matings, males appear to value peak fertility as opposed to peak reproductive value).

Descriptions of the characteristics of desired marital partners or data on actual marriage (Buss, 1989; Epstein & Guttman, 1984) suffer, respectively, from the difficulties of self-report and the unfortunate fact that people cannot always get what they want in a marital or dating partner. Although marital partners are chosen for a variety of reasons in addition to sexual attractiveness, it is of interest that there are substantial correlations between the physical attractiveness ratings of romantically coupled individuals and much smaller correlations between the physical attractiveness of same-sex friends (Feingold, 1988).

Viewing Time

Viewing time, measured unobtrusively while subjects perform some "manifest" task involving the stimuli of interest, has provided orderly data on pornography, sex guilt, and homosexual versus heterosexual interests (Brown, Amoroso, Ware, Pruesse, & Pilkey, 1973; Lang, Searles, Lauerman, & Adesso, 1980; Love, Sloan, & Schmidt, 1976; Martin, 1964; Rosenzweig, 1942; Ware, Brown, Amoroso, Pilkey, & Pruesse, 1972; Zamansky, 1956). Viewing time has been found to be strongly related to ratings of physical attractiveness using both child and adult subjects (Dion, 1977; Power, Hildebrandt, & Fitzgerald, 1982). Recently, Abel (personal communication, November, 1990) and his colleagues have found that viewing time can differentiate homosexual child molesters from other males.

Although viewing time has not yet been tried as a measure of sexual age and gender preferences among children, it appears to be a better candidate for this purpose than other indices. Phallometric measurement is easily ruled out on ethical grounds, as is the use of sexually explicit stimuli. Ratings of sexual attractiveness would be unintelligible to young children and would raise ethical problems with older children. Children have relatively short sexual histories, and there are ethical and practical problems involved in questioning children about their sexual activities. Ratings of physical attractiveness have been used extensively with children, but the evidence for a strong relationship between physical and sexual attractiveness exists only in the case of heterosexual males' ratings of adult female stimuli. The use of children's ratings of physical attractiveness as a measure of sexual preference would be ambiguous concerning age and gender preferences.

COVARIATION AMONG MEASURES
OF SEXUAL INTEREST

Although the above reviewed literature indicates that looking time is a good candidate for studies of sexual preference involving children, considerably more validational and normative work is required before this extension could be made with much confidence. Because it is likely that a variety of factors other than sexual preference influence the amount of time that subjects spend looking at slides of persons, experimental work is needed to identify what features of the experimental situation influence looking time and how close the correspondence is between looking time and other measures of sexual preference.

In order to assess this correspondence, we had male and female subjects rate slides of nude persons of both sexes and different ages on a variety of attractiveness dimensions while the amount of time they illuminated each slide was covertly measured. Subjects rated each stimulus person on physical attractiveness to others, and physical and sexual attractiveness to themselves. It was predicted that the viewing times of male subjects would parallel phallometric data obtained with similar slides, and that viewing time would correlate more highly with sexual attractiveness than physical attractiveness ratings for all subjects. Because of Symons's contention that male sexual arousal is more influenced by visual stimuli than female sexual arousal, it was predicted that the relationship between viewing time and sexual attractiveness ratings would be stronger for male than for female subjects.

METHOD

Subjects

Fifteen male and 15 female subjects were recruited through poster advertisements at Queen's University and were paid to participate. All subjects rated their sexual thoughts and sexual behavior as exclusively or predominantly heterosexual. One female subject's data were discarded because she considered herself a homosexual. Some data from a second additional female subject was discarded due to technical problems with the equipment. Male subjects ranged in age from 21 to 31 years ($m = 27$); females from 20 to 30 years ($m = 26$).

Stimuli

The slide set consisted of 31 slides, half showing a nude female and half showing a nude male of one of four different age categories (7 slides of infants, 8 of children, 8 of pubescents, and 8 of adults). None of the models appeared in flirtatious poses, and none of the male models were shown with erections. Although all subjects viewed 3 neutral slides and 31 stimulus slides, only data from 24 stimulus slides were analyzed. Data from the infant slides were not analyzed, because a number contained technical imperfections.

Previous research in our laboratory (Cannon, 1990) has shown the average estimated age of the models in each category to be: child, 7.67 years ($SD = 1.63$); pubescent, 13.18 years ($SD = 1.87$); and adult, 23.06 years ($SD = 2.77$); there were no significant differences found in the age estimations given by male and female raters and no significant differences attributable to model sex. Cannon also recorded viewing time using age estimation as the manifest task. Unfortunately, the results showed that viewing time simply increased with increasing age of the stimulus person, regardless of whether he or she was of the preferred or nonpreferred gender, suggesting that estimating the age of older persons takes longer because it is more difficult and, therefore, that age estimation is not a good manifest task to use when examining sexual preferences.

Procedure

Each subject viewed the slides in private in a small room. Prior to viewing the slides, each subject was told that he or she should look at all slides, and after seeing all the slides would be asked to make some ratings about each slide. Procedures for illuminating and advancing the slides (via two buttons) were explained to each subject. Instructions were "to get a clear view of the model in each slide before advancing to the next." Subjects were not informed until after all procedures were completed that the amount of time each slide was illuminated was recorded. After each subject had viewed all the slides, the researcher entered the slide viewing room and asked the subject to look at all the slides again, recording his or her judgments about each model's attractiveness. It was explained that the purpose of the study was to find out how physically attractive the models in the slides were, before they were used in other studies. Subjects were asked to rate on a 0 to 100 scale how physically attractive each model would be to people in general, how physically attractive each model was to him or her, and how sexually attractive each model was to him or her. After subjects completed the ratings on the models, they were asked to fill out a Kinsey-type scale, rating sexual thoughts and sexual experiences on two separate scales. This information, together with the judgments about attractiveness, were sealed into envelopes to ensure anonymity.

Treatment of the Data

An average rating (based on four slides) was computed for each age category and model gender for each subject, on each dependent measure (i.e., viewing time, "sexually attractive to me," "physically attractive to me," and "physically attractive to others"). A mixed design (two within-factors, age category and model gender) analysis of variance was applied to these data separately for male and female subjects.

RESULTS AND DISCUSSION

The average ratings and viewing times for male and female subjects are shown in Figure 7.1 and the correlations among the measures for each sex of subject are shown in Table 7.1.

The figure reveals that mean sexual attractiveness ratings varied over age-gender category. For female subjects, only adults of the preferred gender were rated as sexually attractive; for male subjects, both adults and pubescent females were rated as sexually attractive. The results for the male subjects are in accord with findings from phallometric studies, except that the ratings of the pubescent females are higher than would be expected.

Inspection of Figure 7.1 reveals that average viewing time did not show the expected parallels with sexual attractiveness ratings; in particular, the difference in viewing time between the preferred and nonpreferred genders was small for both male and female subjects. Further, the viewing time of male subjects did not mirror phallometric data, again because there was little discrepancy between the sexually preferred and nonpreferred genders.

There were no significant effects for female subjects' ratings of physical attractiveness to others, physical attractiveness to themselves, or viewing time in the analyses of variance based on category means. Female subjects rated only adult males as sexually attractive to them. This was reflected in significant effects for model age ($F(2,24) = 13.74$, $p < .0002$), model sex ($F(1,12) = 13.98$, $p < .003$), and their interaction ($F(2,24) = 15.54$, $p < .0001$) in the sexual attractiveness ratings.

As predicted, single-degree-of-freedom contrasts indicated (all p's $< .05$) that, among the preferred gender, adults were rated by female subjects as more attractive than pubescents and more attractive than children; adults of the preferred gender were also rated as more attractive than members of the

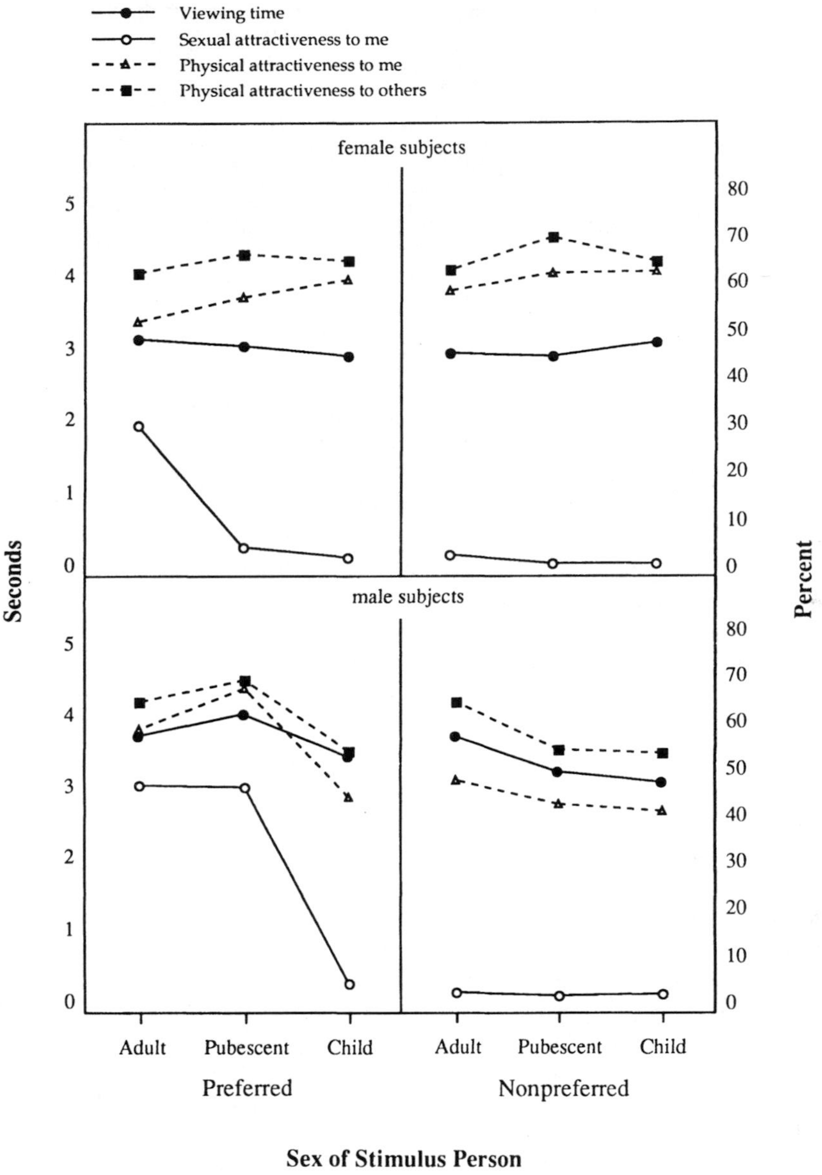

FIGURE 7.1. Viewing time and attractiveness ratings of male and female subjects as a function of stimulus person sex.

TABLE 7.1. Correlations among Category Means for Each Measure Averaged over subjects

Female subjects	Male subjects			
	Physically attractive to others	Physically attractive to me	Sexually attractive to me	Viewing time
Physically attractive to others		.741	.538	.345
Physically attractive to me	.667		.749	.447
Sexually attractive to me	−.055	−.251		.542
Viewing time	.323	.379	.370	

nonpreferred gender. Contrary to predictions, however, pubescents of the preferred gender were neither rated as significantly more attractive than children of the preferred gender nor as more attractive than members of the nonpreferred gender. Identical predictions were made for the viewing-time results, but none were statistically significant.

Turning to the physical attractiveness to others ratings from male subjects, there were significant effects of age ($F(2,14) = 12.27, p < .0003$), model sex ($F(1,14) = 6.08, p < .026$), and their interaction ($F(2,28) = 19.88, p < .0001$). Very similar results were obtained in the ratings of physical attractiveness to themselves. There were significant effects attributable to age ($F(2,14) = 16.66, p < .0001$), model sex ($F(1,14) = 14.91, p < .002$), and their interaction ($F(2,28) = 11.79, p < .0004$). The analysis of male ratings of sexual attractiveness to me yielded significant effects of age ($F(2,14) = 46.14, p < .0001$), gender ($F(1,14) = 84.17, p < .0001$), and age by gender ($F(2,28) = 47.43, p < .0001$).

It was predicted that male subjects would rate adult females as more attractive than pubescent females, but this comparison was not significant. However, as predicted, male subjects rated female adults as more attractive than female children, pubescent females as more attractive than female children, and both adult females and pubescent females as more attractive than all categories of the nonpreferred gender (all p's $< .001$). None of the viewing-time predictions were confirmed, except that both adults and pubescents of the preferred gender were viewed for longer than all categories of the nonpreferred gender ($p < .05$ and $p < .001$, respectively).

Correlations among measures were computed for each subject using the mean for each of the six age-gender categories. These are shown in the table separately for male and female subjects. The relationships tended to be higher for male than for female subjects. As predicted, sexual attractiveness ratings were more closely related to ratings of physical attractiveness to themselves for male than for female subjects (Mann-Whitney U = 171, $p < .01$, one-tailed). It was also predicted that viewing time would be more highly correlated with ratings of sexual attractiveness for males than for females; this comparison, although in the predicted direction, was not significant (Mann-Whitney U = 117, $p < .10$). For male subjects, ratings of sexual attractiveness to themselves and viewing time shared about 29% of the variance, and for female subjects about 14%.

In brief, these data indicate that ratings of physical attractiveness to others (i.e., normative ratings) are very similar to personal ratings of physical attractiveness (to self) for both male and female subjects. Both types of ratings of physical attractiveness were more affected by the age and gender of the stimulus persons for male than for female subjects. As predicted by evolutionary theory, ratings of physical and sexual attractiveness were more closely related for male than for female subjects.

Females rated only adult males as sexually attractive to them, whereas males rated both adult and pubescent females as sexually attractive. Because the high rating of pubescent females by male subjects is not in accord with phallometric data, it is tempting to conclude that the relatively high rating is an artifact of the accidental confounding of model attractiveness with age category. This hypothesis, however, requires that the female subjects also rate the female pubescents as significantly more physically attractive to others and to themselves than other categories of females; this effect was not found.

Viewing time was not found to be as strong a measure of sexual preference as hoped. Although it tended to perform better among male than female subjects, the magnitude of its correlation with sexual attractiveness among males ($r = .546$) is insufficient to allow its use as a substitute for ratings of sexual attractiveness. On the other hand, because viewing time has a real relationship with ratings of sexual attractiveness, further work on procedural details that may increase the size of this relationship is encouraged.

SUMMARY

The literature on ratings of physical and sexual attractiveness, phallometric testing, and sexual partner choice provides some support for an evolutionary account of heterosexual males' sexual preferences. However, because evolutionary theories speak neither to the current mechanisms underlying sexual preferences nor to their development within individuals, a good deal of further ontogenetic research is required. This research would be facilitated if an ethically sound, unobtrusive measure of sexual preference could be developed for use with children of varying ages. Covertly measured viewing time is a good candidate for such a measure, although future research is required to eliminate variables that obscure its relationship with sexual preference. A theory of individual differences in sexual preferences or pathological development of sexual preferences should be facilitated by accurate knowledge of their normal course of development.

ACKNOWLEDGMENTS

This research was supported by a grant from the Advisory Research Council of Queen's University and a contract from the Kingston Psychiatric Hospital. We wish to thank C. Earls for his review of an earlier version of this paper and C. Cannon and A. Olmstead for their help in data collection.

REFERENCES

Adams, G. R. (1977). Physical attractiveness research: Toward a developmental social psychology of beauty. *Human Development, 20*, 217–239.

Barclay, A. M. (1973). Sexual fantasies in men and women. *Medical Aspects of Human Sexuality, 7*, 205–216.

Bateson, P. (Ed.). (1983). *Mate choice.* New York: Cambridge University Press.

Becker, J. V., Cunningham-Rathner, J., & Kaplan, M. S. (1986). Adolescent sexual offenders: Demographics, criminal and sexual histories, and recommendations for reducing future offenses. *Journal of Interpersonal Violence, 1*, 431–445.

Bell, A. P., Weinberg, M. S., & Hammersmith, S. K. (1981). *Sexual preference: Its development in men and women.* Bloomington: Indiana University Press.

Berry, D. S., & McArthur, L. Z. (1985). Some components and consequences of a baby face. *Journal of Personality and Social Psychology, 48*, 312–323.

Berscheid, E. (1981). An overview of the psychological effects of physical attractiveness and some comments upon the psychological effects of knowledge of the effects of physical attractiveness. In R. E. Moyers (Ed.), *Psychological aspects of facial form.* Ann Arbor: Craniofacial Growth Series, University of Michigan Press.

Berscheid, E., & Walster, E. (1974). Physical attractiveness. In L. Berkowitz (Ed.), *Advances in experimental social psychology* (pp. 157–215). New York: Academic Press.

Brown, M., Amoroso, D. M., Ware, E. E., Pruesse, M., & Pilkey, D.W. (1973). Factors affecting viewing time of pornography. *Journal of Social Psychology, 90*, 125–135.

Buss, D. M. (1989). Sex differences in human mate preferences: Evolutionary hypotheses tested in 37 cultures. *Behavioral and Brain Sciences, 12*, 1–49.

Cannon, C. K. (1990). *The relationship of viewing time to ratings of physical and sexual attractiveness in male and female subjects.* Unpublished undergraduate thesis, Queen's University.

Cash, T. F., & Horton, C. E. (1983). Aesthetic surgery: Effects of rhinoplasty on the social perception of patients by others. *Plastic and Reconstructive Surgery, 72*, 543–548.

Cavior, N., & Lombardi, D. A. (1973). Developmental aspects of judgment of physical attractiveness in children. *Developmental Psychology, 8*, 67–71.

Cohn, L. D., Adler, N. E., Irwin, C. E., Jr., Millstein, S. G., Kegeles, S. M., & Stone,

G. (1987). Body-figure preferences in male and female adolescents. *Journal of Abnormal Psychology, 96,* 276–279.

Cross, J. F., & Cross, J. (1971). Age, sex, race, and the perception of facial beauty. *Developmental Psychology, 5,* 433–439.

Cunningham, M. R. (1986). Measuring the physical in physical attractiveness: Quasi-experiments on the sociobiology of female beauty. *Journal of Personality and Social Psychology, 50,* 925–935.

Dion, K. K. (1973). Young children's stereotyping of facial attractiveness. *Developmental Psychology, 9,* 183–188.

Dion, K. K. (1977). The incentive value of physical attractiveness for young children. *Personality and Social Psychology Bulletin, 3,* 67–70.

Dion, K., Berscheid, E., & Walster, E. (1972). What is beautiful is good. *Journal of Personality and Social Psychology, 24,* 285–290.

Ellis, L., & Ames, M. A. (1987). Neurohormonal functioning and sexual orientation: A theory of homosexuality–heterosexuality. *Psychological Bulletin, 101,* 233–258.

Epstein, E., & Guttman, R. (1984). Mate selection in man: Evidence, theory and outcome. *Social Biology, 31,* 243–276.

Fallon, A. E., & Rozin, P. (1985). Sex differences in perceptions of desirable body shape. *Journal of Abnormal Psychology, 94,* 102–105.

Feingold, A. (1988). Matching for attractiveness in romantic partners and same-sex friends: A meta–analysis and theoretical critique. *Psychological Bulletin, 104,* 226–235.

Freund, K. (1967). Erotic preference in pedophilia. *Behaviour Research and Therapy, 5,* 339–348.

Freund, K. (1990). Courtship disorder. In W. L. Marshall, D. R. Laws, & H. E. Barbaree (Eds.), *Handbook of sexual assault: Issues, theories, and treatment of the offender* (pp. 195–207). New York: Plenum Press.

Freund, K., & Blanchard, R. (1989). Phallometric diagnosis of pedophilia. *Journal of Consulting and Clinical Psychology, 57,* 100–105.

Freund, K., & Costell, R. (1970). The structure of erotic preference in the nondeviant male. *Behaviour Research and Therapy, 8,* 15–20.

Freund, K., Langevin, R., Cibiri, S., & Zajac, Y. (1973). Heterosexual aversion in homosexual males. *British Journal of Psychiatry, 122,* 163–169.

Freund, K., Watson, R., & Rienzo, D. (1989). Heterosexuality, homosexuality, and erotic age preference. *Journal of Sex Research, 26,* 107–117.

Goldman, R., & Goldman, J. (1982). *Children's sexual thinking: A comparative study of children aged 5 to 15 years in Australia, North America, Britain, and Sweden.* Boston: Routledge & Kegan Paul.

Horvath, T. (1979). Correlates of physical beauty in men and women. *Social Behavior and Personality, 7,* 145–151.

Horvath, T. (1981). Physical attractiveness: The influence of selected torso parameters. *Archives of Sexual Behavior, 10,* 21–24.

Korthase, K. M., & Trenholme, I. (1982). Perceived age and perceived physical attractiveness. *Perceptual and Motor Skills, 54,* 1251–1258.

Lang, A. R., Searles, J., Lauerman, R., & Adesso, V. (1980). Expectancy, alcohol, and sex guilt as determinants of interest in & reaction to sexual stimuli. *Journal of Abnormal Psychology, 89,* 644–653.

Langlois, J. H., & Roggman, L. A. (1990). Attractive faces are only average. *Psychological Science, 1*, 115–121.

Laws, D. R., & Marshall, W. L. (1990). A conditioning theory of the etiology and maintenance of deviant sexual preference and behavior. In W. L. Marshall, D. R. Laws, & H. E. Barbaree (Eds.), *Handbook of sexual assault: Issues, theories, and treatment of the offender* (pp. 209–229). New York: Plenum.

Love, R. E., Sloan, L. R., & Schmidt, M. J. (1976). Viewing pornography and sex guilt: The priggish, the prudent, and the profligate. *Journal of Consulting and Clinical Psychology, 76*, 624–629.

Marshall, W. A., & Tanner, J. M. (1969). Variations in the pattern of pubertal changes in girls. *Archives of Disease in Childhood, 45*, 291–303.

Marshall, W. A., & Tanner, J. M. (1970). Variations in the pattern of pubertal changes in boys. *Archives of Disease in Childhood, 45*, 13–23.

Marshall, W. L., & Barbaree, H. E. (1990). An integrated theory of the etiology of sexual offending. In W. L. Marshall, D. R. Laws, & H. E. Barbaree (Eds.), *Handbook of sexual assault: Issues, theories, and treatment of the offender* (pp. 257–275). New York: Plenum Press.

Martin, B. (1964). Expression and inhibition of sex motive arousal in college males. *Journal of Applied Social Psychology, 68*, 307–312.

Morse, S. T., Gruzen, J., & Reis, H. (1976). The "eye of the beholder": A neglected variable in the study of physical attractiveness. *Journal of Personality, 44*, 209–225.

Mueser, K. T., Grau, B. W., Sussman, M. S., & Rosen, A. J. (1984). You are only as pretty as you feel: Facial expresssion as a determinant of physical attractiveness. *Journal of Personality and Social Psychology, 46*, 469–478.

Nakdimen, K. A. (1984). The physiognomic basis of sexual stereotyping. American *Journal of Psychiatry, 14*, 499–503.

Patzer, G. L. (1985). *The physical attractiveness phenomena.* New York: Plenum.

Power, T. G., Hildebrandt, K. A., & Fitzgerald, H. E. (1982). Adults' responses to infants varying in facial expression and perceived attractiveness. *Infant Behavior and Development, 5*, 33–44.

Quinsey, V. L. (1984). Sexual aggression: Studies of offenders against women. In D. N. Weisstub (Ed.), *Law and mental health: International perspectives, Vol. 1,* (pp. 84–121). New York: Pergamon Press.

Quinsey, V. L. (1986). Men who have sex with children. In D. N. Weisstub (Ed.), *Law and mental health: International perspectives 2* (pp. 140–172). New York: Pergamon Press.

Quinsey, V. L., & Chaplin, T. C. (1988a). Penile responses of child molesters and normals to descriptions of encounters with children involving sex and violence. *Journal of Interpersonal Violence, 3*, 259–274.

Quinsey, V. L., & Chaplin, T. C. (1988b). Preventing faking in phallometric assessments of sexual preference. In R. A. Prentky & V. L. Quinsey (Eds.), *Human sexual aggression: Current perspectives* (pp. 49–58). New York: New York Academy of Sciences.

Quinsey, V. L., Chaplin, T. C., & Carrigan, W. F. (1979). Sexual preferences among incestuous and non-incestuous child molesters. *Behavior Therapy, 10*, 562–565.

Quinsey, V. L., Chaplin, T. C., Maguire, A. M., & Upfold, D. (1987). The behavioral treatment of rapists and child molesters. In E. K. Morris & C. J. Braukmann (Eds.), *Behavioral approaches to crime and delinquency: Application, research, & theory* (pp. 363–382). New York: Plenum Press.

Quinsey, V. L., & Earls, C. M. (1990). The modification of sexual preferences. In W. L. Marshall, D. R. Laws & H. E. Barbaree (Eds.), *The handbook of sexual assault: Issues, theories, and treatment of the offender* (pp. 279–295). New York: Plenum Press.

Quinsey, V. L., Steinman, C. M., Bergersen, S. G., & Holmes, T. F. (1975). Penile circumference, skin conductance, & ranking responses of child molesters and "normals" to sexual & nonsexual visual stimuli. *Behavior Therapy, 6,* 213–219.

Rosenzweig, S. (1942). The photoscope as an objective device for evaluating sexual interest. *Psychosomatic Medicine, 4,* 150–158.

Snyder, M., Tanke, E. D., & Berscheid, E. (1977). Social perception and interpersonal behavior: On the self-fulfilling nature of social stereotypes. *Journal of Personality and Social Psychology, 35,* 656–666.

Stephan, W., Berscheid, E., & Walster, E. (1971). Sexual arousal and heterosexual perception. *Journal of Personality and Social Psychology, 20,* 93–101.

Sternglanz, S. H., Gray, J. L., & Murakami, M. (1977). Adult preferences for infantile facial features: An ethological approach. *Animal Behavior, 25,* 108–115.

Symons, D. (1979). *The evolution of human sexuality.* New York: Oxford University Press.

Symons, D. (1989). A critique of Darwinian anthropology. *Ethology and Sociobiology, 10,* 131–144.

Tanner, J. M. (1962). *Growth at adolescence.* London: Oxford University Press.

Tanner, J. M. (1971). Sequence, tempo, and individual variation in the growth & development of boys & girls aged 12 to 16. *Daedalus, 100,* 907–930.

Ware, E. E., Brown, M., Amoroso, D. M., Pilkey, D. W., & Pruesse, M. (1972). The semantic meaning of pornographic stimuli for college males. *Canadian Journal of Behavioural Science, 4,* 204—209.

Wiggins, J. S., Wiggins, N., & Conger, J. C. (1968). Correlates of heterosexual somatic preference. *Journal of Personality and Social Psychology, 10,* 82–90.

Zamansky, H. S. (1956). A technique for measuring homosexual tendencies. *Journal of Personality, 24,* 436–448.

CHAPTER 8

The Importance of Attachment Bonds in the Development of Juvenile Sex Offending

William L. Marshall
Stephen M. Hudson
Sharon Hodkinson

In an earlier paper (Marshall, 1989a) we outlined the basis of a theory linking a lack of intimacy in adult relations to a proclivity to engage in offensive sexual behaviors. Evidence that we reviewed at that time suggested that intimacy is pursued or desired by all people. Failure to achieve intimacy leads to the experience of emotional loneliness which, so the limited evidence suggested, increases the likelihood that the person will engage in aggressive behaviors. Subsequently, we evaluated the attainment of intimacy and the experience of emotional loneliness among various groups of sex offenders and matched controls. Sex offenders more frequently failed to report intimacy in their lives and expressed greater feelings of loneliness than did nonoffender controls, thereby offering support for our theory (Marshall, Seidman, & Check, 1991).

It is important to note, however, that our theory suggests that a failure to attain intimacy in relationships is but one aspect of the development and maintenance of sexual deviance. We have, at other times, pointed to sociocultural factors (Marshall, 1984b), the role of pornography (Marshall, 1989b) and biological processes and inherited dispositions (Marshall, 1984a), as well as conditioning (Laws & Marshall, 1990) and developmental experiences (Marshall & Barbaree, 1984a). It is the latter developmental experiences that will be the focus of this chapter, particularly those concerning the relationship between the growing child and his parents. When these particular relationships are strong and effective the child and his parents are said to have formed a strong attachment bond, which is thought to provide the basis for successful and happy future development. When these bonds are weak or unsatisfactory, the child is thought to be at risk for future antisocial or psychiatrically dysfunctional behavior.

In this chapter we begin by briefly outlining the nature of attachment bonds and why they are thought to affect later development, particularly why attachment bonds influence the capacity for intimacy in relationships. Then we will consider the evidence concerning the relationship between poor attachment bonds in early childhood and the later development of antisocial behavior and, more specifically, of sexual offending.

ATTACHMENT AND ITS RELEVANCE FOR DEVELOPMENT

Parent–Child Bonding

Attachment bonds between parents and their young are seen in other mammalian species and are understood to have evolved to protect vulnerable offspring and thereby maximize their inclusive fitness (Hinde & Stevenson-Hinde, 1990). Anxiety over separation serves to keep the infant within the range of the mother's protection and thereby ensures its survival to adulthood. Similar processes seem to occur in humans.

Bowlby (1969, 1973, 1980) has provided the most comprehensive description of attachment bonds in human childhood, and he has elaborated their importance for the developing child. Attachment, according to Bowlby, is the bond between a child and care giver and is the central feature of this developing relationship. This bond serves to provide the child with the security needed to confidently explore the world. Thus, attachments are seen to give rise to positive feelings such as love and a feeling of security. Although a threat to the relationship or a brief separation can generate anxiety, renewal produces joy. If, however, the separation is prolonged or permanent, then a process involving stages characterized by an initial lack of affect, then grief, sorrow, and despair will ensue (Paterson & Moran, 1988). When the bond between child and parent is either disrupted or of poor quality, then all manner of problem behaviors will appear (Bowlby, 1973, 1980).

Bowlby (1973) claims that attachment bonds are the basis for developing internal representations of the relationship between self and others and, accordingly, they serve as templates for future relationships, including those involving intimacy. When the care giver is sensitive to the child's needs and provides warm and loving care, the child's capacity to relate easily to others is maximally developed, as is self-confidence. Such children display warmth toward others, show few if any signs of emotional dysfunction, and rarely engage in antisocial behavior (Grossman & Grossman, 1990).

Secure attachments also seem to be resistant to the negative effects of stressful events, whereas inadequate attachments are more readily disrupted (Egeland & Sroufe, 1981a, 1981b). Thus, early security in attachment bonds is predictive of an enduring good quality in parent–child relationships. In addition, while in general, attachment to the mother seems to be most important, relations with the father also predict future adjustment and may serve to offset problems in the relationship with the mother (Feeney & Noller, 1990). In fact, with respect to the development of delinquent behaviors among boys, perceived closeness to their father is a better predictor than is closeness to their mother (Johnson, 1987). Thus, as far as delinquency is concerned, the father may be the more important figure.

While it seems true that the nature of early attachments is the most powerful predictor of the quality of later relationships, it is also apparent that positive experiences with care givers after early childhood can to some extent offset disruptive attachments (Grossman, Fremmer-Bombik, Rudolph, & Grossman, 1988; Main, Kaplan, & Cassidy, 1985; Myers, 1984; Rutter, 1988). Nevertheless, we would expect children who had been constantly moved from one care giver to another, or who had experienced prolonged separation from a parent, to have difficulties later in life, even if subsequently exposed to a positive care giver. Thus, children adopted after infancy would be expected to have problems.

Perhaps even more importantly, there are significant continuities in level of adaptive functioning from infancy through adulthood (Grossman & Grossman, 1990), in that secure attachment bonds predict how other children will relate to the child and how effective the child will be in relationships as an adult. Jacobson and Wille (1986) found that children who were securely attached at 18 months of age were the recipients of more positive responses from other children when they were older. Consistent relationships were observed between the quality of childhood attachments and adult love relationships (Hendrick & Hendrick, 1989), and Feeney and Noller (1990) found that securely attached children, compared to those with poor attachments, had as adults higher self-esteem, were less self-conscious and anxious, and were more likely to be involved in fulfilling relationships. Indeed, Feeney and Noller found that it was not just adult love relationships that were predictable given knowledge of child–parent attachments, but so also were all adult relationships, including friendships and acquaintanceships. On the other hand, children whose childhood attachments were insecure, whose parents were rejecting, or who experienced prolonged separation suffered all manner of problems both as children and as adults (Bretherton, 1985; Kolvin, Miller, Fletting, & Kolvin, 1988; Loeber, 1990; Paterson & Moran, 1988).

Ainsworth (Ainsworth, Blehar, Waters, & Wall, 1978; Bell & Ainsworth, 1972) has described three different types of attachment styles that reflect the caregiver's sensitivity to the child: (1) secure, (2) avoidant, and (3) anxious-ambivalent. When the parent is warm and sensitive to the child, the child develops a secure way of relating to others. These children have more friends and display reciprocity in relations; they are more sociable, more empathic, and are more frequently imitated by others (La Freniere & Sroufe, 1984; Sroufe, 1983; Waters, Wippman, & Sroufe, 1979). If the quality of the parent–child relationship is poor, then the child will develop an avoidant or anxious-ambivalent style in relating to others. Poor- quality attachments are associated with parents who are absent or rejecting in the way they relate to their children, who are insensitive to the child's needs, who lack warmth and have difficulties in showing affection, and are inconsistent in their responses.

Anxious-ambivalent individuals perceive their parents as offering little or no support or encouragement to them, whereas avoidant subjects see their parents as distant and untrustworthy (Feeney & Noller, 1990). Ainsworth et al. (1978) found that when the mother was unresponsive to the infant, had an aversion to physical contact, and lacked emotional expressiveness, the child developed an avoidant style toward others. When the mother was inconsistent in responding to the infant's signals, the youngster became anxious and ambivalent about relating to others. Actual physical maltreatment by parents may produce either of the inappropriate relationship styles (Lamb, Gaensbauer, Malkin, & Schultz, 1985).

As adults, those with an avoidant attachment history reported either never having been in love or never having experienced strong feelings of love; those with an anxious-ambivalent history had a pattern of brief and unsatisfying love relationships (Feeney & Noller, 1990). Both those subjects with avoidant or anxious-ambivalent attachments in childhood, scored high as adults on an Avoidance of Intimacy Scale (Feeney & Noller, 1990). These poor relationship styles were not only evident at adulthood among those individuals who had insecure attachment bonds, but also during childhood and adolescence (Main et al., 1985; Paterson & Moran, 1988).

In summary then, secure parent–child attachment bonds are formed when the care giver is confident, responsive, sensitive, warm, affectionate, empathic, trustworthy, and consistent. These infants grow up to be themselves sensitive, warm, affectionate, and so on, and to seek out and attain good relations with others, including enduring love relations. When attachment bonds are characterized by insecurity, rejection, a lack of warmth, inconsistency, abuse, or disruptions in continuity, the child will develop either an avoidant or anxious-ambivalent interpersonal style.

From Parental Bonds to Adolescent Peer Relations

As we have seen, the growth of the capacity to form intimate adult relations is understood by attachment theorists (e.g., Weiss, 1982) to depend on the quality of early infant and childhood relationships with care givers. In addition, the shift from attachment bonds with parents to relationships with peers at adolescence is understood to depend, in part, on experiences during this difficult transitional period in the young person's life. Good quality peer relationships during adolescence provide yet another step in the development of the skills and confidence required to attain intimacy as an adult. These formative experiences are facilitated by parents who encourage and support their developing offspring, but these beneficial developments may be missed or retarded if the parents are hostile toward the growing independence of the children or if they are jealous of relationships outside the home. Similarly, parents who constantly argue or fight with each other, or who find difficulties with emotional and affectional expression, will provide poor role models for children at this vulnerable time. Typically, such parents also establish insecure attachments with their children, and in so far as Bowlby (1973) is correct in maintaining that attachment bonds serve as templates for relationships outside the family, these children can be expected to have considerable difficulties in forming peer relations at adolescence.

Weiss (1982) points out that until adolescence, children will maintain the bonds of attachment with their parents, however good or bad they are. With the onset of puberty they begin to desire periods of separation from their parents, away from their scrutiny, and begin to seek the company of peers more and more as time goes on. This is a difficult transition period that can threaten a parent's control over their child and may be seen by some parents as a threat to the continuity of the bond with their child. During this time both child and parents experience some degree of ambivalence about one another, and it may be hard for parents to set clear rules while at the same time being loving and supportive of their somewhat unpredictable child.

Relinquishing parents as their prime attachment figures is clearly critical to the ultimate independence of the child, but it is rarely a smooth transition. Parents who are themselves lonely, and many parents who form inadequate attachment bonds with their children are lonely, may create difficulties for the young person's attempt to transfer his or her attachment to peers. In particular, boys who have experienced insecure attachments will lack the self-confidence and skills necessary to form relations with peers, especially with girls of their own age.

These marked differences in relationship styles between individuals who developed secure or insecure attachment bonds as children are matched by more general, but related, differences in personality and behavior. For instance, securely attached children grow up to be adolescents and adults who are high in self-esteem, un-self-conscious, low in anxiety (Feeney & Noller, 1990), more communicative and socially active (Paterson & Moran, 1988), more empathic (Sroufe, Schork, Frosso, Lawroski, & LaFreniere, 1984), and more socially competent (Sroufe, 1983). Insecure attachments, of course, produce the opposite personalities. In addition to being unempathic, self-conscious, low in self-esteem, anxious, uncommunicative and socially inept, children who have poor attachments develop into adults who are mistrustful and have difficulties in emotional expression (Grossman & Grossman, 1990).

In our most recent papers, theoretical deficiencies in self-confidence, social competence, and empathy were seen as critical to the development and persistence of sexually abusive behavior (Marshall & Barbaree, 1990) and to the development of a more generally criminal lifestyle (Marshall & Barbaree, 1984b). We are not alone in making such claims, but what we (Marshall, 1989a) have attempted to do is to integrate these issues (i.e., attachment bonds, adult intimacy, social and personal functioning) with a propensity to engage in criminal acts. It is to these connections that we now turn.

ATTACHMENT BONDS AND JUVENILE DELINQUENCY

Poor attachment bonds result not only from poor parenting (i.e., inconsistency, lack of warmth, unresponsiveness, insensitivity, rejection, etc.) but also from discontinuities in parenting. If poor attachment can result from disruptions in contact between caregiver and child, then we would expect children who are adopted after the supposed critical period (anywhere up to age 3 years at least, and perhaps up to age 6 years) to be more likely to show problematic behaviors than those adopted at infancy. MacDonald (1985) found that later adoptions are followed by more maladaptive behaviors than are early ones, and multiple mothering during the first 6 months predicts later antisocial behavior (Cadoret & Cain, 1980). Similarly, family breakup during the first 5 years of a child's life is more likely than later breakup to produce delinquency and other problem behaviors (Behar & Stewart, 1982; Wadsworth, 1979), and prolonged separation from the mother between ages 6 months to 3 years is followed by behavioral problems (MacDonald, 1985).

As we might expect, even when there are no discontinuities in parent–child relationships, if attachments are of poor quality, then problem behaviors emerge. Kolvin et al. (1988), for instance, found that poor-quality mothering was related to the number of convictions during adolescence and adulthood. In a series of meta-analyses of a large number of concurrent and longitudinal studies, Loeber and Stouthamer-Loeber (1986) found that the best predictors of juvenile antisocial behavior were parental child-rearing practices. They found that deficiencies in parenting skills (e.g., lack of appropriate supervision, neglect, and parental rejection) were associated with the seriousness of a child's delinquency. Also, a lack of parental involvement with the child, poor discipline, and parental aggression during the early years of a child's life were related to later juvenile delinquency. Furthermore, these effects become more pronounced as the children get older (Loeber, 1990), with the effects showing a "dose-response" relationship according to the number of disruptive factors present (Kolvin et al., 1988).

Interviews with delinquent boys and their parents revealed that in 60% of the cases parental attitudes of indifference were a notable feature, while 31.7% of the boys experienced direct hostility or rejection by their parents (Thilagaraj, 1983). Similarly, Misra (1977) found that separation from parents, neglect by parents, and an absence of warmth and affection in parent–child relations contributed to the development of juvenile delinquency. McCord (1979) found that the strongest predictors of juvenile delinquency were parental conflict, poor parental supervision, and lack of affection by the mothers. In a longitudinal study of 847 families followed since 1947, Kolvin et al. (1988) described a strong relationship between delinquency and poor care by mothers during the early years of life. In fact, they found that the effect of inadequate parenting was far stronger on later delinquency than was marital discord or breakdown. Of particular relevance for our concerns here is the fact that Johnson (1979) observed greater effects for parental factors on male delinquents than on female delinquents. In an interesting analysis of the point of onset of delinquency, Steinberg (1987) determined that early discontinuities in parent–child relations were most likely to result in preadolescent delinquency, excessive parental permissiveness was associated with an early adolescent onset of offending, and a lack of parental monitoring produced delinquency in middle adolescence.

Of course, the disruptive effects of inadequate parenting are not mediated entirely via the emotional impact of poor-quality attachment bonds; inadequate parents also provide models of various inappropriate behaviors. For example, among violent juveniles, Lewis, Shanok, Pincus, and Glaser (1979) found that 78.6% had been exposed to extreme violence in their family, whereas this was true for only 20% of the less violent juveniles. Lewis et al. (1988) noted that only 1 of 14 juveniles sentenced to death in the United States had not been physically abused as a child, and 12 of the 14 had been exposed to extreme violence in the home. These effects seem likely to have arisen as a result of modeling aggression, but of course the destructive effects of such brutal parents extend beyond simple modeling; these parents would certainly not have provided the necessary responses for the development of secure attachments.

We have previously (Marshall, 1989b; Marshall & Barbaree, 1990) argued that although many children are exposed to various negative experiences, only a few develop inappropriate behaviors as a consequence. It is our view that the quality of home life significantly prepares the growing child to be resilient or vulnerable to such influences. The crucial aspect of the quality of home life in this regard is the development of secure or insecure attachment bonds.

This account of the development of juvenile delinquency is, of course, not new. Glueck and Glueck (1962) suggested that parental unconcern, lack of affection by parents, poor discipline, lack of supervision, and broken homes, provide the basis for delinquency, and Schafer and Knudten (1970) point to parental neglect as a cause of juvenile offending. More recently, Loeber (1990) has concluded that secure attachment bonding to adult caretakers helps children learn the prosocial skills that protect them from developing problem behaviors.

There seems, then, to be a growing consensus that features of inadequate parental behaviors, which are understood to be related to a lowered quality of attachment bonds, are predictive of delinquency. The question for us, however, is more specific: Do these features similarly characterize adolescent sex offenders and, if they do, why is it that these boys become sex offenders rather than acting in other antisocial ways?

ATTACHMENT BONDS AND JUVENILE SEX OFFENDING

The fact that many juvenile sex offenders have an extensive history of nonsexual crimes (Fehrenbach, Smith, Monastersky, & Deisher, 1986) suggests that there may not be much difference between juveniles who sexually offend and those who offend in other ways. However, not all adolescent sex offenders have a criminal history.

Adolescent sex offenders seem to be characterized by their poor social relations and, as we have noted, it is understood by attachment theorists that poor social relations are a function of inadequate bonds with parents. These poor social relations not only make the developing boy afraid or mistrustful of others but also fails to instill the skills necessary for productive social behavior. Fehrenbach et al. (1986) found that 65% of their large group ($n = 305$) of juvenile sex offenders showed significant signs of social isolation, indicating that they had serious problems in relating to others. Thirty-two percent of these boys had no friends and another 34% had no close friends. Similarly, Fagan and Wexler (1988) found that juvenile sex offenders were even more socially isolated than chronically violent juveniles, and this isolation was more apparent in their lack of relations with peer-aged females. Among 24 adolescent sex offenders, Awad, Saunders, and Levene (1984) found a high incidence of family instability. Seventy-nine percent of these boys had been separated from parents for prolonged periods, and there were serious problems in the families of 59% of them. Over one-third of Awad et al.'s offenders had been abused or neglected, and more than one-third of the mothers and half of the fathers were judged to have been rejecting. Similarly, half the fathers and 25% of the mothers were described as emotionally detached. Not surprisingly, given this background, almost half of the group of offenders were said to be loners (Awad et al., 1984).

In a careful study where they were able to control for socioeconomic status, age of the offender, and the size of the family of origin, Saunders, Awad, and White (1986) found that sexually assaultive adolescent boys ($n = 63$) had disturbed family backgrounds. The parents of these boys lacked commitment to each other and had weak attachments to their children. Those boys who sexually attacked peer-aged or older victims had experienced long-term separations from parents and were exposed to considerable marital conflict. Those who had assaulted younger children had witnessed high rates of physical violence between their parents. Very few of these adolescent sex offenders had close friends, although there were some apparent inconsistencies here. For instance, while 60% of the exhibitionists and 72% of the child molesters had no close friends, only 32% of the rapists were so isolated (Saunders et al., 1986). On the other hand, Tingle, Barnard, Robbins, Newman, and Hutchinson (1986) reported that 86% of their adult rapists had few or no friends.

The observation that juvenile sex offenders are social isolates is also reported by other researchers. Groth (1977) has noted that adolescent sex offenders have serious problems in relating effectively with peers, and a series of additional studies confirms this (Deischer, Wenet, Paperny, Clark, & Fehrenbach, 1982; Fehrenbach et al., 1986; Shoor, Speed, & Bartlett, 1966). In addition, these latter studies noted that these boys were the victims of family abuse and parental neglect, and this, along with the fact that their families were socially isolated, apparently led these boys to have difficulties relating to others.

ATTACHMENT AND INTIMACY PROBLEMS IN ADULT SEX OFFENDERS

Since many adult sex offenders began their offending in adolescence, or at least developed their deviant interest at a young age (Abel & Rouleau, 1990), it seems reasonable to consider, as relevant to the present issue, evidence indicating attachment problems among these adult offenders.

Adult sex offenders have been found to be insecure in relationships, and they expect their sexual and emotional partners to reject them (Panton, 1978). Generally, these men have problems relating to adult females (Fisher & Howells, 1970; Gebhard, Gagnon, Pomeroy, & Christenson, 1965; Hammer & Glueck, 1957; Mohr, Turner, & Jerry, 1964; Pacht & Cowden, 1974), and we (Marshall, 1989a) took this to indicate an inadequacy in intimate relations. Problems with intimacy as an adult are understood by theorists in this field to indicate failures in the development of attachment bonds in infancy and child-hood (Weiss, 1982). From the earlier considerations in this paper, we would expect these poor attachments to cause problems in relationships throughout life, and we certainly saw that juvenile offenders were social isolates. Consistent with this view is the observation that among adult offenders, 85.7% of rapists and 74.4% of child molesters had few or no friends as youngsters (Tingle et al., 1986), and almost one-third of each group had trouble getting along with classmates while at school (Davidson, 1983). Davidson also found that more than 25% of adult sex offenders said that they had felt neglected by their mothers and an even higher percentage felt neglected by their fathers. Disruptions in the homes of these children who were to grow up to be adult sex offenders was so common and abusive that 66.7% of the rapists and 46.5% of the child molesters ran away from home, and over 20% were placed in institutions or foster homes (Davidson, 1983).

We (Marshall, 1989a) have reported clinical observations of our patients indicating problems in adult intimate relations. Subsequently, we found in a controlled evaluation that rapists, child molesters, and exhibitionists scored far lower on measures of intimacy and far higher on measures of emotional lone-liness than did a matched group of nonoffenders (Marshall et al., 1991). Similarly, among 44 exhibitionists, 19% said they were frequently beaten by parents, 29% said their parents were very strict, and 42% felt emotionally rejected by their parents; only 12% considered their parents to have treated them well (Marshall, Payne, Barbaree, & Eccles, in press). In a matched group of nonoffenders, 11% described their parents as abusive, 20% thought they were excessively strict, and only 14% felt rejected by their parents; 54% of these nonoffenders saw their parents as loving and supportive. These differences between exhibitionists and nonoffenders are quite interesting and suggest that physical abuse by a parent and excessive strictness (neither of which differentiated exhibitionists from nonoffenders) may not be as important in the etiology of exhibitionism as the experience of rejection by parents (which did significantly differ between the two groups). As we saw earlier, parents who are distant and unresponsive to their children, and lack emotional responsiveness toward their offspring, have children who subsequently avoid relationships (Ainsworth et al., 1978; Feeney & Noller, 1990). These negative features of avoidant-attachment parents can be summarized as reflecting rejection. Children with an avoidant-attachment history grow up to be adults who have severe difficulties in forming love relationships (Feeney & Noller, 1990). Thus, it is no surprise to find that exhibitionists, who characteristically report their parents to have been rejecting, have considerable difficulties with intimacy and feel lonely and isolated from love relations (Marshall et al., 1991).

Both adult and juvenile sex offenders, then, seem to have experienced a disproportionate degree of problems or disruptions in the development of appropriate attachment bonds with their parents. In particular, they seem to have been rejected by their parents, which leads them to develop an avoidant or anxious-ambivalent style in relations with peers and in love relationships.

THE RELATIONSHIP BETWEEN ATTACHMENT, INTIMACY, AND SEX OFFENDING

The capacity to form intimate relations in adolescence and adulthood is understood to be largely dependent on early infant and childhood attachments to parents (Weiss, 1982). Whether good or bad, attachment relationships in childhood provide the growing child with a template for the construction of their own future relationships (Bowlby, 1973; Hartup, 1986). When secure attachments are formed in these early years, the individual not only develops confidence in interpersonal relations, but also develops the desire to seek and maintain intimacy with others and the skills necessary to achieve these goals. If parental behaviors lead to insecure attachments, then the individual will be fearful of intimacy, will lack self-confidence, and will not have the skills necessary to establish close relationships.

Such a person will experience what is described as emotional loneliness (Weiss, 1973; Williams, 1983), and there is evidence that this type of loneliness increases the probability that the person will engage in aggression toward others (Zilboorg, 1938). Aggression resulting from emotional loneliness (which in turn arises from a lack of intimacy) has been observed in children (George & Main, 1979), in adult women (De Lozier, 1982; Helfer, 1973), and in adult males (Check, Perlman, & Malamuth 1985; Diamant & Windholz, 1981; Loucks, 1980). Of course, when the problems with early attachments arise as a result of parental aggression, we would expect lonely people to be even more likely to aggress, having been provided as children with models for such behavior.

Poor attachments in childhood, then, lead to an incapacity for intimacy, which produces painful feelings of emotional loneliness, and may ultimately lead to aggressive behavior. But why might a history of insecure attachments lead some adolescents to offend in a sexual way and others to offend in other ways?

It is possible that some adolescent sex offenders also have a biological disposition toward high rates of sexual expression (e.g., higher levels than usual of one or other of the activating sex steroids) and that this, overlying their experiences of insecure attachments, may result in aggression being expressed in a sexual way. That, however, seems unlikely to account for more than a few of these offenders.

Insecurely attached children do not grow up devoid of needs for physical pleasure, for love, and for intimacy; they simply do not have the capacity to meet these needs, or they are afraid to seek it from others. This leaves them in a chronically deprived state, and this yearning is the core of emotional lone-liness. It is highly likely that such individuals will engage in self-stimulation designed to satisfy these goals, but such a tactic, while providing physical gratification, will not meet the additional needs for intimacy and love. However, the damaging effects of insecure attachments and the consequent pursuit of satisfaction through self-stimulation are likely to entrench the view, all too commonly seen in males, that these emotional needs can be fully satisfied by the physical act of sex alone, even in the absence of a reciprocally responsive partner. In addition, all too often, the masturbatory fantasies of males (espe-cially young males) are affectionless scenarios wherein the female is compliant with their every whim. A female who is so compliant will, of course, appeal to these young males who are insecurely attached, as she does not represent a threat to reject their sexual advances. Insecurely attached boys not only do not have the skills to engage in intimate, affectionate relations, they are also very much afraid of rejection, since this has characterized their parent–child rela-tions. Thus impersonal, nonaffectionate themes will appeal to these boys. Responding to these scenarios will tend to entrench a set of beliefs and attitudes that are self-centered, oblivious to the needs or desires of a partner, and show a preoccupation with physical gratification; not the type of disposition that might lead to intimate loving relations but, unfortunately, one that would fail to inhibit tendencies to offend sexually.

The young boy who has insecure attachments will grow up devoid of self-esteem (Bowlby, 1973; Feeney & Noller, 1990). Since self-esteem in males is highly dependent upon their sense of masculinity derived, at least in part, from their sexual experiences (Schimel, 1974), insecurely attached youngsters will seek out, or be attracted to, sexual scripts that depict them, by virtue of being male, as powerful, manly, and in control. Indeed, White and Humphrey (1990) found that insecurity and low self-esteem were predictive of sexual assault, but only when such problems were accompanied by traditional notions of masculinity. Such traditional notions, of course, may appeal to an insecure young boy, and he may derive these notions from his parents, from the media, or from both. Certainly, many parents who display an inability to form effective attachments with their children, and thereby render them insecure, are them-selves authoritarian and traditional in outlook (Baumrind & Black, 1967; Maccoby & Martin, 1983).

Much of the imagery in pornography, advertising, and the general media may be read as testimonies to traditional notions about male–female relations, which may seem attractive, especially to insecure young boys. These images depict women to be compliant with men's sexual desires, as unlikely to be rejecting, and as responsive to coercion. Children may also be seen in these images to be sexual and to be compliant to the wishes of older males.

Circulating levels of the sexually activating hormone testosterone in-creases fourfold among boys during the brief 2-year period of pubescence (Sizonenko, 1978). At this time, therefore, insecure adolescents will be exquisitely responsive to the images we have described, and they may focus only on the aspects of media messages that depict traditional notions because these particular scripts meet the unsatisfied, but distorted, needs of these boys. Forcing a woman to have sex or having sex with a child requires none of the social skills that these boys have failed to acquire; it provides a rare opportunity in the lives of these young males to experience power and control, and to be relatively unconcerned with rejection; and it satisfies those needs that have become focused on physical gratification. Of all the various messages that our society, especially through the media, provides to growing boys, these, in particular, will be most appealing to insecurely attached young males. These boys may subsequently use these images in their masturbatory practices, thereby beginning the process of entrenching a deviant disposition (Marshall & Eccles, Chap. 6, this volume; Laws & Marshall, 1990), thus increasing the probability of overt sexual aggression.

Given the remarkably diverse vagaries of experience, not all boys who suffer poor-quality parenting would be expected to become so responsive to these deviant sexual scripts, or even to fully recognize such scripts, but many will. Others may find the opportunity for self-enhancement in prosocial activities, but it is likely that they will remain lonely individuals who have difficulty in relationships. Still others may find nonsexual aggression or stealing sufficient to meet their desperate needs, at least for some time. When, however, nonsexual delinquency no longer fulfills them, and they have otherwise not overcome their insecurity, these males may turn to sexual aggression. Consistent with this view is the observation that a prior history of nonsexual crimes is commonly observed in sex offenders (Gebhard et al., 1965).

IMPLICATIONS FOR RESEARCH

From this account of the etiology of adolescent sex offending, we can derive some straightforward, testable hypotheses. Obviously, adolescent sex offenders should currently have greater difficulties with intimacy, they should experience more marked feelings of emotional loneliness, they should have fewer close friends, they should have less affectionate sexual experiences than other adolescents, but they should not necessarily differ on these features from juvenile delinquents who have not sexually offended. However, adolescent sex offenders should be more sexually preoccupied than both other delinquents and nondelinquent juveniles. In terms of their family histories, adolescent sex offenders should report poorer attachment bonds and related difficulties with parents than other juveniles, but not other delinquents. Juvenile sex offenders should have poorer social skills, be less confident, and feel more threatened about their masculinity than both other delinquents and nondelinquents.

Some of these hypotheses, derived from our attachment theory of adolescent sex offending, have received some degree of confirmation in the literature and, indeed, these observations provided some of the impetus for our proposal. However, there are many gaps in the data base and even if research does not support the theory, the evidence gathered will expand our meager knowledge of these problematic youths

REFERENCES

Abel, G. G., & Rouleau, J. L. (1990). The nature and extent of sexual assault. In W. L. Marshall, D. R. Laws, & H. E. Barbaree (Eds.), *Handbook of sexual assault: Issues, theories, and treatment of the offender* (pp. 9–21). New York: Plenum Press.

Ainsworth, M. D. S., Blehar, M. C., Waters, E., & Walls, S. (1978). *Patterns of attachment: A psychological study of the Strange Situation.* Hillsdale, NJ: Erlbaum.

Awad, G., Saunders, E., & Levene, J. (1984). A clinical study of male adolescent sex offenders. *International Journal of Offender Therapy and Comparative Criminology, 28,* 105–115.

Baumrind, D., & Black, A. E. (1967). Socialization practices associated with dimensions of competence in preschool boys and girls. *Child Development, 38,* 291–327.

Behar, D., & Stewart, M. A. (1982). Aggressive conduct disorder of children: The clinical history and direct observations. *Acta Psychiatrica Scandinavia, 65,* 210–220.

Bell, S. M., & Ainsworth, M. D. S. (1972). Infant crying and maternal responsiveness. *Child Development, 43,* 1171–1190.

Bowlby, J. (1969). *Attachment and loss: Vol. 1. Attachment.* New York: Basic Books.

Bowlby, J. (1973). *Attachment and loss: Vol. 2. Separation: Anxiety and anger.* New York: Basic Books.

Bowlby, J. (1980). *Attachment and loss: Vol. 3. Loss, sadness, and depression.* New York: Basic Books.

Bretherton, I. (1985). Attachment theory: Retrospect and prospect. *Monographs of the Society for Research in Child Development, 50,* 3–35.

Cadoret, R. J., & Cain, C. (1980). Sex differences in predictors of antisocial behavior in adoptees. *Archives of General Psychiatry, 37,* 1171–1175.

Check, J. V. P., Perlman, D., & Malamuth, N. M. (1985). Loneliness and aggressive behavior. *Journal of Social and Personal Relations, 2,* 243–252.

Davidson, A. T. (1983). Sexual exploitation of children: A call to action. *Journal of the National Medical Association, 75,* 925–927.

Deischer, R. W., Wenet, G. A., Paperny, D. M., Clark, T. F., & Fehrenbach, P. A. (1982). Adolescent sexual offense behavior: Role of the physician. *Journal of Adolescent Health Care, 2,* 279–286.

De Lozier, P. (1982). Attachment theory and child abuse. In C. M. Parkes & J. Stevenson-Hinde (Eds.), *The place of attachment in human behavior* (pp. 95–117). New York: Basic Books.

Diamant, L., & Windholz, G. (1981). Loneliness in college students: Some theoretical, empirical and therapeutic considerations. *Journal of College Students Personality, 22,* 515–522.

Egeland, B., & Sroufe, L. A. (1981a). Attachment and early maltreatment. *Child Development, 52,* 44–52.

Egeland, B., & Sroufe, L. A. (1981b). Developmental sequelae of maltreatment in infancy. In R. Rizley & D. Cicchetti (Eds.), *Developmental perspectives on child maltreatment* (pp. 77–92). San Francisco: Jossey-Bass.

Fagan, J., & Wexler, S. (1988). Explanations of sexual assault among violent delinquents. *Journal of Adolescent Research, 3,* 363–385.

Feeney, J. A., & Noller, P. (1990). Attachment style as a predictor of adult romantic relationships. *Journal of Personality and Social Psychology, 58,* 281–291.

Fehrenbach, P. A., Smith, W. R., Monastersky, C., & Deischer, R. W. (1986). Adolescent sexual offenders: Offender and offense characteristics. *Journal of Orthopsychiatry, 56,* 225–233.

Fisher, G., & Howells, L. (1970). Psychological needs of homosexual pedophiliacs. *Diseases of the Nervous System, 3,* 623–650.

Gebhard, P., Gagnon, J., Pomeroy, W. P., & Christenson, C. V. (1965). *Sex offenders: An analysis of types.* New York: Harper & Row.

George, C., & Main, M. (1979). Social interactions of young abused children: Approach, avoidance and aggression. *Child Development, 50,* 306–318.

Glueck, S., & Glueck, E. (1962). *Family environment and delinquency.* Boston: Houghton Mifflin.

Grossmann, K., Fremmer-Bombik, E., Rudolph, J., & Grossmann, K. E. (1988). Maternal attachment representations as related to patterns of infant–mother attachment and maternal care during the first year. In R. A. Hinde & J. Stevenson-Hinde (Eds.), *Relations within families: Mutual influences* (pp. 241–260). New York: Oxford University Press.

Grossmann, K. E., & Grossmann, K. (1990). The wider concept of attachment in cross-cultural research. *Human Development, 33,* 31–47.

Groth, A. N. (1977). The adolescent sexual offender and his prey. *International Journal of Offender Therapy and Comparative Criminology, 21,* 249–254.

Hammer, E. F., & Glueck, B. C. (1957). Psychodynamic patterns in sex offenders: A four-factor theory. *Psychiatric Quarterly, 31,* 325–345.

Hartup, W. W. (1986). On relationships and development. In W. W. Hartup & Z. Rubin (Eds.), *Relationships and development* (pp. 1–26). Hillsdale, NJ: Erlbaum.

Helfer, R. E. (1973). The etiology of child abuse. *Pediatrics, 51,* 777–779.

Hendrick, C., & Hendrick, S. (1989). Research on love: Does it measure up? *Journal of Personality and Social Psychology, 56,* 784–794.

Hinde, R. A., & Stevenson-Hinde, J. (1990). Attachment: Biological, cultural and individual desiderata. *Human Development, 33,* 62–72.

Jacobson, J. L., & Wille, D. E. (1986). The influence of attachment pattern on developmental changes in peer interaction from the toddler to the preschool period. *Child Development, 57,* 338–347.

Johnson, R. E. (1979). *Juvenile delinquency and its origins.* New York: Cambridge University Press.

Johnson, R. E. (1987). Mother's versus father's role in causing delinquency. *Adolescence, 12,* 305–315.

Kolvin, I., Miller, F. J. W., Fletting, M., & Kolvin, P. A. (1988). Social and parenting factors affecting criminal-offence rates. Findings from the Newcastle Thousand Family Study (1947-1980). *British Journal of Psychiatry, 152,* 80–90.

LaFreniere, P., & Sroufe, L. A. (1984). Profiles of peer competence in the preschool: Interrelations between measures, influence of social ecology, and relation to attachment history. *Child Development, 21*, 56–68.

Lamb, M. E., Gaensbauer, T. J., Malkin, C. M., & Schultz, L. A. (1985). The effects on child maltreatment on security of infant-adult attachment. *Infant Behavior and Development, 8*, 35–45.

Laws, D. R., & Marshall, W. L. (1990). A conditioning theory of the etiology and maintenance of deviant sexual preference and behavior. In W. L. Marshall, D. R. Laws, & H. E. Barbaree (Eds.), *Handbook of sexual assault: Issues, theories, and treatment of the offender* (pp. 209–229). New York: Plenum Press.

Lewis, D. O., Pincus, J. H., Bard, B., Richardson, E., Prichep, L. S., Feldman, M., & Yeager, C. (1988). Neuropsychiatric, psychoeducational, and family characteristics of 14 juveniles condemned to death in the United States. *American Journal of Psychiatry, 145*, 584–589.

Lewis, D. O., Shanok, S. S., Pincus, J. H., & Glaser, G. H. (1979). Violent juvenile delinquents: Psychiatric, neurological, psychological, and abuse factors. *Journal of the American Academy of Child Psychiatry, 18*, 307–319.

Loeber, R. (1990). Development and risk factors of juvenile antisocial behavior and delinquency. *Clinical Psychology Review, 10*, 1–41.

Loeber, R., & Stouthamer-Loeber, M. (1986). Family factors as correlates and predictors of juvenile conduct problems and delinquency. *Crime and Justice: An Annual Review of Research, 7*, 29–149.

Loucks, S. (1980). Loneliness, affect, and self-concept: Construct validity of the Bradley Loneliness Scale. *Journal of Personality Assessment, 44*, 142–147.

Maccoby, E. E., & Martin, J. A. (1983). Socialization in the context of the family: Parent child interaction. In E. M. Hetherington (Ed.), *Handbook of child psychology: Vol. 4. Socialization, personality, and social development* (pp. 1–101). New York: Wiley.

McCord, J. (1979). Some child-rearing antecedents of criminal behavior in adult men. *Journal of Personality and Social Psychology, 9*, 1477–1486.

MacDonald, K. (1985). Early experience, relative plasticity and social development. *Developmental Review, 5*, 99–121.

Main, M., Kaplan, N., & Cassidy, J. (1985). Security in infancy, childhood, and adulthood: A move to the level of representation. *Monographs of the Society for Research in Child Development, 50*, 66–104.

Marshall, W. L. (1984a). L'avenir de la thérapie béhaviorale: Le béhaviorisme bio-social (illustré à patir d'une théorie sur le voil). *Revue de Modification du Comportment, 14*, 136–149.

Marshall, W. L. (1984b, March). *Rape as a socio-cultural phenomenon.* J. P. S. Robertson Lecture. Trent University, Peterborough, Ontario.

Marshall, W. L. (1989a). Invited essay: Intimacy, loneliness and sexual offenders. *Behaviour Research and Therapy, 27*, 491–503.

Marshall, W. L. (1989b). Pornography and sex offenders. In D. Zillman & J. Bryant (Eds.), *Pornography: Recent research, interpretations, and policy considerations* (pp. 185–214). Hillsdale, NJ: Erlbaum.

Marshall, W. L., & Barbaree, H. E. (1984a). A behavioral view of rape. *International Journal of Law and Psychiatry, 7*, 51–77.

Marshall, W. L., & Barbaree, H. E. (1984b). Disorders of personality, impulse and adjustment. In S. M. Turner & M. Hersen (Eds.), *Adult psychopathology: A behavioral perspective* (pp. 406–409). New York: Wiley.

Marshall, W. L., & Barbaree, H. E. (1990). An integrated theory of sexual assault. In W. L. Marshall, D. R. Laws, & H. E. Barbaree (Eds.), *Handbook of sexual assault: Issues, theories, and treatment of the offender* (pp. 257–275). New York: Plenum Press.

Marshall, W. L., Payne, K., Barbaree, H. E., & Eccles, A. (1991). Exhibitionists: Sexual preferences for exposing. *Behaviour Research and Therapy, 29,* 37–40.

Marshall, W. L., Seidman, B., & Check, J. V. (1991). *Intimacy and loneliness in sex offenders and nonoffender males.* Unpublished data.

Misra, S. S. (1977). Juvenile delinquency and parental deprivations. *Indian Journal of Clinical Psychology, 4,* 69–73.

Mohr, J. W., Turner, R. E., & Jerry, M. B. (1964). *Pedophilia and exhibitionism: A handbook.* Toronto: University of Toronto Press.

Myers, B. J. (1984). Mother-infant bonding: The status of this critical-period hypothesis. *Developmental Review, 4,* 240–274.

Pacht, A. R., & Cowden, J. E. (1974). An exploratory study of five hundred sex offenders. *Criminal Justice and Behavior, 1,* 13–20.

Panton, J. H. (1978). Personality differences appearing between rapists of adults, rapists of children, and nonviolent sexual molesters of children. *Research in Communications, Psychology, Psychiatry, and Behavior, 3,* 385–393.

Paterson, R. J., & Moran, G. (1988). Attachment theory, personality development and psychotherapy. *Clinical Psychology Review, 8,* 611–636.

Rutter, M. (1988). Functions of consequences of relationships: Some psychopathological considerations. In R. A. Hinde & J. Stevenson-Hinde (Eds.), *Relationships within families: Mutual influences* (pp. 332–353). Oxford: Oxford University Press.

Saunders, E., Awad, G. A., & White, G. (1986). Male adolescent sex offenders: The offenders and the offense. *Canadian Journal of Psychiatry, 31,* 542–549.

Schafer, S., & Knudten, R. D. (1970). *Juvenile delinquency: An introduction.* New York: Random House.

Schimel, J. L. (1974). Self-esteem and sex. In L. Gross (Ed.), *Sexual behavior: Current issues* (pp. 249–259). Flushing, NY: Spectrum.

Shoor, M., Speed, M. H., & Bartlett, C. (1966). Syndrome of the adolescent child molester. *American Journal of Psychiatry, 122,* 783–789.

Sizonenko, P. C. (1978). Endocrinology in preadolescents and adolescents. *American Journal of Diseases of Children, 132,* 704–712.

Sroufe, L. A. (1983). Infant-caregiver attachment and patterns of adaptation in preschool: The roots of maladaptation and competence. In M. Perlmutter (Ed.), *Minnesota Symposium on child psychology* (Vol. 16) (pp. 41–83). Hillsdale, NJ: Erlbaum.

Sroufe, L. A., Schork, E., Frosso, M., Lawroski, N., & LaFreniere, P. (1984). The role of affect in social competence. In C. E. Izard, J. Kagan, & R. B. Zajonc (Eds.), *Emotions, cognitions, and behavior* (pp. 289–319). Cambridge, England: Cambridge University Press.

Steinberg, L. (1987). Familial factors in delinquency: A developmental perspective. *Journal of Adolescent Research, 2,* 255–268.

Thilagaraj, R. (1983). Parent–child relationship and juvenile delinquency. *Social Defence, 19,* 20–26.

Tingle, D., Barnard, G. W., Robbins, L., Newman, G., & Hutchinson, D. (1986). Childhood and adolescent characteristics of pedophiles and rapists. *International Journal of Law and Psychiatry, 9,* 103–116.

Wadsworth, M. (1979). *Roots of delinquency, infancy, adolescence and crime.* Oxford: Robertson.

Waters, E., Wippman, J., & Sroufe, L. A. (1979). Attachment, positive affect, and competence in the peer group: Two studies in construct validation. *Child Development, 50,* 821–829.

Weiss, R. S. (1973). *Loneliness: The experience of emotional and social isolation.* Cambridge, MA: MIT Press.

Weiss, R. S. (1982). Attachment in adult life. In C. M. Parkes & J. Stevenson-Hinde (Eds.), *The place of attachment in human behavior* (pp. 171–184). New York: Basic Books.

White, J. W., & Humphrey, J. A. (1990). *A theoretical model of sexual assault: An empirical test.* Paper presented at Symposium on Sexual Assault: Research, Treatment and Education, Southeastern Psychology Association, Atlanta.

Williams, E. G. (1983). Adolescent loneliness. *Adolescence, 18,* 51–66.

Zilboorg, G. (1938). *Loneliness.* Atlantic Monthly, 14–19.

CHAPTER 9

Adolescent Sexual Aggression within Heterosexual Relationships: Prevalence, Characteristics, and Causes

Jacquelyn W. White
Mary P. Koss

Available evidence indicates that adolescent males represent a substantial portion of those arrested and convicted of rape (*Uniform Crime Reports*, FBI, 1978–1988). However, this group reflects only a small portion of young men who actually commit acts of sexual aggression (Ageton, 1983; Koss, Gidycz, & Wisniewski, 1987). Mounting evidence indicates that not only do the majority of rapes go unreported, but that these "hidden rapes" most frequently occur among acquaintances, and typically in dating situations (Koss, 1988; Muehlenhard & Linton, 1987; Rabkin, 1979; Russell, 1984).

Understanding adolescent sexual aggression is an urgent matter, given the high levels of physical violence known to occur in marital relationships: One-third of all men hit their wives (Straus, Gelles, & Smith, 1989), and marital rape is not uncommon (Russell, 1982; Yllo & Finkelhor, 1988). Heterosexual skills learned during adolescence set the stage for behaviors in marriage. The focus of this chapter is on adolescent sexual aggression within heterosexual relationships. Following a discussion of definitions of sexual aggression, and a summary of recent incidence and prevalence data, the multiple influences that are related to the occurrence of sexual aggression are reviewed. The focus of this chapter has been limited to sexual assaults involving single rather than multiple perpetrators (see O'Sullivan, 1990, for a discussion of gang rape), and to non-incarcerated offenders (see Davis & Leitenberg, 1987, for a review of the research on adjudicated adolescent sexual offenders).

DEFINITIONS

The *Uniform Crime Reports* defines forcible rape as "the carnal knowledge of a female forcibly and against her will. Assaults or attempts to commit rape by force or threat of force are also included; however, statutory rape (without force) and other sex offenses are excluded." Most jurisdictions employ some variation of this definition and include the elements of carnal knowledge, lack of consent, and threat or use of force. Though this definition appears straightforward, it has proven problematic for both the legal system and researchers interested in studying sexual assault. A perpetrator's judgment of what constitutes "force" and the definition of "her will" often differ from the victim's judgment. A wide variety of variables has been found to affect the likelihood that an instance of forced sex will be labeled rape (Goodchilds, Zellman, Johnson, & Giarusso, 1988). In short, the label *rape* is socially constructed (Burkhart & Bohmer, 1990).

In this chapter the focus has been broadened from strict "legal" definitions of rape. Instead, the continuum of sexual aggression from non-violent forms of coercion (i.e., verbal pressure and intimidation) to violent forms is examined. According to Hall (1990), sexual aggression is any form of unwanted sexual contact between a perpetrator and victim. Research has revealed a variety of tactics that men use to obtain sex from an unwilling partner. These include psychological pressure (i.e., threatening to end the relationship; saying things one does not mean, such as falsely professing love, promising marriage), verbal persuasion, verbal threats, use of alcohol and drugs, physical intimidation, mild physical force (pushing, slapping), severe physical force (beating, choking), and displaying or using a weapon (Kanin, 1985; Miller & Marshall, 1987; Yegidis, 1986). There are two primary reasons for considering a continuum of sexual aggression. First, Muehlenhard and Schrag (1991) have observed that lesser degrees of sexual coercion "have a powerful, insidious effect upon women in our society" (p. 115), even though they would not be legally classified as rape. Second, by conceptualizing rape as an extreme form of sexually aggressive behavior, the frequently "hidden" nature of the crime is highlighted and understanding of the similarities are enhanced between men who commit one type of sexual assault and those who commit others.

INCIDENCE AND PREVALENCE

Four sources of data are available that provide indices of the incidence and prevalence of sexual aggression among adolescent males: the *Uniform Crime Reports*, the National Crime Survey, self-reports based on national samples, and self-reports based on convenience samples.

The *Uniform Crime Reports* (FBI, 1978–1988) reflect only instances of reported forcible rape and other sexual offenses. Of all men arrested for forcible rape approximately 19% were under 19 years of age (1981–1988); for other sexual offenses the comparable figure is 20%. A comparison of the number of men aged 13–21 years old who were arrested for forcible rape to the number of male adolescents in the U.S. population from 1978–1988 (U.S. Bureau of Census, 1978–1988) reveals that the rate per 100,000 has averaged 58, with no discernible pattern of increase or decrease from 1978 to 1986, until recently with a decline from 1986 (62) to 1987 (56) to 1988 (52). An average rate of arrests of adolescents for other sexual offenses for the same time period was 120 per 100,000, with a change pattern similar to the rates for forcible rape. Taken together, the *Uniform Crime Reports* data suggest an average of 160 arrests per 100,000 of men aged 13–21 years for forcible rape and other sexual offenses.

The *Uniform Crime Reports* figures do not reflect unreported instances of sexual assault, and rape is known as the least reported and prosecuted crime (Feild & Bienen, 1980). Data from the National Crime Survey was intended to estimate the true magnitude of crimes. The National Crime Survey was based on interviews with a random sample of the population, and thus included instances that did not come to the attention of the criminal justice system. As well, the National Crime Survey is a victimization survey so that the reported characteristics of perpetrators are based on the victim's perception of the perpetrator's age. The percentage of young men perceived to be 12–20 years old committing a forcible rape averaged 17.7% (1978–1987). Therefore, considering the total number of forcible rapes reported each year to the National Crime Survey and the total male adolescent population, the estimated average rate of rape perpetration for males aged 12–20 years is 125 per 100,000 (1980–1987).

Using offender self-report methodology, Ageton (1983) has conducted the only longitudinal study to date using a national probability sample of youth aged 11–17 years, and her study included seven birth cohorts (1959–1965). Based on face-to-face interviews, men were classified as sexually assaultive if they responded positively to questions dealing with the use of pressure, threat, or force to get women to do something sexual they did not want to do. The percentage of men who reported sexually assaultive behaviors was 3.8% in 1978, 2.9% in

1979, and 2.2% in 1980. These data lead to estimated sexual assault rates per 100,000 of 3,800 in 1978, 2,900 in 1979, and 2,200 in 1980. It is true that these figures contain instances that do not meet legal definitions of rape, but it is also clear that they are enormously higher than National Crime Survey data.

Among college men the best estimates of self-reported sexual aggression have been reported by Koss et al. (1987). In an anonymous paper-and-pencil survey of over 3,000 men sampled from 32 institutions nationwide, Koss et al. found 24.5% of the men admitted that since age 14 they had engaged in some form of sexually aggressive behavior. Of the total sample, 4.6% admitted to behaviors that meet the legal definition of rape; this translates to a rate of 4,600 rapes per 100,000 college males. In addition, a further 3.2% admitted to at least one attempted rape; 6.9% reported using verbal pressure to coerce a woman into sexual intercourse; and 9.8% reported using force or the threat of force to obtain sexual contact, such as kissing and fondling.

A number of surveys of nonrandom samples of college men have reported figures comparable to or higher than Koss et al. (1987). Estimates of college men perpetrating rape have consistently ranged from 4%–7% (Aizenman & Kelley, 1988; Koss, Leonard, Beezley, & Oros, 1985; Lisak & Roth, 1988; Muehlenhard & Linton, 1987; Rapaport & Burkhart, 1984, 1987; White & Humphrey, 1990; White, Humphrey, & Farmer, 1989), with estimates of attempted rape averaging 4% (Koss et al., 1987; Lisak & Roth, 1988; White & Humphrey, 1990; White et al., 1989).

Few studies other than Ageton (1983) have examined self-reported sexual assault among adolescents. Lundberg-Love and Geffner (1989) cited unpublished studies in which 2% of the adolescents surveyed admitted to initiating forced sexual contact. Hall and Flannery (1984) surveyed a random sample of young people in Milwaukee aged 14–17 years and found that 12% of the females had been raped or sexually assaulted. They did not report on sexually aggressive behaviors committed by the males in their sample. Most recently, Humphrey and White (1992) found that 25.6% of a sample of college freshmen self-reported various forms of sexual assault during high school (i.e., since age 14). This included 6.4% admitting to rape and 2.0% reporting attempted rape; the remainder committed other forms of sexually aggressive acts. Furthermore, of those who reported sexual assault during high school, 40% admitted to further sexual assault during their first year in college.

In summary, the adolescent arrest rate for forcible rape is estimated at 58 per 100,000 based on *Uniform Crime Reports* data. National Crime Survey reports, on the other hand, suggest that 125 adolescent males per 100,000 commit a forcible rape. Finally, self-reports suggest considerably higher rates. Ageton's (1983) data suggest a rate of 3,000 per 100,000 for various forms of sexual assault among adolescents. The Koss et al. (1987) data suggest that 2,500 young men per 100,000 have attempted rape in a 6-month period and 900 young men per 100,000 completed a rape in a 6-month period (see Koss, 1988).

CHARACTERISTICS OF SEXUALLY
ASSAULTIVE OFFENDERS

Current conceptualizations of the date rapist are multifactored and focus on several levels of analysis. Available evidence indicates that cultural expectations, attitudes, early experiences, peer influences, personality, and needs and motives all affect the likelihood of engaging in sexually aggressive behaviors, in addition to demographic characteristics of the offender and characteristics of the situation. It appears that a number of these factors must be present before sexually assaultive behavior is likely (Koss & Dinero, 1988; Malamuth, 1986, Malamuth, Sockloskie, Koss, & Tanaka, 1991).

We adopt the "embedded" perspective, suggested by Dutton (1988) to organize presentation of factors affecting the likelihood of sexually assaultive behavior. Sexually assaultive behavior is best understood by considering the intrapsychic characteristics of the individual, called the *ontogenetic level*, within a broader context of interactions with three systems. An individual performs a sexually assaultive act in a *microsystem*, which is the dyadic interpersonal context and includes features of the relationship and situation. The interpersonal interaction in turn is embedded in an *exosystem*, which are the social structures that define and direct the meaning of sex and violence, and includes social structures that directly encroach on the young man's daily life, including family, peer relationships, school, and religion. Finally, these social structures are embedded within the *macrosystem*, the larger social context that includes cultural values, norms, and expectations. Essentially, the interplay of these systems—ontogenetic, microsystem, exosystem, and macrosystem—provide the context within which the process of sexual assault occurs. This perspective demands attention to multilevel analyses and raises questions about how cultural values are transmitted to the family and peer group, and how family and peer values in turn affect the behavior of individuals in specific relationships.

Macrosystem

Cultural Values

At the societal level, rape can be seen as a manifestation of gender inequality and as a mechanism for the subordination of women. Sexist attitudes and values, in conjunction with a general acceptance of violence, contribute to rape (Brownmiller, 1975; Clark & Lewis, 1977; Muehlenhard & Shrag, 1991). Rape-supportive attitudes are socially acquired beliefs that function as releasers and can increase the likelihood of sexually aggressive actions (Mahoney, Shively, & Traw, 1986). A number of macro-analytic studies have found relationships among indices of societal values and rape rates, such as between policies controlling gun ownership and hunting, subscription rates for pornographic magazines and rape rates (Baron & Straus, 1991; Linsky, Straus, & Bachman-

Prehn, 1990). However, there are three reasons why the role of attitudes in predicting sexual aggression is problematic. First, analysis at this level fails to explain why some young men rape and some do not, when all are members of the same stressful, sexist, and violent society. Second, most studies tacitly accept the hypothesis that individual behavior is affected by cultural values that support the subordination of women, without specifying the process whereby these values are transmitted to the individual, become internalized, and affect behavior. Third, studies have varied in the specific attitudinal measures used, making comparison across them difficult. Furthermore, some studies have documented a relationship between various attitudes and sexually aggressive behavior, while others have failed to find one (Ageton, 1983). This research is examined in more detail later in the chapter.

Sexual Scripts

A second societal level variable that influences sexual aggression is a society's expectations about adolescent dating rituals. Scripts about sexual expression can support rape when they deprive a woman of her right to say no to further sexual advances, encourage the man to be a sexual stalker and the woman his prey, and hold a woman responsible for the extent of sexual involvement. Jackson (1978) argues that sexual scripts provide the motivations for sexual conduct:

> Sexual desire is not aroused through a simple stimulus-response mechanism but through the attribution of sexual meanings to specific stimuli and desire alone will not produce sexual behavior unless the actor is able to define the situation as one in which such conduct is appropriate. The same scripts which motivate "normal" sexual behavior also provided a potential vocabulary of motives for the rapist. (p. 30)

LaPlante, McCormick, and Brannigan (1980) have provided evidence that traditional scripts dictate that men should use any strategy to induce dates to have sex, and that women should either passively acquiesce or use any strategy to avoid sex. Furthermore, many young women and men are taught that a woman should pretend she means no even when she means yes. Thus, young men are socialized to believe in "male sexual access rights" (Mahoney et al., 1986). In fact, many date rapists report that they did not realize that what they had done was wrong (Parrot, 1989).

Exosystems

Early Familial Experiences

Developmentally focused theories point to one's early learning histories, specifically focusing on socialization within the family. Witnessing and ex-

periencing family violence have been related to sexual aggression (Koss &
Dinero, 1988). Fagot, Loeber, and Reid (1988) hypothesized that male aggression toward women is highly likely for young men reared in families where
female family members were the targets of male aggression and where attitudes
that devalue women prevailed.

Family attitudes toward sexuality and male–female roles also have been
implicated. Ross (1977) suggested that parents socialize sons to initiate sexual
activity and daughters to resist sexual advances. Sexually assaultive behavior in
young men has been related to fathers' attitudes toward sexual aggression
(Kanin, 1985). As well, White and Shuntich (1990) found significant correlations between college men's self-reported sexually aggressive behavior and
reports of their fathers kissing, fondling, and forcing sexual activity with their
mothers against the mothers' wishes.

Early sexual experiences, including sexual victimization, have been found
to be predictive of sexual aggression (Koss & Dinero, 1988; White & Humphrey, 1990). In a series of longitudinal investigations of sexually abused children, Friedrich and colleagues observed a significant positive correlation between sexual victimization and subsequent sexual aggression in boys
(Friedrich, Beilke, & Urquiza, 1988). Early sexual experiences, especially abusive ones, may shape a young man's notion of normal sex. Furthermore, the
psychological consequences of abuse may include lowered self-esteem, another
factor predictive of sexual assault (White & Humphrey, 1990). In addition,
the earlier sexual experiences increase the opportunity for a sexual assault to
occur. That is, the more sexually active the young man, the longer he is active,
and the greater the number of sex partners, the more likely some assaultive
behavior will occur at least once (Kanin, 1967; Koss & Dinero, 1988; Malamuth, 1986; Mahoney et al., 1986; White & Humphrey, 1990).

Peer Group Influences

Peer group socialization has been identified as a powerful predictor of sexually
assaultive behavior. Ageton (1983) found that delinquent peer group association was the single best predictor of sexual assault. Peer group endorsement of
sexual intercourse and forced sexual behavior were predictors of sexual aggression, as was engagement in various other delinquent behaviors. Other data also
implicate the role of peers (Koss & Dinero, 1988; White & Humphrey, 1990).
Ageton observed that a theory of delinquent behavior is fairly adequate to
distinguish sexual assaulters from nonassaulters, but that no theory yet offered
distinguishes assaulters from nonassaulters within a delinquent subculture.
Here is where the consideration of various intrapersonal characteristics may be
most helpful. There may be individual differences in attitudes, personality,
motives for sex and domination, and opportunities for sexual aggression that

explain why young men in similar circumstances differ in the likelihood of committing a sexually aggressive act.

Other Social Institutions

It is clear that family and peer group characteristics play an important role in predicting sexual assault. But there are other social institutions, though less studied, that have been implicated. Ageton (1983) reported that certain indices of school-related functioning, including academic aspirations, current success, and school normlessness, were significantly related to the probability of committing a sexually assaultive act. She suggested that these variables were indicative of a weak commitment to the conventional school setting. Low commitment to social norms has also been studied by White and Humphrey (1990), who found that lower scores on a measure of religious commitment predicted sexual aggression.

Microsystem

Perpetrator–Victim Relationship

The degree of acquaintanceship between a young man and his potential victim appears to determine whether or not a sexual assault will occur, the type of strategy the perpetrator will use, and the likelihood that the assault will end in a completed rape. Most sexual assaults occur among acquaintances rather than among strangers. Koss (1988) reported that 84% of the rapists she surveyed knew their victims; 61% of the rapes occurred on dates; and 84% of the rapes involved one offender. When a young man rapes an acquaintance, he uses less force and it is less likely that he will use a weapon (Koss, Dinero, Seibel, & Cox, 1988).

Several studies indicate that first dates are riskier than later dates (see Muehlenhard & Linton, 1987), though others have suggested that sexual aggression is more likely to occur in long-term relationships (Kirkpatrick & Kanin, 1957; Russell, 1984; Weis & Borges, 1973). It has been found (Belknap, 1989) that a completed rape is more likely in partners who know each other well (55.8%) than among persons who are acquaintances (40.2%). In addition, relationship status affects perceptions of the assault. The greater the degree of acquaintanceship, the less likely people are to judge an instance of forced sexual intercourse to be rape (Goodchilds et al., 1988). Degree of acquaintanceship is often confounded with level of prior intimacy. That is, the longer a couple has been together, the more likely it is that they have had prior sexual relations. And prior intimacy may increase the likelihood of a sexual assault (Kanin, 1970). Prior intimacy may increase the man's belief, as well as that of others, that rape will not really hurt the woman with whom he was previously intimate (Johnson & Jackson, 1988). Similarly, a victim's prior sexual history is often used to justify the man's use of force in dating situations (Goodchilds et al., 1988).

Victim Characteristics

Research on precipitants of rape has focused on victim characteristics, including her character, past sexual history, attractiveness, style of dress, and provocativeness of behavior. Two tacit assumptions appear to underlie such research. First is the assumption that these factors inform one about the woman's interest in, and consent to, engage in sexual activities. Second is that these characteristics are responsible for the perpetrator's behavior. Schwendinger and Schwendinger (1983) argue that such logic treats the victim as a causal agent and fails to examine the roles of oppressive sexist norms that govern a woman's activities:

> From this standpoint there is something in the psychological makeup of rape victims that differentiates them from nonvictims. Under ordinary conditions, therefore, women [are] catalytic agents. . . . Such underlying ideas obviously short-circuit the woman's rights; consequently, the notion of victim-precipitation itself is a naive reflection of male supremacist standards. It is a normative explanation that chiefly relies on the rapist's judgments "She was asking for it" or "She did not resist strongly enough" or "She changed her mind too late." (p. 66)

Various attempts to find a "victim profile" have yielded null, inconclusive, or mixed results. Koss and Dinero (1989) found that rape victims were not different from nonvictimized women on hypothesized critical risk variables. They concluded:

> Although much has been written about the ways that rape is maintained at a societal level by culturally transmitted beliefs and attitudes, the present study, coupled with other work . . . , offers no justification for continuing to focus on gender-role behavior or rape-supportive attitudes as risk factors by which some women are rendered uniquely vulnerable to victimization." (p. 8)

It would be more productive to examine the situational context of sexual assault, including the perpetrator's perceptions of his victim and the situation.

Miscommunication

Sexual scripts for adolescent heterosexual relationships, described above, contain an inherent tension between the man and woman and create the opportunity for miscommunication in heterosexual relationships (Goodchilds et al., 1988; Lundberg-Love & Geffner, 1989; Muehlenhard & Linton, 1987). Scripts govern the behaviors of young women and men in interpersonal interactions. Abbey (1991) stated:

> Most Americans feel uncomfortable discussing sexual intentions and de-
> sires. . . . Consequently, people try to infer sexual intent from indirect verbal and
> nonverbal cues rather than through frank discussion. Such deductive strategies are
> bound to produce frequent errors. (p. 97)

A man may interpret a woman's friendly behavior in a more sexualized way than she intends (Abbey, 1991), may not take her objections to further sexual contact seriously (Check & Malamuth, 1983), and may perceive her rejection as a threat to his manhood (Beneke, 1982). Abbey (1987) found that two-thirds of the students she surveyed believed that on various occasions their friendliness had been perceived as a sexual invitation, with an average number of incidents of misperception being 4.8. Her survey also revealed that most of the misperceptions were brief and noneventful, but some ended in forced sex. Koss (1988) found that 75% of the men who had raped believed that the victims' nonconsent to have sexual intercourse was "not at all clear," while most women surveyed believed their nonconsent was "extremely clear."

Situational Characteristics

Other situational characteristics that affect the likelihood of a sexual assault are those that create the opportunity for sexual activity and contribute to the ambiguity of cues. Victims in Ageton's (1983) adolescent sample cited time of day, location, and offenders' being drunk and sexually excited as the major precipitants of the assault. They did not believe their behavior, dress, or appearance played a role in the assault. From the perspective of the adolescent offender, his sexual arousal and desire for sexual pleasure, the victim's physical build, and her flirting and teasing were the primary reasons for the assault.

According to Belknap (1989), the riskiest season for acquaintance rape is summer (31.3%) and the riskiest time of day is between 6:00 P.M. and midnight. Assaults frequently occur in the victim's home (42.5%), or other locations, such as the man's home, his car (i.e., "parking"), or any secluded place that allows for privacy (Ageton, 1983; Goodchilds et al., 1988; Lott, Reilly, & Howard, 1982; Muehlenhard & Linton, 1987). Women have reported that sexual assault is also likely at parties, especially when alcohol is involved (Muehlenhard & Linton, 1987).

Alcohol and drugs have been implicated frequently in sexual assaults. It is likely that alcohol may serve multiple functions: as a disinhibitor for the male, as an excuse for the male after the fact, and as a strategy to reduce victim resistance (Richardson & Hammock, 1991). Furthermore, alcohol may function as a cue; women who drink might be perceived as "loose" or more interested in sex. One- to two-thirds of rapists and many rape victims have consumed alcohol prior to the rape (Lott et al., 1982; Wilson & Durrenberger, 1982; Wolfe & Baker, 1980). Many young men and women also feel that forced sex is more justifiable if the woman is drunk or "stoned" (Goodchilds et al., 1988).

It is well documented that high school and college students think forced sex is acceptable when the man spends a lot of money on the woman (Goodchilds et al., 1988; Muehlenhard, Friedman, & Thomas, 1985). Muehlenhard and Linton (1987) reported that men who initiate the date, pay all expenses, and drive are more likely to be sexually aggressive. Apparently, a man may feel justified in using force if necessary to obtain sex because of his "investment."

Ontogenetic Level

Demographic Characteristics

The typical image of a rapist, in the United States, derived primarily from crime statistics, is that of a young, black, urban male, often of lower class status. However, data from other sources suggest that this image is misleading. Ageton (1983), and others (Hall & Flannery, 1984; Rouse, 1988), found no significant differences in the incidence or prevalence of sexual assault as a function of race, social class, or place of residence. On the other hand, Koss et al. (1987) in their college sample found that rate of self-reported rape was significantly related to ethnic group and region of the country where attending school, but not related to religion or family income. Rape was reported by 4% of white men, 10% of black men, 7% of Hispanic men, 2% of Asian men, while no Native American men reported committing rape. Given that more black men attend schools in the South, which in general had the highest rape rate, this ethnic-regional confound remains to be sorted out in future research. As well, relationships between rape-supportive attitudes and ethnicity have been reported by a number of investigators (Fischer, 1987; Giacopassi & Dull, 1986; Goodchilds et al., 1988) and these attitudes may affect willingness to self-report.

Attitudes

Sexually aggressive young men more strongly subscribe to traditional sex-role stereotypes (Burt, 1980; Malamuth, 1988; Mosher & Anderson, 1986; Rapaport & Burkhart, 1984) than sexually nonaggressive men. Specific aspects of sex-role stereotypes on which sexually aggressive and nonaggressive men are most likely to differ include the acceptance of male dominance, acceptance of rape-supportive myths, acceptance of interpersonal violence as a strategy for resolving conflicts, and hostility toward women (Koss et al., 1985; Malamuth, 1986, 1988; Malamuth & Ceniti, 1986; Rapaport & Burkhart, 1984, 1987). Sexually aggressive men are more reluctant to view forced sexual relations on a date as rape; rather, rape is judged to be normal and acceptable. They are more likely to perceive a rape victim as seductive and desiring sexual relations, and thus more blameworthy. They are more likely to judge rape to be justifiable under various circumstances (Jenkins & Dambrot, 1987; Koss & Dinero, 1988; Muehlenhard et al., 1985; Muehlenhard & Linton, 1987). Koss et al. (1985) sum it up:

> The more sexually aggressive a man has been, the more likely he was to attribute adversarial qualities to interpersonal relationships, to accept sex-role stereotypes, to believe myths about rape, to feel that rape prevention is a woman's responsibility, and to view as normal an intermingling of aggression and sexuality. (p. 989)

As clear as the attitudinal differences between sexually aggressive and non-aggressive men appear to be, attitudes have not been shown to be adequate predictors of sexually aggressive behavior. That is, though studies find statistically significant relationships between attitudes and sexual aggression, the amount of variance accounted for is small (see Ageton, 1983; Malamuth, 1986, for examples). Two explanations may account for the low explanatory power of attitudes. First, there may be individual differences in the importance of attitudes. For example, Niles and White (1989) found significantly higher correlations between attitudes and self-reported sexual aggression among men for whom the attitudes were highly accessible, while the correlations between attitudes and behavior were lower and nonsignificant among men for whom the attitudes were of low accessibility. Accessibility in this context refers to how likely the attitude will be retrieved automatically from memory and will influence subsequent perceptions and behavior. Second, in addition to attitudes, various other inhibitory and disinhibitory factors (such as personality characteristics, needs, motives, and situational features) are operating. Current research suggests that many of these variables are more powerful predictors than attitudes, and may in fact help shape the attitudes that sexually aggressive men hold.

Antisocial Personality and Behavioral Characteristics

Antisocial tendencies (Malamuth, 1986), low socialization and low responsibility (Rapaport & Burkhart, 1984), nonconformity (Rapaport & Burkhart, 1987), impulsivity (Calhoun, 1990), and self-monitoring (Yescavage & White, 1989) have been correlated with sexual aggression. Other data suggest that sexual aggression is part of a constellation of various antisocial tendencies. For example, Ageton (1983) and Humphrey and White (1992), using adolescent samples, and White et al. (1989), using a college sample, found correlations between reports of sexual aggression and delinquent behaviors, including alcohol and drug use at levels significantly beyond those of sexually nonaggressive men. Of particular interest in this regard are correlations between scores on a hypermasculinity scale and self-reported drug use, aggressive behaviour, danger-ous driving, delinquent behaviour during high school (Mosher & Sirkin, 1984), and a history of sexual aggression (Mosher & Anderson, 1986).

Masculinity and Gender Schema

In general, sexually aggressive men describe themselves in more traditional masculine terms than do sexually nonaggressive men (Koss & Dinero, 1988; Tieger, 1981; White & Humphrey, 1990; see Burke, Stets, & Pirog-Good, 1988, for an exception). White and Humphrey (1990) found that only when in-security accompanied traditional masculinity was sexual aggression predicted. Sexual aggression may overcome emotional insecurity in traditionally masculine males. This finding is consistent with others that report self-esteem to be lower in sexually aggressive than in sexually nonaggressive men (Parrot, 1989; White & Humphrey, 1990).

Quackenbush's (1989) conceptualization of masculinity in gender-sche-matic terms provides a valuable framework. A gender schema serves as a generalized expectancy that selectively organizes and guides, and even biases, perceptions of the world. Individual differences in the use of masculine and feminine schemata as a basis for processing social information should affect behavior. Quackenbush found that men who lacked the feminine gender schema were more sexually aggressive than those who had it. He said these men "lacked the social skills of femininity, which encompass such expressive com-petencies as concern for, and ability to empathize with other persons" (p. 336), and they would rely on social myths in negotiating social interactions, with sexual aggression being one consequence. Abbey (1991) stated that "once males develop a sexual schema about women, they are likely to interpret ambiguous evidence as confirming their pre-existing beliefs" (p. 104). Others too have suggested that sexually aggressive men lack empathy (Deitz, Black-well, Daley, & Bentley, 1982).

Rape Proclivity and Attraction to Sexual Aggression

Sexually aggressive men are likely to find aspects of sexual aggression attractive, to report a likelihood of raping a woman in the future (Malamuth, 1989a, 1989b), and to engage in coercive sexual fantasies (Greendlinger & Byrne, 1987). Malamuth (1989a, 1989b) developed an Attraction to Sexual Aggres-sion Scale and demonstrated that men high on this measure were likely to believe that they might aggress sexually if the fear of punishment and other inhibitory factors were absent. He defined the attraction to sexual aggression construct as the belief that sexual aggression is likely to be a sexually arousing experience to both perpetrators and victims. Studies have shown that sexually aggressive men scored higher on this scale than nonsexually aggressive men.

Furthermore, higher attraction to sexual aggression scores were associated with various attitudes supportive of violence against women. However, not all high scorers had been sexually aggressive. Malamuth found that the difference between men who were highly attracted to sexual aggression but had not aggressed as compared to those who had actually aggressed was due in part to the nonaggressors having had fewer "opportunities" to aggress due to youth and/or inexperience.

Sex and Power Motives

As theories of sexual aggression have moved from psychiatric models to sociocultural models, there has been an accompanying rejection of the notion that sexual assault is a solely sexually motivated act. Rather, it is viewed as a violent act motivated by a need to dominate and control (see Palmer, 1988, for a review of the history of theories of rape). However, recent evidence suggests that the sexual motive may have been rejected prematurely (Palmer, 1988). Some argue that sexual assault is fulfillment of a sexual urge via violent behavior (Ellis, 1989; Shields & Shields, 1983). Others see sexually aggressive actions as extensions of normative heterosexual practices (Jackson, 1978; Russell, 1982, 1984; Weis & Borges, 1973).

Taking a sociobiological perspective, Ellis (1989) has argued that only men whose sex drive and need to control others surpass some threshold have any likelihood of committing sexually aggressive acts. Once that biological threshold is surpassed, the actual commission of the acts will be influenced by the strength of the drives and by various environmental factors, including opportunities and societal sanctions. The stronger the drives, the less effective environmental restraints will be. Ellis notes that research to date has not been able to establish which motive, sex or power, is stronger. However, several studies that have included paper-and-pencil measures of both suggest that the motives other than sex, such as power and anger, are stronger (Lisak & Roth, 1988). Such research has relied on self-reported indices of sexual desires, motives, and frustrations.

Other studies have examined patterns of sexual arousal to depictions of consensual and nonconsensual sex. Much of this work has been limited to the comparison of incarcerated rapists, nonrapists, and other sex offenders. This research has shown consistently that some "normal" males (i.e., those with no known history of sexual aggression) may be aroused by rape stimuli involving adults. Based on a careful examination of this research, Hall (1990) concluded that "diagnosis of sexual deviance solely based on deviant physiological arousal may result in an unacceptably high number of false positives" (p. 232). This does not rule out the possibility that sexual motives contribute something to the likelihood of sexual aggression.

A number of studies have shown that self-reported sexually aggressive college men, and men who score high on attraction to sexual aggression, compared with sexually nonaggressive college men, show higher levels of physiological and self-reported sexual arousal to depictions of forced sex (Malamuth, 1989b; Malamuth, Check, & Briere, 1986; Malamuth, Feshbach, Fera, & Kunath, 1988) and to rape pornography (Rapaport & Burkhart, 1987; Rapaport & Posey, 1990). Rapaport and Posey (1991) stated that "it appears that sexually coercive males, including acquaintance rapists, are generally more sexually arousable, whether to consenting or rape stimuli" (p. 225).

Kanin (1985) reported date rapists have higher sexual expectations than their sexually nonaggressive peers, and though sexually active they remain chronically sexually frustrated. This frustration may disinhibit aggression as a tactic to achieve sexual fulfillment. Findings of a relationship between dominance as a motive for sex and sexual aggression (Malamuth, 1988; White, et al., 1989) are not inconsistent with Kanin's claim. It is possible that men who engage in sexual behavior because of the feelings of power and control are more likely to use force when other tactics fail. Recently, White et al. (1989) reported that sexually aggressive men scored higher than nonaggressive men on motives other than dominance, including conformity, recognition, hedonism, and novelty.

CONCLUSION

The levels of analysis approach suggests that various factors combine during the life of a young man to increase the risk of sexual aggression. Familial and peer group attitudes and behaviors that condone violence as an interpersonal strategy and that degrade women appear to be important. Acceptance of the male sex role and accompanying sexual scripts that govern the dating game encourage the misinterpretation of women's behaviors, justify the use of force in sexual interactions, and trivialize the consequences of sexual assault for the victim. The features of a typical date—the man initiating the date, paying all expenses, and providing transportation, and the use of intoxicants, the couple being alone, kissing and/or petting, and lack of open communication about sexual intentions—are conducive to acquaintance sexual assault. Such a perspective suggests a multilevel intervention strategy (see Rozee, Batemen, & Gilmore, 1991, for recommendations).

There are three general impressions one retains from the material reviewed in this chapter. First is that the causation of sexual aggression is multifactorial and there will never be a simple answer to the question "Why do men rape?" Second is the notable lack of data on adolescent sexual aggression in community- and school-based samples, in spite of convincing evidence that sexual aggression is occurring with great frequency. Third is the almost total absence of longitudinal or prospective data that will be necessary to sustain causal arguments about the genesis of sexual aggression.

It is heartening to see the growth in research on sexual aggression among acquaintances, which is a topic that was virtually unstudied prior to the 1980s. Now that much descriptive data have proliferated, it seems a good point in the development of the field to suggest that researchers turn more of their attention toward adolescents and younger children. These potential research participants are in the active period of sexual socialization and closer to the traumatic experiences that have been linked to aggressive adult outcomes. There is great need to improve the data base on adolescents including prevalence data on sexual aggression, descriptive characteristics of the incidents that occur during junior high and high school, and measurement of those variables with predictive power for adult sexually aggressive behavior.

In this review we have described the levels of analysis and specific variables that appear promising. Research on adolescents will not be an easy task given the institutional barriers that block research access to adolescents and our society's discomfort with children's sexuality. We can only hope that some will be encouraged to try.

REFERENCES

Abbey, A. (1987). Misperceptions of friendly behavior as sexual interest: A survey of naturally occurring incidents. *Psychology of Women Quarterly, 11*, 173–194.

Abbey, A. (1991). Misperceptions as an antecedent of acquaintance rape: A consequence of ambiguity in communication between women and men. In A. Parrot & L. Bechhofer (Eds.), *Acquaintance rape: The hidden crime* (pp. 96–112). New York: Wiley.

Ageton, S. (1983). *Sexual assault among adolescents.* Lexington, MA: Lexington Books.

Aizenman, M., & Kelley, G. (1988). The incidence of violence and acquaintance rape in dating relationships among college men and women. *Journal of College Student Development, 29*, 305–311.

Baron, L., & Straus, M. A. (1991). *Four theories of rape in American society.* New Haven: Yale University Press.

Belknap, J. (1989). The sexual victimization of unmarried women by nonrelative acquaintances. In M. A. Pirog-Good & J. E. Stets (Eds.), *Violence in dating relationships: Emerging social issues* (pp. 205–218). New York: Praeger.

Beneke, T. (1982). *Men who rape.* New York: St. Martin's Press.

Brownmiller, S. (1975). *Against our will: Men, women, and rape.* New York: Simon & Schuster.

Burke, P. J., Stets, J. E., & Pirog-Good, M. A. (1988). Gender identity, self-esteem, and physical and sexual abuse in dating relationships. *Social Psychology Quarterly, 51*, 272–285.

Burkhart, B., & Bohmer, C. (1990). Hidden rape and the legal crucible: Analysis and implications of epidemiological, social, and legal factors. *The Expert Witness, the Trial Lawyer, the Trial Judge, 5*, 3–6.

Burt, M. R. (1980). Cultural myths and supports for rape. *Journal of Personality and Social Psychology, 38*, 217–230.

Calhoun, K. (1990, March). *Lies, sex, and videotapes: Studies in sexual aggression.* Presidential address, presented at the Southeastern Psychological Association, Atlanta.

Check, J. V. P., & Malamuth, N. M. (1983). Sex role stereotyping and reactions to depictions of stranger versus acquaintance rape. *Journal of Personality and Social Psychology, 45,* 344–356.

Clark, L., & Lewis, D. (1977). *Rape: The price of coercive sexuality.* Toronto: Woman's Press.

Davis, G. E., & Leitenberg, H. (1987). Adolescent sex offenders. *Psychological Bulletin, 101,* 417–427.

Deitz, S. R., Blackwell, K. T., Daley, P. C., & Bentley, B. J. (1982). Measurement of empathy toward rape victims and rapists. *Journal of Personality and Social Psychology, 43,* 372–384.

Dutton, D. (1988). *The domestic assault of women: Psychological and criminal justice perspectives.* New York: Allyn & Bacon.

Ellis, L. (1989). *Theories of rape: Inquiries into the causes of sexual aggression.* New York: Hemisphere.

Fagot, B. I., Loeber, R., & Reid, J. B. (1988). Developmental determinants of male-to-female aggression. In G. W. Russell (Ed.), *Violence in intimate relationships* (pp. 91–105). New York: PMA.

Federal Bureau of Investigation. (1978–1988). *Crime in the United States: Uniform crime reports.* Washington, DC: U.S. Deptartment of Justice.

Feild, H. S., & Bienen, L. B. (1980). *Jurors and rape: A study in psychology and law.* Lexington, MA: Heath.

Fischer, G. J. (1987). Hispanic and majority student attitudes toward forcible date rape as a function of differences in attitudes toward women. *Sex Roles, 17,* 93–101.

Friedrich, W. N., Beilke, R. L., & Urquiza, A. J. (1988). Behavior problems in young sexually abused boys: A comparison study. *Journal of Interpersonal Violence, 3,* 21–28.

Giacopassi, D. J., & Dull, R. (1986). Gender and racial differences in the acceptance of rape myths within a college population. *Sex Roles, 15,* 63–75.

Goodchilds, J. D., Zellman, G. L., Johnson, P. B., & Giarrusso, R. (1988). Adolescents and their perceptions of sexual interactions. In A. W. Burgess (Ed.), *Rape and sexual assault,* (Vol. 2, pp. 245–270). New York: Garland.

Greendlinger, V., & Byrne, D. (1987). Coercive sexual fantasies of college men as predictors of self-reported likelihood to rape and overt sexual aggression. *Journal of Sex Research, 23,* 1–11.

Hall, E. R., & Flannery, P. J. (1984). Prevalence and correlates of sexual assault experiences in adolescents. *Victimology, 9,* 398–406.

Hall, G. C. (1990). Prediction of sexual aggression. *Clinical Psychology Review, 10,* 229–245.

Humphrey, J. A., & White, J. W. (1992, November). *Perpetration of sexual assault: Social psychological predictors.* Paper presented at American Society of Criminology, New Orleans, LA.

Jackson, S. (1978). The social context of rape: Sexual scripts and motivation. *Women's Studies International Quarterly, 1,* 27–38.

Jenkins, M. J., & Dambrot, F. H. (1987). The attribution of date rape: Observer's attitudes and sexual experiences and the dating situation. *Journal of Applied Social Psychology, 17,* 875–895.

Johnson, J. D., & Jackson, L. A. (1988). Assessing the effects of factors that might underlie the differential perception of acquaintance and stranger rape. *Sex Roles, 19,* 37–45.

Kanin, E. J. (1967). Reference groups and sex conduct norm violations. *Sociological Quarterly, 8,* 495–504.

Kanin, E. J. (1970). Sexual aggression by college men. *Medical Aspects of Human Sexuality, 4,* 25–40.

Kanin, E. J. (1985). Date rapists: Differential sexual socialization and relative deprivation. *Archives of Sexual Behavior, 14,* 218–232.

Kirkpatrick, C., & Kanin, E. J. (1957). Male sex aggression on a university campus. *American Sociological Review, 22,* 52–58.

Koss, M. P. (1988). Hidden rape: Sexual aggression and victimization in a national sample of students in higher education. In A. W. Burgess (Ed.), *Rape and sexual assault,* (Vol. 2, pp. 3–25). New York: Garland.

Koss, M. P., & Dinero, T. E. (1988). Predictors of sexual aggression among a national sample of male college students. In R. A. Prentky & V. L. Quinsey (Eds.), *Human sexual aggression: Current perspectives* (pp. 133–147). New York: New York Academy of Sciences.

Koss, M. P., & Dinero, T. E. (1989). Discriminant analysis of risk factors for sexual victimization among a national sample of college women. *Journal of Consulting and Clinical Psychology, 57,* 242–250.

Koss, M. P., Dinero, T. E., Seibel, C. A., & Cox, S. L. (1988). Stranger and acquaintance rape: Are there differences in the victim's experience? *Psychology of Women Quarterly, 12,* 1–24.

Koss, M. P., Gidycz, C. A., & Wisniewski, N. (1987). The scope of rape: Incidence and prevalence of sexual aggression and victimization in a national sample of higher education students. *Journal of Consulting and Clinical Psychology, 55,* 162–170.

Koss, M. P., Leonard, K. E., Beezley, D. A., & Oros, C. J. (1985). Nonstranger sexual aggression: A discriminant analysis of the psychological characteristics of undetected offenders. *Sex Roles, 12,* 981–992.

Laplante, M. N., McCormick, N., & Brannigan, G. G. (1980). Living the sexual script: College students' views of influence in sexual encounters. *Journal of Sex Research, 16,* 338–355.

Linsky, A. S., Straus, M., & Bachman-Prehn, R. (1990). *Social stress and the cultural context of rape in the United States.* Paper presented at the International Conference on Social Stress Research, London.

Lisak, D., & Roth, S. (1988). Motivational factors in nonincarcerated sexually aggressive men. *Journal of Personality and Social Psychology, 55,* 795–802.

Lott, B., Reilly, M. E., & Howard, D. R. (1982). Sexual assault and harassment: A campus community case study. *Signs, 8,* 296–319.

Lundberg-Love, P., & Geffner, R. (1989). Date rape: Prevalence, risk factors, and a proposed model. In M. A. Pirog-Good & J. E. Stets (Eds.), *Violence in dating relationships: Emerging issues* (pp. 169–184). New York: Praeger.

Mahoney, E. R., Shively, M. D., & Traw, M. (1986). Sexual coercion and assault: Male socialization and female risk. *Sexual Coercion and Assault, 1,* 2–8.

Malamuth, N. M. (1986). Predictors of naturalistic sexual aggression. *Journal of Personality and Social Psychology, 50*, 953–962.

Malamuth, N. M. (1988). A multidimensional approach to sexual aggression: Combining measures of past behavior and present likelihood. In R. A. Prentky & V. L. Quinsey (Eds.), *Human sexual aggression: Current perspectives* (pp. 123–132). New York: New York Academy of Sciences.

Malamuth, N. M. (1989a). The attraction to sexual aggression scale: Part one. *Journal of Sex Research, 26*, 26–49.

Malamuth, N. M. (1989b). The attraction to sexual aggression scale: Part two. *Journal of Sex Research, 26*, 324–354.

Malamuth, N. M., & Ceniti, J. (1986). Repeated exposure to violent and nonviolent pornography: Likelihood of raping ratings and laboratory aggression against women. *Aggressive Behavior, 12*, 129–137.

Malamuth, N. M., Check, J. V. P., & Briere, J. (1986). Sexual arousal in response to aggression: Ideological, aggressive, and sexual correlates. *Journal of Personality and Social Psychology, 50*, 330–340.

Malamuth, N. M., Feshbach, S., Fera, T., & Kunath, J. (1988). Aggressive cues and sexual arousal to erotica. In G. W. Russell (Ed.), *Violence in intimate relationships* (pp. 239–251). New York: PMA.

Malamuth, N. M., Sockloskie, R. J., Koss, M. P., & Tanaka, J. S.(1991). Characteristics of aggressors against women: Testing a model using a national sample of college students. *Journal of Consulting and Clinical Psychology, 59*, 670–681.

Miller, B., & Marshall, J. C. (1987). Coercive sex on the university campus. *Journal of College Student Personnel, 28*, 38–47.

Mosher, D. L., & Anderson, R. D. (1986). Macho personality, sexual aggression, and reactions to guided imagery of realistic rape. *Journal of Research in Personality, 20*, 77–94.

Mosher, D. L., & Sirkin, M. (1984). Measuring a macho personality constellation. *Journal of Research in Personality, 18*, 150–163.

Muehlenhard, C. L., Friedman, D. E., & Thomas, C. M. (1985). Is date rape justifiable? The effects of dating activity, who initiated, who paid, and men's attitudes toward women. *Psychology of Women Quarterly, 9*, 297–309.

Muehlenhard, C. L., & Linton, M. A. (1987). Date rape and sexual aggression in dating situations: Incidence and risk factors. *Journal of Counselling Psychology, 34*, 186–196.

Muehlenhard, C., & Schrag, J. (1991). Nonviolent sexual coercion. In A. Parrot & L. Bechhofer (Eds.), *Acquaintance rape: The hidden crime* (pp. 115–128). New York: Wiley.

National Crime Survey. (1978–1987). *Criminal victimization in the United States.* Washington, DC: U.S. Department of Justice, Bureau of Statistics.

Niles, P. L., & White, J. W. (1989, March). *Correlates of sexual aggression and their accessibility.* Paper presented at the Southeastern Psychological Association meeting, Washington, DC.

O'Sullivan, C. S. (1991). Acquaintance gang rape on campus. In A. Parrot & L. Bechhofer (Eds.), *Acquaintance rape: The hidden crime* (pp. 140–156). New York: Wiley.

Palmer, C. T. (1988). Twelve reasons why rape is not sexually motivated: A skeptical examination. *Journal of Sex Research, 25*, 512–530.

Parrot, A. (1989). Acquaintance rape among adolescents: Identifying risk groups and intervention strategies. Special Issue: Adolescent sexuality: New challenges for social work. *Journal of Social Work and Human Sexuality, 8,* 47–61.

Quackenbush, R. L. (1989). A comparison of androgynous, masculine sex-typed, and undifferentiated males on dimensions of attitudes toward rape. *Journal of Research in Personality, 23,* 318–342.

Rabkin, J. G. (1979). The epidemiology of forcible rape. *American Journal of Orthopsychiatry, 49,* 634–647.

Rapaport, K., & Burkhart, B. R. (1984). Personality and attitudinal characteristics of sexually coercive college males. *Journal of Abnormal Psychology, 93,* 216–221.

Rapaport, K., & Burkhart, B. R. (1987). *Male aggression symposium: Responsiveness to rape depictions.* Paper presented at the Society for the Scientific Study of Sex, Atlanta, GA.

Rapaport, K. R., & Posey, C. D. (1991). Sexually coercive college males. In A. Parrot & L. Bechhofer (Eds.), *Acquaintance rape: The hidden crime* (pp. 217–228). New York: Wiley.

Richardson, D., & Hammock, G. (1991). The role of alcohol in acquaintance rape. In A. Parrot & L. Bechhofer (Eds.), *Acquaintance rape: The hidden crime* (pp. 83–95). New York: Wiley.

Ross, V. M. (1977). Rape as a social problem: A byproduct of the feminist movement. *Social Problems. 25,* 75–89.

Rouse, L. P. (1988). Abuse in dating relationships: A comparison of blacks, whites, and Hispanics. *Journal of College Student Development, 29,* 312–319.

Rozee, P., Bateman, P., & Gilmore, T. (1991). The personal perspective: How to avoid acquaintance rape. In A. Parrot & L. Bechhofer (Eds.), *Acquaintance rape: The hidden crime* (pp. 337–354). New York: Wiley.

Russell, D. E. H. (1982). *Rape in marriage.* New York: Macmillan.

Russell, D. E. H. (1984). *Sexual exploitation: Rape, child sexual abuse, and workplace harrassment.* Beverly Hills, CA: Sage.

Schwendinger, J. R., & Schwendinger, H. (1983). *Rape and inequality.* Beverly Hills, CA: Sage.

Shields, W. M., & Shields, L. M. (1983). Forcible rape: An evolutionary perspective. *Ethology and Sociobiology, 4,* 115–136.

Straus, M., Gelles, R., & Smith, C. (1989). *Physical violence in American families: Risk factors and adaptations to violence in 8,145 families.* New Brunswick, NJ: Transaction.

Tieger, T. (1981). Self-rated likelihood of raping and the social perception of rape. *Journal of Research in Personality, 15,* 147–158.

U.S. Bureau of Census. (1978–1988). Current population reports. 1978 (Series P-20, No. 336); 1979 (Series P-20, No. 350); 1980–1988 (Series P-25, No. 1045). Washington, DC: U.S. Government Printing Office.

Weis, K., & Borges, S. S. (1973). Victimology and rape: The case of the legitimate victim. *Issues in Criminology, 8,* 71–115.

White, C., & Shuntich, R. (1990, March). *Some relationships between the father's approach to sexuality and the son's propensity to date rape.* Paper presented at Southeastern Psychological Association, Atlanta.

White, J. W., & Humphrey, J. A. (1990, March). *A theoretical model of sexual assault: An empirical test.* Paper presented at symposium on Sexual Assault: Research,

Treatment, and Education. Southeastern Psychological Association meeting, Atlanta, GA.

White, J. W., Humphrey, J. A., & Farmer, R. (1989, March). *Anti-social behavioral correlates of self-reported sexual aggression.* Paper presented at the Southeastern Psychological Association, Washington, DC.

Wilson, W., & Durrenberger, R. (1982). Comparison of rape and attempted rape victims. *Psychological Reports, 50,* 198.

Wolfe, J., & Baker, V. (1980). Characteristics of imprisoned rapists and circumstances of the rape. In C. Warner (Ed.), *Rape and sexual assault: Management and intervention* (pp. 265–278). London: Aspen.

Yegidis, B. L. (1986). Date rape and other forced sexual encounters among college students. *Journal of Sex Education and Therapy, 12,* 51–54.

Yescavage, K. M., & White, J. W. (1989, March). *Relating self-monitoring and sexual aggression.* Paper presented at the Southeastern Psychological Association, Washington, DC.

Yllo, K., & Finkelhor, D. (1988). *Stopping family violence: Research priorities for the coming decade.* Newbury Park, CA: Sage.

CHAPTER 10

The Relationship Between Substance Use and Abuse and Sexual Offending in Adolescents

Lynn O. Lightfoot
Howard E. Barbaree

T he relationship between alcohol and other drug use and aggressive and sexual behavior has been the subject of much debate and conjecture. Substance use has consistently been found to be highly related to a wide variety of violent criminal behaviors in men (Bartholomew, 1968; Blum & Braunstein, 1967; Nicol, Gunn, Gristwood, Fogg, & Watson, 1973; Pernanen, 1976; Chaiken & Chaiken, 1982; Hodgins & Lightfoot, 1988; Lightfoot & Hodgins, 1988; Ross & Lightfoot, 1987). Studies of adult offenders have frequently found that more severe offenses tend to follow drug use, particularly alcohol use (Pernanen, 1976). Although the evidence regarding the strength of the relationship is mixed, alcohol use has been found to be particularly associated with sexual offenses, including rape and pedophilia (Amir, 1971; Gebhard, Gagnon, Pomeroy, & Christenson, 1965; Rada, 1975; Selling, 1940; Shupe, 1954; Johnson, Gibson, & Linden, 1978). Despite this consistent picture of a positive relationship, some have argued that this does not necessarily indicate that drugs or alcohol cause violence or crime. Rather, it is argued, the relationship is a spurious one due to the high rate of substance use and abuse in antisocial individuals.

Substance use and abuse is also highly prevalent in delinquent youth (Elliott & Huizinga, 1984; Hawkins, Lishner, Jensen, & Catalano, 1987; Hartstone & Hansen, 1984; Walters, Reinarman, & Fagan, 1985), and is one of the factors that contributes to a diagnosis of Conduct Disorder (Bornstein, Schuldberg, & Bornstein, 1987). Although controversial, there is increasing speculation by some that substance use may be a significant factor in sex offending by some adolescents (Vinogradov, Dishotsky, Doty, & Tinklenberg, 1988; Tinklenberg & Woodrow, 1974; Tinklenberg, Murphy, Murphy, & Pfefferbaum, 1981). In order to explore this relationship, in this chapter we first define and describe current perspectives on substance use and abuse in adolescents. We then describe experimental and descriptive studies which examine the effects of substance use on both aggressive and sexual behaviors and examine the evidence that links substance abuse to delinquency and to sex offending in adolescents. We end by discussing the implications of this association between substance abuse and sexual offenses for future research and for the treatment of adolescent sexual offenders.

DEFINING SUBSTANCE ABUSE

The third revised edition of the *Diagnostic and Statistical Manual of Mental Disorders* (DSM III-R) (American Psychiatric Association, 1987) distinguishes between substance abuse and dependence in adults. Substance abuse is defined as a pattern of pathological use that causes an impairment in social or occupational functioning that lasts for at least a month. A diagnosis of substance dependence requires, in addition to the above, evidence of tolerance or withdrawal symptoms upon cessation of use. DSM-III-R also describes four possible courses of the disorder, including continuous, episodic, in remission, or unspecified. No distinction is made however, between adult substance abuse disorders and those observed in childhood and adolescence. Some would argue that any use of a substance by a child or adolescent should be considered abuse. However, North American surveys have consistently demonstrated that experimentation with substances, particularly alcohol, tobacco, and marijuana, is still a normative rather than pathological behavior in adolescence and is associated with the normal developmental process of individuation and separation from the family (e.g., Jessor & Jessor, 1977; Johnston, O'Malley, & Bachman, 1985; Miller et al., 1983; Smart & Adlaf, 1989). At present there is little agreement as to the diagnostic criteria for identification of adolescents whose alcohol or drug use constitutes a disorder requiring treatment (Institute of Medicine, 1990). However, there is some agreement that substance dependence is multidimensional and that dependence problems vary in severity. As a result, classification schemas have been proposed for adolescents that address the differences between the infrequent user, the experimental user, recreational user, and the chronic habitual or addicted user (George & Skinner, 1991). Thus, although most adolescents indicate some use of alcohol, tobacco, and marijuana, few adolescents engage in regular use more than one to two times per month. Use of hallucinogens, stimulants, inhalants, and opioids is relatively uncommon (Smart & Jansen, 1991).

ALCOHOL, DRUGS, AND AGGRESSIVE BEHAVIOR

As Collins (1981) and others have noted, there is a long history of inferring a causal link between alcohol consumption and violent criminal behavior. The early work of the 19th-century criminologist Lombroso (1968) reflects his belief that alcohol is an important cause of assaultive crime:

> Alcohol, then, is a cause of crime, first, because many commit crime in order to obtain drinks, further, because men sometimes drink the courage necessary to commit crime, or an excuse for their misdeeds; again, because it is by the aid of drink that young men are drawn into crime; and because the drink shop is the place for meeting of accomplices, where they not only plan their crimes but also squander their gains . . . it appears that alcoholism occurred oftenest in the case of those charged with assaults, sexual offenses, and insurrections. (pp. 95–96)

In his writing, Lombroso was not clear about how drinking exerts its criminogenic influence, and we are still unable to be very specific about how alcohol, or for that matter drugs, exert their influence on aggressive and violent behavior in humans. However, it is fair to say that we now recognize that the influence of alcohol on aggressive behavior is a complex phenomenon, and is not a simple or straightforward relationship.

EPIDEMIOLOGICAL LITERATURE

The epidemiological literature on the link between alcohol and violence has found consistently that alcohol use is prevalent among perpetrators of violent crime. This finding obtains whether one examines event-based literature (e.g., police, court records), or if one interviews incarcerated offenders. The crimes most frequently involving alcohol abuse are homicide, forcible rape, and aggravated assault. Shupe (1954) examined urine or blood samples for persons arrested immediately after commission of alleged felonies and found alcohol was present in 82% of assaults or homicides: 25 of 30 murders, 92 of 100 assaults, and 27 of 33 nonfatal shootings. Wolfgang (1958) reviewed 588 cases of homicide in Philadelphia over a 4-year period and found that alcohol was present in either victim, offender, or both in 64% of cases. Similarly, Mayfield

(1976), in a study of 307 convicted assaultive offenders, found that 58% were "not sober" at the time of the crime. Chaiken and Chaiken (1982) found that 83% of violent offenders were taking drugs daily in the month prior to their offense. Lightfoot and Hodgins (1988) found that 80% of incarcerated offenders reported being under the influence of at least one substance when they committed their index offense. MacDonald (1961) reviewed ten studies of homicide offenders and found a range of 19%–83% of cases in which alcohol was involved (mode = 50%–60%). In the case of rape, estimates of alcohol use among the perpetrators range from 34% (Amir, 1967), to 50% (Christie, Marshall, & Lanthier, 1979), to 72% (Johnson et al., 1978). Of course, the use of alcohol by perpetrators of violent crime does not mean that alcohol intoxication per se caused the crime. However, these findings are suggestive, and other research has explored possible mechanisms in a causal link between alcohol and violence.

THEORETICAL MODELS

Although, as noted earlier, the associations between alcohol and aggression is well established in the literature, there is little agreement about how alcohol exerts its effects on behavior. Several theoretical models have been proposed, and most identify biological, psychological, and social components. Major disagreements stem primarily from the relative weight assigned to each of these components in producing aggressive behavior.

According to biological theorists, alcohol directly causes aggressive behavior as a result of the pharmacological effects of the drug on the brain. Psychological theorists, on the other hand, explain the effects of alcohol on aggression as indirect, resulting from the effects of alcohol on cognition and affect. Some of these well-documented effects include increased arousal levels and emotional lability. A subtype of psychological theories includes anxiety reduction and power motivation theories. According to these theories, drinking can be motivated by a desire to reduce anxiety, which may be associated with an increase in aggressive behavior. McClelland is responsible for the power motivation view of alcohol use, which postulates that men drink to feel stronger and more powerful (McClelland, Davis, Kalin, & Wanner, 1972). Social-cultural theorists contend that in many societies drinking situations are culturally agreed upon time-out periods where violence and other antisocial behaviors are tolerated. Interactionist theories, on the other hand, contend that aggressive behavior occurs as a result of an interaction between biological psychological and/or sociocultural variables. In this framework, alcohol increases the probability of violence in individuals depending on their psychological status when in particular sociocultural situations. In the section that follows, we examine experimental evidence for each of these perspectives in turn.

THE BIOLOGICAL PERSPECTIVES: CHEMICAL DISINHIBITION THEORY

It has generally been assumed that, because alcohol depresses the socalled higher brain centers before affecting the lower more primitive brain centers, that alcohol affects moral reasoning and judgment. Under the influence of alcohol, it is said, inhibitions are released, resulting in that well-known spectrum of drunken behavior that characterizes intoxicated individuals. In a seminal text on drug effects, Jacobs and Fehr (1987) have summarized the effects of alcohol on humans. Large individual variations in drunken behavior occur in the low to moderately high range of blood alcohol concentrations (.03–.25 mg/%). Some individuals become extremely gregarious and their mood is euphoric, while others become morose or withdrawn, and wide swings in mood and aggressive behavior may become evident. These individual differences appear to be related to a wide variety of factors including the drinker's mood before beginning drinking, his or her expectations, the setting, the extent of individual tolerance, the behavior of others, and past learning experiences (Jacobs & Fehr, 1987).

THE SOCIOCULTURAL PERSPECTIVE

While the Lapps of northern Finland and the Scots engage in periodic binges during which they may become aggressive, the Camba of Bolivia, who are described as heavy binge drinkers, do not become aggressive but rather the drinking binges appear to act as "time-out periods" from tedious daily labor (MacAndrew & Edgerton, 1969). These data and other cross-cultural studies suggest that the cultural meanings and the expected effects of drinking affect the individual's expression of violent behavior while intoxicated. In addition, social structure and social control influence an individual's behavior while drinking. Drunken brawling is more common in loosely organized societies with relatively powerless leaders, but is uncommon in highly structured societies with clearly defined roles and status, and where there is an emphasis on authority and respect in interpersonal relationships (Ahlstrom-Laakso, 1976; MacAndrew & Edgerton, 1969). It is clear that attitudes toward alcohol and drug use and abuse, and the rules that govern behavior after the ingestion of a particular substance, are variable across cultures, subcultures, and social settings. Thus, individuals growing up in cultures where violence is the expected normative behavior following the ingestion of a substance learn the norm as well as the cultural rules prescribing how, where, and with whom that behavior is to be expressed (Heath, 1976).

While there is this variability in drug effects across cultures, it is clear that the variability could easily be exaggerated. Mayfield (1976) has argued that the extreme sociological perspective would lead to the conclusion that assaultive behavior could just as well result from lemonade, were it consumed in the right setting and embellished with the appropriate beliefs, rituals, and societal expectations as is the case for alcohol. Although the frequency and expression of alcohol-related assaults vary widely across cultures, the relationship between alcohol and aggression seems to be somewhat consistent across time and place. The psychopharmacological properties of alcohol clearly have a causal role to play in violent, aggressive behavior. In the experimental literature on animals, although there are problems from study to study in the lack of precise definitions of the terms *aggression*, *violence*, and *addiction*, some generalizations are possible. In most studies, amphetamine, phencyclidine, and alcohol at low to moderate doses seem to increase certain "attack" and threat behaviors, while at intermediate to higher doses, a sedating effect is usually seen, and cannabis (THC) and the opiates are usually found to suppress aggressive behavior (Alioto, 1984; Taylor et al., 1976; Tinklenberg et al., 1981).

THE PSYCHOLOGICAL PERSPECTIVE

Experimental studies of human subjects have used two research paradigms which bear description here. In the laboratory, direct physical aggression has been studied using a teacher–learner task (Buss, 1961), or a reaction time task (Taylor, 1967). In the learning task, subjects are required to "teach" a confederate of the experimenter by providing feedback for incorrect responses. Feedback is delivered by electric shocks that the subject controls in terms of their frequency and sometimes intensity. Aggression is measured as increases in the intensity or frequency of shocks set after some experimental manipulation, say, the confederate's insulting the subject or the subject being administered an alcoholic beverage.

In the balanced placebo design (Marlatt & Rohsenow, 1980), subjects are randomly divided in half, with one-half designated to receive an alcohol beverage and the other half to receiving an nonalcoholic beverage. Then each group is again randomly split, with half of each group told the beverage will contain alcohol and the other half told the beverage will not contain alcohol. Therefore, when examining the eventual effects of the beverages on performance, the effects of alcohol intoxication can be separated from the effects of the alcohol expectancy.

Experimental studies with humans indicate that alcohol is a potent causal antecedent of aggressive behavior; however, it is neither a sufficient nor a necessary cause. For example, although subjects on average perform more aggressively the higher the dose of alcohol, some intoxicated subjects never set intense shocks (Boyatzis, 1974; Taylor & Leonard, 1983). When conditions are "nonthreatening," intoxicated subjects were not found to inflict more pain on an opponent that were nonintoxicated subjects (Boyatzis, 1974, 1977). Even when provoked by having an opponent deliver high shock, intoxicated men are responsive to social pressure to reduce the severity of their aggressive behavior (Sears, 1977, cited in Taylor, 1983). These studies suggest that alcohol increases one's preparedness to aggress (Boyatzis, 1974) or decreases the threshold for aggression (Moyer, 1971), but that additional factors are required to elicit violent behavior. It also seems from these studies that alcohol increases the perception or attribution of threat, such that intoxicated subjects expect more aggression than nonintoxicated subjects.

Consistent with numerous studies in the literature, Taylor and Leonard (1983) found that intoxicated subjects consistently behaved more aggressively than subjects who received either placebo, or a no-beverage group, with higher doses producing higher levels of aggression. However, it is not clear that alcohol intoxication per se is solely responsible. For example, subjects who received distilled spirits rather than beer demonstrated more aggression despite having comparable blood alcohol levels (Takala, Pihkanen, & Markkanen, 1957). In this same study, alcohol placebo was found to produce more aggressive behavior than beer placebo or beer. For these and other reasons, the effects of expectancy have been much discussed in the psychological literature.

Bushman and Cooper (1990) recently conducted a meta-analysis of the effects of alcohol on human aggression. Thirty experimental studies that used between subject designs with male social drinkers were included in the main meta analysis. They found a significant average effect size for alcohol versus no alcohol (.25) and for alcohol versus placebo (.61). These effect sizes are significantly greater than zero and are comparable to the effect sizes reported for other independent variables in aggression research. These findings led them to assert that "alcohol does indeed cause aggressive behavior" (p. 348). However, they also found that when the effects of antiplacebo (told no alcohol/given alcohol) are compared to control conditions, the average effect size is .06 and is not significantly different from zero. They then assert "there is little support for the hypothesis that alcohol *directly* affects aggression." Similarly placebo versus control conditions yielded an average effect of .10, which was not significantly greater than zero, indicating that the "pure" psychological expectancy of alcohol does not increase aggressive behavior. These authors guardedly concluded that the physiological and psychological effects must occur together for alcohol to cause aggression.

In summary, a large number of variables, only some of which have been discussed here, are hypothesized to be links between the ingestion of alcohol and violent behavior. Collins (1981) suggested that two major psychological variables, specifically an overt style of exercising personal power and a culturally based belief in the aggression-producing properties of alcohol, interact with the physiological effects of alcohol on human cognition to increase the likelihood that interpersonal violence will occur after drinking.

ALCOHOL AND SEXUAL AROUSAL

The effects of alcohol use on sexual behavior received little attention until the 1970s. In 1981, Wilson reviewed this literature and drew the following conclusions. In general, there is a negative linear relationship between alcohol dose and penile tumescence. Men generally believe, however, that alcohol has no influence on their arousal level or that they become more aroused when consuming alcohol than when sober. At low doses, males who consume alcohol or who believe that they have consumed alcohol show increased sexual arousal to erotic stimuli and devote more attention to sexual stimuli than when they are sober.

Briddell et al. (1978) assigned male social drinkers to one of four conditions in a balanced placebo design. Penile tumescence was recorded while subjects listened to three tape recordings of erotic narratives. The taped narratives described mutually enjoyable heterosexual intercourse, forcible rape, and nonsexual sadistic aggression. Subjects who believed that they had consumed alcohol experienced greater levels of penile tumescence than subjects who believed that they were sober. While there were no significant effects of alcohol per se, subjects who believed that they had consumed alcohol had arousal levels to the forcible rape scenes, which were comparable to the levels observed to mutually consenting sex. Subjects who believed that they were sober were less aroused by the forcible rape than by the mutually consenting scenario. In conclusion, these authors suggested that normal heterosexual males may exhibit sexual arousal patterns indistinguishable from that seen in (some) rapists when they believe they have consumed alcohol.

This study has been criticized on a number of grounds. First, the study did not use properly counterbalanced stimuli (Lansky & Wilson, 1981). Second, it is possible to explain the Briddell et al. findings on the basis of increased sexual arousal to all cues (Barbaree, Marshall, Yates, & Lightfoot, 1983) due to general increases in arousal caused by alcohol expectancy (Lansky & Wilson, 1981; Wilson & Lawson, 1976). Also, Briddell et al. used a low dose of alcohol, which might account for the absence of an alcohol effect. Finally, the validity of the balanced placebo design in actually producing an alcohol expectancy has been questioned (Knight, Barbaree, & Boland, 1986).

Barbaree et al. (1983) used the balanced placebo design in a study much like that of Briddell et al. (1978). After being tested in a base-line session, subjects returned to the laboratory and were administered their expectancy instructions and a beverage to consume. The dose of alcohol increased blood alcohol levels to 0.07% BAC during arousal assessment, a higher dose then that used by Briddell et al. After drinking, subjects were again presented with rape and consenting cues while their arousal was monitored. There were no effects of alcohol expectancy. Further, there were no effects of alcohol on overall levels of rape arousal. However, subjects who were intoxicated failed to show the increase in discrimination between consenting and rape cues that we have previously seen in nonoffenders and that we saw in this study in the men who had not drunk alcohol.

It is not clear what implications these results might have for our understanding of sexual assault. If the increase in discrimination in nonintoxicated men results from their responses to experimenter demands, and the failure of this to occur in the intoxicated men indicates less sensitivity to experimenter demands, then alcohol intoxication might facilitate sexual assault by reducing men's sensitivity to societal demands for appropriate behavior. Wydra, Marshall, Earls, and Barbaree (1983) have begun an examination of this proposition. These authors asked nonoffenders—both sober and intoxicated—and rapists to indicate when during presentation of the rape verbal descriptions the behavior of the man was inappropriate. Intoxicated nonoffenders seemed to indicate inappropriate behavior earlier in the sequence than did either rapists or nonintoxicated nonoffenders. So if alcohol intoxication interferes with the sensitivity of subjects in responding to experimenter demands, it is not because they are impaired in their ability to identify inappropriate sexual behavior. Therefore, it is likely that alcohol intoxication disrupts normal stimulus control of sexual arousal, but we do not know enough yet to specify clearly the nature of this interaction.

In a follow-up study, Briddell, Cash, and Wunderlin (1979) assessed the effect of cognitive set on arousal to taped descriptions of mutually consensual sex or forcible rape, in male social drinkers. Subjects were given either a permissive set (told most people show arousal to the tapes) or a restrictive set (told arousal to tapes was unusual or unacceptable). Subjects were all sober, but half were told they had consumed alcohol; the other half were told they had received no alcohol. Subjects given the permissive cognitive set showed significantly greater arousal to the rape than subjects given the restrictive set. Alcohol expectancy had no significant effect on arousal.

Indirect measures of sexual behavior have found similar effects of alcohol and expectancy. Lang, Searles, Lauerman, and Adesso (1980) assessed sex guilt in male social drinkers, and assigned them to one of four conditions in a balanced placebo design. Subjects viewed and rated pornographic color slides. Viewing times increased linearly with the pornographic content of the slides. High "sex guilt" subjects who thought they had consumed alcohol viewed the slides for a significantly longer time than those who believed that they had not had alcohol, irrespective of the actual alcohol content of their drinks. Only high sex guilt subjects who believed they had not consumed alcohol failed to increase their viewing time to the more sexually explicit slides.

As indicated earlier in the discussion of the effects of alcohol on aggressive behavior, the physical disinhibition theory has often been raised to explain the changes in sexual behavior seen under the influence of alcohol. The studies described above, which demonstrate the effect of alcohol expectancy and cognitive set, indicate that a simple disinhibition model, at least at the low blood alcohol levels usually obtained in the human experimental research, cannot account for the changes in arousal observed (Crowe & George, 1989). Wilson (1981) has proposed that social learning theory, which acknowledges the role of self-evaluative cognitive processes, may have a profound impact on sexual behavior. In most circumstances people avoid engaging in activities that would elicit negative self-evaluations. "Among the many means whereby the regulatory function of negative self-evaluative consequences can be disengaged is the attribution of responsibility to something or to someone other than oneself. Alcohol is one such source of misattribution of personal responsibility" (Wilson, 1981, p. 35). McCaghy's (1968) finding that alcohol attributions allow child molesters to admit their deviant behavior while excusing themselves from personal responsibility is a prime example of this "disavowal of deviance" effect.

SUBSTANCE USE AND VIOLENT SEXUAL BEHAVIOR: PUTTING THE PIECES TOGETHER

In summary, our examination of the relationship between alcohol and sexual and aggressive behavior reveals a complex process involving both cognitive and physiological responses. Alcohol and many other drugs are known to disrupt performance on complex tasks, particularly those that require central processing and complex problem solving. Alcohol increases the probability of an aggressive response and has a disinhibition effect on sexual behavior. These combined effects create a potent combination, in which the probability of sexually aggressive behavior becomes more likely. Adolescent sex offenders have repeatedly been described as being more likely to be socially isolated with low to borderline intellectual functioning. They are, therefore, at higher risk for inappropriate behavior if they consume alcohol and are subsequently exposed to a social situation that involves a combination of complex, subtle cues.

THE RELATIONSHIP BETWEEN DELINQUENCY AND DRUG ABUSE

The relationship between the frequent use and abuse of drugs and chronic delinquent behavior has been consistently reported in the literature (Elliott, Huizinga, & Ageton, 1985). The U.S. National Youth Study (Elliott & Huizinga, 1984) found that in 1980, almost half of "serious" juvenile offenders (i.e., those who committed three or more index offenses in the past year) were also users of multiple illicit drugs. In this sample, 82% reported use of at least one illicit drug. Rates for alcohol use were 4–9 times higher, rates for marijuana use were 14 times higher, and rates for use of other illicit drugs were 36 times higher in serious delinquents than nonoffenders.

A 1985 survey of institutionalized delinquents found higher lifetime and current prevalence rates for the use of all illicit drugs than a national (U.S.) probability survey of high school seniors also surveyed that year (Hawkins et al., 1987). Cocaine use was twice as high in the delinquent sample, and heroin use was ten times greater in delinquents than in high school seniors (11.7% vs. 1.2%). Alcohol was the only substance for which use among high school seniors exceeded that of delinquents. Hartstone and Hansen (1984), in a study of violent juvenile offenders, found that half reported using alcohol or drugs prior to violent behaviors, and 40% reported using drugs immediately prior to offending.

As Hawkins et al. (1987) have pointed out, while minor delinquency and occasional use of alcohol and marijuana have become normative behavior among young people (Baumrind, 1985; Johnston, O'Malley, & Bachman, 1984; Kaplan, Martin, Johnson, & Robbins, 1986), serious and persistent delinquency and the *regular* use of illicit drugs have not.

THE RELATIONSHIP BETWEEN SEXUAL OFFENDING AND SUBSTANCE USE AND ABUSE IN ADOLESCENTS

In a recent survey of institutional juvenile delinquents (Hawkins et al., 1987), the most frequent type of offense was the sexual offense. However, there is little agreement in the literature as to the extent of alcohol and drug involvement in juvenile sexual offenses. As can be seen in Table 10.1, prevalence rates vary from very low to very high. In a review of the literature on adolescent sex offenders, Davis and Leitenberg (1987) assert that "there are no data to indicate whether adolescents who commit sexual offenses are more likely than other adolescents to have a history of alcohol or drug use problems, or whether there is a higher incidence of adolescent sex offenders in the drug or alcohol abusing population of adolescents than in the general population of adolescents" (p. 420). They go on to assert that intoxication at the time of the offense is uncommon. In support of this view they refer to Groth (1977), who reported an 11% rate, Wasserman and Kappel (1985), who reported a 10% rate, and Fehrenbach, Smith, Monastersky, and Deisher (1986), who reported a 6% rate. Davis and Leitenberg suggest that claims of being drunk or stoned may be used more frequently as a way to avoid responsibility, and that this might account for the 55% figure reported for incarcerated adolescents (Van Ness, 1984).

In contrast to this view, Vinogradov et al. (1988) in a study of 63 adolescent rapists (pedophilics, statutory rape, and three individuals denying the

TABLE 10.1. The Relationship between Substance Use and Adolescent Sex Offending Summary, 1970–1991

Authors	Description	Relationship to drug use
Tinklenberg, Murphy, Darley, Roth, & Kopell, 1974	Sample: 50 male assaultive adolescents (sexual and non) offenders compared for drug use and criminal behavior with 50 nonassaultive offenders; mean age 18.5 years; semistructured interview/records	65% of assaults, assailants under influence; assaults more sustained under drug; nonassaultive used greater A/D variety and more frequently than assaultive offenders
Groth, 1977	Sample: 26 male adolescent offenders and 37 adult offenders with juvenile history; clinical interviews	11% of offenses involved A/D use
Tinklenberg, Murphy, Murphy, & Pfefferbaum, 1981	293 juvenile male offenders compared to California moderate security serious offenders, 63 sexually assaultive (SA), 93 physically assaultive (PA), 135 delinquents; review of official records and semistructured interview	All three groups had similar levels of use; alcohol and cannabis most often used; pattern was typically binge; 71% of SA A/D; 69% of PA used A/D
Hartstone & Hansen, 1984 (cited in Hawkins, Lishner, Jenson, & Catalano, 1987)	Sample: juvenile violent offenders	50% reported A/D use prior to violent behavior; 40% reported using drugs immediately prior to their committing offense
Van Ness, 1984	Sample: incarcerated juvenile offenders	55% under the influence during the offense
Awad, Saunders, & Levene, 1984	Sample: 24 juvenile sex offenders compared to control group of matched nonsexual delinquents; average age 14 years; interview and psychological testing	1 under the influence of drugs; 8% of sexual offenders, 33% of delinquents had a history of A/D abuse
Wasserman & Kappel, 1985 (cited in Davis & Leitenberg, 1987)	Sample: adolescent sex offenders	10% under the influence of A/D at time of the offense

(cont.)

TABLE 10.1 *(cont.)*

Authors	Description	Relationship to Drug Use
Fehrenbach, Smith, Monastersky, & Deisher, 1986	Sample: 305 adolescent sexual offenders; 297 male, 8 female, average age 14.8 years; between 1976 and 1981; interview and official reports	6% of cases appeared to involve A/D use by offender or victim
Mio, Nanjundappa, Verleur, & De Rios, 1986	Sample: 7 male sex offenders at residential treatment in California; average age 15.66 years; 6 were incest offenders	6/7 abused drugs; 4/7 polydrug users; 5/7 parents abused substances
Awad & Saunders, 1989	Sample: 29 adolescent sexual offenders	1 (3.4%) was under influence of A/D at the time of offense
Fagan & Wexler, 1988	Sample: 34 juvenile sexual offenders from sample of 242 chronic/violent offenders	Sexual offenders lower incidence of A/D problems than violent offenders
Vinogradov, Dishotsky, Doty, & Tinklenberg, 1988	Sample: 63 adolescent rapists; interview and file review	48/67 (72%) under influence of one or more drugs at time of rape; majority were regular users
Hsu & Starzynski, 1990	Sample: 14 adolescent rapists, 17 adolescent child sexual assaulters	Frequent use of A/D by rapists

Note. A/D = alcohol and drug.

charge were eliminated from the sample), found that the large majority of adolescent offenders reported the regular (not defined) use of alcohol and other drugs. In 48 of 67 rape episodes, the offender described himself as under the influence of one or more psychoactive drugs at the time of the offense, and 15% reported taking a drug less than 15 minutes before the rape.

The authors suggest that their findings replicate the well-described association between alcohol and rape in adult offenders. They pay particular attention to the "high number" of assailants who report marijuana use, a drug that is not usually associated with impulsive aggressive behavior. However, it should be noted that only 6 out of 48 cases (12.5%) reported marijuana use alone. They suggest that programs aimed at the treatment of alcohol and drug abuse in high-risk adolescent populations would be important in the primary prevention of rape as well as other violent crimes. They further recommend that ongoing alcohol and drug programming should be a condition of parole for adolescents with a history of substance abuse who committed the offense while intoxicated. "In general, the need for these kinds of alcohol and drug treatment programs in the rehabilitation of sex offenders has not received sufficient attention and the possible role of treatment programs for marijuana abuse have been almost totally ignored" (p. 185).

There are a number of methodological factors in these studies that probably account for the wide discrepancies in reported prevalence rates. The measures of alcohol and drug use vary greatly from study to study, with most relying on unsubstantiated interview data. Very few appear to use standardized assessment tools. There also seems to be little attempt to examine the pattern of substance abuse, with no differentiation made between adolescents who are infrequent versus those who are chronic users. Studies that specifically examine the relationship between substance use and sex offending are more likely to report higher rates than those studies that have addressed alcohol and drug use in a minor descriptive way. It is likely that the former studies include many more specific questions designed to elicit information about alcohol and drug use than the latter. There are also major differences in the characteristics of the samples studied that may result in very different prevalence rates.

IMPLICATIONS FOR THE ASSESSMENT AND TREATMENT OF ADOLESCENT SEX OFFENDERS

Our review of the literature indicates that alcohol and or drug abuse is probably an important factor in the sex offending of some adolescents. Because of the methodological limitations of the present studies, however, it is not clear what the nature of this relationship is. In our studies of adult offenders (Hodgins & Lightfoot, 1988; Lightfoot & Hodgins, 1988), we identified, through the use of clustering algorithms, four types of substance-abusing offenders. These groups varied significantly in the type and levels of substances used, and associated problems. One group of offenders abused primarily alcohol and had limited involvement with a criminal lifestyle. The offenders in the second group were primarily drug abusers, had multiple problems related to their drug use, and were heavily involved in a criminal lifestyle. The third and fourth groups were also polydrug users with multiple life problems related to their substance abuse, but were differentiated from the other two groups and from each other. One of these groups had evidence of organic impairment of intellectual function, and the other had evidence of current psychological distress. Based on the treatment outcome literature, which indicates that outcomes are enhanced when clients are matched to treatment interventions, we have identified the different treatment needs of each of these types (Lightfoot, 1993; Lightfoot & Hodgins, in press). We recommended that offenders with evidence of psychopathology (which has consistently been associated with poorer outcomes in both adults (McLellan, 1983) and adolescents (Harrison & Hoffman, 1987) require comprehensive assessment and treatment for the presenting symptoms before initiating substance abuse treatment. Offenders with evidence of organic impairment or low to below-average intellectual function will require treatment that is simple and concrete and that allows for a great deal of rehearsal and built-in strategies to enhance generalization of the skills that are targeted in treatment.

A typology of substance-abusing rapists was proposed by Rada (1973), who distinguished between alcoholic and nonalcoholic rapists. For the alcoholic rapist, the addiction is the primary problem, and the sexual deviance represents one aspect of general social disorganization. In the latter type of offender, the sexual deviance is the primary disorder with alcohol use serving to increase the rapist's personal sense of power and control.

In the case of adolescent sex offenders, we do not know what proportion of adolescent sex offenders are infrequent versus chronic users. Even in the absence of abuse or dependence, for adolescents with poor impulse control, limited problem-solving abilities, and poor social skills, even a small amount of alcohol or some other drugs may seriously impair their cognitive abilities, hence significantly increasing the risk for sex offending. For those who are chronic users, their high frequency of substance use may impair the development of appropriate heterosexual behaviors and problem-solving abilities, and increase the probability of affiliation with a delinquent peer group, thus increasing their risk of sex offending.

Because adolescent sex offenders will have varying degrees of alcohol and drug involvement, sex offender treatment programs must be able to assess and plan treatment that is appropriate to the offender's needs. The adoption of standardized screening and assessment instruments that quantify the amount and frequency of use and related problems is highly recommended. It has been recently recognized that screening and assessment instruments originally developed for adults may be very inappropriate for adolescents, and the National Institute on Drug Abuse has funded the development of a manual for adolescent substance abuse assessment and treatment referral (Tarter, 1988). The Drug Use Screening Instrument and the Personal Experience Screening Questionnaire (Winters, 1988a; Winters, 1988b) are both examples of screening instruments developed for adolescent populations.

With regard to treatment, Wilkinson and Martin (1991), in their review of substance abuse treatment for youth, noted that there are "almost no experimental assessments of treatment efficacy in the literature of drug dependent youth, and even evaluation studies of treatment outcome are sparse" (p. 119). Given the state of our knowledge about effective strategies for substance abuse problems in adolescents, let alone adolescent sex offenders, the following recommendations about the intensity and type of treatment are considered tentative. In keeping with the view that more intensive and costly treatment should be reserved for those with more severe problems, infrequent substance users could likely benefit from preventive programming that stresses any substance use as a risk factor for reoffending. The chronic abuser (abuse/dependence), on the other hand, will likely require more intensive treatment geared toward the reduction or elimination of substance use and the development of adaptive coping strategies and skills, combined with long-term aftercare and maintenance. With regard to the modalities of treatment, given that adolescents are highly susceptible to peer influence, perhaps group therapy formats within structured milieus are likely to be among the more effective treatment techniques (Wilkinson, Leigh, Cordingley, Martin, & Lei, 1987). Involvement of the family in treatment is also likely to be important given the high rates of family dysfunction including violence, sexual abuse, and substance abuse in delinquent and substance-abusing youths.

SUMMARY AND CONCLUSION

Alcohol and many other drugs have powerful psychological and physical effects that increase sexual and aggressive behaviors. It is therefore not surprising that substance use has been implicated as a contributing factor in the sex offending of some adolescents. Widely divergent prevalence rates linking adolescent substance use to sex offending have been reported in the literature. This variability is not surprising, however, given that the methods of data collection have relied primarily on interview techniques, with few researchers or clinicians adopting the systematic use of more reliable and valid screening and assessment tools that would allow for quantification of alcohol and drug dependence and related problems.

Alcohol and drug problems in adult offenders are heterogeneous, and it is therefore likely that they will be so in youthful sex offenders. Although most treatment programs for adolescent sex offenders give lip service to the need to target alcohol and drug use in pretreatment assessment, there is little evidence that these assessments are designed to provide sufficient information about the nature and extent of alcohol and drug use to make appropriate decisions about the intensity and type of treatment required. Most assessments seem to be designed to address a dichotomous question, "Is there or is there not an alcohol or drug problem?" whereas the more important question should be, "Is substance use a risk factor for offending, independent of the presence of a substance abuse or dependence?" In other words, was alcohol and or another drug used before the current and previous offenses? If yes, then substance use is part of the offense cycle and must be identified and targeted in treatment. If there is evidence of abuse or dependence (i.e., chronic use), then more focused substance abuse treatment, possibly in a residential facility, may be required in order to interrupt substance use, perhaps prior to participation in a sex offender treatment program. Youth whose intellectual abilities are repeatedly impaired by the use of substances are unlikely to gain the maximum benefit from sex-offender treatment. Outpatient treatment programs may need to carefully monitor substance use by participants in order to both contain risk and to maximize treatment impacts.

Both future research and clinical practice with adolescent sex offenders could benefit greatly from the consistent utilization of valid and reliable substance-related screening and assessment techniques. These data could be used to achieve a variety of objectives including the following: a description of the population of adolescent offenders in terms of their alcohol and drug use patterns, the relationship of substance use and sex offending, the development of appropriate individualized treatment and referral plans, and the evaluation of treatment outcomes. The relationship between sexual and substance use behavioral outcomes for different types of adolescent offenders could eventually be related in cost-effectiveness studies. Refinements in the assessment and treatment of adolescent sex offenders will ultimately require the refinement of substance abuse prevention, identification assessment, and treatment techniques.

REFERENCES

Ahlstrom-Laakso, S. (1976). European drinking habits: A review of research and some suggestions for conceptual integration of findings. In M. W. Everett, J. O. Waddell, & D. B. Heath (Eds.), *Cross-cultural approaches to the study of alcohol.* The Hague: Mouton.

Alioto, J. T. (1984). The effects of expectancy of receiving either marijuana or alcohol on subsequent aggression in provoked high and low users of these drugs. *Dissertation Abstracts International, 35,* 4637B (University Microfilms No. ADG74-27722,0000).

American Psychiatric Association. (1987). *Diagnostic and statistical manual of mental disorders* (3rd ed., rev.). Washington, DC: Author.

Amir, M. (1967). Alcohol and forcible rape. *British Journal of Addictions, 62,* 219–232.

Amir, M. (1971). *Patterns in forcible rape.* Chicago: University of Chicago Press.

Awad, G. A., Saunders, E. (1989). Adolescent child molesters: Clinical observations. *Child Psychiatry and Human Development, 19,* 195–206.

Awad, G. A., Saunders, E., & Levene, J. (1984) A clinical study of male adolescent sex offenders. *International Journal of Offender Therapy and Comparative Criminology, 28,* 105–116.

Barbaree, H. E., Marshall, W. L., Yates, E., & Lightfoot, L. O. (1983). Alcohol and deviant sexual arousal in male social drinkers. *Behavior Research and Therapy, 21,* 365–373.

Bartholomew, A. A. (1968). Alcoholism and crime. *Australia and New Zealand Journal of Criminology, 1,* 70–99.

Baumrind, D. (1985). Familial antecedents of adolescent drug use: A developmental perspective. In C.L. Jones & R.J. Battjes (Eds.), *Etiology of drug abuse: Implications for prevention* (National Institute on Drug Abuse Research Monograph 56, DHHS Publication No. ADM 85-1335, pp. 13–44). Washington, DC: U.S. Government Printing Office.

Blum, R. H., & Braunstein, L. (1967). Mind-altering drugs and dangerous behavior: Alcohol. In *The President's Commission on Law Enforcement and Administration of Justice, Task Force on Drunkenness, Task force report: Drunkenness: Annotations, consultants' papers and related materials* (pp. 29–49). Washington, DC: U.S. Government Printing Office.

Bornstein, P. H., Schuldberg, D., & Bornstein, M. P. (1987). Conduct disorders. In V. Van Hasselt & M. Hersen (Eds.), *Handbook of adolescent psychology*. New York: Pergamon Press.

Boyatzis, R. E. (1974). The effect of alcohol consumption on the aggressive behavior of men. *Quarterly Journal of Studies in Alcohol, 35,* 959.

Boyatzis, R. E. (1977). Alcohol and interpersonal aggression. In M. Gross (Ed.), *Advances in experimental medicine and biology: Vol. 85B. Alcohol intoxication and withdrawal IIIb, Studies in alcohol dependence*. New York: Plenum Press.

Briddell, D. W., Cash, T. F., & Wunderlin, R. J. (1979). *Effects of alcohol cognitive set and appropriateness instruction on sexual arousal to normal and deviant stimuli.* Unpublished manuscript, Old Dominion University.

Briddell, D. W., Rimm, D. C., Caddy, G. R., Krawitz, G., Sholis, D., & Wunderlin, R. J. (1978). Effects of alcohol and cognitive set on sexual arousal to deviant stimuli. *Journal of Abnormal Psychology, 87,* 418–430.

Bushman, B., & Cooper, H. (1990). Effects of alcohol on human aggression: An integrative research review. *Psychological Bulletin, 7,* 341–354.

Buss, A. H. (1961). *The psychology of aggression*. New York: Wiley.

Chaiken, J., & Chaiken, M. R. (1982). *Varieties of criminal behavior*. Santa Monica, CA: Rand.

Christie, M. M., Marshall, W. L., & Lanthier, R. D. (1979). *A descriptive study of incarcerated rapists and pedophiles.* Report to the Solicitor General of Canada, Ottawa.

Collins, J. (1981). Alcohol use and expressive interpersonal violence: A proposed explanatory model. In E. Gottheil, K. Druley, T. Skiolada, & H. Waxman (Eds.), *Alcohol, drug abuse & aggression*. Springfield, IL: Charles C. Thomas.

Crowe, L. C., & George, W. H. (1989). Alcohol and human sexuality: Review and Integration. *Psychological Bulletin, 105,* 374–386.

Davis, G. E., & Leitenberg, H. (1987). Adolescent sex offenders. *Psychological Bulletin, 101,* 417–427.

Elliott, D. S., & Huizinga, D. (1984). *The relationship between delinquent behavior and ADM problem behaviors.* Paper prepared for the ADAMHA/OJJDP State of the Art Research Conference on Juvenile Offenders with Serious Drug/Alcohol and Mental Health Problems; Bethesda, MD.

Elliott, D. S., Huizinga, D., & Ageton, S. S. (1985). *Explaining delinquency and drug use*. Beverly Hills, CA: Sage.

Fagan, J., & Wexler, S. (1988). Explanations of sexual assault among violent delinquents: Special Issue. Adolescent sexual behavior. *Journal of Adolescent Research, 3*, 363–385.

Fehrenbach, P. A., Smith, W., Monastersky, C., & Deisher, R. (1986, April). Adolescent sexual offenders: Offender and offence characteristics. *American Journal of Orthopsychiatry, 56*, 225–233.

Gebhard, P. H., Gagnon, J. H., Pomeroy, W. B., & Christenson, C. V. (1965). *Sex offenders. An analysis of types.* New York: Harper & Row.

George, M., & Skinner, N. (1991). *Drug use by adolescents: Identification, assessment and intervention.* In H. Annis & C. Davis (Eds.), Youth and Drugs (pp. 95–105). Book of Readings. Supply & Services. Canada, and Addiction Research Foundation, Toronto.

Groth, A. N. (1977). The adolescent sexual offender and his prey. *International Journal of Offender Therapy and Comparative Criminology, 21*, 249–254.

Harrison, P. A., & Hoffman, N. G. (1987). *Adolescent residential treatment: Intake and follow-up findings* (CATOR 1987 Report). St. Paul, MN: Chemical Abuse/Addiction Treatment Outcome Registry.

Hartstone, E., & Hansen, K. V. (1984). The violent juvenile offender: An empirical portrait. In R. A. Mathias, P. Demura & R. S. Allinson (Eds.), *Violent juvenile offenders: An anthology* (pp. 83–112). San Francisco, CA: National Council on Crime & Delinquency.

Hawkins, J. D., Lishner, D., Jenson, J., & Catalano, R. F. (1987). Delinquents & drugs: What the evidence suggests about prevention & treatment planning. In B. Brown & R. Mills (Eds.), *Youth at high risk for substance abuse.* Rockville, MD: U.S. Department of Health & Human Services.

Heath, D. B. (1976). Anthropological perspectives on alcohol: An historical review. In M. W. Everett, J. O. Waddell, & D. B. Heath (Eds.), *Cross-cultural approaches to the study of alcohol.* The Hague: Mouton.

Hodgins, D. C., & Lightfoot, L. O. (1988). Types of male alcohol and drug abusing incarcerated offenders. *British Journal of Addictions, 83*, 1201–1213.

Hsu, L., & Starzynski, J. (1990). Adolescent rapists and adolescent child sexual assaulters. *International Journal of Offender Therapy and Comparative Criminology, 34*, 23–30.

Institute of Medicine. (1990). *Broadening the base of treatment for alcohol problems.* Washington, DC: National Academy of Sciences.

Jacobs, M. R., & Fehr, K. (1987). *Drugs and drugs abuse: A reference text* (2nd ed.). Toronto: Addiction Research Foundation.

Jessor, R., & Jessor, S. L. (1977). *Problem behavior and psychosocial development: A longitudinal study of youth.* New York: Academic Press.

Johnson, S. D., Gibson, L., & Linden, R. (1978). Alcohol and rape in Winnipeg, 1966–1975. *Journal of Studies on Alcohol, 39*, 1887–1894.

Johnston, L. D., O'Malley, P. M. & Bachman, J. G. (1984). *Highlights from drugs & American high school students, 1975–1983.* Rockville, MD: National Institute on Drug Abuse.

Johnston, L. D., O'Malley, P. M., & Bachman, J. G. (1985). *Use of licit and illicit drugs by America's high school students, 1975–84.* Rockville, MD: National Institute on Drug Abuse.

Kaplan, H. B., Martin, S. S., Johnson, R. J., & Robbins, C. A. (1986). Escalation of
    marijuana use: Application of a general theory of deviant behavior. *Journal of
    Health and Social Behavior, 27*, 44–61.
Knight, R., Barbaree, H. E., & Boland, F. J. (1986). Alcohol and the balanced placebo
    design: The role of experimenter demands in expectancy. *Journal of Abnormal
    Psychology, 95*, 335–340.
Lang, A. R., Searles, J., Lauerman, R., & Adesso, V. (1980). Expectancy, alcohol and
    sex guilt as determinants of interest in and reaction to sexual stimuli. *Journal of
    Abnormal Psychology, 89*, 644–653.
Lansky, D., & Wilson, G. T. (1981). Alcohol, expectations, and sexual arousal in males:
    An information processing analysis. *Journal of Abnormal Psychology, 90*, 35–45.
Lightfoot, L. O. (1993). The offender substance abuse pre-release program: An empir-
    ically based model of treatment for offenders. In J. Baer, A. Marlatt, & R.
    McMahon Eds.), *Addictive behaviors across the life span* (pp. 184–201). Newbury
    Park, CA: Sage.
Lightfoot, L. O., & Hodgins, D. (1988). A survey of alcohol and drug problems in
    incarcerated Canadian offenders. *International Journal of the Addictions, 23*, 687–
    706.
Lightfoot, L. O., & Hodgins, D. C. (in press). Characteristics of substance abusing
    offenders: Implications for treatment programming. *International Journal of Of-
    fender Therapy & Comparative Criminology.*
Lombroso, C. (1968). *Crime: Its causes & remedies.* Montclair, NJ: Patterson Smith.
MacAndrew, C., & Edgerton, R. (1969). *Drunken compartment: A social explanation.*
    Chicago: Aldine.
MacDonald, J. M. (1961). *The murderer and his victim.* Springfield, IL: Charles C.
    Thomas.
McCaghy, C. N. (1968). Drinking and deviance disavowal: The case of child molesters.
    Social Problems, 16, 43–49.
McClelland, D. C., Davis, W., Kalin, R., & Wanner, E. (Eds.). (1972). *The drinking man.*
    New York: Free Press.
McLellan, A. T. (1983). *Patient characteristics associated with outcome* (National Institute
    on Drug Abuse: Treatment Research Monograph, DHHS Publication No.
    ADM 83-1281) (pp. 500–529). Rockville, MD: NIDA.
Marlatt, G. A., & Rohsenow, D. J. (1980). Cognitive processes in alcohol use: Ex-
    pectancy and the balanced palcebo design. In N. K. Mello (Ed.), *Advances in
    substance abuse: Behavioral and biological research* (pp. 159–199). Greenwich, CT:
    JAI Press.
Mayfield, D. (1976). Alcoholism, alcohol intoxication and assaultive behavior. *Diseases
    of the Nervous System, 37*, 288–291.
Miller, J. D., Cisin, I. N., Gardner-Keaten, H., Harrel, A. V., Wirtz, P. W., Abelson, H.
    I., & Fishburne, P. M. (1983). *National survey on drug abuse: Main findings, 1982.*
    Rockville, MD: National Institute on Drug Abuse.
Mio, J. S., Nanjundappa, G., Verleur, D. E., & De Rios, M. D. (1986). Drug abuse and
    the adolescent sex offender: A preliminary analysis. *Journal of Psychoactive Drugs,
    18*, 65–72.
Moyer, K. E. (1971). A psychobiological model of aggressive behavior: Substance abuse

implications. In E. Gottheil, M. D. Keith, A. Druley, T. E. Skoloda, & H. M. Waxman (Eds.), *Alcohol, drug abuse and aggression* (pp. 189–202). Springfield, IL: Charles C. Thomas.

Nicol, A. R., Gunn, J. C., Gristwood, J., Fogg, R. H., & Watson, J. P. (1973). The relationship of alcoholism to violent behavior resulting in long term imprisonment. *British Journal of Psychiatry, 123*, 47–51.

Pernanen, F. (1976). Alcohol & crimes of violence. In B. Kissin & H. Begleton (Eds.), *Social aspects of alcoholism* (pp. 351–444). New York: Plenum Press.

Rada, R. T. (1973). Alcoholism and forcible rape. *American Journal of Psychiatry, 132*, 444–446.

Rada, R. T. (1975). Alcohol and rape. *Medical Aspects of Human Sexuality, 9*, 48–65.

Ross, R., & Lightfoot, L.O. (1987). *Treatment of the alcohol abusing offender.* Springfield, IL: Charles C. Thomas.

Sears, J. (1977). *The effects of social pressure on the aggressive behavior of intoxicated and nonintoxicated subjects.* Unpublished Master's thesis, Kent State University.

Selling, L. S. (1940). The role of alcohol in the commission of sex offenses. *Medical Records, 151*, 289–291.

Shupe, L. M. (1954). Alcohol and crime: A study of the urine alcohol concentration found in 882 persons arrested during or immediately after the commission of a felony. *Journal of Criminal Law, Criminology & Police Science, 44*, 661–664.

Smart, R. G., & Adlaf, E. M. (1989). *The Ontario student drug use survey: Trends between 1977–1989.* Toronto: Addiction Research Foundation.

Smart, R. G., & Jansen, V. A. (1991). Youth substance abuse. In H. Annis & C. Davis (Eds.), *Drug use by adolescents: Identification, assessment and intervention* (pp. 25–46). Toronto: Supply & Services Canada & Addiction Research Foundation.

Takala, M., Pihkanen, T. A., & Markkanen, T. (1957). *The effects of distilled and brewed beverages: Physiological, neurological and psychological study* (Publication No. 4). Helsinki: Finnish Foundation for Alcohol Studies.

Tarter, R. (1988). *Adolescent substance abuse: Assessment and treatment referral guide* (pp. 109–124). Pittsburg: Westover Consultants Incorporated.

Taylor, S. P. (1967). Aggressive behavior and physiological arousal as a function of provocation and the tendency to inhibit aggression. *Journal of Personality, 35*, 297–310.

Taylor, S. P. (1983). Alcohol and human physical aggression. In E. Gottheil, K. A. Druley, T. E. Skoloda, & H. M. Waxman (Eds.), *Alcohol, drug abuse and aggression* (pp. 280–291). Springfield, IL: Charles C. Thomas.

Taylor, S. P., & Leonard, K. E. (1983). Alcohol and human physical aggression. In R. G. Geen & E. I. Donnerstein (Eds.), *Aggression: Theoretical and empirical reviews: Vol. 2. Issues in Research.* New York: Academic Press.

Taylor, S. P., Vardaris, R. M., Rawtich, A. B., Gammon, C. B., Cranston, J. W., & Lubetkin, A. I. (1976). The effects of alcohol and delta-9-tetrahydrocannabinol on human physical aggression. *Aggressive Behavior, 2*, 153–161.

Tinklenberg, J. R., Murphy, P., Murphy, P. L. & Pfefferbaum, A. (1981). Drugs and criminal assaults by adolescents: A replication study. *Journal of Psychoactive Drugs, 13*, 277–287.

Tinklenberg, J. R., Murphy, P. L., Darley, C. F., Roth, W. T., & Kopell, B. S. (1974). Drug involvement in criminal assaults by adolescents. *Archives of General Psychiatry*, *30*, 685–689.

Tinklenberg, J. R., & Woodrow, K. M. (1974). Drug use among youthful assaultive and sexual offenders. *Aggression*, *52*, 209–224.

Van Ness, S. R. (1984). Rape as instrumental violence: A study of youth offenders: Special issue. Gender issues, sex offenses, and criminal justice: Current trends. *Journal of Offender Counselling, Services and Rehabilitation*, *9*, 161–170.

Vinogradov, S., Dishotsky, N. I., Doty, A. K., & Tinklenberg, J. R. (1988). Patterns of behavior in adolescent rape. *American Journal of Orthopsychiatry*, *58*, 179–187.

Wasserman, J., & Kappel, S. (1985). *Adolescent sex offenders in Vermont*. Burlington: Vermont Department of Health.

Walters, J. K., Reinarman, C., & Fagan, J. (1985). Causality, context and contingency relationships between drug abuse and delinquency. *Contemporary Drug Problems*, *12*, 351–373.

Wilkinson, D. A., Leigh, G. M., Cordingley, J., Martin, G. W., & Lei, H. (1987). Dimensions of multiple drug use and a typology of drug users. *British Journal of Addiction*, *82*, 259–273.

Wilkinson, D. A., & Martin, G. (1991). Intervention methods for youth with problems of substance abuse. In H. E. Annis & C. Davis (Eds.), *Drug use by adolescents: Identification, assessment and intervention*. Toronto: Supply & Services & Addiction Research Foundation.

Wilson, G. T. (1981). The effects of alcohol on human sexual behavior. In N. Mellon (Ed.), *Advances in substance abuse* (Vol. 2, pp. 1–40). Greenwich, CT: JAI.

Wilson, G. T., & Lawson, D. M. (1976). Expectancies, alcohol and sexual arousal in male social drinkers. *Journal of Abnormal Psychology*, *85*, 587–594.

Winters, K. (1988a). *Personal Experience Screen Questionnaire (PESQ)*. Chemical Dependency Adolescent Assessment Project, St. Paul, MN.

Winters, K. (1988b). *Personal Experience Screen, (PESQ) Information Sheet*. Wilder Research Center, St. Paul, MN.

Wolfgang, M. E. (1958). *Patterns in criminal homicide*. Philadelphia: University of Pennsylvania Press.

Wydra, A., Marshall, W. L., Earls, C. M., & Barbaree, H. E. (1983). Identification of cues and control of sexual arousal by rapists. *Behavior Research and Therapy*, *21*, 469–476.

CHAPTER 11

The Conduct Disorders and the Juvenile Sex Offender

Karyn G. France
Stephen M. Hudson

T he exploration of the relationship between nonsexual disturbances of conduct and juvenile sex offending is important; a significant number of juvenile sex offenders engage in other criminal acts or may be diagnosed as conduct disordered. The literature on these conditions is more striking in its similarities than its differences. Each condition shares several important distal causative and prognostic factors and, not surprisingly, there are similarities in the various attempts to subclassify both. It is possible that theoretical and treatment formulations for nonsexual disturbances of conduct may have useful explanatory power for at least some types of juvenile sex offending. The coexistence of disturbances of conduct and juvenile sex offending may be significant for predicting risk of reoffending. The composite behaviors may also be related—for example, when a sex offense is committed during a burglary. Other developmental events during adolescence may link both—for example, the role of group behavior and peer pressure.

The present chapter reviews the literature on nonsexual disturbances of conduct and their association with juvenile sex offending. We do this by defining both, describing the rates of nonsexual antisocial behavior in juvenile sex offenders; summarizing similarities and differences in associated factors, treatment, and prognosis; and finally examining attempts at subclassification.

NONSEXUAL DISTURBANCES OF CONDUCT

In this chapter, the broad term *nonsexual disturbances of conduct* subsumes the diagnostic term *conduct disorder* (American Psychiatric Association, 1987; Kazdin, 1987) as well as the sociolegal term *delinquency* (Kazdin, 1987; West, 1985). The term *conduct disorder* includes a range of behavior such as lying, petty thieving, aggression, and truancy, in addition to repetitive illegal behavior by minors leading to impairment of everyday functioning. *Delinquency* refers to behavior that leads to contact with the courts. Unlike conduct disorder, delinquency need not be repetitive nor lead to impairment of everyday functioning (Kazdin, 1987).

The discussion of conduct disorder and delinquency is plagued by problems similar to those involved in the discussion of sex offending. They are heterogeneous phenomena, marked by a wide range of behavioral expressions. However, the inclusion of such diverse behaviors under one term can be justified. Wolfe (1985), for instance, comments that delinquent and non-delinquent disturbances of conduct have fruitfully been examined together for epidemiological purposes because they share so many associated factors. Kazdin (1987) says that they are considered together because they often go together and that the most important considerations in the diagnosis of conduct disorders are the stability, breadth, and intensity of the behaviors, rather than the presence of any particular behavior.

NONSEXUAL DISTURBANCES OF CONDUCT IN JUVENILE SEX OFFENDERS

Several studies have sought to establish the rates of nonsexual disturbances of conduct in juvenile sex offenders by examining records of delinquency or through diagnoses of conduct disorder based on psychiatric or psychological assessment. These studies have established that approximately half of juvenile sex offenders have a history of nonsexual arrests and that the majority can be described as conduct disordered. Becker, Kaplan, Cunningham-Rathner, and Kavoussi (1986), for example, found that 50% of their sample of juvenile male incest perpetrators had a record of previous non-sexual arrests, and that 63% of those available for psychiatric assessment could be diagnosed as conduct disordered. This rate of nonsexual arrests is higher than the self-reported rate (28%) among a more varied group of juvenile sex offenders studied by Becker, Cunningham-Rathner, and Kaplan (1986), but is similar to figures for non-sexual delinquencies reported in other samples of juvenile sex offenders (Awad & Saunders, 1989; Awad, Saunders, & Levene, 1984; Fehrenbach, Smith,

Monastersky, & Deishner, 1986; Kavoussi, Kaplan, & Becker, 1988; Pierce & Pierce, 1987). A much higher rate (100%) was found by Lewis, Shankok, and Pincus (1979).

The range of rates for non–sexual offending found in these studies is partly explained by the type of sex offending. More serious and aggressive hands-on offending is associated with higher rates of non–sexual offending (Kavoussi et al., 1988; Lewis et al., 1979; Smith, 1988). Unfortunately, these are the only studies that have differentiated juvenile sex offenders on the basis of type of sex offense, and this is a significant omission (Davis & Leitenberg, 1987).

The temporal relationship between juvenile sex offending and other delinquency has also been considered by McDermott and Hindelang (1981), who found a slightly higher rate of thefts (12%) concomitant with rapes committed by adolescents compared with those committed by adults. Van Ness (1984), however, reports that 90% of the rapes committed by the subjects in her study followed an anger-provoking incident such as an argument.

Several theories of delinquency underscore the importance of peer relationships subsequent to disruption of normal bonding (Blaske, Borduin, Henggeler, & Mann, 1989). The role of peer relationships in the commission of nonsexual antisocial acts is considered so important that it has become part of the classification system for these problems, with group offending being a predominant feature of many such acts. Several authors, however, have found that juvenile sex offenders, in contrast to perpetrators of nonsexual disturbances of conduct, are likely to be socially isolated with serious disruptions in their ability to form peer relationships (Awad & Saunders, 1989; Awad et al., 1984; Blaske et al., 1989; Fehrenbach et al., 1986; Groth, 1977; Shoor, Speed, & Bartelt, 1966)

Studies investigating whether sex offenses are committed with peers, however, have confined themselves to rapists. Davis and Leitenberg (1987) found in their review, a vast difference in the reported proportion of lone offenders; for example, from 93% (Groth, 1977), to 14% (Amir, 1971). Most of the studies reported by Davis and Leitenberg, however, indicate that although group rape may be more prevalent in adolescents than in adults, it is by no means a feature of most such crimes. With respect to female adolescents, the only study focusing on these particular sex offenders found that they invariably offended alone. This finding is in contrast to observations of adult female offenders who typically offend with an adult male who has often coerced them into offending (Fehrenbach & Monastersky, 1988).

A significant number of juvenile sex offenders engage in other antisocial behavior; however, a large group, particularly nonaggressive and hands-off perpetrators, do not. In addition, sex offending differs from non–sex offending in that it is less likely to be associated with the commission of other offenses or to occur in the company of peers.

FACTORS ASSOCIATED WITH NONSEXUAL
DISTURBANCES OF CONDUCT AND JUVENILE
SEX OFFENDING

Attempts to elucidate the etiology of both nonsexual disturbances of conduct and sex offending in juveniles have been confined to a description of correlated or associated factors.

Awad et al. (1984) compared 24 male juvenile sex offenders with a group of other matched delinquents and found that the similarities in associated factors outweighed the differences between the groups. The two groups were more alike than not on measures of the prevalence of psychiatric disturbance and psychiatric history, violence, and sexual deviance among their parents, disruptions in parent–child relationships, inadequate parenting, a chronic history of school problems, and past delinquencies. The few differences comprised a higher prevalence of middle-class boys, lower intellectual functioning and less truancy, alcohol abuse, and temper tantrums among the sex offenders.

Intellectual functioning is one factor that has received considerable attention, with most studies finding lower intellectual functioning in juvenile sex offenders than in other juvenile offenders, and particularly higher rates of individuals with IQ's less than 80 (Atcheson & Williams, 1954, Lewis, Shankok, & Pincus, 1981), although studies by Lewis et al., (1979), and Tarter, Hegedus, Alterman, and Katz-Garris (1983) dispute this. It is likely that intellectual functioning is of etiological significance only for a subgroup of low IQ, juvenile sex offenders who differ from most juvenile sex offenders on other dimensions as well (Awad et al., 1984).

The general findings of this literature appear to support a common etiology for both sex offending and nonsexual disturbances of conduct; however, Blaske et al. (1989) dispute this. They compared a group of aggressive hands-on juvenile sex offenders with assaultive offenders, nonviolent offenders, and nondelinquent adolescents. Blaske et al.'s goal was to evaluate contentions derived from previous studies, most of which were deemed to be of poor methodological quality. These studies concluded that both violent offenders and sex offenders show emotional and interpersonal deficits that are generally consistent with contemporary theories of delinquency. These latter theories typically emphasize the importance of differential affective ties to conventional and deviant socializing agents. Blaske et al. (1989) found that sex offenders were different from other juvenile offenders in that their emotional functioning and peer relationships were more disturbed, whereas their family relationships and behavioral functioning was more similar to that of nondelinquents. These authors therefore concluded that sex offenders did not fit contemporary models of delinquency.

The etiological significance of prior experience of sexual abuse in the development of sex offending is an important question that has been subject to much conjecture but sparse research. It is possible that juvenile sex offenders, although sharing some etiological features with other antisocial offenders, differ from them in the amount of prior sexual abuse they have experienced.

However, one of the biggest problems is obtaining valid information. One of the sequelae of sexual abuse is dissociation, and disclosure in and of itself may be traumatic (Finkelhor, 1987). Awad et al. (1984) for example, found that none of their sample of 24 sex offenders and matched juvenile delinquents reported prior sexual abuse, a finding the authors themselves doubted. In addition, it is possible that some sex offenders may overreport sexual abuse as a factor mitigating their own unacceptable behavior. Other studies report an incidence of prior sexual abuse in juvenile sex offenders ranging from 11% (Fehrenbach et al., 1986) to 26% (Awad & Saunders, 1989), 43% (Pierce & Pierce, 1987), and 49% (Johnson, 1988). These figures range from equal to that found in delinquents and the general population (Awad & Saunders, 1989), to considerably more.

Although it is clear that sexual abuse can lead to sexual behavior problems in children (Friedrich, Beilke, & Urquiza, 1988; Friedrich & Lueke, 1988), its role in the etiology of juvenile sex offending is far from clear.

ATTEMPTS TO SUBCLASSIFY

There have been several attempts to identify subtypes of nonsexual disturbances of conduct within the literature on conduct disorders. The third edition of the *Diagnostic and Statistical Manual of Mental Disorders* (DSM-III) (American Psychiatric Association, 1980) subdivided conduct disorders into four subtypes: undersocialized aggressive, undersocialized nonaggressive, socialized aggressive, and socialized nonaggressive. These categories referred to the presence or absence of affection, empathy, or an emotional bond with others, as well as to the degree of physical aggression or confrontation involved in the problematic behavior. However, this classification has been changed because of mixed findings regarding the predictive validity of these categories (Kazdin, 1987). The third revised edition of the *Diagnostic and Statistical Manual of Mental Disorders* (DSM-III-R) (APA, 1987) emphasises the importance of group relationships in the commission of the offenses and misdemeanors. It has three categories: group type (conduct problems that occur mainly as a group activity with peers, with or without aggression), solitary aggressive type (predominance of aggressive behavior, initiated by the person alone), and undifferentiated type (not clearly solitary aggressive or group type). Kazdin (1987) identifies several other approaches to subclassification (Jesness & Wedge, 1984; Loeber, 1985; Patterson, 1982; Quay, 1964). All of these systems make a distinction between overt, aggressive behavior, such as fighting, arguing, and temper tantrums, and more covert acts such as stealing, truancy, lying, and fire setting.

Attempts to subclassify juvenile sex offenders have also typically used an aggressive/nonaggressive distinction but have seldom utilized social bonding as a means of classification (Groth, 1977; Monastersky & Smith, 1985; Shoor et al., 1966). Monastersky and Smith (1985), for example, place the offenses of juvenile sex offenders along a continuum that includes nonaggressive hands-off (e.g., indecent exposure), aggressive hands-off (e.g., breaks in to steal underwear), nonaggressive hands-on (e.g., fondling of young child), and aggressive hands-on (e.g., forcible rape).

There is some evidence that aggressive, hands-on offenders are different from other groups of juvenile sex offenders. They are twice as likely to be diagnosed as conduct disordered, or to have committed other acts of violence than are other adolescent sex offenders (Kavoussi et al., 1988; Van Ness, 1984). Rapists engage in more substance abuse (Vinogradov, Dishotsky, Dotty, & Tinklenberg, 1988), are less likely to be acquainted with their victims (Groth, 1977; Vinogradov et al., 1988; Van Ness, 1984), and use, along with assaultive pedophiles, more coercion than some other offenders (Becker, Cunningham-Rathner, & Kaplan, 1986; Saunders, Awad, & White, 1986); they are more likely to use a weapon (Groth, 1977), and are less likely to have offended similarly in the past (Awad et al., 1984; Groth, 1977; Fehrenbach et al., 1986). Juvenile rapists also occupy a narrower age range (Groth, 1977), have slightly higher IQ scores (Groth, 1977), and perpetrate a greater proportion of interracial crimes (Groth, 1977). There is also evidence that adolescent offenders who use excessive force have different personalities as measured by the Minnesota Multiphasic Personality Inventory (MMPI) than other offenders (Smith, Monastersky, & Deisher, 1987) and have a more disturbed family background, with a high rate of parent–child separations, (Saunders et al., 1986).

Hands-on juvenile sex offenders, in their increased use of violence, substance abuse, and in their personality profiles and lack of acquaintance with victims, appear to be more similar to other antisocial adolescents than are other groups of juvenile sex offenders. However, the similarity is not complete, as differences have been demonstrated between juvenile rapists and other juvenile offenders in their peer relationships, emotional adjustment, family functioning, and type of non–sexual offending (Awad et al., 1984; Blaske et al., 1989).

PROGNOSIS

Considerable work on prognosis has been carried out in the conduct disorder literature. Conduct-disordered youths with mixed (covert and overt) presentations have a poorer long-term outcome than youths with only covert or only overt features (Kazdin, 1987; Loeber, Lahey, & Thomas, 1991). The importance of conduct disorder as a prognostic indicator in juvenile sex offending, however, has received scant attention and shows conflicting results. Henderson, English, and MacKenzie (1988) found about half of the youths in their treatment program, who had victim-related criminal histories prior to the sex offense, continued to exhibit assaultive or sexually aggressive behaviors afterward. Smith and Monastersky (1986), however, found no more than a trend relating a history of aggressive or destructive behavior, to the likelihood of reoffending. This latter study, however, was limited by difficulties in detecting such low-rate, covert events over a relatively short period of time.

DISCUSSION

The major problem in attempting to elucidate the relationship between nonsexual disturbances of conduct and juvenile sex offending is the failure of studies to differentiate those juvenile sex offenders who have other disturbances of conduct from those who do not. It may be that juvenile sex offenders without other conduct disturbances are a group with unique characteristics that are obscured in current research.

Furthermore, those juvenile sex offenders who have nonsexual disturbances of conduct need to be further examined to determine which is the primary diagnosis. The increased likelihood of conduct-disturbed juveniles to offend sexually was reflected in the inclusion of sex offending in DSM-III criteria for conduct disorder. Is the sex offense merely one of a range of antisocial behaviors exhibited by conduct-disordered juveniles, or is it the predominant problem presented by a juvenile with other adjustment difficulties as well? Once conduct-disordered youths who offend sexually, and juvenile sex offenders with and without other antisocial behavior, have been differentiated, meaningful research comparing these groups can be carried out. Similarly, previous research has failed to delineate different subtypes of sex offenses (e.g., aggressive hands-on vs. nonaggressive hands-off) and of nonsexual behavioral disturbances, and to systematically apply the same research questions to these different groups.

An additional methodological problem is the difficulty of ascertaining the true rate of antisocial behavior in juvenile sex offenders. There is a high rate of isolated antisocial behavior in the general population (Kazdin, 1987; West, 1985) such that the severity and persistence of the antisocial behavior is an important consideration. A further complication is that existing research often reports the proportion of juvenile sex offenders exhibiting various antisocial behaviors but does not indicate whether these cluster sufficiently in the one person to justify a diagnosis of conduct disorder.

The search for oversimplified relationships between juvenile sex offending and other disturbances of conduct has merely served to confuse the issue. Further progress in understanding the complex relationships between the two and the prognostic importance of the presence of other antisocial behavior in juvenile sex offenders will depend on research that overcomes the serious methodological and conceptual problems that are a feature of much of the previous research.

REFERENCES

American Psychiatric Association. (1980). *Diagnostic and statistical manual of mental disorders* (3rd ed.). Washington, DC: Author.

American Psychiatric Association. (1987). *Diagnostic and statistical manual of mental disorders* (3rd. rev. ed.). Washington, DC: Author.

Amir, M. (1971). *Patterns of forcible rape*. Chicago: University of Chicago Press.

Atcheson, J. D., & Williams, D. C. (1954). A study of juvenile sex offenders. *American Journal of Psychiatry, 111*, 366–370.

Awad, G. A., & Saunders, E. (1989). Adolescent child molesters: Clinical observations. *Child Psychiatry and Human Development, 19*, 195–206.

Awad, G. A., Saunders, E., & Levene, J. (1984). A clinical study of male adolescent sex offenders. *International Journal of Offender Treatment and Comparative Criminology, 28*, 105–116.

Becker, J. V., Cunningham-Rathner, J., & Kaplan, M. S. (1986). Adolescent sexual offenders: Demographics, criminal and sexual histories and recommendations for reducing future offenses. *Journal of Interpersonal Violence, 1*, 431–443.

Becker, J. V., Kaplan, M. S., Cunningham-Rathner, J., & Kavoussi, R. (1986). Characteristics of adolescent incest sexual perpetrators: Preliminary findings. *Journal of Family Violence, 1*, 85–97.

Blaske, D. M., Borduin, C. M., Henggeler, S. W., & Mann, B. J. (1989). Individual, family, and peer characteristics of adolescent sex offenders and assaultive offenders. *Developmental Psychology, 25*, 846–855.

Davis, G. E., & Leitenberg, H. (1987). Adolescent sex offenders. *Psychological Bulletin, 101*, 417–427.

Fehrenbach, P. A., & Monastersky, C. (1988). Characteristics of female adolescent sex offenders. *American Journal of Orthopsychiatry, 58*, 148–151.

Fehrenbach, P. A., Smith, W., Monastersky, C., & Deisher, R. W. (1986). Adolescent sexual offenders: Offender and offense characteristics. *American Journal of Orthopsychiatry, 56*, 225–233.

Finkelhor, D. (1987). The trauma of child sexual abuse: Two models. *Journal of Interpersonal Violence, 2*, 348–366.

Friedrich, W. N., Beilke, R. L., & Urquiza, A. J. (1988). Behavior problems in young sexually abused boys: A comparison study. *Journal of Interpersonal Violence, 3*, 21–28.

Friedrich, W. N., & Luecke, W. J. (1988). Young school-age sexually aggressive children. *Professional Psychology Research and Practice, 19*, 155–164.

Groth, A. N. (1977). The adolescent sex offender and his prey. *International Journal of Offender Therapy and Comparative Criminology, 21*, 249–254.

Henderson, J. E., English, D. J., & MacKenzie, W. R. (1988). Family centered casework practice with sexually aggressive children. *Treatment of Sex Offenders in Social Work and Mental Health Settings, 7*, 89–109.

Jesness, C. F., & Wedge, R. F. (1984). Validity of a revised Jesness Inventory I-level classification with delinquents. *Journal of Consulting and Clinical Psychology, 52,* 997–1010.

Johnson, T. C. (1988). Child perpetrators—children who molest other children: Preliminary findings. *Child Abuse and Neglect, 12,* 219–229.

Kavoussi, R. J., Kaplan, M., & Becker, J. V. (1988). Psychiatric diagnoses in adolescent sex offenders. *Academy of Child and Adolescent Psychiatry, 27,* 241–243.

Kazdin, A. E. (1987). *Conduct disorders in children and adolescence.* Newbury Park, CA: Sage.

Lewis, D. O., Shankok, S. S., & Pincus, J. H. (1979). Juvenile male sexual assaulters. *American Journal of Psychiatry, 136,* 1194–1196.

Lewis, D. O., Shankok, S. S., & Pincus, J. H. (1981). Juvenile male sexual assaulters: Psychiatric, neurological, psychoeducational and abuse factors. In D. O. Lewis (Ed.), *Vulnerabilities to delinquency.* New York: S. P. Medical & Scientific Books.

Loeber, R. (1985). Patterns and development of antisocial child behavior. In G. J. Whitehurst (Ed.), *Annals of Child Development* (Vol. 2). Greenwich, CT: JAI Press.

Loeber, R., Lahey, B. B., Thomas, C. (1991). *The diagnostic conundrum of oppositional defiant disorder and conduct disorder.* Unpublished manuscript, Western Psychiatric Institute and Clinic School of Medicine, Pittsburgh.

McDermott, M. J., & Hindelang, M. J. (1981). *Juvenile criminal behavior in the United States: Its trends and patterns* (Analysis of National Crime Victimization Survey Data to Study Serious Delinquency Behavior Monograph No. 1). Washington, DC: Office of Juvenile Justice and Delinquency Prevention.

Monastersky, C., & Smith, W. (1985). Juvenile sexual offenders: A family systems paradigm. In E. M. Otey & G. D. Ryan (Eds.), *Adolescent sex offenders: Issues in research and treatment* (pp. 164–175). Rockville, MD: U.S. Department of Health & Human Services.

Patterson, G. R. (1982). *Coercive family process.* Eugene, OR: Castalia.

Pierce, L. H., & Pierce, R. L. (1987). Incestuous victimization by juvenile sex offenders. *Journal of Family Violence, 2,* 351–364.

Quay, H. C. (1964). Personality dimensions in delinquent males as inferred from factor analysis of behavior ratings. *Journal of Research in Crime and Delinquency, 1,* 33–37.

Saunders, E., Awad, G. A., & White, G. (1986). Male adolescent sexual offenders: The offender and the offense. *Canadian Journal of Psychiatry, 31,* 542–548.

Shoor, M., Speed, M. H., & Bartelt, C. (1966). Syndrome of the adolescent child molester. *American Journal of Psychiatry, 122,* 783–789.

Smith, W. R. (1988). Delinquency and abuse among juvenile sex offenders. *Journal of Interpersonal Violence, 3,* 400–413.

Smith, W. R., & Monasterski, C. (1986). Assessing juvenile sex offenders' risk for re-offending. *Criminal Justice and Behavior, 13,* 115–140.

Smith, W. R., Monastersky, C., & Deisher, R. M. (1987). MMPI-based personality types among juvenile sex offenders. *Journal of Clinical Psychology, 43,* 422–430.

Tarter, R. E., Hegedus, A. M., Alterman, A. I., & Katz-Garris, L. (1983). Cognitive capacities of juvenile violent, nonviolent, and sexual offenders. *Journal of Nervous and Mental Disorders, 171,* 564–567.

Van Ness, S. R. (1984). Rape as instrumental violence: A study of youth offenders. *Journal of Offender Counselling, Services, and Rehabilitation, 9,* 161–170.

Vinogradov, S., Dishotsky, N. I., Dotty, A. K., & Tinklenberg, J. R. (1988). Patterns of behavior in adolescent rape. *American Journal of Orthopsychiatry, 58,* 179–187.

West, D. (1985). Delinquency. In M. Rutter & L. Hersov (Eds.), *Child and adolescent psychiatry* (pp. 414–420). London: Blackwell.

Wolfe, S. (1985). Non-delinquent disturbances of conduct. In M. Rutter & L. Hersov (Eds.), *Child and adolescent psychiatry* (pp. 400–413). London: Blackwell.

CHAPTER 12

The Developmentally Disabled Adolescent Sex Offender

Lana Stermac
Peter Sheridan

F ew clinical and research studies of developmentally disabled sex offenders have focused on the adolescent population and its special needs. Despite this dearth of information, mental health professionals are faced with increasing demands to treat this population of sexual offenders. It is estimated, for example, that 20–30% of rapes and 30–50% of incidents of child sexual abuse in North America are committed by adolescents (Davis & Leitenberg, 1987; Stermac & Matthews, 1987; Rogers, 1990). Canadian data suggest 25% of sexual offenses are committed by adolescents and that one in seven men imprisoned for sexual offenses against children is under the age of 21 (Matthews, 1987).

Several studies have proposed that there is a greater-than-expected incidence of developmental delay in populations of adolescent sex offenders (Awad, Saunders, & Levene, 1984; Saunders, Awad, & White, 1986). Approximately 23% of developmentally disabled adolescents in treatment were found to have engaged in sexually abusive behavior (Gilby, Wolf, & Goldberg, 1989). While there may be no clear evidence of an overrepresentation of disabled persons within the sex offender population (Gilby et al., 1989; Murphy, Coleman, & Abel, 1983), Griffiths, Hinsburger, and Christian (1985) suggest that the prevalence of sex offending is at least as common, if not more common, in the disabled population.

Although there has been recent interest in both adolescent sex offenders and in developmentally disabled adult sex offenders, this interest has not yet been extended to the area of developmentally disabled adolescent sex offenders. There is virtually no information, clinical or research, available on this group of sex offenders. This chapter attempts to integrate some preliminary information and clinical impressions about the developmentally disabled adolescent sex offender. Treatment possibilities and special issues in the treatment of this population will also be considered.

AN INTRODUCTION TO THE DEVELOPMENTALLY DISABLED ADOLESCENT SEX OFFENDER

We are aware of only one published research study on the developmentally disabled adolescent sex offender. Gilby et al. (1989) found that, among adolescents seen at a children's psychiatric research institute, developmentally disabled individuals showed a similar proportion of sexual problems overall as nondisabled individuals. Although developmentally disabled adolescents were as likely to engage in assaultive sexual behaviors as adolescents of normal intelligence, they were significantly more likely to display inappropriate, nonassaultive "nuisance" behaviors such as public masturbation, exhibitionism, and voyeurism. This is consistent with our clinical impression of frequent nonviolent sexual misconduct among this group. Developmentally disabled adolescents in residential treatment were as likely as nondisabled adolescents to be involved in consensual sexplay, but tended to be less discriminating in their choice of partner, as evidenced by greater frequency of homosexual and heterosexual activities.

Comparing small groups of developmentally disabled adolescent offenders, nondisabled adolescent sex offenders, and disabled nonoffenders, Gilby et al. (1989) found that the disabled adolescents offended equally against males and females, whereas nondisabled adolescents chose primarily female victims. Griffiths et al. (1985) found a similar pattern of victim choice; the developmentally disabled offender tends to be less discriminating, choosing both male and female victims, adults and children, and less often than nondisabled adolescents, they choose a victim who is known. Gilby et al. (1989) found that the nondisabled adolescent sex offenders exhibited greater delinquent behavior other than the sexually anomalous behaviors and reported greater family disruption. On these issues, the authors did not find any significant differences between developmentally disabled adolescent offenders and nonoffenders.

Given the paucity of literature on the developmentally disabled adolescent sex offender, it is necessary to examine the clinical and research literature on nondisabled adolescent offenders and disabled adult offenders. Adolescent sex offenders are assumed to display deviant sexual interest patterns and cognitive distortions (Becker, Kaplan, & Kavoussi, 1988), and are thought to lack sexual knowledge (Becker & Abel, 1985; Davis & Leitenberg, 1987), to have poor control over their anger and sexual impulsivity (Kavoussi, Kaplan, & Becker, 1988; Davis & Leitenberg, 1987), and to be deficient in social and assertiveness skills (Stermac & Matthews, 1987). They are also said to experience feelings of low self-esteem and social isolation (Groth, 1977). Developmentally disabled adult sex offenders have likewise been found to display deviant sexual arousal patterns and distorted cognitions (Murphy, Coleman, & Abel, 1983; Rowe, Savage, Ragg, & Wigle, 1987), and are often deficient in sexual knowledge and skill (Hinsburger, 1987; Murphy, Coleman, & Abel, 1983). They are also thought to lack impulse control, have poor peer relations and inadequate social skills (Hinsburger, 1987), as well as low self-esteem (Lackey & Knopp, 1989). Adolescent sex offenders have also been found to have experienced family dysfunction such as marital discord, parental rejection, and physical discipline (Awad et al., 1984), and a significant number have themselves been victims of sexual abuse (Awad et al., 1984; Stermac & Matthews, 1987). These latter conditions appear approximately as frequently in the families of developmentally disabled adolescent sex offenders as in the families of nondisabled sex offenders according to Gilby et al.'s (1989) research.

Unfortunately, there are too few published research studies, and those studies that are reported lack adequate comparison groups to provide a demonstrative profile of the developmentally disabled adolescent sex offender. Our impression is that developmentally disabled offenders share many of the diagnostic and clinical characteristics common to most sex offenders. Self-esteem issues, common in many groups of offenders, are particularly salient among this population as few areas of competence exist or are emphasized (Haaven, Little, & Petre-Miller, 1990).

TREATMENT OF THE DEVELOPMENTALLY DISABLED ADOLESCENT SEX OFFENDER

A review of the literature on the treatment of developmentally disabled adult and adolescent sex offenders has highlighted the dearth of work in this area. The majority of treatment studies to date have been conducted with adult offenders and have focused on behaviorally oriented treatments (Rowe et al., 1987). Operant techniques such as facial screening (Barmann & Murray, 1981), contingent application of lemon juice (Cook, Altman, Shaw, & Blaylock, 1978) and overcorrection (Foxx, 1976) have been used to treat severely and profoundly developmentally disabled individuals. Aversion-suppression methods such as covert sensitization (with or without pairing of a noxious odor), satiation, and electrical aversion adapted for the developmentally disabled offender are described by Murphy, Coleman, and Haynes (1983). These authors also describe masturbatory reconditioning and imagery techniques utilizing pictures of appropriate-age partners.

Pharmacological interventions have also been used in the treatment of developmentally disabled sex offenders. These interventions most commonly include the use of the sex-drive-reducing (SDR) agents medroxyprogesterone acetate (MPA; Provera) or cyproterone acetate (CPA; Androcur) in Canada. The overall efficacy of SDR medication in reducing deviant urges and sexual fantasies among sex offenders in general has been demonstrated in numerous studies (Berlin, 1983; Bradford, 1985, 1987; Gagne, 1981; Hucker, Langevin, & Bain, 1988; Tennent, 1984). Of particular interest is the reported efficacy of treating developmentally disabled or organically impaired offenders with SDR medication. Bradford (1985) reports that CPA treatment was effective in controlling the expression of a serious sexual deviation with poor prognosis in a developmentally disabled sex offender.

Although there exist significant ethical considerations for the use of SDR medications on developmentally disabled sex offenders, particularly adolescents, this treatment does appear promising for certain competent developmentally disabled offenders (Gilby et al., 1989). A general sexual calming effect is attributed to both drugs, with minimal and reversible side effects, except for the potential for long-term impotency. These SDR medications are best administered in outpatient settings, where consent is likely to be freely given, and should be used in conjunction with psychotherapy. Gilby et al. (1989) suggest that a guardian's consent and the capacity to report differences in sexual interest and activity should be further considerations in decisions regarding SDR prescription.

Recent approaches to the psychological treatment of sex offenders who are developmentally disabled have used a modification of existing treatment programs for sex offenders (Murphy, Coleman, & Abel, 1983; Murphy, Coleman, & Haynes, 1983; Griffiths, Quinsey, & Hinsburger, 1989; Swanson & Garwick, 1990). These programs include both inpatient and institutionally based programs (e.g., Haaven et al., 1990) as well as community-based programs (e.g., Griffiths et al., 1989). In particular, treatments designed to enhance learning and generalization of skills or coping strategies have been advocated. Targeted are social and hetero- or homosocial skills (depending on the sexual orientation of the client), assertiveness and self-esteem training, anger management, cognitive restructuring around sexual myths and beliefs, human sexuality education, victim empathy training, and relapse prevention. We feel that these modifications offer particular promise for the developmentally disabled adolescent sex offender, who may come to the attention of mental health workers at a point of intervention prior to conviction and sentencing. Modifications of treatment programs for developmentally disabled sex offenders must be made on the basis of an understanding and familiarity with both the typical treatment approaches for sex offenders and the specific cognitive, behavioral, and emotional abilities of the developmentally disabled population.

Relapse prevention training for sex offenders was originally developed to provide an approach that would optimize the transfer of skills and coping strategies from a treatment setting to the community (Pithers, Marques, Gibat, & Marlett, 1983). This approach is based on the identification and recognition of precursors and risk situations for offending. A modified form of relapse prevention training has been used effectively on sex offenders with developmental disabilities (Griffiths et al., 1989). Our experience has confirmed the value of adapting components of this model for the treatment of disabled sex offenders (Stermac & Glancy, 1991). The model's emphasis on self-management, although not appropriate for all developmentally disabled offenders, allows for greater autonomy, enhances self-esteem, and fosters a sense of responsibility over behavior, all of which are particularly salient issues in the treatment of this population.

SPECIAL NEEDS OF THE DEVELOPMENTALLY DISABLED ADOLESCENT SEX OFFENDER

Although we have pointed out many of the similarities between the developmentally disabled adolescent sex offender and other sex offender populations, it is important to understand the differences between those offenders with developmental disabilities and those who are nondisabled. Of particular importance in treatment'planning are differences in sexual experiences (including histories of abuse), sexual knowledge, and opportunities for sexual expression.

Estimates of sexual abuse in the developmental histories of adolescent sex offenders range from 10% to 50% (Awad et al., 1984; Stermac & Matthews, 1987). Developmentally disabled adolescents may be particularly vulnerable to victimization; the developmentally disabled are reportedly four times more likely than the nondisabled to be victims of sexual abuse (Cowardin, 1986, reported in Senn, 1988).

Sexuality in the developmentally disabled is an area replete with myths, stereotypes, and misunderstanding among the general population, and often among caretakers of the disabled. Caretakers are often reluctant to provide socio-sexual skills training or to explain and assign masturbatory activities to the developmentally disabled (Murphy, Coleman, & Haynes, 1983). Few of those with developmental disabilities are encouraged to date, express their sexual needs, cohabit or marry (Brantlinger, 1985), and there is widespread ignorance on sexuality among developmentally disabled adults (Edmondson, McCombs, & Wish, 1979). In our experience, the sexual knowledge, experiences, and opportunities of the developmentally disabled adolescent are particularly important areas to be considered when working with this population.

A final issue involves a recognition of the diversity among the developmentally disabled population. Individuals scoring similarly on tests of intellectual functioning may have had varied experiences ranging from lifelong institutionalization to community living and educational "streaming" (normalization). Treatment and intervention strategies must be targeted to the client's social sophistication as well as to any specific behavioral deficits that he might have. Our emphasis is always on the client assuming responsibility for his own behavior, and we require him to be an active agent in his treatment.

REFERENCES

Awad, G., Saunders, E., & Levene, J. (1984). A clinical study of male adolescent sexual offenders. *International Journal of Offender Therapy and Comparative Criminology*, 28, 105–116.

Barmann, B. C., & Murray, W. J. (1981). Suppression of inappropriate sexual behavior by facial screening. *Behavior Therapy*, 12, 730–735.

Becker, J. V., & Abel, G. G. (1985). Methodological and ethical issues in evaluating and treating adolescent sexual offenders. In E. M. Otey & G. D. Ryan (Eds.), *Adolescent sex offenders: Issues in research and treatment*. Rockville, MD: U.S. Department of Health & Human Services.

Becker, J. V., Kaplan, M. S., & Kavoussi, R. (1988). Measuring the effectiveness of treatment for the aggressive adolescent sexual offender. In R. A. Prentky & V. L. Quinsey (Eds.), *Human sexual aggression: Current perspectives* (pp. 215–222). New York: New York Academy of Sciences.

Berlin, F. S. (1983). Sexual offenders: A biomedical perspective and a status report on biomedical treatment. In J. G. Greer & I. R. Stuart (Eds.), *The sexual aggressor: Current perspectives on treatment* (pp. 88–123). New York: Van Nostrand Reinhold.

Bradford, J. M. W. (1985). Organic treatments for the male sexual offender. *Behavioral Sciences and the Law*, 3, 355–375.

Bradford, J. M. W. (1987). Sadistic homosexual pedophilia: Treatment with cyproterone acetate: A single case study. *Canadian Journal of Psychiatry*, 32, 22–30.

Brantlinger, E. (1985). Mildly mentally retarded secondary students' information about and attitudes toward sexuality and sexuality education. *Education and Training of the Mentally Retarded*, 20, 99–108.

Cook, J. W., Altman, K., Shaw, J., & Blaylock, M. (1978). Use of contingent lemon juice to eliminate public masturbation by a severely retarded boy. *Behavior Research and Therapy*, 16, 131–134.

Cowardin, N. W. (1986). *Preventing sexual exploitation of adolescents with exceptional needs*. Unpublished manuscript.

Davis, G. E., & Leitenberg, H. (1987). Adolescent sex offenders. *Psychology Bulletin*, 101, 417–427.

Edmondson, B., McCombs. K., & Wish, J. (1979). What retarded adults believe about sex. *American Journal of Mental Deficiency, 84,* 11–18.

Foxx, R. M. (1976). The use of overcorrection to eliminate the public disrobing (stripping) of retarded women. *Behavior Research and Therapy, 14,* 53–61.

Gagne, P. (1981). Treatment of sexual offenders with medroxyprogesterone acetate. *American Journal of Psychiatry, 138,* 644–646.

Gilby, R., Wolf, L., & Goldberg, B. (1989). Mentally retarded adolescent sex offenders. A survey and pilot study. *Canadian Journal of Psychiatry, 34,* 542–548.

Griffiths, D., Hinsburger, D., & Christian, R. (1985). Treating developmentally handicapped sexual offenders: The York behaviour management services treatment program. *Psychiatric Aspects of Mental Retardation Reviews, 4,* 49–54.

Griffiths, D., Quinsey, V. L., & Hinsburger, D. (1989). *Changing inappropriate sexual behavior.* New York: Paill H. Brookes.

Groth, A. N. (1987). The adolescent sexual offender and his prey. *International Journal of Offender Therapy and Comparative Criminology, 21,* 249–254.

Haaven, J., Little, R., & Petre-Miller, D. (1990). *Treating intellectually disabled sex offenders.* Orwell, VT: Safer Society Press.

Hinsburger, D. (1987). Sex counselling with the developmentally handicapped: The assessment and management of seven critical problems. *Psychiatric Aspects of Mental Retardation Reviews, 6,* 41–46.

Hucker, S., Langevin, R., & Bain, J. (1988). A double blind trial of sexual drive reducing medication in pedophiles. *Annals of Sex Research, 1,* 227–242.

Kavoussi, R. J., Kaplan, M., & Becker, J. V. (1988). Psychiatric diagnosis in adolescent sex offenders. *Journal of the American Academy of Child and Adolescent Psychiatry, 27,* 241–243.

Lackey, L. B., & Knopp, F. H. (1989). A summary of selected notes from the working sessions of the First National Training Conference on the Assessment and Treatment of Intellectually disabled Juvenile and Adult Sexual Offenders. In F. H. Knopp (Ed.), *Selected readings: Sexual offenders identified as intellectually disabled.* Orwell, VT: Safer Society Press.

Matthews, F. (1987). *Adolescent sex offenders: A needs study.* Toronto: Central Toronto Youth Services.

Murphy, W. D., Coleman, E. M., & Abel, G. G. (1983). Human sexuality in the mentally retarded. In J. L. Matson & F. Andrasik (Eds.), *Treatment issues and innovations in mental retardation* (pp. 581–643). New York: Plenum Press.

Murphy, W. D., Coleman, E. M., & Haynes, M. R. (1983). Treatment and evaluation issues with the mentally retarded sex offender. In J. G. Greer & I. R. Stuart (Eds.), *The sexual aggressor: Current perspectives on treatment* (pp. 22–41). New York: Van Nostrand Reinhold.

Pithers, W. D., Marques, J. K., Gibat, C. C., & Marlett, G. A. (1983). Relapse prevention with sexual aggressives. In J. G. Greer & I. R. Stuart (Eds.), *The sexual aggressor: Current perspectives on treatment* (pp. 214–239). New York: Van Nostrand Reinhold.

Rogers, R. (1990). *Reaching for solutions: The report of the Special Advisor to the Minister of National Health and Welfare on child sexual abuse in Canada.* Ottawa: National Clearinghouse on Family Violence.

Rowe, W., Savage, S., Ragg, M., & Wigle, K. (1987). *Sexuality and the developmentally handicapped: A guidebook for health care professionals*. New York: Edwin Mellen.

Saunders, E., Awad, G. A., & White, G. (1986). Male adolescent sexual offenders: The offender and the offense. *Canadian Journal of Psychiatry, 31*, 542–549.

Senn, C. (1988). *Vulnerable: Sexual abuse and people with an intellectual handicap*. Toronto: G. Allan Roeher Institute.

Stermac, L., & Glancy, G. (1991). *Issues and approaches to the treatment of developmentally disabled sexual offenders*. Unpublished manuscript.

Stermac, L., & Matthews, F. (1987). *Adolescent sex offenders: Towards a profile*. Toronto: Central Toronto Youth Services.

Swanson, C. K., & Garwick, G. B. (1990). Treatment for low-functioning sex offenders: Group therapy and interagency coordination. *Mental Retardation, 28*, 155–161.

Tennent, G. (1984). Review of research into the use of drugs and the treatment of sexual deviations with special reference to the use of cyproterone acetate (Androcur). In H. Stancer, P. Garfinkel, & V. Rakoff (Eds.), *Guidelines for the use of psychotropic drugs* (pp. 411–426). Toronto: Spectrum.

CHAPTER 13

Treatment of the Juvenile Sex Offender within the Criminal Justice and Mental Health Systems

Howard E. Barbaree
Franca A. Cortoni

Increasingly, criminal justice and mental health professionals have come to recognize the importance of treatment of the adolescent sex offender. There are a number of reasons for this. A substantial proportion of all sex offenses can be attributed to adolescents. It is estimated that 20% of all rapes and as much as 50% of assaults against children are committed by juveniles (Deisher, Wenet, Paperny, Clark, & Fehrenbach, 1982; Showers, Farber, Joseph, Oshins, & Johnson, 1983). Moreover, professionals working with adult sex offenders have become increasingly aware of the proportions of their clients who have begun their deviant careers in adolescence. Approximately 50% of adult sex offenders report sexually deviant behavior in adolescence (Abel, Mittleman, & Becker, 1985; Becker & Abel, 1985; Longo & Groth, 1983; Groth, Longo, & McFadin, 1982). Therefore, if treatment is effective in reducing deviant behaviors, treatment of the juvenile offender could go a long way toward reducing the impact of sexual assault in our society.

In response to this perceived need for treatment, services for juvenile sex

offenders have multiplied throughout North America. In 1982, there were
only 20 recognized programs in the United States; but by 1988, this had
increased to over 520 programs specifically prepared to treat the juvenile sex
offender (National Adolescent Perpetrator Network, 1988). Unfortunately,
our knowledge of juvenile offenders and how to treat them lags behind the
perceived need for treatment. The literature contains numerous descriptions
of extant treatment programs (e.g., Becker, 1988; Elliot, 1987; Fillmore, 1987;
Groth, Hobson, Lucey, & St. Pierre, 1981; Johnson & Berry, 1989; Kahn &
Lafond, 1988). As well, the literature contains a number of articles promoting
particular kinds of treatment for juveniles, and arguing for the importance of
various components in treatment or the context in which treatment is given
(e.g., Groth et al., 1981; Margolin, 1984; Rowe, 1988; Stenson & Anderson,
1987). However, the literature contains very few reports of systematic research
evaluating the effectiveness of different treatment approaches. Therefore, it is
not known how effective treatment is for the juvenile sex offender, nor which
form of treatment is more effective, nor which contextual factors facilitate or
disrupt treatment.

In this uncertain environment, one might expect a good deal of controversy. However, it seems there is consensus on many issues. The National
Adolescent Perpetrator Network is a group of 800 professionals involved in the
treatment and assessment of the juvenile sex offender in the United States.
This group established the National Task Force on Juvenile Sexual Offending,
consisting of 20 participating members and 20 advisory members. The task
force was commissioned to develop professional standards for the assessment
and treatment of the juvenile sex offender. However, at an early stage in the
process, it was decided that the lack of substantive research in the area pre-
cluded the immediate setting of standards. Accordingly, the task force was
directed to suggest principles or common assumptions among professionals in
the area that might lay the groundwork for eventual standards. The preliminary report of the task force (National Adolescent Perpetrator Network,
1988) presented 221 assumptions that were endorsed by at least 90% of the
task force participants, with many of the stated assumptions receiving unan-
imous support. The assumptions were grouped according to various categories,
including: community protection, system and legal response, assessment, and
treatment. The assumptions covered all aspects of criminal justice and clinical
intervention in cases of sexual assault by juveniles.

The present chapter provides an overview of issues relating to the assessment and treatment of the juvenile sex offender, and its role in the criminal
justice system. The chapter depends heavily on the preliminary report of the
task force described above, but it is beyond the scope of the present chapter to
provide complete coverage of the report. Instead, we use the task force report
as a framework for raising what we feel are the more salient issues.

DENIAL AND MINIMIZATION AMONG
JUVENILE SEX OFFENDERS

For clinicians and professionals working with the sex offender, it comes as no surprise that many juvenile offenders deny their offenses (Becker, 1988; Bethea-Jackson & Brissett-Chapman, 1989; Fillmore, 1987; French, 1989; Margolin, 1984; McConaghy, Blaszczynski, Armstrong, & Kidson, 1989; Rowe, 1988; Ryan, Lane, Davis, & Isaac, 1987; Shoor, Speed, & Bertelt, 1966). Even if the offender admits to an offense, he is very likely to distort the truth by minimizing the frequency, severity, and variety of his criminal sexual behavior. Much of what we currently know about denial and minimization comes from studies of adults. In a nonrandom survey of 114 volunteer incarcerated rapists, Scully and Marolla (1984) divided the sample into those men who admitted to the offense for which they had been convicted (41%), and those who denied committing a sexual offense (59%). Both groups presented justifications that were intended to support their denial, or to minimize responsibility for the offense. For example, among the deniers, 31% reasoned that they had not committed an offense, because the victim provoked them by being seductive. Thirty-four percent of the deniers and 24% of the admitters argued that their victims meant yes even though they said no. Of the deniers 69% claimed that their victims eventually relaxed and enjoyed the rape, and the same argument was put forward by 20% of the admitters. Sixty-nine percent of the deniers and 22% of the admitters alluded to the victim's unsavory sexual reputation as excuses for their crimes. Seventy-seven percent of admitters and 84% of deniers excused their behavior by attributing it to alcohol intoxication, while 40% of deniers and 33% of admitters explained their crimes by pointing to emotional problems caused by an unhappy childhood or current marital conflict.

Similar findings have been reported for the adult child molester. In a recent Canadian study of child molesters, Pollock and Hashmall (1991) focused on the thematic content and logical structure of the excuses of child molesters. Over 250 justificatory statements were taken from the records of 86 child molesters referred for psychiatric assessment and submitted to analysis. A total of 21 distinct excuses and six thematic categories were identified, and the authors were able to devise an "excuse syntax" to define the structure of the offenders' reasoning about their sexual improprieties.

Based in part on these findings, we have attempted to develop a typology of denial and minimization that would be applicable to both child molesters and rapists. The following discussion presents the typology in summary form. First, denial and minimization represent different degrees of the process; whereas denial is extreme and categorical, minimization is graded. Second, denial usually concerns either the facts in the case, or whether or not the offender has a "problem" that needs treatment, whereas minimization concerns the extent of the man's responsibility for the offense, the extent of his past offending, and the degree of harm his victim(s) suffered.

Denial of the facts can take different forms. First, the offender may deny that he committed the offense at all, claiming that he never had sexual relations with the victim. He may rationalize the fact that he has been convicted in a court of law by saying that he was framed, that the victims or the police were out to get him. Second, he may claim that although he did have sexual interactions with the victim, it was not an offense, because she consented, because she did not resist, because the victim somehow received some emotional benefit from the sexual experience, or because he was tricked into believing that she was older. Finally, the offender will admit to the act he is alleged to have committed, but deny that the interaction was sexual in nature. For example, he may claim that he was touching the victim for some legitimate reason (e.g., applying skin medication to a child), or that the assault was a nonsexual assault.

Minimization can take three basic forms: The offender will minimize the harm done to his victim(s), the extent of his previous offensive behavior, and the extent of his responsibility for the offenses. In minimizing victim harm, the offender will argue that the victim will recover and not suffer any long-term effects, that the victim had so many previous partners that the offense was of no consequence, or that the benefits the victim received from the experience outweighs the harm. In minimizing the extent of his previous offensive behavior, the offender may underestimate the number of his past victims, the frequency of his past offenses, the degree of force he has used, and the intrusiveness of the offensive behaviors he has committed.

Offenders minimize their own responsibility for their offenses in three ways: attributing blame to the victim, making external attributions, and making irresponsible internal attributions. The offender may absolve himself of any blame by attributing his behavior to external or situational factors, such as alcohol intoxication, stressful circumstances, social pressure, or provocation. The offender will absolve himself of blame by pointing to nonsexual personal problems that led to the offense, such as his past victimization, his deprived childhood, or his hormones or sex drive. Perhaps the most important way in which the offender absolves himself is to blame the victim. Offenders will claim that the victim was sexually provocative, or they will claim that the victim made them angry and therefore deserved her fate.

Based on the above typology of denial and minimization, we have developed the Denial and Minimization Checklist. The checklist was designed to be appropriate for use with both child molesters and rapists, and with both adults and adolescents. The checklist was completed by a psychometrist during assessment of offenders at the Kingston Sexual Behavior Clinic, a community-based outpatient clinic for sex offenders of all ages. On the checklist, the psychometrist indicated whether or not the offender denied the offense. If so, he or she then recorded the subcategory of denial. If the offender accepted that he had committed a sexual offense, but minimized the offense, then the psychometrist indicated as many ways in which the offender achieved his minimization by checking the appropriate subcategories. According to our use of the checklist, there is only one kind of denial checked for each man, but an offender may minimize his offenses in a variety of ways.

The checklist was completed for 50 consecutive cases attending the clinic. We divided the subject sample into adult and adolescent offenders, with adults being defined as men over the age of 18 years. As it happened, there were 30 adults and 20 juveniles in the sample. Table 13.1 presents some of the characteristics of each sample. The average age of the adult group was 40 years, and the average age of the juvenile group was almost 16, with a range from 12 to 17 years. The subject samples differed in some ways by offense history. The adults were predominantly incest offenders, while the adolescents were predominantly nonfamilial child molesters. The adolescents, of course, did not have their own children to offend against, so that category was not open to them. The subject samples were similar to the extent that they had both offended against children.

Table 13.2 presents the results of the Denial and Minimization Checklist on these samples. Sixty percent of the adults and 40% of the adolescents denied committing an offense. The majority of the adults denied having any interaction with the victim, while the various forms of denial were equally represented in

TABLE 13.1 Fifty Consecutive Admissions to an Outpatient Community-Based Treatment Program for Sex Offenders

	Adults	Adolescents
Number	30	20
Mean age (years)	40	15.89 (12–17)
Mean number of victims	1.5	2.47
Mean victim age (years)	9.25	7.45
Offense type (%)		
Non–familial child molest		
Against female	7	50
Against male	20	5
Against both	3	20
Incest		
Against female	53	0
Against male	10	0
Attempt rape	0	5
Other paraphilias	7	20
	100%	100%

TABLE 13.2 Denial and Minimization among 50 Consecutive Admissions to an Outpatient Community-Based Treatment Clinic for Sex Offenders

	Adults (n = 30)	Adolescents (n = 20)
Denial	18 (60%)	8 (40%)
Denial of any interaction	12	3
Denial interaction was sexual	4	2
Denial interaction was offense	2	3
Minimization	11 (37%)	10 (50%)
Of responsibility		
Victim blame	7	4
External attributions	5	2
Irresponsible internal attributions	3	3
Of extent		
Frequency	9	2
Number of previous victims	3	3
Force used	1	3
Intrusiveness	3	2
Of harm		
No long-term effects	3	1
Victim education	2	0
No denial or minimization	1 (3%)	2 (10%)

the adolescents. Thirty-seven percent of the adults and 50% of the adolescents agreed with the allegations that they had committed a sexual offense, but, in their explanation of their offense, they minimized their deviant behavior in some way. Men may minimize their offenses in numerous ways, so the column totals will be greater than the number of men who minimize in each group. There seem to be some trends in these data, but they are not statistically significant. A Chi Square test testing for dependence between deny/no deny and adult/adolescent was not significant χ^2 (1 d.f.) = 1.92, n.s. Very few individuals in each sample were judged to accept full responsibility for their offenses. Only 1 adult of 30, and 2 of 20 adolescents neither denied nor minimized their offenses. Again, there is a trend toward adolescents showing less denial and minimization. These data show clearly that only a very small minority of sex offenders accept full responsibility for their behavior. And this statement seems to be true for both adolescent and adult subgroups.

While these data characterize the nature of denial and minimization, they do not describe the psychological processes that lead to denial. Since the results of assessment often have important consequences for sentencing, parole decisions, and child custody and access disputes, offenders frequently lie about their offenses as a self-protective strategy. While denial of the offense, obfuscation of facts, and suppression of responses during assessment are conscious components of the offender's denial, as well, there may be aspects of this denial that the offender does not purposefully control and of which he is at best only marginally aware. Subconscious denial and minimization are the result of psychological processes involving distortion, mistaken attribution, rationalization, and selective attention and memory. The process serves to reduce the offender's self-blame and sense of responsibility for his offenses. And it seems to be successful, since only 14% of sexual offenders report being remorseful for their offense (Wormith, 1983).

These denials and distortions compromise both the accurate assessment and the effective treatment of sex offenders of all ages. Therapists depend on the offender's veridical descriptions of events leading to past offenses in order to determine which behaviors need to be targeted in therapy. In assessing progress in therapy, the therapist depends on faithful accounts of the offender's ongoing fantasies and sexual behaviors. Denial is generally regarded as an important impediment to successful therapy and as a consequence, many treatment programs exclude juvenile offenders who steadfastly deny their offense (Lombardo & DiGiorgio-Miller, 1988; Stenson & Anderson, 1987). While in denial, the offender often concludes that he has no problems and that there is no reason for him to enter treatment. In addition, family members and friends of the offender often support him in his denial (Stevenson, Castillo, & Sefarbi, 1989), often against the allegations of another family member. Important differences have been found between the family structures of admitters and deniers (Sefarbi, 1990). Denial and minimization create an environment in which the offender does not want to be assessed or treated, and he is opposed to the suggestions and concerns expressed by the professional. The offender will behave as if he is the victim, self-righteously protesting his innocence and demanding that his rights be recognized and respected. Offenders are often litigious, and their litigiousness will interfere with treatment progress (Miller, Maier, Blancke, & Doren, 1986).

PRIMARY OBJECTIVES OF INTERVENTION: PROTECTION OF THE COMMUNITY

The earlier permissive view that adolescent sex offending was the result of sexual experimentation or that it was somehow just a part of normal development (Maclay, 1960; Markey, 1950; Roberts, Abrams, & Finch, 1973) encouraged earlier clinicians to suggest decriminalizing sexual offenses among adolescents. The suggestion was made that these crimes be investigated and adjudicated by mental health professionals and that the appropriate response to the adolescent sex offender was a nonprosecutorial response such as diversion. However, in contrast to this earlier permissive view, by far the greater concern among contemporary professionals is that treating the juvenile offender as a noncriminal would encourage the offender and his family in their denial and minimization (National Adolescent Perpetrator Network, 1988).

At the present time, professionals in the area argue that the primary objective of intervention with the juvenile sex offender is the protection of the community (National Adolescent Perpetrator Network, 1988). With this in mind, the initial stages of intervention must involve the criminal justice system, with law enforcement agencies investigating cases, and proceeding with criminal charges when sufficient evidence is available. The current view is that criminal charges for juvenile sex offenses should reflect the actual sexual behavior alleged to have been committed, and should reflect the degree of force or violence used by the offender (National Adolescent Perpetrator Network, 1988). When the strength of the evidence permits, plea bargaining should be avoided, since it can be used later by the offender and his family in denial and minimization. When the offender and his family adopt a position of strong denial or minimization, the criminal justice system should proceed to trial when the evidence warrants (Stenson & Anderson, 1987). These responses are desirable to convey the seriousness of sexual offenses to the offender and the community, and to respond in a way that is commensurate with the harm done to the victim. It is hoped that the consequence of these actions by the criminal justice system will be to increase young men's accountability for their sexual behavior.

Beyond prosecution, further steps must be taken to ensure the safety of the victim(s) in particular and the community in general. These precautions must be taken in the short term during prosecution, and in the long term, while a sentence is being served. As soon as an investigation begins, steps must be taken to protect the victim, and these steps should include separation of the offender from the victim and monitoring of attempts by the offender to contact or threaten the victim (National Adolescent Perpetrator Network, 1988). These steps may include the appointment of a victim advocate. When an offender is ordered by the court to a community-based residence, or if the offender is on bail awaiting trial, the court should specifically address the issue of safety of the victim by placing restrictions on the offender's movements and contacts (Stenson & Anderson, 1987). If the victim resides in the same home as the offender, the offender should be removed from the home until a final disposition is made by the court (Rowe, 1988; Saunders & Awad, 1988).

Some juvenile offenders are dangerous to the point where they cannot be safely kept or treated in the community, and they may require varying degrees of residential security and supervision (Groth et al., 1981). At the same time, decisions concerning placement for the juvenile have to consider the safety of the offender, who may be vulnerable to reprisals from other offenders, or the family of the victim (Groth et al., 1981). However, when the needs of the offender for security and treatment are in conflict with the needs of the victim(s) and the community for security, the needs of the community should be given the higher priority (National Adolescent Perpetrator Network, 1988).

In most jurisdictions, penalties for juveniles are greatly reduced compared with adults, including reduced or limited sentence lengths. The length of sentences possible for juveniles may be as short as 1–2 years, and as such, may not provide adequate long-term protection of society. In these jurisdictions, juvenile offenders who have committed very serious offenses, such as brutal sexual assaults and murder, should be transferred to adult court for trial so that sentencing can provide for the long-term safety of the community (National Adolescent Perpetrator Network, 1988).

THE CRIMINAL JUSTICE SYSTEM SUPPORT FOR TREATMENT

There is widespread acceptance of the notion that incarceration alone, or any other penalty imposed by the criminal justice system, does not change sexual offending behavior (Fillmore, 1987; Saunders & Awad, 1988). It is generally accepted that treatment, in concert with the criminal justice system, can reduce the risk these young men pose to society (National Adolescent Perpetrator Network, 1988). But effective treatment requires support from the criminal justice system, and the following section shows how this support can be accomplished.

As described above, denial and minimization are serious problems among this population. Consequently, there is wide agreement that juvenile sex offenders do not possess sufficient internal motivation for treatment and behavior change. Therefore, it is commonly felt that court-mandated treatment is necessary. Beyond this external motivation for treatment, internal motivation may improve the prognosis; but it should not be seen as a prerequisite for entrance into treatment nor should it be considered a guarantee of success (Fillmore, 1987; Groth et al., 1981). The mandate for treatment may require the offender to choose between treatment and incarceration. Later, release from incarceration may be made contingent on successful participation in treatment. In addition, family members of the offenders may require a court order forcing their compliance with the offender's treatment requirements, and prohibiting them from interfering with treatment (Fillmore, 1987; Lombardo & DiGiorgio-Miller, 1988; Saunders & Awad, 1988).

Further, it is not sufficient to simply mandate treatment at sentencing or in preparation for release from incarceration. The criminal justice system should provide for the longest possible period of follow-up monitoring (probation and parole). Probation and parole officers should file violations for offenders who have not complied with the demands of treatment, either in terms of work accomplished or progress made (National Adolescent Perpetrator Network, 1988).

TREATMENT SUPPORT FOR THE CRIMINAL JUSTICE SYSTEM

While successful treatment of the juvenile offender requires support from the criminal justice system, as described above, effective management of the offender in the criminal justice system requires reciprocal support from treatment professionals. Among treatment professionals, their obligation to ensure the safety of the community takes precedence over all other conflicting considerations (Fillmore, 1987; Johnson, & Berry, 1989; Ryan et al., 1987), including the treatment professional's broad range of responsibilities to their client, the sex offender.

This obligation to protect the community may include the reporting of incidents of sexual offenses by juveniles disclosed during treatment (Margolin, 1984). Because of the high rate of sexual offenses and the low rate of reporting of sexual offenses, it is very likely that offenders in treatment will have committed a number of unreported offenses. It is almost always advantageous for the treatment professional to have knowledge of these unreported offenses, and most treatment professionals will encourage additional disclosures. Disclosure of additional offenses during treatment should not necessarily result in reports by the professional unless the disclosure changes the assessment of risk and a new charge is necessary to protect the public, or to ensure victim safety (National Adolescent Perpetrator Network, 1988). If new disclosures change the assessment of risk and needs, these reports should be made to both law enforcement and social service agencies (National Adolescent Perpetrator Network, 1988), and new charges and prosecution should be pursued to achieve a more appropriate intervention. In this instance, it is the duty of the treatment provider to advocate for the offender's continuation in treatment (Margolin, 1984). But when community safety and treatment concerns are not compatible, community safety must take the highest priority (National Adolescent Perpetrator Network, 1988).

Disclosing offenses that have not been previously reported may have benefits in therapy. It has been argued that confidentiality cannot apply in the treatment of this population, because it promotes the secrecy that supports offending and may endanger the community. The offender must be willing to give up secrecy if he is to succeed in treatment (Margolin, 1983).

Treatment providers have the obligation to demand that the offender participate actively in and successfully complete treatment (Margolin, 1983). Offenders should not be considered to have complied with mandated treatment simply by attending the clinic. When offenders drop out of treatment, or when they attend without expending effort at treatment, the treatment provider must notify an authority in the criminal justice system, such as the court, parole officer, and so on (National Adolescent Perpetrator Network, 1988). Similarly, when treatment providers see signs of increased risk during treatment, they are under a clear obligation to notify the criminal justice authorities and to ensure that appropriate action is taken (National Adolescent Perpetrator Network, 1988).

CLINICAL ASSESSMENT

Current authoritative opinion is that assessment of the juvenile sex offender is necessary to inform a variety of decisions regarding the management of the offender, but also that it is a demanding and difficult task. At the present time, the research literature is lacking validation for any particular assessment instruments or criteria with which to assess risk in the juvenile sex offender. The strategies and instruments for suggested risk assessment (e.g., Ross, Loss, & Associates, 1988; Smith & Monastersky, 1986), and the typologies which have been presented (e.g., Smith, 1990) are in a preliminary stage of development and should be used with caution (Lombardo & DiGiorgio-Miller, 1988; Rowe, 1988; Saunders & Awad, 1988). At the same time, there is overwhelming support for the importance of assessment, particularly when an offender is being considered for some kind of treatment or for reduced security or less supervision (Becker, 1988; Bethea-Jackson & Brissett-Chapman, 1989; Gilbey, Wolf, & Goldberg, 1989; Groth et al., 1981; Lombardo & DiGeorgio-Miller, 1988; Saunders & Awad, 1988; Stenson & Anderson, 1987).

Assessments should be comprehensive, covering all aspects of the juvenile's behavior and functioning, and assessment of risk for future offending must be based on a complete account of the offender's history of offending (Saunders & Awad, 1988). A comprehensive assessment would include multiple sessions with the offender and should also include a review of the testimony or statements of the victim(s), interviews with family members, teachers and school officials, and any other individuals who would have important information in a particular case (Becker, 1988; Bethea-Jackson & Brissett-Chapman, 1989; Lombardo & DiGiorgio-Miller, 1988; Gilbey et al., 1989; Johnson & Berry, 1989).

Phallometric assessment has become a standard part of the assessment of the adult sex offender (Barbaree, 1990; Earls & Marshall, 1983). However, use of the phallometric test with juveniles has been an issue of some controversy. Some programs and clinicians use phallometric assessment as a standard part of their assessment battery with juveniles, and testing of adolescents with this method has been done with offenders as young as 11 years of age (e.g., Becker, Hunter, Stein, & Kaplan, 1989). Becker (1988) claims that the adolescents tolerate the tests well and show responses comparable to those shown by adults. On the other hand, some other clinicians use this method of assessment in a very cautious way. Saunders and Awad (1988) use phallometric assessment only in cases where the offender has committed a very serious offense. These authors base their caution on the following: (1) There are no published studies demonstrating the reliability, validity, or predictive power of the phallometric test with juveniles; (2) these authors have found it difficult to obtain consent to the testing, not only from the offender but from his parents; and (3) exposing boys under the age of 16 to explicit descriptions of deviant sexual acts through the use of audio and videotapes raises ethical issues that they have not been able to resolve. At the very least, testing of older juveniles with less explicit and less deviant stimuli is commonly accepted and justifiable.

TREATMENT

Following disclosure of the offense(s), and the identification of the offender, treatment intervention should begin as soon as possible (National Adolescent Perpetrator Network, 1988). The level of intervention and the kind of treatment should be determined individually on the basis of the comprehensive assessment of the individual offender's behavioral deficits and excesses. The needs assessment should be updated periodically as the treatment provider becomes more familiar with the individual case (Gilby et al., 1989; Rowe, 1988).

Treatment for the sex offender should be highly structured (Groth et al., 1981; Margolin, 1983; Ryan et al., 1987). It may include written treatment contracts, involving the therapist and parole (probation) officer on the one hand and the offender and his family on the other. Treatment aims at increasing the offender's accountability and his sense of responsibility for his own treatment and prevention of further offending. However, in addition, the treatment provider, in conjunction with the appropriate criminal justice authority, is responsible for setting appropriate external controls in place to allow for the monitoring of high-risk situations and verification of the offender's whereabouts and movements (Margolin, 1983).

Treatment of the juvenile sex offender should be sex-offender specific and it should be conducted in a sex-offender-specific treatment setting (Margolin, 1983; Saunders & Awad, 1988; Stenson & Anderson, 1987). If possible, the juvenile sex offender should be treated within the context of his sex-offender peer group (Fillmore, 1987; Johnson & Berry, 1989; Margolin, 1983; Stenson & Anderson, 1987). Within the group setting, treatment should involve direct confrontation, but such confrontation must be done in a controlled and supportive environment, and confrontation should not be confused with humiliation or abusive attacks, which are unacceptable (Margolin, 1983; Ryan et al., 1987; Stenson & Anderson, 1987).

Treatment that is not sex-offender specific, such as insight-oriented individual psychotherapy, is not seen to be sufficient to modify sexually abusive behaviors. According to the consensus of modern professionals, this kind of psychotherapy may be detrimental to the offender's treatment and may even increase the risk to the community if used exclusively in response to sexual offenses (National Adolescent Perpetrator Network, 1988). The juvenile sex offender treatment provider has unique requirements of training. Some of the training and background common for generic mental health workers may predispose professionals to make errors in their treatment of the juvenile sex offender (Margolin, 1983; Ryan et al., 1987; National Adolescent Perpetrator Network, 1988). Often, the generic mental health professional's overriding concern for confidentiality and his or her allegiance and perceived professional obligations to the sex-offender client outweighs the legitimate concern for the safety of victims and the community. The misplaced loyalty will often inhibit the professional from reporting crimes when they should be reported and from making appropriate demands for adherence to treatment requirements. Unfortunately, at present, there are very few educational settings that provide appropriate training for the aspiring sex-offender professional.

Treatment specific to the juvenile sex offender must target certain issues that have been identified by numerous clinicians during many years working with this population (Becker, 1988; Davis & Leitenberg, 1987; Gilby et al., 1989; Hains, Herrman, Baker, & Graber, 1986; Lombardo & DiGiorgio-Miller, 1988; Rowe, 1988; Ryan et al., 1987; Saunders & Awad, 1988; Stenson & Anderson, 1987). In the present chapter, we are reviewing the literature on treatment components, but are presenting them in the context of a staged model of treatment, and this is presented in Table 13.3.

As mentioned earlier, the problem of denial and minimization is serious in this population (Becker, 1988; Bethea-Jackson & Brissett-Chapman, 1989; Fillmore, 1987; French, 1989; Margolin, 1984; McConaghy et al., 1989; Rowe, 1988; Ryan, 1987; Shoor et al., 1966). As long as the offender denies his offense, he will not be motivated to engage in treatment as a sex offender. As well, victim blame precludes victim empathy, or at least limits the development of victim empathy. As soon as denial and minimization is successfully reduced, the offender can then begin to develop victim empathy and is more motivated to work toward change in his behavior. We consider that these two components of therapy, denial/minimization and victim empathy, as together forming a first step that increases the offender's motivation for treatment and behavior change. Therefore, the first stage in treatment targets denial and minimization and successful completion of this stage is a prerequisite to successful treatment.

Once the offender has attained an acceptable level of treatment motivation, treatment aimed at changing sexually deviant behaviors begins. Relapse prevention has been suggested as a way to maintain the behavior change produced in the treatment of individuals suffering from various forms of addic-

TABLE 13.3. Stages of Treatment of the Sex Offender

Pretreatment: Developing Motivation for Behavior Change
1. Denial
2. Minimization
3. Victim blame → Victim empathy

Treatment Planning
4. Understanding precursors to offending and the offense cycle

Treatment: Achieving Behavior Change
Deviant sexual behavior
5. Reducing deviant sexual arousal
6. Eliminating cognitive distortions
7. Addressing issues of their own victimization
8. Enhancing healthy sexuality, including increasing sexual knowledge

Nonsexual contributions to offending
9. Increasing social competence and anger control
10. Decreasing criminal thinking, life-style, and behavior
11. Substance abuse treatment
12. Family dysfunction and peer support for offending

Posttreatment: Preventing the Recurrence of Sex Offending
13. Developing a relapse prevention plan
    a. Internal self-management
    b. External supervision
14. Relapse prevention
15. Follow-up

tions. Marlatt and Gordon (1980, 1985) have outlined a strategy for assisting individuals who have completed treatment to prevent the recurrence of substance-abusing behavior. The strategy involves (1) identifying situations in which the individual is at high risk for relapse, (2) teaching the individual to identify these high-risk situations and how to avoid them, (3) identifying lapses as behaviors that do not constitute full-fledged relapses (e.g., drinking alcohol) but that constitute approximations to the drug-taking behavior and that may be a precursor to a relapse (e.g., frequenting bars), (4) teaching the individual to identify a lapse, and (5) teaching the individual various coping strategies that might be used in response to both high-risk situations and lapses to minimize the chances of a relapse.

Pithers, Marques, Gibat, and Marlatt (1983) have extended the relapse prevention strategy for use with sex offenders, and this approach has had broad clinical appeal. An edited volume has recently been published describing various aspects of the use of relapse prevention with sex offenders (Laws, 1989).

The principles involved are similar to those used with addicts. First, high-risk situations are identified for each offender (MacDonald & Pithers, 1989; Pithers, Beal, Armstrong, & Petty, 1989), and he is taught to identify their occurrence. Second, he is taught to identify lapses or decisions he makes that lead him closer to a relapse (Jenkins-Hall & Marlatt, 1989). Finally, he is taught to cope with high-risk situations and lapses to prevent the occurrence of a relapse (Carey & McGrath, 1989; Steenman, Nelson, & Viesti, 1989). As yet, no studies of outcome have been reported for relapse prevention, but most clinicians are optimistic that relapse prevention will eventually be shown to be an effective component in therapy.

Ryan et al. (1987) have described the sexual assault cycle as a framework for juvenile sex offenders to conceptualize and understand the cognitive, behavioral, psychological, and situational factors that have led to their deviant behavior in the past. These authors also point to the fact that the sexual assault cycle offers a means of demonstrating to offenders how their behavior is similar to other sex offenders. The sexual assault cycle is thought to be an important framework for treatment of the juvenile offender by numerous authors (e.g., Fillmore, 1987; Groth et al., 1981; Lombardo & DiGiorgio-Miller, 1988).

One of the important developments during the assault cycle among sex offenders is sexual arousal, and the arousal among offenders to deviant sexual cues is well known (Barbaree, 1990; Freund & Blanchard, 1989). Treatment of deviant arousal is a central component of the treatment of the adult sex offender (e.g., Abel, Levis, & Clancy, 1970; Laws, 1989), and Abel and Becker, and their associates (Becker, 1988; Becker & Abel, 1985; Becker et al., 1989) have pointed to the importance of treatment of deviant arousal in the juvenile offender.

The way the adult offender thinks of sexuality and his role in the sexual relationship is often supportive of his deviant sexual behavior, including seeing children as sexually motivated, seeing victims as responsible for their own victimization, and so on (Abel, Becker, & Cunningham-Rathner, 1984), and it is generally accepted that these distorted beliefs and attitudes must be changed in any effective treatment of the sex offender (Murphy, 1990). Many clinicians who have had experience with juvenile offenders argue for a component in therapy that targets these distorted cognitions (Lombardo & DiGiorgio-Miller, 1988; Ryan et al., 1987).

An important issue that needs to be targeted in the treatment of the juvenile offender is the offender's own victimization (Ryan et al., 1987; Showers et al., 1983). It has been suggested that the offender's own victimization is causally related to deviant sexual arousal (Becker et al., 1989). Sex education and other therapeutic efforts have been directed toward the development in the juvenile of a "healthy sexuality" (Groth et al., 1981; Hains et al., 1986; Lombardo & DiGiorgio-Miller, 1988).

Besides issues relating directly to deviant or nondeviant sexual behavior, many clinicians point to the contribution of nonsexual behaviors and motivations as they contribute to sexual offenses. These nonsexual contributors to sexual abuse may include (1) deficits in social competence; (2) anger and hostility (3) criminal thinking, life-style, and behavior, (4) substance abuse; and (5) family dysfunction. Clinicians have argued that a comprehensive treatment for the juvenile sex offender should include anger and stress management (Fillmore, 1987; Groth et al., 1981; Hains et al., 1986; Lombardo & DiGiorgio-Miller, 1988; Ryan et al., 1987). Margolin (1983) has argued convincingly that an effective treatment for the juvenile offender must deal with the aggressive and exploitive aspects of sexual offenses. In a related vein, some authors have pointed to the diverse criminal behaviors among the juvenile sex offenders they have seen and have argued that treatment should target criminal thinking and behavior (Davis & Leitenberg, 1987; Vinogradov, Dishotsky, Doty, & Tinklenberg, 1988). Many authors have focused on substance abuse among the juvenile offenders in their samples and have specified treatment for this abuse as being an important component of the comprehensive treatment of the juvenile offender (Awad & Saunders, 1989; Fagan & Wexler, 1988; Hsu & Starzynski, 1990; Milier, 1973; Mio, Nanjundappa, Verleur, & de-Rios, 1986; Tinklenberg, Murphy, Murphy, & Pfefferbaum, 1981; Tinklenberg & Woodrow, 1974; Van Ness, 1984; Vinogradov et al., 1988). Finally, the issue of family dysfunction, and the contribution of family disorder to sexual abuse by juveniles, has been specified (Becker, Cunningham-Rathner, & Kaplan, 1986; Blaske, Borduin, Henggeler, & Mann, 1989; Fehrenbach, Smith, Monastersky, & Deisher, 1986; Fillmore, 1987; Henderson, English, & MacKenzie, 1988).

Blaske et al. (1989) have reported that juvenile sex offenders and their mothers reported high rates of neurotic symptoms, and the peer relations of sex offenders showed relatively low levels of emotional bonding. And Sefarbi (1990) has reported the results from structured interviews with juvenile sex offenders and their families that deniers tended to be caught in an enmeshed family organization, while admitters were in a disengaged family system. For the whole group, there were significant positive correlations between the extent of parental nurturance and adolescent self-esteem and between lack of clear communication and mixed messages about sexuality. An adequate treatment of the juvenile offender will target family dysfunction when the assessment indicates that these problems have contributed to the sexual offense, when these family problems act to support denial and minimization, or when the family acts to disrupt treatment.

CONCLUSION

The successful treatment of the juvenile sex offender depends on numerous factors. First, treatment must be provided within a criminal justice framework that supports treatment by giving the offender and his family incentives for participating in treatment. These incentives may include treatment while on probation as an alternative to incarceration, or early release from incarceration as an outcome of successful treatment. Second, treatment must support the rehabilitative and control functions of the criminal justice system through appropriate reporting of risk and adherence to treatment requirements. Third, an adequate treatment intervention will be based on a detailed comprehensive assessment of the offender and his risk for reoffense. Fourth, treatment of the juvenile sex offender will be (1) comprehensive, targeting a broad range of issues; (2) cognitive-behavioral in format with relapse prevention; (3) sex-offender specific in that it targets issues directly related to sexual assault; and (4) administered by an appropriately trained professional. Finally, we need to conduct well-designed treatment outcome studies with juveniles to assess the efficacy of the treatment approach describe here.

REFERENCES

Abel, G. G., Becker, J. V., & Cunningham-Rathner, J. (1984). Complications, consent and cognitions in sex between children and adults. *International Journal of Law and Psychiatry, 7*, 89–103.

Abel, G. G., Levis, D. J., & Clancy, J. (1970). Aversion therapy applied to taped sequences of deviant behavior in exhibitionism and other sexual deviations. *Journal of Behavior Therapy and Experimental Psychiatry, 1*, 59–66.

Abel, G. G., Mittleman, M. S., & Becker, J.V. (1985). Sex offenders: Results of assessment and recommendations for treatment. In M. H. Ben-Aron, S. J. Hucker, & C. D. Webster (Eds.), *Clinical criminology: The assessment and treatment of criminal behavior* (pp. 207–220). Toronto: M & M Graphics.

Awad, G. A., & Saunders, E. (1989). Adolescent child molesters: Clinical observations. *Child Psychiatry and Human Development, 19*, 195–206.

Barbaree, H. E. (1990). Stimulus control of sexual arousal: Its role in sexual assault. In W. L. Marshall, D. R. Laws, & H. E. Barbaree (Eds.), *Handbook of sexual assault: Issues, theories, and treatment of the offender* (pp. 115–142). New York: Plenum Press.

Becker, J. V. (1988). Adolescent sex offenders. *Behavior Therapist, 11*, 185–187.

Becker, J. V., & Abel, G. G. (1985). Methodological and ethical issues in evaluating and treating adolescent sexual offenders. In E. M. Otey & G. D. Ryan (Eds.), *Adolescent sex offenders: Issues in research and treatment* (pp. 109–129). Rockville, MD: Department of Health & Human Services.

Becker, J. V., Cunningham-Rathner, J., & Kaplan, M. S. (1986). Adolescent sexual offenders: Demographics, criminal and sexual histories, and recommendations for reducing future offenses. *Journal of Interpersonal Violence, 1*, 431–445.

Becker, J. V., Hunter, J. A., Stein, R. M., & Kaplan, M. S. (1989). Factors associated with erection in adolescent sex offenders. *Journal of Psychopathology and Behavioral Assessment, 11*, 353–362.

Bethea-Jackson, G., & Brissett-Chapman, S. (1989). The juvenile sexual offender: Challenges to assessment for outpatient intervention. *Child and Adolescent Social Work Journal*, 6, 127–137.

Blaske, D. M., Borduin, C. M., Henggeler, S. W., & Mann, B. J. (1989). Individual, family, and peer characteristics of adolescent sex offenders and assaultive offenders. *Developmental Psychology*, 25, 846–855.

Carey, C. H., & McGrath, R. J. (1989). Coping with urges and craving. In D. R. Laws (Ed.), *Relapse prevention with sex offenders* (pp. 188–196). New York: Guilford Press.

Davis, G. E., & Leitenberg, H. (1987). Adolescent sex offenders. *Psychological Bulletin*, 101, 417–427.

Deisher, R. W., Wenet, G. A., Paperny, D. M., Clark, T. F., & Fehrenbach, P. A. (1982). Adolescent sexual offense behavior: The role of the physician. *Journal of Adolescent Health Care*, 2, 279–286.

Earls, C. M., & Marshall, W. L. (1983). The current state of technology in the laboratory assessment of sexual arousal patterns. In J. G. Greer & I. R. Stuart (Eds.), *The sexual aggressor: Current perspectives on treatment* (pp. 336–362). New York: Van Nostrand Reinhold.

Elliot, J. G. (1987). The treatment of serious juvenile delinquents in Massachusetts. *Educational Psychology in Practice*, 3, 49–52.

Fagan, J., & Wexler, S. (1988). Explanations of sexual assault among violent delinquents Special Issue: Adolescent sexual behavior. *Journal of Adolescent Research*, 3, 363–385.

Fehrenbach, P. A., Smith, W., Monastersky, C., & Deisher, R. W. (1986). Adolescent sexual offenders: Offender and offense characteristics. *American Journal of Orthopsychiatry*, 56, 225–233.

Fillmore, A. (1987). Treatment of the juvenile sex offender. *Health Visitor*, 60, 97–98.

French, D. D. (1989). Distortion and lying as defense processes in the adolescent child molester. *Journal of Offender Counseling, Services and Rehabilitation*, 14, 161–167.

Freund, K., & Blanchard, R. (1989). Phallometric diagnosis of pedophilia. *Journal of Consulting and Clinical Psychology*, 57, 100–105.

Gilby, R., Wolf, L., & Goldberg, B. (1989). Mentally retarded adolescent sex offenders: A survey and pilot study. *Canadian Journal of Psychiatry*, 34, 542–548.

Groth, A., Longo, R. E., & McFadin, J. (1982). Undetected recidivism among rapists and child molesters. *Crime and Delinquency*, 28, 450–458.

Groth, A. N., Hobson, W. F., Lucey, K. P., & St. Pierre, J. (1981). Juvenile sexual offenders: Guidelines for treatment. *International Journal of Offender Therapy and Comparative Criminology*, 25, 265–275.

Hains, A. A., Herrman, L. P., Baker, K. L., & Graber, S. (1986). The development of a psycho-educational group program for adolescent sex offenders. *Journal of Offender Counseling, Services and Rehabilitation*, 11, 63–76.

Henderson, J. E., English, D. J., & MacKenzie, W. R. (1988). Family centered casework practice with sexually aggressive children. *Journal of Social Work and Human Sexuality*, 7, 89–108.

Hsu, L., & Starzynski, J. (1990). Adolescent rapists and adolescent child sexual assaulters. *International Journal of Offender Therapy and Comparative Criminology*, 34, 23–30.

Jenkins-Hall, K. D., & Marlatt, G. A. (1989). Apparently irrelevant decisions in the relapse process. In D. R. Laws (Ed.), *Relapse prevention with sex offenders* (pp. 47–55). New York: Guilford Press.

Johnson, T. C., & Berry, C. (1989). Children who molest: A treatment program. *Journal of Interpersonal Violence, 4,* 185–203.

Kahn, T. J., & Lafond, M. A. (1988). Treatment of the adolescent sexual offender. *Child and Adolescent Social Work Journal, 5,* 135–148.

Laws, D. R. (Ed.). (1989). *Relapse prevention with sex offenders.* New York: Guilford Press.

Lombardo, R., & DiGiorgio-Miller, J. (1988). Concepts and techniques in working with juvenile sex offenders. *Journal of Offender Counseling, Services and Rehabilitation, 13,* 39–53.

Longo, R. E., & Groth, A. N. (1983). Juvenile sexual offenses in the histories of adult rapists and child molesters. *International Journal of Offender Therapy and Comparative Criminology, 27,* 150–155.

McConaghy, N., Blaszczynski, A. P., Armstrong, M. S., & Kidson, W. (1989). Resistance to treatment of adolescent sex offenders. *Archives of Sexual Behavior, 18,* 97–107.

MacDonald, R. K., & Pithers, W. D. (1989). Self-monitoring to identify high-risk situations. In D. R. Laws (Ed.), *Relapse prevention with sex offenders* (pp. 96–104). New York: Guilford Press.

Maclay, D. T. (1960). Boys who commit sexual misdemeanours. *British Medical Journal, 11,* 186–190.

Margolin, L. (1983). A treatment model for the adolescent sex offender. *Journal of Offender Counseling, Services and Rehabilitation, 8,* 1–12.

Margolin, L. (1984). Group therapy as a means of learning about the sexually assaultive adolescent. *International Journal of Offender Therapy and Comparative Criminology, 28,* 65–72.

Markey, O. B. (1950). A study of aggressive sex misbehavior in adolescents brought to juvenile court. *American Journal of Orthopsychiatry, 20,* 719–731.

Marlatt, G. A., & Gordon, J. R. (1980). Determinants of relapse: Implications for the maintenance of behavior change. In P. O. Davidson & S. M. Davidson (Eds.), *Behavioral medicine: Changing health lifestyles* (pp. 410–452). New York: Brunner/Mazel.

Marlatt, G. A., & Gordon, J. R. (Eds.) (1985). *Relapse prevention: Treatment strategies in the treatment of the addictive behaviors.* New York: Guilford Press.

Miller, D. (1973). The treatment of adolescent sexual disturbances. *International Journal of Child Psychotherapy, 2,* 93–126.

Miller, R. D., Maier, G. J., Blancke, F. W., & Doren, D. (1986). Litigiousness as a resistance to therapy. *Journal of Psychiatry and the Law, 14,* 109–123.

Mio, J. S., Nanjundappa, G., Verleur, D. E., & de-Rios, M. D. (1986). Drug abuse and the adolescent sex offender: A preliminary analysis. *Journal of Psychoactive Drugs, 18,* 65–72.

Murphy, W. D. (1990). Assessment and treatment of cognitive distortions in sex offenders. In W. L. Marshall, D. R. Laws, & H. E. Barbaree (Eds.), *Handbook of sexual assault: Issues, theories, and treatment of the offender* (pp. 331–342). New York: Plenum Press.

National Adolescent Perpetrator Network. (1988). Preliminary report from the National Task Force on Juvenile Sexual Offending. *Juvenile and Family Court Journal, 39*, 1–67.

Pithers, W. D., Beal, L. S., Armstrong, J., & Petty, J. (1989). Identification of risk factors through clinical interviews and analysis of records. In D. R. Laws (Ed.), *Relapse prevention with sex offenders* (pp. 77–87). New York: Guilford Press.

Pithers, W. D., Marques, J. K., Gibat, C. C., & Marlatt, G. A. (1983). Relapse prevention with sexual aggressives: A self-control model of treatment and maintenance of change. In J. G. Greer & I. R. Stuart (Eds.), *The sexual aggressor: Current perspectives on treatment* (pp. 214–239). New York: Von Nostrand Reinhold.

Pollock, N. L., & Hashmall, J. M. (1991). The excuses of child molesters. *Behavioral Sciences and the Law, 9*, 53–59.

Roberts, R. E., Abrams, L., & Finch, J. R. (1973). Delinquent sexual behavior among adolescents. *Medical Aspects of Human Sexuality, 7*, 162–183.

Ross, Loss, & Associates (1988). *Risk assessment/interviewing protocol for adolescent sex offenders.* Mystic, CT: Ross, Loss & Associates.

Rowe, B. (1988). Practical treatment of adolescent sexual offenders. *Journal of Child Care, 3*, 51–58.

Ryan, G., Lane, S., Davis, J., & Isaac, C. (1987). Juvenile sex offenders: Development and correction. *Child Abuse and Neglect, 11*, 385–395.

Saunders, E. B., & Awad, G. A. (1988). Assessment, management, and treatment planning for male adolescent sexual offenders. *American Journal of Orthopsychiatry, 58*, 571–579.

Scully, D., & Marolla, J. (1984). Convicted rapists' vocabulary of motive: Excuses and justifications. *Social Problems, 31*, 530–544.

Sefarbi, R. (1990). Admitters and deniers among adolescent sex offenders and their families: A preliminary study. *American Journal of Orthopsychiatry, 60*, 460–465.

Shoor, M., Speed, M. H., & Bertelt, C. (1966). Syndrome of the adolescent child molester. *American Journal of Psychiatry, 122*, 783–789.

Showers, J., Farber, E. D., Joseph, J. A., Oshins, L., & Johnson, C. F. (1983). The sexual victimization of boys: A three-year survey. *Health Values: Achieving High Level Wellness, 7*, 15–18.

Smith, W. R. (1990). *Toward an empirical typology of adolescent sex offenders.*

Smith, W. R., & Monastersky, C. (1986). Assessing juvenile sexual offenders' risk for reoffending. *Criminal Justice and Behavior, 13*, 115–140.

Steenman, H., Nelson, C., & Viesti, C., Jr. (1989). Developing coping strategies for high risk situations. In D. R. Laws (Ed.), *Relapse prevention with sex offenders* (pp. 178–187). New York: Guilford Press.

Stenson, P., & Anderson, C. (1987). Treating juvenile sex offenders and preventing the cycle of abuse. *Journal of Child Care, 3*, 91–102.

Stevenson, H. C., Castillo, E., & Sefarbi, R. (1989). Treatment of denial in adolescent sex offenders and their families. *Journal of Offender Counseling, Services and Rehabilitation, 14*, 37–50.

Tinklenberg, J. R., Murphy, P., Murphy, P. L., & Pfefferbaum, A. (1981). Drugs and criminal assaults by adolescents: a replication study. *Journal of Psychoactive Drugs, 13*, 277–287.

Tinklenberg, J. R., & Woodrow, K. M. (1974). Drug use among youthful assaultive and sexual offenders. *Aggression, 52,* 209–224.

Van Ness, S. R. (1984). Rape as instrumental violence: A study of youth offenders. Special Issue: Gender issues, sex offenses, and criminal justice: Current trends. *Journal of Offender Counseling, Services and Rehabilitation, 9,* 161–170.

Vinogradov, S., Dishotsky, N. I., Doty, A. K., & Tinklenberg, J. R. (1988). Patterns of behavior in adolescent rape. *American Journal of Orthopsychiatry, 58,* 179–187.

Wormith, J. (1983). A survey of incarcerated sexual offenders. *Canadian Journal of Criminology, 25,* 379–390.

CHAPTER 14

Cognitive Behavioral Treatment of the Juvenile Sex Offender

Judith V. Becker
Meg S. Kaplan

Recently, the research and clinical literature has paid a great deal of attention to the treatment of adult sex offenders (Furby, Weinrott, & Blackshaw, 1989; Greer & Stuart, 1983; Laws, 1989; Marshall, Laws, & Barbaree, 1990). At present, the most popular and widely recognized therapy for the adult sex offender is cognitive-behavioral therapy, including relapse prevention. A number of authoritative chapters and articles have detailed the components of this therapy, which seem to be required for it to be effective (e.g., Abel, Becker & Skinner, 1986; Marshall & Barbaree, 1990). Surprisingly, little such attention has been paid to the treatment of the adolescent sex offender. This lack of attention is especially surprising given the fact that (1) adolescent males represent a significant number of those arrested and convicted of sexual crimes (*Uniform Crime Reports*, FBI, 1985), and (2) the majority of adult sex offenders can trace the origins of their sexual deviance to their adolescence (Longo & Groth, 1983).

We have been conducting a cognitive-behavioral treatment program for adolescent sex offenders at the Sexual Behavior Clinic, New York State Psychiatric Institute in New York City for a period of 7 years. The present chapter provides a summary and overview of this program as it has evolved in our setting. We will begin with a discussion of the intake process and assessment of the offender, and then describe the treatment program.

ASSESSMENT

Adolescents seen at our clinic are between the ages of 13–18 (x = 15.4) years. The racial composition is 66% black, 23% Hispanic, and 9% Caucasian. The majority of adolescents are from a lower socioeconomic status. Approximately 70% of the adolescents have molested young children, and 30% have committed sexual assaults.

Upon referral to the Sexual Behavior Clinic, each adolescent undergoes a comprehensive evaluation to determine treatment needs. An available parent is included in the assessment process. Approximately 85% of the adolescents are accompanied by a parent or guardian. In the majority of cases (80%) the mother accompanies the child.

Prior to clinical assessment, the following materials are reviewed when available: victim statement, hospital records, police/criminal justice system records, and prior psychological/psychiatric records. Also, both the adolescent and the parent(s) sign a consent form. The consent form outlines the nature of the entire assessment process. Both the adolescent and parent must indicate consent before any evaluation will be conducted. If either or both refuse to consent, the assessment will not be conducted.

The assessment at the Sexual Behavior Clinic consists of three components: a structured clinical interview, psychometric testing, and physiological evaluation. The structured clinical interview collects information concerning demographic characteristics, family background, criminal history, social history, drug and alcohol history, a history of all sexual behavior including all deviant sexual behaviors and fantasies, and a history of sexual and/or physical abuse.

Psychometric testing involves a number of self-report measures. The Adolescent Sexual Interest Cardsort is a 64-item self-report measure of sexual interest developed at the Sexual Behavior Clinic to determine the presence of deviant sexual interests. An example of an item is, "I've forced a 10-year-old boy to suck my penis. It's getting hard." The adolescent is asked to rate this vignette on a Likert Scale from −2 (really turns me off) to +2 (really turns me on). The Adolescent Cognitions Scale (ACS), is a 32-item true-false test developed at the Sexual Behavior Clinic to determine if the adolescent offender has any distorted cognitions regarding sexual behaviors. A sample item is, "Showing my penis to a stranger in a public place will get me into trouble." To assess the adolescent's sexual knowledge, we administer the Math Tech Sex Test (Kirby, 1984), which is divided into two parts: (1) sexual knowledge and (2) attitudes and values.

Social skills are assessed by the Matson Evaluation of Social Skills in Youngsters (Matson, Esveldt-Dawson, & Kazdin, 1983), which is designed to assess the social and assertive skills of adolescents. It is a 62-item self-report measure that assesses five factors: (1) appropriate social skills, (2) inappropriate assertiveness, (3) impulsive-recalcitrant traits, (4) overconfidence, and (5) jealousy withdrawal.

The Beck Inventory is used to assess depressive symptomatology (Beck, Ward, Mendelson, Mock, & Erbough, 1961). It is conducted to objectively evaluate the sexual interest patterns of these young offenders. It is important to note that, to date, data are not available on a non-sex-offending adolescent population. Reliability and validity on erectile assessment of adolescents have yet to be established. Consequently, risk management and treatment decisions should never be made solely on the basis of physiological assessment.

It is imperative that the adolescent and parent or guardian have the procedure described in detail prior to their signing the consent form. At our clinic, we only conduct this assessment on postpubertal males (they are usually between the ages of 13 and 18 years old). The stimuli consist of 19 audiotaped passages, each lasting 2 minutes, recorded by an adult male. The tapes, which are narrated in the second person, are descriptions of various sexual activities with a variety of targets. Each passage describes the age and sex of the target and an interaction scene. Two of the tapes describe a non-sexual social inter-action among a group of adolescents (neutral). Because we have a multi-ethnic population, the use of audiotapes allows the client to imagine the specific characteristics of his victim.

We have found that our adolescent population tolerates this procedure very well. Preliminary research using this assessment technique has found that deviant erectile responding is common among adolescents who have molested young boys, and who have a history of sexual victimization themselves (Becker, Hunter, Stein, & Kaplan, 1989). Although our research is in preliminary stages, we have found that adolescents who admit to their deviant sexual behaviour are more likely to show deviant arousal in the laboratory. We are continuing to document erection profiles for the adolescent sex offender population (Becker & Kaplan, 1988).

TREATMENT PROGRAM

Entry Criteria

In order to be accepted into the program, an adolescent must either admit that he has engaged in deviant sexual behavior, or his sexually deviant behavior must be documented by a victim statement, a court finding, or a reliable valid witness such as a parent.

In addition, at intake the following variables are used to assess treatment needs:

1. Distorted cognitions
2. Self-report of deviant sexual fantasies
3. Significant inappropriate sexual arousal during the psychophysiological assessment

4. Having been found guilty of a sexual offense
5. Lack of remorse regarding inappropriate sexual behavior
6. Failure to accept responsibility for the inappropriate sexual behavior

THE PROGRAM

Our treatment is a multicomponent program utilizing a cognitive behavioral model that was initially developed for, and evaluated on, an adult sex offender population (Abel, Becker et al., 1984). After attempting to utilize this adult model with an adolescent sex offender population, it became apparent that numerous modifications had to be made to make the intervention more appropriate given the level of cognitive, emotional, and social development these adolescents displayed. The following section will describe the components of our therapy program and discuss issues to be considered.

Verbal Satiation

This technique teaches the offender how to utilize deviant thoughts in a repetitive manner to the point of boring or fatiguing themselves with the very stimuli to which they had previously become aroused.

In our earlier work with adults, clients were instructed to complete 20 hours of masturbatory satiation (described in detail in Abel et al., 1984). This technique proved most difficult to utilize with our adolescent sex offenders for the following reasons: (1) The majority of the adolescents seen at our clinic reported that they did not masturbate and that to do so would be in violation of religious or ethical practices. We do not feel that a clinician should require clients to engage in any form of sexual behavior with which they feel uncomfortable; therefore, the masturbation segment of satiation was dropped. (2) The majority of adolescents either share rooms with their siblings or others, or have no privacy in which to conduct the satiation sessions; therefore, these sessions could not be conducted at home. (3) Many of the adolescents seen at our clinic cannot be relied upon to carry out therapeutic homework assignments. (4) The majority of adolescents protested that 1 hour (the time required for adults to complete one satiation tape) was too long for them to focus on a topic.

Given the above issues, we modified the procedure as follows: each adolescent is required to complete a minimum of eight, 30-minute verbal satiation tapes that are conducted at our clinic. The adolescent is presented a slide depicting a naked male or female child or male or female adult, corresponding to the gender and age of his victim. While viewing the slide, the adolescent is requested to repeat, over a period of 30 minutes, a phrase describing the nature of the deviant sexual activity he engaged in with his victim(s). When beginning this procedure, most of the adolescents have been unable or unwilling to verbalize their deviant sexual fantasies. In these cases, the therapist chooses a particular phrase that is relevant to their offense and which is as close as possible to the adolescent's own colloquial language. In each of the eight sessions, a different phrase and a different slide is used. One fantasy is eliminated at a time. Every effort is made to attempt to elicit any additional deviant thought or fantasies from each adolescent. Examples of phrases typically used in our treatment are:

Target—Young Children (girls or boys)

I'm feeling this girl all over.
I want to be with this girl.
I'm telling this girl to take off her clothes.
I'm telling this girl to sit on my lap.
Me and this girl are going to have some fun.
I'm going to have sex with this girl.
I'm going to rape this girl.
I'm about to touch this girl.
I'm holding this little girl.
This little girl wants me.

Rape—Adult Woman

I'm sneaking up behind this woman.
I'm going to rape her.
I'm holding this lady down.
I'm ripping her clothes off.
I'm telling this woman to take off her clothes.
I'm staring at this woman.
I want to rape this woman.
I'm beating this woman up.
I'm punching this woman.

These are only suggestions. If no violence was involved in the offense, we do not recommend using violent phrases.

While the adolescent is engaged in the satiation procedure, his erectile responding is measured by a penile plethysmograph. Although it has rarely been the case, there have been adolescents who at the end of one 30-minute session have still shown significant arousal (20% or more of a full erection) to the deviant stimuli. When this occurs, the adolescent must continue with the session until all or most deviant arousal has dissipated (as measured by the plethysmograph) before he can end the session.

Preliminary results indicate that arousal to deviant sexual stimuli declines after eight sessions for those adolescents who have offended against females less than 8 years of age. If erectile responding has not declined after eight sessions, the adolescent is required to complete another eight sessions. In general, a maximum of 16 sessions is sufficient to lower arousal.

GROUP TREATMENT

Upon completion of the satiation sessions, adolescents are entered into a 40-week closed-group treatment led by a male and female cotherapist team. We have found that 7 clients constitute an optimal group; however, due to absences and dropouts, we begin with 12 and typically finish with between 7 to 9 members. Initially, we had designed the groups to be an hour and one-half in length (based on the adult model); however, we found that with the limited attention span of our clients an hour was more optimal. We have observed that it is less threatening for the adolescents to be seated around a table as opposed to having a seat with nothing in front of them.

The first group session begins by group members introducing themselves (first name only). They are then given group rules, which are as follows:

1. Each group member must show respect for everyone else, no put-downs are allowed.
2. Once the group starts, no leaving (for the men's room or any other reason) until the group is over, unless it is an emergency.
3. One person speaks at a time—no interrupting.
4. No shouting or yelling.
5. Everyone must stay seated.
6. Coming in late disrupts the group. If you're continually late you can be dropped from the program.
7. Any physical fighting will result in being dropped from the program.

For adolescents who are court mandated to receive treatment, there are consequences from the Juvenile Justice System if they are dropped from treatment. After the rules have been explained, everyone is informed that all group participants have committed different types of sexual offenses and that no one sexual offense is better or worse than another. For instance, we have observed that the adolescent rapists tend to "put down" the child molesters. Members are cautioned against these kinds of unnecessary criticisms.

Group members are then informed that it is usual for everyone to be wondering what type of sex offense the other members have committed and that it is usual for young men to worry about having to discuss their offenses in the group setting. Each adolescent is then asked to state the age and gender of his victim(s), whether the victim was related to him, and whether the abuse

occurred once or more than once. While adolescents are compliant in presenting this information, they usually do so in a low voice and with their eyes
downcast. At the completion of this session, cotherapists emphasize the need
for strict confidentiality ("What goes on in here stays in here"). The clients are
thanked for engaging in a difficult task.

The next step in the group program is aimed at modifying cognitive
distortions and this segment runs for five sessions. Cognitive restructuring
involves confronting the adolescent with his maladaptive beliefs about his
deviant sexual behaviour. The cotherapists inform participants that for the next
4 weeks the group will talk about "things that you told yourself to make it okay
to do what you did." The adolescents are given the following example: "If I
speed in a car, I know that it is against the law, because speeding is illegal. So
if I feel bad about breaking the law, I tell myself reasons that it is okay for me
to do it, so I won't feel bad. One example is that it's no big deal because
everyone else speeds." The cotherapists then ask group members what other
reasons they would use to make it "okay to speed."

Group members then engage in role-play enactments where one of the
therapists plays a child molester who uses typical rationalizations for his behavior. The adolescents take the role of therapists, court personnel, judges, and
psychiatrists; they either agree with the "molester's" rationalizations or disagree.
At the completion of each role play, the group discusses the rationalizations or
distortions that were used and "why they were wrong." For the first few sessions
the maladaptive beliefs that the cotherapists role play are taken from the
Adolescent Cognition Scale, which was described earlier.

During the course of these sessions, the following topics are role-played:
child molestation, incest, date rape, non–date rape, voyeurism, exhibitionism,
and frotteurism. For those adolescents who have abused young children, issues
of the children's inability to consent to a sexual act are emphasized throughout
the group. The adolescents are also informed that people who are high on drugs
or alcohol, or are developmentally disabled are legally unable to give informed
consent.

At approximately the third session, the clients are asked to write down
how they rationalized their sexually deviant behaviors. Examples of typical
responses from child molesters are: "What the hell, nobody is here so why
not—I can't get laid" (this is an example from someone who molested a female
child). "Nobody will see me and I will get away." "Since somebody put me in
pain, I might as well put someone else in pain" (this is an example of an
adolescent who had been sexually abused and then acted out sexually.) "A
young person wouldn't know better so she would do what you asked her to do."
The following statements were made by adolescents who raped their peers: "I
asked a cute girl, does she want to have sex with me, the girl said 'no because
I'm only 13,' but I kept forcing her so she finally said yes." "It was fun." "If I
forced a girl to have sex with me, if she didn't fight back it was okay, if she didn't

yell it was no trouble, and if she fought back she didn't like it." The following statements were made by adolescents who had participated in gang rapes. "Friends were doing it and said it was all right." "I'm not responsible because two other guys held her down and one raped her, I only touched her and I thought it might be all right because she wasn't making any noises."

The above statements reflect the following themes: (1) lack of empathy, (2) objectification of females, (3) viewing sex as something that one does to another person for personal gratification as opposed to a shared consensual experience, (4) lack of remorse, and (5) acceptance of violence as part of their lives.

There are numerous ways by which children develop these beliefs, including personal experience of having been neglected or victimized, being exposed to coercive models within their homes and communities; associating with antisocial peers; and societal messages about females and about the acceptance of violence.

In general, we have observed during these sessions that the mixture of different categories of offenses (e.g., child molesters with rapists) facilitates confrontation and changing belief systems. For example, when the therapist role-plays an adolescent who has had sex with a 7-year-old girl, the rapists in the group are horrified in their role as court personnel and immediately insist on that person being sent to jail. The adolescents in the group who have had sex with children listen to the reactions of their peers, and that helps them learn how others view their behavior. By engaging the adolescents in role-playing in these first sessions, a sense of cohesion in the group is facilitated.

The next several sessions (four to five) are spent developing and utilizing covert sensitization scripts. The purpose of covert sensitization is to teach each adolescent to recognize his own thought processes and behaviors that place him at risk to abuse someone, and to interrupt these thought processes and behaviors by substituting negative rather than positive consequences. Several group sessions are spent in which individuals write their own "scripts" of risk factors and negative consequences. We entitle this component of treatment "risk and consequences." An example is: *Risk:* I arrive home; no one is there; I feel lonely. I sit at the kitchen table watching young kids playing in the park—they look so happy. I think I'll go down and play with them. *Switch—Consequences:* I'm sitting in jail wondering what the judge will do. I'm really scared. All because I went down to the park to play with young kids.

From these scripts each adolescent makes eight individual tapes at the clinic, apart from time spent in the group. Each tape is 15 minutes in duration. The tapes are reviewed by the therapist with the client, and feedback is given. The tapes are then erased.

The next several sessions (five) focus on developing assertiveness and learning to control anger. Many of these clients have difficulty recognizing and controlling their aggressive impulses and may resort to either verbal or physical aggression as a means of problem solving. During the early developmental years, many parents help children direct their aggressive impulses in socially appropriate ways. However, some adolescents have not received or been able to integrate parental training or have learned dysfunctional modeling from adults and peers.

The purpose of this section of group treatment is to teach adolescents to recognize the differences between passive, assertive, and aggressive behaviors, to recognize their own anger, and to develop appropriate alternative responses. Adolescents are given examples from each of three categories of responses (i.e., passive, assertive, and aggressive). For example: "A friend asks to borrow your favorite piece of clothing. You do not want to give it to him." The client is then told that he may respond in one of the following ways: "You say okay or you say you can't find it when you know you can" (nonassertive); "You explain why you do not want to lend it to him" (assertive); or "You yell at your friend for asking" (aggressive).

The next session concentrates on learning to handle emotions. An example of an iceberg is used, in that the largest part of an iceberg is under the water and cannot be seen. Group members are taught that emotions are very similar; when someone "icebergs" or "blows off steam," the only emotion that shows is anger—but there are other feelings that need to be recognized and expressed appropriately. Group members are asked if they have ever been upset about something and then taken it out on someone else. An example would be failing a test and then coming home, tripping on a dog bone, and kicking the dog and taking it out on him.

We explain that many times people abuse others because they are feeling frustrated. An example would be a boy whose dad has remarried and then had an infant girl who gets all the attention. This boy was angry at his father for remarrying, hated his stepmother for getting his father's attention, and was angry at the little girl for being so loved. Subsequently, he sexually abused his half-sister, as a means of expressing his anger.

In one of the sessions, the video, *Rethink Workout for Teens: Learning to Manage Anger* (Silverman, 1988) is used. The main premise of this tape is expressed in the acronym "RETHINK":

Recognize when you are feeling angry; why you are angry.
Empathize; try to see things from the other person's point of view and to step into the other person's shoes.
Think about the situation another way, from another point of view.
Hear what the other person is saying.
Integrate respect and love in what you say even when you are angry.
Notice how your body reacts and how you calm yourself.
Keep you attention on here and now and the problem to be solved.

Group members are encouraged to anonymously write down their own difficult situations. They role-play from a common pool. Common examples are: "I loaned my basketball to a friend and he lost it, what should I do?"; "My mother is always asking me to go to the store. How can I tell her I don't want to go? (She yells at me when I say no)"; "My mother bought me new sneakers, I don't know why. What should I say?"

Our experience with adolescent sex offenders has also shown that many are undersocialized and have difficulty in establishing peer relationships, both platonic and nonplatonic (sexual). Other adolescent offenders have adequate social skills, but use these skills to manipulate peers. Consequently, these deficits or excesses must be addressed in treatment. Topics that are covered during these sessions (four to five sessions) of social skill training are starting conversations, open-ended versus closed-ended questions, and listening skills. Other sessions deal with communication in relationships. Topics that are covered include having adolescents describe their ideal romantic relationship, defining love, exploring differences between infatuation, "being" in love, and loving someone.

It is also important for the group members to learn that sexual communication is not confined to words alone. Body language may also convey a great deal of information, such as:

The extent to which they face you
The extent to which they sit close to you
Whether they touch you with their body
Whether their arms are wrapped around their bodies (reflecting being closed off)
Whether their hands are down to the side or even stretched out along the furniture, reflecting an acceptance

Again, several situations are role-played in which the group members are asked to identify what message the girl's body is giving to the boy in particular situations. This is extremely helpful, since it gives the group members an opportunity to role-play talking about sex with their partner so that when they get into the situation they will feel less anxious about sexual communication.

Even though sex education is taught in the school system, it has been our experience that adolescents still have a lot of misinformation regarding human sexuality. The purpose of this component of therapy is to help adolescent sex offenders better understand themselves by focusing on social, sexual, and health issues currently facing them. We attempt to (1) increase their knowledge about adolescent sexual development and sexual anatomy and physiology; (2) broaden their knowledge about sexual myths and learn ways to prevent unwanted pregnancy and sexually transmitted diseases; and (3) become more aware of their own attitudes and feelings concerning sexuality, and clarify their values about sexuality.

In order for adolescents to explore and clarify their attitudes about sexuality, the atmosphere must be one of openness. In each session, we encourage clients to ask questions. We point out that we know it is sometimes difficult for them to ask questions; therefore, 10 minutes before each sex education class ends, all students are asked to write down anonymous questions about sex that they were reluctant to ask in class. Throughout these sex education sessions the following points are made:

All group members should be treated with respect—no put-downs allowed. Some people will know more than others about some things, but not about everything.
Different viewpoints, opinions, and values are expected and encouraged.
It is wrong to force someone to do something sexually or to have sex with anyone who cannot give consent.

A list of 20 sexual myths is made up on index cards. An example of a myth is, "If a boy pulls out before he comes, the girl will not get pregnant." The first student picks an index card from among the deck which is face-down on the table; he reads it aloud, and then says whether he thinks it is true or false. After he answers, the others are encouraged to respond. In one of the sex education sessions a film on anatomy and physiology is shown in order to educate the adolescents about sexual physiology and anatomy.

Another session explores why teens have sex. We break the group into two small groups and make it a contest to see which of the two groups can come up with the longest list of reasons that they can think of for having sex. The therapist then explains that there are many different reasons and many different meanings for sex, and it varies at different times and in different situations. The therapist then writes answers on the board. Some of the typical reasons proffered include to prove masculinity or femininity, to get pleasure physically or give pleasure, to keep up with friends (or show off), to show anger or degrade someone, to show love, to relieve physical tension, curiosity, get acceptance, to keep a boyfriend or make a commitment, to have children, or to have fun. When all the reasons are on the board, we ask the group what they think about each of the reasons and which are positive and valuable.

The remaining sex education sessions concentrate on birth control decisions and methods, sexually transmitted diseases, and values clarification. For values clarification, we explain to students that the following exercise is designed to explore opinions about a variety of sexual issues. We emphasize that there are no right or wrong answers, only opinions. Everyone has a right to take a turn expressing his own opinion, as long as no one is put down for having a different opinion. Some sample opinions that get frequently expressed are "Homosexuals are sick" and "Most men want to marry a virgin."

Our clinic is located in New York City, which has a high HIV-positive population. Some of the adolescents in our clinic have known HIV-positive people, either relatives, friends, or acquaintances. We recently assessed pretreatment general knowledge about AIDS in a population of adolescent sex offenders and male runaways. Sex offenders scored significantly lower than runaways in general knowledge about AIDS in an adolescent sex-offender population and male runaway population and were not able to discriminate safer sexual behaviors from those that were less safe (Rotheram-Borus, Becker, Koopman, & Kaplan, 1991). Therefore, we provide four sessions focusing on AIDS prevention.[1]

The content of these sessions review briefly the entire treatment. Each individual writes his own "plan" to avoid relapse. Safety measures that are covered include the following:

1. Avoid unsupervised contact with young children.
2. If you are not sure if someone is too young, ask him or her questions such as what grade he or she is in, what school he or she goes to. If you have to, ask for identification. A good rule to follow is to date someone no more than 4 years younger than you are.
3. Never test yourself (don't stay around kids to see if you get excited; if you want a test, come to the lab).
4. Always remember that children cannot give consent because they do not know the consequences.
5. Be sure that your partner consents to any sexual interaction.
6. Remember the bad consequences of your behavior—for you and the people who are close to you.
7. If you are not sure if your sexual behavior is appropriate, ask someone who is not involved, such as a friend, a parent, or a teacher for an opinion. Be aware of your attitudes about sex; do not fool yourself.
8. Increase contact with kids your own age.
9. Practice social skills.
10. Be assertive by expressing your negative and positive feelings; don't keep them to yourself.
11. Do not use thoughts of children or rape while having sexual intercourse or masturbating.
12. If inappropriate sexual urges return, it is not the end of the world; call

---

[1]If this is to be included in your program, we suggest you become familiar with M. Quackerbush & P. Sargent, *Teaching AIDS: A Resource Guide on Acquired Immune Deficiency Syndrome* (Santa Cruz, CA: Network Publications, 1986).

us. Do not wait to ask for help. If you are thinking you might need help, call immediately. Always have our telephone number with you.

13. Take care of yourself; you are the only one who can do it.

Following treatment, we assess each individual on four occasions: after treatment and at 3, 6, and 12 months following treatment discharge.

TREATMENT OUTCOME

Becker and Kaplan (1988) reported 1-year posttreatment follow-up data, which indicate that treatment is effective, according to self-reports, rearrests, and plethysmographic data. Of the first 300 adolescents evaluated, 68.3% (205) entered treatment. Although only 27.3% (56) attended 70–100% of the scheduled therapy sessions, recidivism rates at 1-year posttreatment were low. According to self-reports and reports from parents and criminal justice agencies, only 9% had recommitted sexual crimes (Becker, 1990).

CONCLUSION

Although clinical research of adolescent sexual offenders is at an early stage, preliminary results such as described here are promising (Becker, 1990). Further research needs to concentrate on the development of adolescent sex offender typologies and the evaluation of treatments relative to those typologies. Controlled therapy outcome studies are also needed.

Finally, then, the challenge to clinical researchers is to conduct studies that will inform us about the development of sexual interest patterns in children and adolescents, and how individual, familial, and environmental factors interplay.

REFERENCES

Abel, G. G., Becker, J. V., Cunningham-Rathner, J., Rouleau, J., Kaplan, M., & Reich, J. (1984). *Treatment manual: The treatment of child molesters.* Tuscaloosa, AL: Emory University Clinic, Deptartment of Psychiatry.

Abel, G. G., Becker, J. V., & Skinner, L. (1986). Behavioral approaches to the treatment of the violent sex offender. In L. H. Roth (Ed.), *Behavioral approaches to treatment of the violent person* (95–117). New York: Guilford Press.

Beck, A. T., Ward, C., Mendelson, H., Mock, J., & Erbough, J. (1961). An inventory for measuring depression. *Archives of General Psychiatry, 4,* 53–63.

Becker, J. V. (1990). Treating adolescent sexual offenders. *Professional Psychology Research and Practice, 21,* 362–365.

Becker, J. V., Hunter, J. A., Stein, R. M., & Kaplan, M. S. (1989). Factors associated with erection in adolescent sex offenders. *Journal of Psychopathology and Behavioral Assessment, 11,* 353–362.

Becker, J. V., & Kaplan, M. S. (1988). The assessment of adolescent sexual offenders. In R. Prinz (Ed.), *Advances in behavioral assessment of children and Families* (pp. 97–118). Greenwich, CT: JAI Press.

Federal Bureau of Investigation. (1985). *Uniform crime reports.* Washington, DC: U.S. Government Printing Office.

Furby, L., Weinrott, M. R., & Blackshaw, L. (1989). Sex offender recidivism: A review. *Psychological Bulletin, 105,* 3–30.

Greer, J. G., & Stuart, I. R. (1983). *The sexual aggressor: Current perspectives on treatment.* New York: Van Nostrand Reinhold.

Kirby, D. (Ed.). (1984). *Sexuality education: An evaluation of programs and their effects.* Santa Cruz, CA: Network.

Laws, D. R. (1989). *Relapse prevention with sex offenders.* New York: Guilford Press.

Longo, R. E., & Groth, A. N. (1983). Juvenile sexual offenses in the histories of adult rapists and child molesters. *International Journal of Offender Therapy and Comparative Criminology, 27,* 150–155.

Marshall, W. L., & Barbaree, H. E. (1990). Outcome of comprehensive cognitive-behavioral treatment programs. In W. L. Marshall, D. R. Laws, & H. E. Barbaree (Eds.), *Handbook of sexual assault: Issues, theories, and treatment of the offender* (pp. 363–385). New York: Plenum Press.

Marshall, W. L., Laws, D. R., & Barbaree, H. E. (1990). Issues in sexual assault. In W. L. Marshall, D. R. Laws, & H. E. Barbaree (Eds.), *Handbook of sexual assault: Issues, theories, and treatment of the offender* (pp. 3–7). New York: Plenum Press.

Matson, J. L., Esveldt-Dawson, K., & Kazdin, A. (1983). Evaluating social skills with youngsters. *Journal of Clinical Child Psychology, 12,* 174–180.

Rotheram–Borus, M. J., Becker, J. V., Koopman, C., & Kaplan, M. S. (1991). AIDS knowledge, attitudes and sexual behaviors of sexually delinquent and nondelinquent adolescents. *Journal of Adolescence, 14,* 229–244.

Silverman, D. (Producer). (1988). *Rethink Workout for Teens: Learning to Manage Anger* (Video). Washington, DC: Institute for Mental Health Services.

CHAPTER 15

The Pharmacological Treatment of the Adolescent Sex Offender

John M. W. Bradford

Adolescence is a unique time for the intervention and treatment of the sex offender. Most of the paraphilias that are later manifested in sexually deviant behavior have their onset during adolescence, starting at the time of puberty. Further, as has been stated many times before, paraphilias are almost exclusively seen in males. The usual sequence of events is the onset of deviant sexual fantasy, which is later accompanied by masturbation and then, in late adolescence, the development of sexually deviant behavior with the victimization of others. It follows, therefore, that a successful intervention during adolescence would dramatically reduce the number of victims of sexual abuse, as it would prevent adolescents with some initial manifestations of the paraphilias progressing to sexual offenses against women and children. At the same time, however, adolescence is unique with regard to sexual development. Puberty is a dynamic process with dramatic hormonal changes, which need to be taken into account if the treatment approach to adolescent sex offenders is to be placed on a scientific footing.

In the prepubertal years the plasma levels of the various sex hormones, particularly the gonadotropins and the androgens, are low. The earliest sign of the onset of puberty is an increase in the secretion of the adrenal androgens, dehydroepiandrosterone and androstenedione, starting usually prior to age 10 and antedating the maturation of the hypothalamic-pituitary-gonadal axis (Griffin & Wilson, 1985). Some of the early secondary sex differentiation seen in adolescents is generated by adrenal androgens, in particular the growth spurt and the development of axillary and pubic hair. Prior to the onset of puberty, the levels of plasma gonadotropins are low and there are low levels of androgens produced by the testes. This state appears to be due to the increased sensitivity of androgen receptors in the hypothalamus to the plasma testosterone levels. What occurs at puberty is not fully understood, but it is most likely that changes in the sensitivity of androgen receptors occur and the hypothalamic-pituitary axis reacts, which then results in increases in luteinizing hormone secretion and, to a lesser extent, in follicle-stimulating hormone secretion, mostly during sleep. This gradually increases so that the levels are maintained throughout the day and there are subsequent increases in plasma testosterone and dihydrotestosterone. The increase in gonadotropin secretion is secondary to an increase in luteinizing hormone-releasing hormone secreted from the hypothalamus. The physiological changes that occur at puberty are primarily generated by the gonadal steroids, particularly testosterone and dihydrotestosterone through their action on the androgen receptors. At puberty anatomical changes occur, including increased folds in the scrotal skin; growth of the testes, penis, and scrotum, with increased pigmentation; increase in the size of the seminal vesicles, prostate and epididymis; onset of hair growth; the development of a moustache and beard; some regression of the scalp line; the extension of pubic hair to the abdomen and the growth of axillary and pubic hair; the enlargement of the larynx and the thickening of the vocal cords; and the growth spurt, with a rapid gain in height and an accompanying increase in body mass, particularly of muscle bulk (Griffin & Wilson, 1985). With these anatomical changes there are also behavioral and psychological changes, particularly in the development of libido and sexual potency. To what extent the behavioral changes are directly related to the outpouring of gonadal steroids and the increase in the activity of the hypothalamic-pituitary-gonadal system is poorly understood even at this time. Another factor is that there is large variability both in the onset of puberty and in the general time frame during which the process is completed. A fundamental understanding of the behavioral effects of puberty is seen in a variety of pathological conditions that can occur during puberty. One area, which is an interesting focus of study, is that of sexual precocity. This can result from a variety of disorders and manifests as virilization in boys and, in other circumstances, in feminization. Precocious sexual development is usually defined as sexual development prior to age 9 (Griffin & Wilson, 1985). Puberty is generally regarded as being delayed if there is no onset prior to age 15. In general terms, in the male, a documented increase in testosterone production is usually seen at around a bone age of 12 years. After this point it rises steeply until the ages of 15 to 17 and then further slight increases occur into early adulthood (Bancroft, 1983b). Luteinizing hormone and follicle-stimulating hormone levels having risen during this period, start to decline in late adolescence to reach adult levels in the early 20s. There is also a fall in sex hormone binding globulin, during adolescence, to adult levels. As already outlined the development of secondary sex characteristics accompany these hormonal changes and are dependent on them. In particular, the growth spurt is variable and can occur anywhere from approximately 10.5 years to 16 years of age, with a deceleration of growth starting about 18 months later. The considerable individual variability in both the onset and progress of these pubertal changes have to be very carefully taken into account in the pharmacological treatment of the adolescent sex offender (Griffin & Wilson, 1985).

These hormonal changes and their effects on human sexual behavior need further consideration, although a full discussion is beyond the scope of this chapter. Because of the extreme complexity of the endocrine system and ethical barriers to human research, the effects on sexual behavior have mostly been studied in primates and other mammals. Sexual behavior in these species is very strongly controlled by the endocrine system, particularly in females, and slightly less so in males. In primates, a variety of castration studies suggest that sexual behavior is clearly androgen dependent. Castration leads to a deterioration in the various components of sexual behavior, with the initial effects being the reduction of ejaculation, erections, and mounting behavior. With the replacement of androgens these responses are restored. The impact on any individual's sexual behavior is quite variable. This is in turn most likely based on the sensitivity of the hypothalamic-pituitary axis, which is likely genetically determined. If the prepubertal androgen surge does not take place or is delayed for some reason, this is not entirely critical in the long term, so long as androgen replacement is delayed but not entirely absent. The three relevant sites of action of androgens are the anterior hypothalamus, the spinal cord where erectile and ejaculatory reflexes are androgen-sensitive, and in the penis (Bancroft, 1983a, 1983b).

As already outlined, the onset of paraphilic arousal and behavior occurs during adolescence, and this may be the ideal time for intervention, be it pharmacological or cognitive-behavioral treatments. Abel, Mittelman, and Becker (1985) report that 42% of paraphilics exhibited deviant arousal by age 15 and 57% by age 19. Homosexual pedophilia had the earliest onset with 53% reporting arousal by age 15 and 74% by age 18.

Basic understanding of the hormonal aspects of puberty, as well as the pharmacological principles involved in the treatment of the paraphilias, is crucial when considering the pharmacological treatment of adolescent sex offenders. In broad terms, the pharmacological approach would be (1) the use of antiandrogens and hormonal agents and (2) the use of other pharmacological agents.

ANTIANDROGEN AND HORMONAL AGENTS

The use of antiandrogens and a variety of hormonal agents forms part of a pharmacological approach to the reduction of paraphilic behavior through the suppression of the sexual drive. The impact on deviant sexual behavior, in clinical terms, is assumed to be related to the suppression of libido and secondary effects on the levels of arousability, but not necessarily any change in the direction of the sexual drive. However, there is at least some evidence that cyproterone acetate (CPA), an antiandrogen, can have effects, not only on the general suppression of sexual arousal, but possibly also on the direction of that arousal (Bradford & Pawlak, 1987). The principal agents that have been used for this pharmacological approach have been estrogens, initially used for sex-drive reduction, then medroxyprogesterone acetate, cyproterone acetate, and more recently other antiandrogens such as flutamide and the use of luteinizing hormone-releasing hormone agonists and antagonists.

The various estrogen derivatives are no longer used other than in the treatment of transsexualism, where the specific aim of treatment is feminization. Nonetheless, they have been shown to be effective in reducing the sexual drive in sexually deviant males, although there are no indications for their use in adolescents at this time (Foote, 1944; Golla & Hodge, 1949; Heller, Laidlaw, Harvey, & Nelson, 1958; Whittaker, 1959).

The use of antiandrogens in adolescents, as already acknowledged, is restricted, although not absolutely contraindicated. In the Sexual Behaviors Clinic at Ottawa antiandrogens or hormonal agents are not used prior to age 16, which is the outside limit for the expected development of puberty. At the same time, the developmental status of the adolescent is closely examined, as precocious puberty can be a cause of secondary sexually deviant behavior in adolescence. Although a full discussion of precocious puberty is beyond the scope of this chapter, idiopathic precocious puberty is relatively rare and instances of this have often proved to be secondary to premature activation of the hypothalamic-pituitary axis due to a tumor. If precocious puberty is suspected, a careful clinical evaluation of the central nervous system and the endocrine system is indicated, and, in addition, specialized imaging techniques need to be used to ensure a brain disorder is not present. The other complication is that intracerebral tumors can act in different ways, in some cases delaying puberty and in other cases bringing on precocious puberty. The reason for the cautious use of medroxyprogesterone acetate, cyproterone acetate, or other antiandrogens is that, to a degree, these drugs interfere with the development of puberty. This is only partially true as, although the virilizing affects of puberty are slowed, there does not appear to be any effect on epiphyseal closure with either cyproterone acetate or medroxyprogesterone acetate. Both of these agents have been used to treat precocious puberty, with the more recent treatment involving luteinizing hormone-releasing hormone analogs. The clinical indication for the use of antiandrogens in adolescence in the 16- to 17-year age group is the presence of very serious sexual deviation. This in most cases would be the potential for serious sexual aggression as in the sexual sadism described on Axis I of the third revised edition of the *Diagnostic and Statistical Manual of Mental*

Disorders (DSM-III-R) (American Psychiatric Association, 1987). An actual case study of the use of CPA in a 16-year-old is the following:

> A. M., a mildly mentally retarded 16-year-old adolescent, presented with a fetish for plastic bags and pedophilic attraction for younger children. He would place the bags over his own head, severely endangering his life. As he was a very unreliable historian, it was difficult to be certain what motivated him, although a component of autoerotic asphyxia was felt to be present as masturbation appeared to accompany his use of plastic bags. In addition his behavior was potentially homicidal in that he placed plastic bags over the heads of young children and fondled them sexually. A detailed sexual behaviors evaluation was completed. Plethysmographic assessment of his penile tumescence was limited to avoid exposing him to sadistic stimuli and thus avoid coaching him in further sexually deviant behavior. He showed a clear pedophilic sexual preference. As he was not cooperative he was not suitable for other treatment approaches. He denied the deviant behavior or even any interest in plastic bags. This was despite supervisory residential staff who observed the behavior and noted that he continued to steal plastic bags. As he was in a community group home with coresidents, some of whom were younger, serious concerns were raised as to whether or not he could be managed in the community at all. In this case, cyproterone acetate, at a therapeutic dose, reduced this behavior and allowed him to continue in the community with careful supervision. He has now been treated for close to 5 years without any major difficulties. In this instance, institutionalization would have been certain if antiandrogen treatment had not been used. The use of cyproterone acetate in this case has been intermittent rather than continuous, with good success.

The other indication for the use of cyproterone acetate in adolescents would be pedophilia where other treatments have failed. In this instance cyproterone acetate would be the final treatment approach indicated. Another clinical indication for the use of cyproterone acetate in adolescents would be where rapid and immediate control of sexually deviant behavior is required. Cyproterone acetate, in low dosages and in the short term (i.e., less than 3 months) can be used to immediately suppress the sexually deviant behavior while other treatment options (i.e., cognitive-behavioral treatment) can be started. This situation is likely to develop as a valid use of cyproterone acetate in adolescent sexual offenders, provided a careful evaluation of endocrine status and the clinical status of puberty is done. In addition, careful monitoring of the patient's clinical status must occur after the implementation of treatment.

Cyproterone acetate was the first commercially available antiandrogen and has antiandrogen, antigonadotropic, and progestational effects. It acts as a true antiandrogen in that it acts on the intracellular androgen receptors in various parts of the body. The androgen receptor response is blocked by cyproterone acetate, and, in addition, it has a principal effect on receptors with a high affinity for dihydrotestosterone. It actually has both an antiandrogen and a synandrogen effect as the pure antiandrogens such as cyproterone and flutamide, used therapeutically, register an androgen deficit in the hypothalamus, leading to an increased secretion of luteinizing hormone-releasing hormone, luteinizing hormone, and an increase in plasma testosterone. Cyproterone acetate, because of its actions, has a number of uses in males. Its principal use, aside from the treatment of the paraphilias, is in the treatment of carcinoma of the prostate. Its effects against virilization has led to its use in females for the treatment of a variety of endocrine states where there is an overproduction of androgens in females—for example, hirsutism, alopecia, acne, and seborrhea. Cyproterone acetate has also been used for the treatment of precocious puberty in children (Gupta, 1977), with both desirable and undesirable effects (Bradford, 1985; Chapman, 1982; Flanigni et al., 1977; Mahesh, 1977). There are a number of side effects on sexual behavior, notably its reduction, that are desirable. Within the first 2 months of treatment, often beginning in the first 10 days, the plasma testosterone level is decreased, with subsequent decreases in erections, ejaculate, spermatogenesis, sexual fantasies, sexual drive, and overall sexual arousal.

Within the first 2 months of treatment there are likely to be undesirable side effects such as fatigue, an increased need for sleep, a general decrease in physical activity, and, occasionally, depression. A transient negative nitrogen balance, returning to normal by 3 months, has been described. Weight gain has also been noted but it is dose related and can easily be managed by diet and exercise. Protracted or temporary gynecomastia is possible, although it is mainly dose related and in most cases is reversible on the discontinuation of the drug. From clinical experience it appears more likely to occur in individuals who have spontaneous gynacomastia during puberty. There is also some decrease in body hair, some increase in scalp hair, and decreases in the secretion of sebum. Using large doses of cyproterone acetate, Neumann (1977) reported liver damage in rats. Also, cyproterone acetate has been reported to produce hepatomas in laboratory animals, which is similar to all progestagens. Although some studies have shown some increases in some of the liver enzymes, there has been no report of hepatomas in humans as a result of cyproterone acetate administration, and no evidence of long-term liver damage. Animal studies have shown that suppression of the adrenal function can occur with cyproterone acetate, and in some children treated for precocious puberty, there have been decreases in basal plasma cortisol and adrenal corticotrophic hormone levels, as well as decreased adrenal responses to insulin-induced hypoglycemia. However, there are no reports of adrenal crisis or severe impairment in adrenal function, and it has not been a contraindication for the use of cyproterone acetate in the treatment of precocious puberty. It would appear that this is not a substantial risk for adults, but that there is some risk for children and possibly adolescents. It appears to be dose related and can be monitored and managed medically.

Subjectively, many patients treated with cyproterone acetate report reductions in anxiety and irritability. More significantly there have been reports of positive effects on sexual behavior, particularly reductions in recidivism (Bradford, 1985; Bradford & Pawlak, 1987, in press-a, in press-b). The usual dose of cyproterone acetate is 50 mg, orally once a day, or an injection of 300 mg every 10 days to 2 weeks.

Medroxyprogesterone acetate is available in both oral and long-acting depot forms, known as Depo-Provera, and has been used to treat the paraphilias in the United States. It is principally a progestational agent which suppresses gonadotropic secretion but does not appear to be a true antiandrogen—that is, having its action on the androgen receptors. It reduces the plasma level of testosterone through increases in the metabolic clearance or breakdown of testosterone (Bradford, 1985). The plasma testosterone level is reduced typically to prepubertal levels, this having direct effects on sexual behavior.

Medroxyprogesterone acetate's mechanism of action works principally through the induction of testosterone-A reductase in the liver, thereby accelerating the metabolism of testosterone. This progestational agent affects the production rate of testosterone through an increased clearance in the plasma and also has an antigonadotropic effect. It has also been shown that medroxyprogesterone acetate reduces the production of testosterone from precursors. Medroxyprogesterone acetate is administered in a depot injection, usually at dosage levels of 300 or 400 mg intramuscularly every 7 to 10 days. It can also be given in an oral format of 100–200 mg daily in divided dosages.

There are some potential side effects of medroxyprogesterone acetate treatment that need to be considered, particularly with adolescents. Hawker and Mayer (1981) reviewed a series of studies of medroxyprogesterone acetate and found weight gain in nearly 50% of subjects; sperm production was decreased initially but returned to normal levels; basal insulin levels were normal, although there was a hyperinsulinemic response to glucose load; gastrointestinal functioning, including functioning of the gall bladder, was also in question. There were headaches reported and, in addition, diabetes mellitus was precipitated in at least one case. Gagne (1981) reported fatigue, weight gain, hot and cold flushes, phlebitis, nausea, vomiting, headaches, and sleep disturbances in the sample of men treated with medroxyprogesterone acetate. Berlin and Menicke (1981) also reported nightmares, hypoglycemia, leg cramps and some other side effects similar to those reported by Gagne. However, it is clear from the studies involving medroxyprogesterone acetate that it does have an effect on sexual functioning, reducing sexual drive, decreasing erotic fantasies, reducing sexual activity, and possibly reducing irritability and aggressiveness (Blumer & Migeon, 1975). The first clinical studies of medroxyprogesterone acetate were reported by Money and his colleagues, starting in 1968 (Money et al., 1975). Medroxyprogesterone acetate was used in the treatment of paraphilics with effects on sexual behavior, including decreased frequencies of erections, reductions in sexual drive, and reduced orgasm rates. Most significant is that some of these patients were followed for 8 years and numbers of them still reported beneficial side effects (Money, 1968, 1970, 1972; Money, Weideking, Walker, & Gain, 1977; Money et al., 1975). Other studies have also described similar effects (Berlin & Menicke, 1981; Gagne, 1981).

Effective clinical management of either cyproterone acetate or medroxyprogesterone acetate is even more critical in adolescents than adults. It is important to select patients most likely to benefit, with a minimum of unwanted side effects, particularly with younger adolescents. Patients should be carefully screened for any medical contraindications to the use of antiandrogens. Whether the medication should be used intermittently or continuously is a matter of some debate. My own clinical experience suggests there is certainly very dramatic success, even at follow-up, where patients use it intermittently, maybe for 2 or 3 months a year. At the same time, highly dangerous individuals, where any relapse may lead to very serious difficulties, may need to be on the medication continuously. This could also apply to adolescents and therefore would have to be part of the treatment decision.

THE USE OF OTHER PHARMACOLOGICAL AGENTS

When dealing with adolescents, the use of other pharmacological agents that may suppress the sexual drive is important, as these may provide a more acceptable alternative to antiandrogens. For example, thioridazine (Mellaril) is used in adolescents for various therapeutic reasons without any problems. The use of thioridazine is relatively readily accepted in adolescents, with the usual concerns with regard to tardive dyskinesia and the other potential side effects of neuroleptics. A number of phenothiazines have been reported to reduce sexual drive, including benperidol.

Although anecdotal at this stage, on occasions I have successfully used clomipramine (Anafranil) in cases of severe paraphilia in adolescents. For example, I recently had a 17-year-old adolescent referred for fetishism. He also exhibited pervasive fantasies of lust-murder directed towards 10-year-old girls. There was no evidence of any enactment of these fantasies, but he was following girls. He was regarded as presenting a high risk for sexual violence in the future. He had already been assessed at a Department of Psychiatry in a university teaching hospital and had been placed on medroxyprogesterone acetate at age 16 on the basis that the potential for serious sexual violence was very high. He had, however, discontinued himself as a result of some minor, breast enlargement. He therefore remained untreated, and concerns with regard to his potential for violent sexual behavior remained high. He was referred for an inpatient evaluation and treatment under my care. It was clear that he continued to have highly pervasive, sexually violent fantasies directed toward strangling or suffocating 10-year-old girls, and then raping them while they were unconscious. Some of these fantasies included the homicidal strangulation with sexual activity after death. In addition, investigations showed that he had reduced temporal lobe perfusion, minor electroencephalogram (EEG) abnormalities, and subtle evidence of an organic brain syndrome. The reduced cerebral perfusion to the temporal lobe, using single photon emission computerized tomography, has been found in sadistic sex offenders. His sexual behaviors assessment showed mostly a normal sex hormone profile. The pen-and-pencil tests showed very little in the way of abnormalities. Penile tumescence testing of his sexual arousal patterns confirmed very strong pedophilic and sadistic tendencies. He was highly aroused by rape stimuli, pedophilic stimuli, and pedophilic assault stimuli. Because of his reluctance to go on antiandrogens, although this was the treatment of choice in his case, and given anecdotal success reported previously for individuals treated with clomipramine, I proceeded to place him on clomipramine. Within a relatively short period of time (2 to 3 weeks) he reported a complete reduction of the sexual fantasies and that he felt quite relieved. He also tolerated clomipramine very well at dosage levels of 150 mg PO QHS. Repeating penile tumescence testing showed reduced levels of arousal overall. His rape arousal was almost completely suppressed, and there was some improvement in his pedophilic patterns.

The success of clomipramine in this particular case, and in a number of others may, of course, be incidental, although as is well described, paraphilias have a strongly compulsive element to them, and the use of clomipramine in obsessive-compulsive disorder is well accepted. That is, it is possible there may be a compulsive factor to the paraphilias that is responding to clomipramine. If this is the case, clomipramine, which is a relatively safe drug in adolescents, may be a useful future pharmacological treatment for the paraphilias in adolescents; however, treatment trials will have to be conducted before this could be said with any scientific certainty.

In certain cases where there is evidence of irritability, brain damage, and an organic personality disorder, carbamazepine (Tegretol) has also been used with some success, with subjective reporting of reductions in deviant sexual fantasy and sexual interest, and some evidence of reduction of deviant sexual arousal patterns in penile tumescence testing. This could also be used in adolescents, but again it would be necessary to perform clinical trials to establish its effectiveness in treating the paraphilias, particularly those with a sadistic or sexually aggressive component to it.

In conclusion, the pharmacological treatment of the adolescent sex offender is a new field, an unexplored area neglected by the scientific community. It is a treatment approach that must be used with caution in adolescents, particularly when it comes to the use of antiandrogens and neuroleptics. If the anecdotal evidence of success with carbamazepine and clomipramine is supported empirically in the future, it may form a basis for pharmacological interventions in adolescents in the future.

REFERENCES

Abel, G. G., Mittelman, M. S., & Becker, J. V. (1985). Sexual offenders: Results of assessment and recommendations for treatment. In M. H. Ben-Aron, S. J. Hucker, & C. D. Webster (Eds.), *Clinical criminology: The assessment and treatment of criminal behaviour* (pp. 191–206). Toronto: M and M Graphics.

American Psychiatric Association. (1987). *Diagnostic and statistical manual of mental disorders* (3rd rev. ed.). Washington, DC: Author.

Bancroft, J. (1983a). *Human sexuality and its problems.* Edinburgh: Churchill Livingstone.

Bancroft, J. (1983b). The hormonal and biochemical basis of human sexuality. I. In J. Bancroft (Ed.), *Human sexuality and its problems* (pp. 64–107). Edinburgh: Churchill Livingstone.

Bancroft, J. (1989). *Human Sexuality and its Problems* (2nd Ed.). Edinburgh: Churchill Livingstone.

Berlin, F. S., & Menicke, C. F. (1981). Treatment of sex offenders with antiandrogen medication: Conceptualization, review of treatment modalities and preliminary findings. *American Journal of Psychiatry, 138*, 601–607.

Blumer, D., & Migeon, C. (1975). Hormone and hormonal agents in the treatment of aggression. *Journal of Nervous and Mental Disorders, 160*, 127–137.

Bradford, J. M. (1985). Organic treatments for the male sexual offender. *Behavioral Sciences and the Law, 3*, 355–375.

Bradford, J. M., & Pawlak, A. (1987). Sadistic homosexual pedophilia: Treatment with cyproterone acetate: A single case study. *Canadian Journal of Psychiatry, 32*, 22–30.

Bradford, J. M., & Pawlak, A. (in press-a). *Treatment with cyproterone acetate: A double blind placebo crossover study.* Archives of Sexual Behavior.

Bradford, J. M., & Pawlak, A. (in press-b). *The effects of cyproterone acetate on the sexual arousal patterns of pedophiles.* Archives of Sexual Behavior.

Chapman, M. G. (1982). Side effects of antiandrogen therapy. In E. Jeffcoat (Ed.), *Androgen and antiandrogen therapy* (pp. 169–178). New York: Wiley.

Flanigni, C., Venturoli, S., Lodi, S., Bolelli, G., Nardi, M., & Di Leo, A. (1977). Role of androgens in clinical disorders. In L. Martini & M. Motta (Eds.), *Androgens and antiandrogens* (pp. 201–229). New York: Raven Press.

Foote, I. M. (1944). Diethylstilbestrol in the management of psychopathological states in males. *Journal of Nervous and Mental Disorders, 99*, 928–935.

Gagne, P. (1981). Treatment of sex offenders with medroxyprogesterone acetate. *American Journal of Psychiatry, 138*, 644–646.

Golla, F. L., & Hodge, S. R. (1949). Hormone treatment of sexual offenders. *Lancet, 1*, 1006–1007.

Griffin, J. E., & Wilson, J. D. (1985). Disorders of the Testes and Male Reproductive

Tract. In J. D. Wilson & D. W. Foster (Eds.), *Textbook of endocrinology* (7th ed., pp. 259–311). Philadelphia: Saunders.

Gupta, D. (1977). Androgens and antiandrogens in relation to human sexual maturity. In L. Martini & M. Motta (Eds.), *Androgens and antiandrogens* (pp. 295–309). New York: Raven Press.

Hawker, P. A., & Mayer, W. J. ,(1981). Medroxyprogesterone acetate treatment for paraphilic sex offenders. In J. R. Hayes, T. K. Roberts, & K. S. Solway (Eds.), *Violence and the violent individual* (pp. 353–373). New York: S P Medical and Scientific Books.

Heller, C. G., Laidlaw, W. M., Harvey, H. T., & Nelson, W.O. (1958). Effects of progestational compounds on the reproductive processes of the human male. *Annals of the New York Academy of Sciences, 71,* 649–655.

Mahesh, V. (1977). Excessive androgen secretion and the use of antiandrogens in endocrine therapy. In L. Martini & M. Motta (Eds.), *Androgens and antiandrogens* (pp. 321–327). New York: Raven Press.

Money, J. (1968). Discussion of the hormonal inhibition of libido in male sex offenders. In R. Michael (Ed.), *Endocrinology and human behaviour* (pp. 169–174). London: Oxford University Press.

Money, J. (1970). Use of androgen-depleting hormone in the treatment of male sex offenders. *Journal of Sex Research, 6,* 165–172.

Money, J. (1972). The therapeutic use of androgen depleting hormone. *International Psychiatric Clinics, 8,* 165–174.

Money, J., Weideking, C., Walker, P., Migeon, C., Mayer, W., & Borgaonkar, D. (1975). 47 XYY and 46 XY males with antisocial and/or sex offending behaviour: Antiandrogen therapy plus counselling. *Psychoneuroendocrinology, 1,* 165–178.

Money, J. M., Weideking, C., Walker, P. A., & Gain, D. (1977). Combined antiandrogen and counselling program for treatment of 46 XY and 47 XYY sex offenders. In E. Sachar (Ed.), *Hormones, behaviour and psychopathology* (pp. 105–120). New York: Raven Press.

Neumann, F., Gräf, K. J., Hasan, S. H., Schenok, B., & Steinbeck, H. (1977). Central actions of antiandrogens. In L. Martini & M. Motta (Eds.), *Androgens and Antiandrogens.* New York: Raven Press.

Whittaker, L. H. (1959). Estrogens and psychosexual disorders. *Medical Journal of Australia, 2,* 547–549.

CHAPTER 16

Relapse Prevention with Sexually Aggressive Adolescents and Children: Expanding Treatment and Supervision

Alison Stickrod Gray
William D. Pithers

T reating adolescents who have sexually abused was once regarded as an easier challenge than treating adult offenders. The unvoiced societal view considered adolescent sex offending to be a single overzealous mistake occurring during a confusing exploration of awakening sexuality. Learning theorists regarded the less prolonged reinforcement history of adolescent abusers as a favorable prognostic sign for behavioral change. From a developmental perspective, the abundant energy and youthful resources of adolescents were believed to offer vast hope for change at later stages of growth. Regardless of one's perspective, a safe conclusion was that treating juvenile sex abusers would be easier than similar efforts with adults.

Over the past decade, the notion that juveniles are easier to treat than adults has been recognized as yet another myth about sex offenders. The desire to view all instances of juvenile sexual abuse as isolated events is not supported by research data.

ONSET OF ABUSIVE SEXUALITY: ADOLESCENCE

Working with 561 adult offenders whose disclosures of previously unreported sexual abuse were protected by a Federal Certificate of Confidentiality (*Federal Register*, 1975), Abel and Rouleau (1990) found that "53.6% reported the onset of at least one deviant sexual interest prior to age 18 . . . . Of the 53.6% of adult offenders reporting the onset of deviant sex interest prior to age 18, each reported two different paraphilias and an average commission of 380 sexual offenses by the time he reached adulthood" (p. 13). By age 16, 50% of the same-sex pedophiles were aware of their interest in abusing boys.

Interviewing adolescent sex offenders, Abel and Rouleau discovered an average of 1.9 paraphilias and 6.8 sex offenses, with child sexual abuse or rape accounting for 54.1% of these offenses. Our clinical experience suggests that as juvenile offenders progress through treatment there is an increase in their reported numbers of victims and abusive acts. In one therapy group for adolescent abusers, the number of reported victims increased 800% during the course of treatment. These data suggest that figures obtained during research interviews, even those conducted by the most highly skilled experts, may underestimate the actual number of victims and offenses.

Efforts to Differentiate Adolescent Sex Abusers

Not all juvenile sex abusers experience deeply ingrained problems. Recognizing that not all adolescent abusers are alike, several efforts have been made to differentiate subtypes. The first schemata for subtyping juvenile abusers was developed by O'Brien and Bera (1986). Each subgroup was typified by specific offense characteristics and treatment needs. At the least extreme end of the continuum, O'Brien and Bera's Naive Experimenters were believed to benefit from sex education and family therapy in community-based programs. More extreme subtypes, such as the "Sexual Aggressor," were thought to be most appropriately treated in a highly specialized, residential setting where intensive group and behavioral therapies are employed. Building on O'Brien and Bera's work, the Oregon Children's Services Division published "Guidelines for Treatment of Juvenile Sex Offenders" in *The Oregon Report on Juvenile Sexual Offenders* in 1986. Known as the "Oregon Matrix," this effort attempted to identify the ideal treatment placement for juveniles on the basis of their therapeutic, educational, recreational, and supervision needs. Therapeutic goals were specified for individual, family, adolescent group, parent group, and substance abuse issues. Both typologies identified a range of juvenile sex abusers, many of whom were believed to benefit from weekly, outpatient, educational groups and some of whom require intensive, residential treatment followed by prolonged, outpatient treatment and supervision.

ONSET OF ABUSIVE SEXUALITY: PREADOLESCENCE

More recently, practitioners have discovered that the onset of sexually abusive behaviors can precede adolescence. Between 1984 and 1989 in Vermont, nearly 200 children under 10 years of age were discovered to have sexually abused others. In 1991 alone, nearly 100 sexually aggressive children were identified in Vermont. Since these figures include only forceful or repetitive acts, they underestimate the magnitude of sexually abusive behaviors performed by children. Lieb and Felver (1991) report that the State of Washington identified 691 children who were considered sexually aggressive youth.

Mental health professionals have clearly recognized this problem. The First National Conference on Sexually Aggressive and Sexually Reactive Children (Gray & Knopp, 1991) was attended by more than 450 treatment providers who came from 38 States and 3 Canadian Provinces. Though practitioners recognized the existence of this population, statistics on prevalence are extremely limited. The *Preliminary Report from the National Task Force on Juvenile Sex Offending* (National Adolescent Perpetrator Network, 1988) commented on this issue:

> Identification and reporting of child offending has been almost nonexistent prior to 1985 . . . . In a society which denies all sexuality in childhood and attempts to repress sexual behavior in adolescence, it is not surprising that we would minimize and deny sexual offending by children. The histories of adult and adolescent offenders, however, have indicated that sexual offending develops over time (Longo; Groth; Abel); and recent work with children has confirmed that sexual offending may begin in early childhood (Isaac; Cavanaugh-Johnson). (p. 42)

One contributing factor to underreporting is that preadolescent sex abuse is defined on a case-by-case basis, with abusiveness being judged on vaguely defined criteria such as differences in stature, sophistication, coerciveness, and force. Across the country, various criteria have been used to define child-on-child sexual abuse. The long-standing tendency to view much of the perpetrating behavior as child play also remains with us. Some child protection workers, concerned about the potential stigmatization of children referred to as "perpetrators," may identify such children as victims only. In other settings, sexually aggressive children receive little attention, since they fall outside the mandates of both the child protection and juvenile justice systems. As a result of these factors, the scope of the problem may be difficult to estimate. However, the best available evidence suggests that our previous estimates greatly minimize the extent of the problem.

Efforts to Differentiate Sexually Aggressive Children

Some theorists have proposed that typologies of adolescent sex offenders may be applicable to the treatment of sexually aggressive children. Rasmussen, Burton, and Christopherson (1990) modified O'Brien and Bera's adolescent typology for application to sexually aggressive children. Rasmussen and colleagues identified six subtypes: (1) sexually curious, (2) reenacting trauma, (3) socially motivated, (4) egocentric, (5) behaviorally disordered, and (6) group influenced.

Developing a typology specifically for child sexually behavior problems, Johnson (1988) distinguished four subtypes of behavior: (1) within normal limits, (2) sexually reactive, (3) mutual, and (4) child perpetrator. Criteria employed to define subtypes include (1) sexual behavior, (2) other behaviors, (3) relationship to other, (4) age difference/coercion, (5) affect regarding sexuality, (6) motivation for sexual behavior, and (7) possible etiology.

Berliner, Manaois, and Monastersky (1986) defined three levels of "Child Sexual Behavior Disturbance": (1) coercive sexual behavior, (2) developmentally precocious behavior, and (3) inappropriate sexual behavior. Coercive sexual behavior involved use of force or implied force to gain the victim's submission, whereas developmentally precocious behavior included attempted intercourse without use of coercion. Inappropriate sexual behavior subsumed a wide variety of acts (e.g., public masturbation, exposure, sexualized play) that did not necessarily suggest psychological disturbance or the need for intensive intervention.

The existing taxonomies represent useful heuristic devices, since they are based on the clinical impressions of very respected therapists. However, research has yet to be performed to empirically validate these clinical impressions. Efforts to empirically validate these subtypes clearly represent an important direction for additional research.

RELAPSE PREVENTION

Regardless of subtype, offense precursors to sexually abusive behaviors exist and appear specific to each juvenile. The abuser's subtype may be reflected in the number or variety of offense precursors as well as the swiftness with which they progress through their precursive pattern. For example, abuse-reactive children may manifest relatively few precursors. Simply recalling the sensation of sexualized touch may elicit such behavior toward others. In contrast, sexually compulsive adolescents may exhibit an extensive and ritualized pattern of precursors to abusing. Since distinct sequences of precursors to sexually abusive acts exist, treatment can assist abusers to learn specific coping responses that may be invoked to disrupt the progression toward another offense.

Relapse prevention (Pithers, Kashima, Cumming, Beal, & Buell, 1988) and offense cycles (Isaac & Lane, 1990) are theoretical treatment models based on the concept that offense precursors can be identified and addressed. These theoretical models have created substantial change in our understanding and treatment of juvenile sex offenders. These theories assert that sexual abuse is not committed on impulse or as a result of severe psychiatric disorders. The likelihood that precursors associated with sexual abuse will recur is now widely accepted.

Relapse prevention (RP) was originated to strengthen the self-management skills of substance abusers (Chaney, O'Leary, & Marlatt, 1978; Marlatt, 1982; Marlatt & Gordon, 1980, 1985). The first step toward this goal was accomplished by providing clients with structured methods for identifying decisions and situations that could precipitate compulsive behavior. Following this assessment, clients learned methods of avoiding or coping more effectively with risky circumstances. RP was designed to assist maintenance of behavioral change in clients who had already been in other treatment for substance use disorders. More recently, RP has been applied with highly varied clinical populations, including juvenile and adult sex offenders.

Although RP was initially designed to be solely a self-management model of behavioral maintenance, the model has been modified extensively for application with sex offenders. RP has served three distinct functions in sex offender treatment: (1) an Internal, Self-Management Dimension used to enhance the client's self-control; (2) an External, Supervisory Dimension used by a "prevention team" of professional and collateral contacts who monitor the juvenile's behaviors and who model appropriate behaviors; and (3) a conceptual framework, which integrates highly specific therapeutic interventions within a unifying theory. Each of these functions of RP is discussed in this chapter.

AN OVERVIEW OF THE RELAPSE PREVENTION MODEL

RP is a theory-based model. In order to implement the model in assessing and treating juvenile abusers, an understanding of its underlying concepts is essential. The following section of this chapter summarizes RP theory. More detailed information about RP theory is provided in other publications (Marlatt & Gordon, 1985; Pithers, 1990).

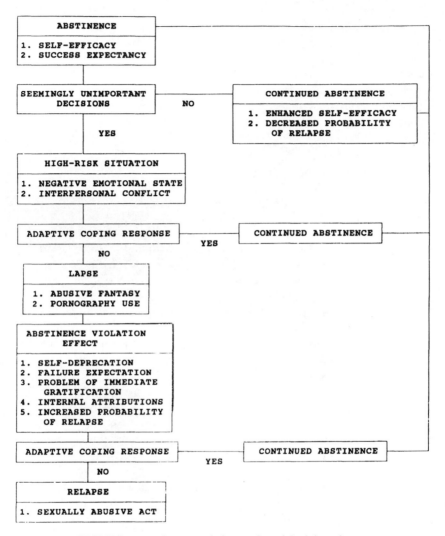

FIGURE 16.1. Cognitive-behavioral model of the relapse process.

THE RELAPSE PROCESS

RP proposes that sex offenses are not impulsive acts but rather the culmination of a process that builds across time. A graphical depiction of the relapse process is presented in Figure 16.1.

Although some juveniles reoffend in situations that would have been difficult to anticipate, most set the stage for sexual abuse by making decisions that allow them access to High-Risk Situations. Juvenile abusers generally get into High-Risk Situations by making a series of Seemingly Unimportant Decisions (SUDs). Taken individually, each SUD may *seem* unrelated to the ultimate choice of whether or not to sexually abuse someone; however, each decision changes the subsequent array of choices available to the juvenile. The importance of the cumulative impact of a series of SUDs can be seen in Figure 16.2. Since few people make consistently good or bad decisions, most juveniles fall toward the middle of this diagram, having made some decisions that move toward High-Risk Situations and others that take them away from heightened risk of offending. Clients making a preponderance of ill-considered choices will come closer to the left side of Figure 16.2, while those more consistently making good decisions will fall toward the right side.

Risk of lapsing or relapsing increases when the juvenile encounters High-Risk Situations. High-Risk Situations contain stimuli associated with past offenses or that could enable another offense. If the juvenile successfully copes with a High-Risk Situation, his sense of self-efficacy increases and the probability of relapse decreases. If the juvenile reacts maladaptively to a High-Risk Situation, the potential consequences may include (1) another SUD that permits access to a still Higher Risk Situation; (2) a lapse into one of the thoughts, feelings, fantasies, or behaviors that precede sex offenses; or (3) a prolonged exposure to a High-Risk Situation that may encourage the juvenile to passively yield to an urge to abuse.

Clients who lapse into an abuse-related thought, feeling, fantasy, or behavior are often reluctant to divulge what they perceive as a "failure." At such

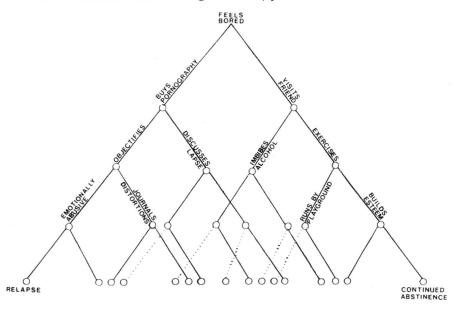

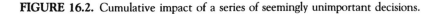

FIGURE 16.2. Cumulative impact of a series of seemingly unimportant decisions.

times, juveniles frequently adhere to one of two erroneous beliefs: "What I do not acknowledge does not exist" or "What they don't know won't hurt me," and attempt to hide the error from therapists and family. The juvenile may fear that acknowledging even a momentary abusive fantasy will suggest to others that he or she is totally out of control. The problem with such attempts to "bury" lapses is that buried lapses rarely stay underground. More commonly, hidden lapses give the juvenile freedom to enter Higher Risk Situations and engage in additional lapses that are closer to another offense. In the RP model, engaging in thoughts, feelings, fantasies, or nonabusive behaviors that are precursors to sex offenses are called *lapses*. Recurrence of abusive sexual behavior is considered a *relapse*.

When juveniles lapse they commonly experience the Abstinence Violation Effect. The Abstinence Violation Effect is essentially a conflict between the juvenile's developing self-image as someone who manages behaviors effectively and his previous self-image as someone who acts abusively toward others. The juvenile's response to a lapse plays a major role in determining whether he will engage in another offense. Left unprepared to cope with the lapse, the juvenile, thinking in an overly generalized and rigid manner, may either deny that he has acted imperfectly or consider himself a hopeless failure. Under such circumstances, the adolescent may first become physically or emotionally abusive, setting the stage for continued failure, culminating in sexual abuse.

Another factor influencing the extent of the Abstinence Violation Effect is the juvenile's selective recall of only the positive aspects of having abused in the past. To the degree that juveniles selectively remember outcomes that were perceived as positive (e.g., increased power, social competence, release of rage) while forgetting the delayed negative consequences (e.g., arrest, decreased self-respect, public blaming, humiliation at school, feeling "weird"), the probability of relapse increases. Due to the strength of this aspect of the Abstinence Violation Effect, it has been labeled the Problem of Immediate Gratification.

A final factor affecting the occurrence of the Abstinence Violation Effect is the individual's expectation about the likelihood of encountering lapses. If the juvenile believes that successful treatment should permanently erase all semblances of his abusive interests, a momentary loss of control can have a devastating effect. In contrast, if the juvenile accepts that lapses in control are a common human trait, then he may recognize that he can learn by reviewing poor decisions, and he may realize that his self-management skills can be increased through disclosure and open discussion.

A Common Sequence of Precursors to Sexual Abuse

With many adolescent perpetrators a common sequence of risk factors appears to precede sexually abusive behaviors. The initial change from the abuser's usual behaviors is emotional. In our clinical work, boredom appears among the most common emotional precursors to sex offenses by adolescents. Other common emotional precursors are social or sexual embarrassment, anger, fear of rejection, and numbness.

The second stage of the relapse process is marked by an increase in the frequency or strength of abusive sexual fantasies. Adolescents sometimes experience abusive fantasies while masturbating in a maladaptive effort to escape from a strong emotional state, or from feeling unsuccessful, or as a result of being unable to express their feelings. Photographs or drawings, including sexually explicit and nonsexual images, are sometimes used to heighten arousal to abusive fantasies.

Abusive sexual fantasies are transformed into cognitive distortions in the third stage of the relapse process. Rationalizations objectifying women or attributing overly mature characteristics to children minimize the deviance of the fantasized behavior. In fact, cognitive distortions appear to link the entire sequence of offense precursors. However, in this stage of the sequence, distortions allow the juvenile to move from feeling entitled to entertain a sexually abusive *fantasy* to feeling entitled to perform the abusive *behavior*.

Having justified their fantasies with cognitive distortions, offenders "passively" develop plans to perform the behavior. Nuances in offense setting, timing, and grooming behaviors were developed to decrease the chance of detection or to permit the abuse to be depicted as impulsive if they are discovered. We use the term *planned impulsiveness* to refer to this phenomenon.

The plan is enacted in the final step of the relapse sequence. Occasionally, substances are used in the first step of this stage. Juveniles use substances to sedate inhibitions against the act or to attempt to minimize their culpability.

Thus, a distinct sequence of offense precursors is often discerned: Unpleasant Affect → Deviant Fantasy → Passive Planning → Cognitive Distortion → Disinhibition → Deviant Act. The relapse process entails identifiable precursors that can be addressed during treatment, or that can be targeted to enhance supervision of the offender.

Potential Uses of Identified Offense Precursors

Identification of precursive risk factors by clients and therapists serves several important functions. Risk factors may point to behavioral excesses and deficits that may be addressed therapeutically. By monitoring risk factors during treatment, therapists may be better able to confront and inform clients about elements of their relapse processes. Such monitoring also allows us to assess the efficacy of treatment in an ongoing fashion.

Since RP asserts that juvenile abusers engage in precursors to sexual assault and that these risk factors represent distinct changes from the offender's typical behaviors, family members and probation officers may discern periods when a juvenile is at risk to relapse by monitoring these "high-risk" factors. In this fashion, RP enhances efficacy of external supervision. Since *specific* risk factors related to the juvenile's sex offenses are monitored by collateral contacts (e.g., family members, guidance counselors, employers), probation officers gain information that otherwise might not be available to them.

Currently, as seen in Figure 16.3, three categories of risk factors are defined within the the relapse prevention model (Pithers & Gray, 1991). *Predisposing* risk factors are those occurring during early development or that fall very early in the abuser's sequence of precursors (i.e., Affect → Fantasy → Passive Planning → Cognitive Distortion → Disinhibition → Act). *Precipitating* risk factors generally occur shortly before the sexually abusive behavior and tend to determine that the type of abuse performed will involve coercive sexuality. *Perpetuating* risk factors increase the likelihood that sexually abusive behaviors will continue in the future.

Although far from absolute, these categories appear to be addressed by different therapeutic responses. Predisposing risk factors generally are addressed by relatively traditional and supportive individual, group, and family therapies that delve into historical issues. Precipitating risk factors are the focus of more specialized interventions devised for application with sexual abusers (e.g., behavioral therapies to alter arousal to abusive fantasies, victim empathy building). Perpetuating risk factors are managed through the creation of environmental structure, prevention team supervision, modeling of prevention skills, and knowledge of trauma effects and the relapse process.

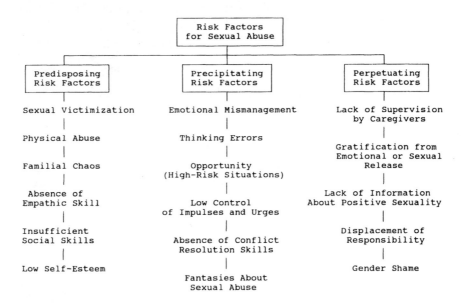

FIGURE 16.3. Examples of predisposing, precipitating, and perpetuating risk factors.

INTERNAL, SELF-MANAGEMENT DIMENSION OF
RELAPSE PREVENTION

When first modified for application to sex offenders within the Vermont Treatment Program for Sexual Aggressors (Pithers, 1982; Pithers, Marques, Gibat, & Marlatt, 1983), RP remained solely a means of enhancing offenders' self-management skills to prevent future abuse. This aspect of the modified RP model now is referred to as the Internal, Self-Management Dimension.

Abusers derive the greatest benefit from the Internal, Self-Management Dimension of RP if they have previously participated in a group designed to enhance accountability for the effects of their offenses and to establish empathy. A high degree of motivation and integrity is required for a client to continually monitor signs of his relapse process and to invoke coping strategies, even when it feels like a sacrifice to do so. Without the dedication derived from the empathy for sexual abuse victims developed in treatment, RP risks becoming an intellectual exercise that educates offenders about what they need to do to avoid reoffending but that finds offenders lacking the motivation to use this knowledge.

With adolescents, the overall goals of the Internal, Self-Management Dimension are increased awareness of the range of choices affecting their behavior, development of specific coping skills and heightened self-control capacities, creation of a general sense of self-mastery, enhancement of empathic skills, and prevention of further victimization. These goals, adapted to the child's level of developmental competence, also apply to sexually aggressive children. While an individual's unique characteristics determine the different emphasis placed on development of self-management skills and the supervision network, external supervision generally receives greater emphasis with children. Internal, Self-Management Interventions also can be used to assist both children and adolescents to manage trauma effects if they have been victims of abuse.

To attain these goals, RP employs structured procedures designed to help clients anticipate and cope with the occurrence of lapses, and to modify the early antecedents of lapses.

Introducing the Internal, Self-Management
Dimension of RP to the Client

In beginning RP, dispelling the juvenile's misconceptions about the outcome of treatment is essential. Many sex offenders enter treatment expecting that their desire for unacceptable sex acts will be eliminated. In the RP model, although the client participates in procedures designed to reduce abusive interests, he is also prepared for the possible return of these problems.

In introducing RP to the client, we emphasize development of realistic expectations about therapy by teaching clients that treatment is an active, problem-solving process. We directly tell clients that they have engaged in a criminal behavior for which no cure exists, but that they can learn to control their decision making and behavior. Clients are told that treatment may decrease their attraction to abusive sexual behaviors, but that abusive fantasies may recur at least momentarily in the future. Clients are informed that the return of an abusive fantasy does not necessarily signify that they are going to reoffend. They learn that a crucial part of their treatment involves learning what to do when they feel drawn to abusive sexual behaviors again. We instruct clients that they will discover SUDs that allow them to move closer to offending again, or which take them away from that danger. They are assisted in developing the ability to recognize these situations and enact alternatives that will reduce the likelihood that they will abuse again.

The RP therapist encourages responsibility on the part of the client by fostering an atmosphere of collaboration without collusion. This firm, but noncondemnatory, approach has several goals. By encouraging the client to serve as his own cotherapist, we foster a greater sense of objectivity in the client's consideration of his own behaviors. As a result, the client feels freer to discuss threatening emotions and behaviors. By adopting this objective and detached approach, the client and therapist mutually begin to explore problematic behaviors without the extreme defensiveness that otherwise might be engendered. The absence of moral indictment and the focus upon behaviors enable the client to see that sexually aggressive behavior is an unacceptable act that he has performed, rather than an indication of something he *is* (and always will be), a sex offender. This therapeutic style has been referred to as "compassionate accountability" (Pithers & Gray, 1991). The therapist holds the client responsible for his or her abusive behaviors, but does so with an understanding recognition of the client's life experiences. Compassionate accountability does not allow clients' to excuse abusive behavior, nor does it endorse abuse of the abuser under the guise of treatment.

A wide variety of assessment and treatment activities are subsumed by the Internal, Self-Management Dimension of RP. Many of these are skill training procedures designed to equip the offender to act effectively when he/she recognizes that he/she is at risk. Information about these procedures is presented in other sources (Pithers et al., 1988; Pithers, Cumming, Beal, Young, & Turner, 1989; Pithers, Martin, & Cumming, 1989) and, therefore, they are not reviewed here. We consider here only those procedures designed specifically to train offenders in recognizing those factors that increase their risk to reoffend.

The Internal, Self-Management Treatment Group

A special treatment group is used to introduce juveniles to RP as a method of deterring their abusive patterns. This group provides a structured process through which juveniles become increasingly aware of their SUDs, High-Risk

Factors, Lapses, Abstinence Violation Effect, and coping strategies. A similar approach, adapted for developmental level, is used with sexually aggressive children. This treatment process also is employed to enhance management of fear and anxiety with offenders who have been victimized.

Stage 1: Explanation of the RP model

The first group session educates juveniles about core RP concepts including offense precursors, planned impulsiveness, SUDs, High-Risk Situations, Risk Factors, the Problem of Immediate Gratification, Coping Strategies, Lapses, the Abstinence Violation Effect, and Relapse. Juveniles must demonstrate knowledge of these concepts before continuing in the group.

Stage 2: Identifying risk factors

Once knowledge of RP concepts has been demonstrated, group members complete a homework assignment by preparing a list of their own risk factors for sex offenses. Upon hearing the assignment, occasionally a juvenile will acknowledge that he performed a sex offense but insist that he did not mean to do it. The implication is that abuse somehow occurred without his awareness or intent, that no precursors to his sexual abuse exist. Clients reluctant to acknowledge risk factors often can be encouraged to do so through the following discussion.

Therapist: Have you ever sneezed?

Client: Sure. So what?

Therapist: Would you agree with me that a sneeze is probably one of the most reflexive, automatic acts that a human being could ever perform? I mean, you probably didn't wake up this morning thinking that you would unleash a good sneeze today in order to feel really good about yourself, did you?

Client: Not very likely.

Therapist: So you'd agree that a sneeze is probably a very reflexive, automatic act that you don't think much about before you do it?

Client: Yes.

Therapist: What do you do whenever you're in public and you realize that you're about to sneeze?

Client: I put my hand over my mouth and nose or grab a tissue out of my back pocket.

Therapist: You've agreed that a sneeze is a very automatic reflexive act that you don't think about before it happens. Whenever you realize that you're about to sneeze, you still have time to raise your hand to your nose and mouth or to get a tissue from your back pocket. Yet you're asking me to believe that when you were about to abuse your victim you didn't at any point in time realize what you were about to do and that you didn't make the decision to go ahead with the abuse. Would you ask your grandmother to believe that?

Client: No, I guess not.

Therapist: Okay, then I'd ask you not to expect me to believe it either.

Other juveniles may be reluctant to admit their awareness of offense precursors out of fear that they will be judged more harshly. They may become more open if permitted to acknowledge fleeting precursive fantasies that were not cultivated over a prolonged time.

"A lot of people think that in order to call something a sexual fantasy it needs to be as long, action-packed, and detailed as a Hollywood movie. Other people think that sexual fantasies are the thoughts they have when they are doing something sexual.

"The reality is that there are all sorts of sexual fantasies. Some of them really can be long, action-packed, daydreams. It's also possible to have sexual fantasies that occur in less than a second.

"Have you ever looked out the window at nighttime when it's raining and lightning? Whenever there is a flash of lightning, for just a moment you can see trees and buildings almost as clearly as in the daytime. And then just as quickly the image is gone. Some sexual fantasies are like the image you see during a flash of lightning; there for only a moment, then gone. I call these 'flash fantasies.' How many times did you have these kinds of flash fantasies about what your offenses?"

Pithers, Beal, Armstrong, and Petty (1989) offer other suggestions about interview procedures that foster the client's acknowledgment of offense precursors.

Stage 3: Recording risk factors

In sequence, each group member reads aloud his highest risk factor. Group members discuss each risk factor to ensure understanding and assist differentiation among risk factors. A group leader writes each risk factor on a flip chart. This process continues until each client's list of risk factors has been exhausted. A partial list of risk factors generated by one group is shown in Table 16.1.

Stage 4: Individual review of risk factors

As a homework assignment, group members review the complete list of risk factors. Juveniles look at the risk factors generated by the entire group, since

TABLE 16.1. Partial List of Risk Factors for Sexual Abuse Identified by one Treatment Group.

Rushing into relationships	Believing I'm cured
Fear of rejection	Compartmentalization
Loneliness	Depression
Substance use	Overworking
Passivity	Abusive sexual fantasies
Misreading social cues	Misuse of leisure time
Allowing myself to be bored	Emotional isolation
Negative self-statements	Going to playgrounds
Nude swimming areas	Hitchhiking
Use of pornography/erotica	Skipping school
Feeling inferior	Staring at crotches
Talking about sex with victim	Hanging out in restrooms
Ending relationships	Unexpressed anger
Keeping secrets	Role-playing
Masturbating to abusive fantasies	Lack of empathy

others may have noted risk factors that they had not listed but that apply to them.

Each client identifies his five most problematic risk factors rating them along two dimensions: (1) How frequently does the risk factor occur and (2) how strongly does it influence his behavioral choices? Some risk factors are like drops of water glancing off granite; the immediate impact is negligible, but the cumulative effect erodes even the strongest resistance. Other risk factors seldom are encountered but have an irresistibly magnetic influence over behavioral choices.

Stage 5: Identification of most common risk factor

Each juvenile describes his highest risk factor. As each factor is written on a flip chart, all clients having that risk factor as one of their five most problematic raise their hands and a tally is taken. After the first group member has described his highest risk factor, another group member describes the highest risk factor remaining on his list and another tally is taken. The exercise continues until every group member has listed his five highest risk factors. This process identifies the risk factors most common to the entire group. The structure of this exercise requires all group members to participate in the process.

Stage 6: Cue identification

As homework, clients identify cues enabling them to detect the presence, or imminence, of the group's most common risk factor. At least one of the cues must be externally observable. This requirement ensures that cues identifiable by the prevention team will be listed.

The importance of identifying reliable cues and remaining vigilant for their presence is stressed using the metaphor of a stop sign.

"When someone first learns to drive a car, it takes a great deal of attention to make sure they stop at stop signs. The driver first needs to be aware of cues signifying they are approaching a stop sign. Some of these cues include the octagonal shape of the sign, its red color, its location on a 6-foot-high pole at the right-hand side of an intersection, taillights illuminating on other vehicles approaching the sign, and pedestrians crossing nearby.

"When learning to drive, noticing these cues while also steering, keeping just the right amount of pressure on the gas or brake pedal, conversing with a friend, and watching for pedestrians and other cars takes a lot of work and can cause some anxiety. As people grow more accustomed to driving, it takes less work to stop at stop signs because we grow so accustomed to the cues for stop signs that using the correct coping response of gently applying the brakes seems almost automatic. If you fail to notice these cues at an important intersection, you could be responsible for someone's tragedy.

"It's also important to identify reliable cues to your risk factors for sex offenses. Just like stopping a car at a stop sign, it may take considerable work and cause some anxiety as you begin looking for these cues. Eventually, you'll find that identifying the cues to your sexually abusive behaviors will become nearly as automatic as stopping a car. Just like with the car, you will be responsible for a tragedy if you realize too late that you've carelessly gone through an important intersection in your life."

Stage 7: Analysis of cues

Group members sequentially list their cues to the most common risk factor. Group discussion fosters understanding of the meaning of each cue, differentiation among cues, and disclosure of secrets. Some of the cues identified for a risk factor that one group labeled, "Not Feeling Good about Myself," are shown in Table 16.2.

Group members often begin to notice that some cues occur in clusters. For example, one juvenile might observe that when angry (risk factor), he isolates himself, scowls, sighs a lot, feels bored, and develops a headache (cues). Such observations allow the introduction of the concept of cue convergence.

The overlap of several different cues to a single risk factor is called cue convergence. While any one cue might suggest the presence of a risk factor, the simultaneous presence of several cues to a risk factor is certain evidence. Since

TABLE 16.2. Cues to the Risk Factor "Not feeling Good about Myself."

Self-Statements	Behavioral Cues
"Nothing is going right"	Staying by myself
"I should have done . . . "	Pacing
"I can't . . . "	Skipping school
"There I go again"	Taking off work
"I always (or never) . . . "	Horseplaying
	Risky driving
Physical Cues	Being passive
Queasy stomach	Procrastinating
Sleepiness or insomnia	Solitary activities
Feeling drained	
Not shaving	Interpersonal Cues
Having a "long face"	Needing to win
Disregard for personal appearance	Getting others to feel sorry for me
Physically hurting myself	Bragging
	Exaggerating stories
Emotional Cues	Snap judgments about other people
Feeling all alone	
Worrying	Cognitive Cues
Fear of expressing feelings	Dwelling on the past
Feeling angry	Suicidal thoughts
Feeling jealous	Thinking about drugs
Feeling depressed	Comparing self to people to whom I
Faking happiness	feel inferior
Withholding feelings	

some individuals are more sensitive to cues from one sensory modality than others, juveniles are encouraged to attend to their most reliable cues first and then to look for others cues that may converge on a risk factor.

Stage 8: Identification of coping responses

As homework, group members identify potential coping strategies for the group's most common risk factor. The assignment calls for the juveniles to create as many potential coping strategies as possible.

Stage 9: Brainstorming of coping strategies

Group members brainstorm potential coping strategies for the most common risk factor, using the list from their homework assignment as a starting point. No criticism of suggested coping strategies is permitted, since one objective of the exercise is to help juveniles expand their ability to generate many options toward creative resolution of problems. The process continues until all suggestions are exhausted. A partial list of coping strategies for the risk factor "rejection" are shown in Table 16.3.

TABLE 16.3. Partial List of Coping Strategies for Risk Factor of Rejection Generated by One Treatment Group.

Call someone	Use a relaxation fantasy
Accept limitations	Be aware of distorted thinking
Accept no for answer	Look elsewhere for acceptance
Accept disappointment	Don't role play for acceptance
Respect other's position	Be aware of need to control
Ask for clarification	Express anger appropriately
Journal feelings	Remember self-worth
Think of other's feelings	Accept feelings as they are
Take deep breaths	Think positively
Don't blame or pass judgment	Allow others their space

Stage 10: Analysis of coping strategies

As homework, each client analyzes the potential coping responses identified by the group. Coping responses are rated on a seven-point scale along two dimensions: (1) the likelihood that the coping response will effectively deal with the risk factor and (2) the client's ability to perform the coping strategy.

Stage 11: Review of optimal coping strategies

Each group member presents his five optimal coping strategies to the group. His own ratings of the likely success and his ability to use each strategy are discussed. Group members challenge unrealistic ratings and suggest alternate coping strategies.

Stage 12: Preparation of reminder card

As homework, each client is requested to prepare a reminder card for the group's most common risk factor. The name of the risk factor is written on one side of a 3" x 5" index card. The five most reliable cues and the five optimal coping strategies are written in two columns on the reverse side. Clients prepare two sets of reminder cards, keeping one and giving the other to the therapists. Clients are instructed to review the cards several times every day.

Stage 13: Processing other risk factors

Clients repeat the processing of other risk factors common to group members (i.e., identification of cues, potential coping strategies, rating of potential coping strategies, and preparation of reminder cards). Throughout this period, clients may be quizzed about risk factors, cues, and coping strategies by the therapists or other group members.

Stage 14: Testing preparedness

Without warning, clients may be requested to engage in a relapse fantasy. At any point in the relapse fantasy, a therapist may interrupt and ask the client to state how he would cope with the imagined High-Risk Situation. Clients are pressured to respond as quickly as possible. Proposed coping responses that are unrealistic are confronted. At unexpected moments, therapists use reminder cards to quiz group members about the cues and coping strategies for their risk factors.

Stage 15: Analysis of effectiveness

Group members are asked to report any risk factors they have encountered and to discuss how they identified the risk factor and how well they were able to cope. If group members are reluctant to self-report risk factors or lapses, they are asked to confront other group members whom they have observed in lapses or risk behaviors. The group analyzes the risk factor, cues, and coping strategies and makes suggestions about how the offender may deal with precursors to the risk factor more effectively in the future.

Stage 16: Informing the prevention team

The last stage of the RP group is also the next step in strengthening the effectiveness of the External, Supervisory Dimension of RP. The client is required to meet with his care providers, probation supervisor, selected family members, and collateral community advocacy members to provide them with a full disclosure of his relapse process. The juvenile presents his reminder cards to the prevention team and asks for their assistance in identifying cues and risk factors. This has been rehearsed in developmental segments as the juvenile has progressed through the group. The juvenile is expected to state that others may assist his monitoring of cues and risk factors, but that he alone is responsible for his decisions and behaviors. The prevention team and juvenile then discuss who else needs to be informed about his offense history and relapse process to widen his advocacy community.

By following this group therapy format, juvenile sex offenders become acutely aware of their relapse process and the steps they can take to interrupt that process. However, since sex offenders are at times unreliable informants, creating other methods of gaining access to information about the juvenile's behaviors in the community was considered essential. In order to enhance community safety, the External, Supervisory Dimension of the RP model was developed (Pithers et al., 1988; Pithers, Cumming, et al., 1989).

SPECIAL ISSUES WHEN WORKING WITH SEXUALLY AGGRESSIVE CHILDREN

Treatment of sexually aggressive children is at a pioneering stage. To provide adequate care for a sexually aggressive child, therapists need to be aware of the traumatic effects of sexual victimization. In addition, attention needs to be paid to the child's competence in attachment, moral reasoning, empathic ability, and autonomy. When working with sexually aggressive children, a balanced approach (Gray, 1991a) is essential.

As previously discussed, three broad categories of risk factors (or precursors) can be identified: predisposing, precipitating, and perpetuating. Figure 16.4 shows how four responses (i.e., self-managed, trauma induced, compensatory, and external supervision) affect the extent to which each category of precursors influences a sexually aggressive child's behaviors. Depending on the specific qualities, each response may promote either the child victim's safe recovery (indicated by "+" in Figure 16.4) or the externalization of negative emotions through abuse of others (indicated by "−"). For example, compensatory responses to a feeling of powerlessness could include abusing others or becoming an advocate for abuse victims. Both behaviors involve a heightened sense of personal power. One response promotes victimization; the other works to resolve it.

The balanced approach, presented in Figure 16.4 (Gray, 1991a), demonstrates that abuse-related tendencies may be addressed by the following prevention structures: (1) enhancing self-management skills of sexually aggressive children, (2) resolving trauma resulting from the child's own victimization, (3) addressing compensatory reactions often associated with externalization of difficult emotions through problematic behaviors, and (4) increasing the extent to which prevention team members model abuse-preventive beliefs and intervene when abuse-related behaviors are observed.

The balanced approach suggests that abuse-prone characteristics can be addressed either directly or indirectly. Consider a child whose compensatory response to fear associated with his victimization is to punch his brother in the nose. In this case, the compensatory response to fear precipitated physical abuse. This response momentarily may reduce fears, increasing his sense of powerfulness and ability to defend himself. However, the behavior is clearly unacceptable.

Within the balanced approach, this compensatory display of precipitating fear can be dealt with in several ways. From a self-management perspective, the behavior could be considered to represent the problem of immediate gratification. The good feeling of the immediate sense of power can be contrasted with the harm done to the brother and the unpleasantness of even the most appro-

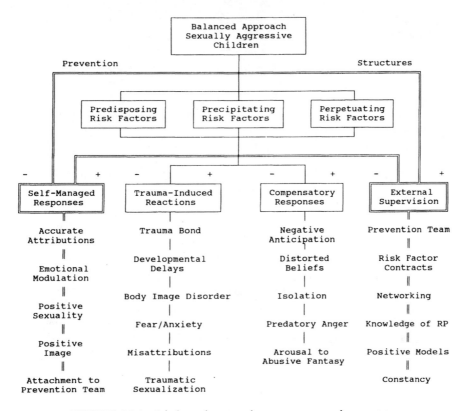

FIGURE 16.4. A balanced approach to treatment and supervision.

priate discipline. From the perspective of external supervision, care givers may be asked what observations they made about the situational characteristics or the child's emotions and behaviors (e.g., Was he isolating? Did he appear sad? Was anything on television at the time?). In the future, these observations may result in early identification of the pattern and preventive intervention. The behavior also can be viewed as a sign that abuse-related memories have been recalled. From this perspective, the child may be provided an opportunity to discuss his fears or to take part in activities designed to inoculate him from the effects of stress. Finally, the destructive compensatory behavior of hitting his brother could be replaced with a more constructive response. A child can be encouraged to understand that it takes great courage to admit that one is afraid and that his ability to voice his feelings will be taken as a sign that he is stronger than others who are afraid to admit their fears.

In summary, the balanced approach allows one to consider that four elements (i.e., self-managed responses, trauma-induced reactions, compensatory responses, and external supervision) interact to increase or decrease concerns about a juvenile's risk factors and abuse deterrents. The juvenile's (and the prevention team's) status on these four elements needs to be addressed throughout treatment as a child may progress in one competence yet regress in another. Likewise, over time, some abuse precursors will shift progressively toward prevention and safety, while others suggest movement toward risk and lapses. By using the balanced approach, creativity and flexibility in responding to these needs can be maximized.

EXTERNAL, SUPERVISORY DIMENSION OF RELAPSE PREVENTION

The External, Supervisory Dimension serves three functions: (1) fostering development of a collaborative relationship between mental health professionals treating the offender, probation officers supervising the offender, and family members who witness the offender's daily behaviors; (2) increasing the efficiency of supervision by creating an informed network of collateral contacts who monitor the offender's behaviors; and (3) enhancing efficacy of supervision by specifying distinct offense precursors that can be monitored by professional and collateral contacts. The External, Supervisory Dimension of RP establishes a "prevention team" that works collaboratively with the juvenile to diminish the potential of another sex offense.

Building the Prevention Team

Construction of a prevention team is a developmental process. During early contacts, the team may include parents, siblings, caseworker or probation officer, and therapist. As interventions progress, the circle of the prevention team expands to include school guidance counselors, community members, and even peers who model abuse prevention attitudes and behaviors.

A solid prevention team offers assurance that the adolescent will receive enduring support from a community that clearly understands his risk factors and is educated to effectively support prevention of relapse. They agree to give feedback to the juvenile about risk behaviors observed in the home, community, and school.

A student's right to confidentiality needs to be balanced with his right to effective treatment and supervision. RP is founded on a marriage of internal self-management and external supervision. Favorable treatment outcome is reliant on an informed and respectful prevention team representing different spheres of influence in the adolescent's world.

It is possible to conceptualize the prevention team as a series of expanding concentric circles, each of which represents a distinct sphere of influence. Sphere one would include one's immediate family, treatment provider, and caseworker or probation officer. Extended family and close friends might represent sphere two. Sphere three may be constituted by school personnel and immediate neighbors. Sphere four may include selected church members, acquaintances, and recreational personnel. Generally, spheres expand as treatment and maintenance of change endure.

Decisions about who to include in the outer spheres of influence are made primarily by members of sphere one. Gray (1991c) has presented guidelines that may help the prevention team decide how to balance internal self-management with external supervision. A summary of these guidelines is presented later in this chapter.

In order to function effectively, all members of the prevention team must be knowledgeable about RP concepts. Prevention team members accept the belief that assisting the juvenile's identification of his relapse process will decrease the likelihood of another offense. In the juvenile's presence, the prevention team is encouraged to report lapses to the therapist or probation officer. This feedback is also an intervention framed as concern for the best interests of the adolescent and support for abuse prevention.

Specification of the juvenile's SUDs, High-Risk Situations, and risk factors provides the prevention team with identifiable precursors to relapse. Since these risk factors are specific to the juvenile's sex offenses, supervision becomes more meaningful and effective than when the prevention team is expected to monitor all of the juvenile's behaviors. Whenever a prevention team member detects an offense precursor, the juvenile is known to be involved in his relapse process.

Since offense precursors appear most commonly in a distinct sequence (i.e., Emotion → Fantasy → Cognitive Distortion → Passive Planning → Act), the type of precursor exhibited provides an indication of the imminence of potential relapse. With this information, the prevention team may determine the type of intervention required by an offender's lapse (e.g., curfew, additional form of treatment, probation violation). Generally, early precursors (e.g., emotion) require less intrusive interventions than later precursors (e.g., planning).

As mentioned previously, the juvenile informs his prevention team about his offense precursors. This accomplishes two goals. The completeness of information presented by the juvenile can be evaluated, enabling the prevention team to gauge how well the juvenile understands his precursors and the importance of the team to his behavioral maintenance. Informing the prevention team about his offense precursors also destroys the secrecy that promotes sexual abuse. Behaviors that once seemed unimportant but that are central to the relapse process can then be recognized as signs for concern.

Guidelines for Balancing Internal Self-Management and External Supervision

Gray (1991b) developed a comprehensive approach to risk factor assessment that pairs ratings of the client's self-management skills with ratings of the adequacy of external supervision. By making independent ratings, one can determine for each adolescent whether an emphasis should be placed on enhancing self-management skills, external supervision, or both. Gray's approach recognizes that both self-management and supervision are important and that their relative emphasis will vary across clients.

A youthful offender's comprehensive risk factor analysis includes a two-tier assessment protocol. The first tier identifies the juvenile's risk factors and his ability to cope with these factors. The second tier examines the extent to which the external supervisory network is prepared to identify the adolescent's risk factors, willing to intervene when risk factors are detected, and able to model abuse prevention attitudes and behaviors. Ratings result in an estimate of low, moderate, or high risk on each tier.

On the basis of these ratings, independent conclusions can be drawn about intervention strategies needed for each risk condition. If an adolescent lacks strong self-management skills (a moderate to high risk on tier one) but is supported by a strong supervision team (low risk on tier two), therapeutic interventions aimed at strengthening self-management skills may be the initial focus of intervention.

Tier one assessment focuses on issues related to the client's self-management skills including number of offense precursors, awareness of seemingly unimportant decisions, ability to modulate affective risk states, extent of arousal to sexually or physically abusive fantasies, prevalence of cognitive distortions, and the degree to which the offense pattern is rehearsed in fantasies. Tier one also evaluates a youth's view of environmental factors such as extent and ease of access to victims, extent and ease of access to prevention team resources, and realistic plans for implementation of his relapse prevention plan. As mentioned previously, these factors are integrated and the client receives a rating of low, moderate, or high risk. Tier two assessment rates factors related to the adequacy of the adolescent's external supervision. Ratings can be completed separately on the spheres of influence noted earlier in this chapter (e.g., immediate family members, supervising agent, therapist, school environment, and specific community members). Adequacy of external supervision within each of these spheres can be rated on five factors: relapse prevention knowledge, ability to effectively apply intervention strategies, modeling of empathic attitudes and behaviors, degree of permanence or constancy, and willingness to network with other prevention team members. Tier two results in a rating of low, moderate, or high risk of enabling perpetuation of the abusive pattern.

As an example of a tier two assessment, a low-risk rating of a residential placement may be earned by the following characteristics: Full responsibility for the abuse is placed on the offender; the victim's report is considered to reflect accurately the nature of the offense; staff members model healthy empathy and emotional modulation; staff are familiar with relapse prevention and corrective procedures for thinking errors; staff participate in supportive education and supervision, refute sexist attitudes, and dispel gender and other myths; staff model respect for rights of victims; and staff disavow expression of sexualized violence.

By conducting a two-tier assessment, one can identify the emphasis that needs to be placed on treatment and supervision. While not identifying specific treatment needs in the same manner as a comprehensive psychosexual assessment, this information can be useful to guide decisions to permit community access, visitation to specific locations, movement within the community, and minimal supervision required in various situations.

Special Issues When Working with Parents

Several standards have proven helpful while working to gain the cooperation of parents of sexually abusive adolescents. We suggest that parents adopt the belief that "knowledge is power." In the initial session, we discuss the initial shock or numbness that is part of experiencing a major loss in one's view of their world. We focus on processes of healthy self-care, concerns about unknowns, and immobilizing emotions. We assist parents in seeing that they are influential in a discovery and recovery process. We create safe opportunities for parents to assert themselves, to take the risk of feeling uncertain and vulnerable, and to volunteer to explore the unknown.

Willingness to become involved in their child's treatment is framed as an indication of the parents' personal power, integrity, and concern. We emphasize the importance of their role as valued investigators and coaches on the prevention team. Parents are provided with a safe setting in which their fears of powerlessness, failure, shame, and humiliation can be expressed and acknowledged. We instruct parents that even though these emotions sometimes allow one to feel out of control, it is healthier to accept these feelings for what they are rather than to convert them into anger which may provide the illusion of control. We ask parents to discuss their losses, that healthy grieving can be important to the ongoing process of taking care of themselves and letting go of the desire to assume responsibility for their child's behaviors. We encourage parents to accept an attitude of caring detachment and to apply this attitude in situations that feel "crazy making."

When parents deny the abusiveness of their child, we inform them that denial is a common initial reaction when people are asked to accept distressing news. We also assert that shame and denial become maladaptive if prolonged because they block a positive resolution of distress by distorting reality. We ask parents to accept an attitude that "anything is possible," that they can be good parents and still not know everything their child does or has done. We encourage parents to replace "either/or" thinking with an attitude of "exploring possible options." We also provide reading materials (Gil, 1987) that they may refer to when feeling less pressured.

Parents have given us recommendations about the resources and interventions that they have found useful. Among these resources are (1) written information on relapse prevention, cognitive distortions, and the consequences of sexual abuse; (2) educational videotapes of adolescent abusers discussing their relapse process and the need to be held accountable; (3) literature on the recovery process of sexual abuse victims; (4) referrals to treatment groups for adult survivors of sexual abuse; (5) the opportunity to be included periodically in sessions of the adolescent abuser group; (6) support groups for parents of abusive adolescents; and (7) attention to the concerns of the juvenile's nonabusive siblings in the treatment process.

Care must be exercised when working with parents of abusive adolescents. Some parents identify their child's lapses and reliably report them to treatment providers. Other parents may not possess the ability to identify lapses; others detect the lapse and are reluctant to report it; still others may feel such anxiety or anger that they exaggerate misbehaviors. Stepparents of abusive juveniles may fear their spouse's wrath when contemplating reporting their stepchild's precursors. Other adults may worry about reprisals from the juvenile's parents, who may be known to have problems managing anger. Developing a prevention team demands good judgment and careful attention.

Many resistant parents may be encouraged to become members of the prevention team. Occasionally, parents genuinely want to help their child but do not wish to be identified as being on the same "team" as a mental health professional or a representative of a social services agency. In such cases, we may define the prevention team as subsuming "home" and "away" teams that compete to identify the juvenile's offense precursors most quickly and accurately in order to give the parent room to grow toward joining the larger "prevention league."

In practice, it has been important for professional members of the prevention team to meet regularly. By reviewing case-specific information, the professional prevention team may discern inconsistencies in the juvenile's behaviors or statements. Early in treatment, it is commonly discovered that the juvenile has depicted a single event very differently to two members of the prevention team. Such inconsistencies may reflect efforts to manipulate, split, or deceive prevention team members. Regular meetings ensure that each professional possesses all available information. Since regularly scheduled meetings allow exchange of routine information, telephone messages between meetings may indicate a critical event that must be dealt with immediately.

RELAPSE PREVENTION AS A UNIFYING
THEORETICAL FRAMEWORK

RP has been used as a treatment procedure and supervisory process for sex offenders for several years. Recently, Laws (1989) referred to RP as a "core, unifying concept" that may be used to structure use of other therapeutic interventions. Within this perspective, RP offers a comprehensive analysis of the sex offender's life-style and functioning. The offender's unique excesses (e.g., arousal to sexually abusive stimuli) and deficits (e.g., inability to tolerate distress without acting out) are considered risk factors that potentiate abuse. Specific therapeutic interventions can then be invoked to reduce the effect of these risk factors.

RP thus permits the integration of distinct treatment approaches for specific behavioral excesses and deficits within a single comprehensive therapeutic framework. Treatment within the RP model becomes an individualized program tailored to meet each client's unique needs comprehensively. Figure 16.5 illustrates how RP can serve as a unifying framework for treatment of the following juvenile abuser.

> Allan D. is a 14-year-old who was adjudicated delinquent after attempting to rape a female peer at knife point. Allan asserts that the assault was his first attempt to experience intercourse. He expresses a desire to "have sex" and admits that he does not know much about dating or sexuality. He thinks the victim encouraged his behavior by wearing "an outfit like Madonna," with an exposed bra and short skirt, and by "looking at me like she wanted it." Allan does not think his victim was harmed by the attempted assault stating, "She obviously has had it before. I guess she just didn't want it from me. No one thinks I'm good enough."
>
> Allan has never dated, has no extracurricular activities at school, works 5 hours a week drying vehicles at a car wash, and spends his free time with drug-involved friends. He admits buying them drugs just to be able to spend time with them. He mentions "boredom" as being his most common emotion. When pressed, he indicates that he masturbates while looking at lingerie catalogs when bored. He volunteered that he is bored a lot. Sometimes when masturbating he feels angry that no female his age will have him and he imagines forcing one to have sex with him.
>
> Allan indicated that he has run away from home on three occasions. He began to cry when he described how his father, when intoxicated, has beaten his mother and him. Allan said that he thinks his father has "been weird" with his sister because he has heard his sister say through her closed bedroom door, "But you promised you'd never do anything like this again, Dad! It hurts me!" Allan added very quickly that his father has never abused him like that. He mentioned that he plans to beat up his father as soon as he builds himself up."

Some of the risk factors identified in this synopsis of Allan D. are shown in the boxes at the top of Figure 16.5. Risk factors include (1) cognitive precursors (victim's clothing considered to have provoked the assault; eye contact from victim interpreted as sexual overture; assumptions about victim's sexual history, thoughts, and feelings); (2) mismanagement of emotions (ex-

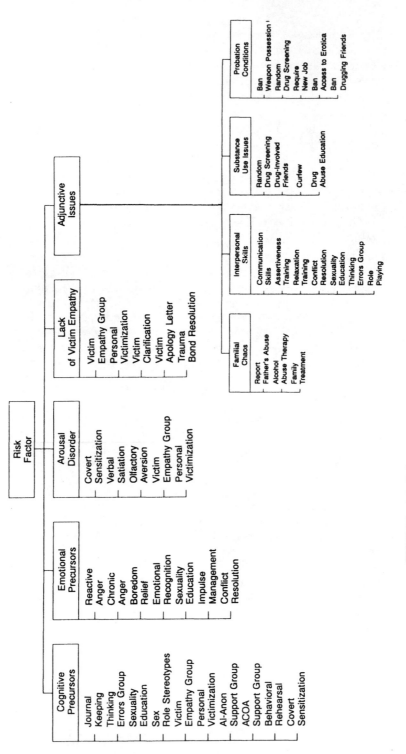

FIGURE 16.5. Relapse prevention as an integrative framework.

cessive boredom, boredom masking other emotions, masturbation to gain relief from unexpressed emotion); (3) arousal to rape fantasies; (4) lack of empathy for sexual abuse victims; and (5) a variety of concerns including familial physical and sexual abuse, poor interpersonal skills, possession of weapons, exposure to drug-involved peers, possible drug use, and a potential high-risk working environment.

Following the concept of the balanced approach, Figure 16.5 also demonstrates how RP can structure a combination of treatment components and environmental controls to address risk factors. While any of several treatment components could be employed to deal with each risk factor, the therapist would chose the component (or identify a new one) that most completely addresses the client's needs. Environmental controls would be designated as diversion, probation, or parole conditions. The prevention team would monitor adherence to these conditions.

Since the client's treatment and supervision needs change across time, the prevention team should remain vigilant for emergence of new risk factors. These risk factors, and the appropriate interventions, can be added to the program design.

REFERENCES

Abel, G. G., & Rouleau, J. L. (1990). The nature and extent of sexual assault. In W. L. Marshall, D. R. Laws, & H. E. Barbaree (Eds.), *Handbook of sexual assault: Issues, theories, and treatment of the offender.* New York: Plenum Press.

Berliner, L., Manaois, O., and Monastersky, C. (1986). *Child sexual behavior disturbance: An assessment and treatment model.* Seattle: Sexual Assault Center and University of Washington.

Chaney, E. F., O'Leary, M. R., & Marlatt, G. A. (1978). Skill training with alcoholics. *Journal of Consulting and Clinical Psychology, 46,* 1092–1104.

Federal Register. (1975, December 5). *Protection of identity: Research subjects* (Vol. 40, No. 234). Washington, DC: U.S. Government Printing Office.

Gil, E. (1987). *Children who molest: A guide for parents of young sex offenders.* Walnut Creek, CA: Launch Press.

Gray, A. S. (1991a, November). *A balanced approach to intervention with children molesting children.* Paper presented at the Tenth Annual Research and Treatment Conference of the Association for the Treatment of Sexual Abusers, Fort Worth, TX.

Gray, A. S. (1991b). *A framework for a comprehensive two-tier analysis of risk: Rating internal self-management skills and external supervision.* Unpublished manuscript, Center For Prevention Services, Underhill Center, VT.

Gray, A. S., & Knopp, F. H. (1991, October). The First National Conference on Sexually Aggressive and Sexually Reactive Children. Burlington, VT.

Gray, A. S. (1991c, October). *Modifying relapse prevention with sexually agressive and sexually reactive children: Building the prevention team.* Paper presented at the First

National Conference on Sexually Aggressive and Sexually Reactive Children. Burlington, VT.

Isaac, C., & Lane, S. (1990). *The sexual abuse cycle in the treatment of adolescent sexual abusers*. Shoreham, VT: Safer Society Program and Press.

Johnson, T. C. (1988). Child perpetrators-children who molest other children. *Child Abuse and Neglect, 12*, 219–229.

Laws, D. R. (Ed.). (1989). *Relapse prevention with sex offenders*. New York: Guilford Press.

Lieb, R., & Felver, B. (1991, February). *The 1990 Community Protection Act: One year later*. Olympia, WA: Washington State Institute for Public Policy.

Marlatt, G. A. (1982). Relapse prevention: A self–control program for the treatment of addictive behaviors. In R. B. Stuart (Ed.), *Adherence, compliance, and generalization in behavioral medicine*. New York: Brunner/Mazel.

Marlatt, G. A., & Gordon, J. R. (1980). Determinants of relapse: Implications for maintenance of change. In P. O. Davidson & S. M. Davidson (Eds.), *Behavioral medicine: Changing health lifestyles*. New York: Brunner/Mazel.

Marlatt, G. A., & Gordon, J. R. (1985). *Relapse prevention*. New York: Guilford Press.

National Adolescent Perpetrator Network. (1988). Preliminary report from the National Task Force on Juvenile Sex Offending. *Juvenile and Family Court Journal, 39*, 1–67.

O'Brien, M., & Bera, W. (1986, Fall). Adolescent sex offenders: A descriptive typology. *Preventing Sexual Abuse, 1*, 1–4.

Oregon Children's Services Division. (1986, December). Guidelines for treatment of juvenile sexual offenders. In *The Oregon Report on Juvenile Sexual Offenders* (pp. 35–39). Salem, OR: Author.

Pithers, W. D. (August, 1982). *The Vermont Treatment Program for Sexual Aggressors: A program description*. Waterbury, VT: Vermont Department of Corrections.

Pithers, W. D. (1990). Relapse prevention with sexual aggressors: A method for maintaining therapeutic gain and enhancing external supervision. In W. L. Marshall, D. R. Laws, & H. E. Barbaree (Eds.), *The handbook of sexual assault: Issues, theories, and treatment of the offender* (pp. 343–361). New York: Plenum Press.

Pithers, W. D., Beal, L. S., Armstrong, J., & Petty, J. (1989). Identification of risk factors through records analysis and clinical interview. In D. R. Laws (Ed.), *Relapse prevention with sex offenders* (pp. 77–87). New York: Guilford Press.

Pithers, W. D., Cumming, G. F., Beal, L. S., Young, W., & Turner, R. (1989). Relapse prevention. In B. Schwartz (Ed.), *A practitioner's guide to treating the incarcerated male sex offender* (pp. 123–140). Washington, DC: National Institute of Corrections.

Pithers, W. D., & Gray, A. S. (1991, May). *The Pre-Adolescent Sexual Abuser Research Project*. Grant proposal submitted to the National Center on Child Abuse and Neglect.

Pithers, W. D., Kashima, K. M., Cumming, G. F., Beal, L. S., & Buell, M. M. (1988). Relapse prevention of sexual aggression. In R. A. Prentky, & V. L. Quinsey (Eds.), *Human sexual aggression: Current perspectives. Annals of the New York Academy of Sciences* (Vol. 528 pp. 244–260). New York: New York Academy of Sciences.

Pithers, W. D., Marques, J. K., Gibat, C. C., & Marlatt, G.A. (1983). Relapse prevention: A self-control model of treatment and maintenance of change for sexual aggressives. In J. Greer, & I. R. Stuart (Eds.), *The sexual aggressor: Current perspectives on treatment* (pp. 214–239). New York: Van Nostrand Reinhold.

Pithers, W. D., Martin, G., & Cumming, G. F. (1989). The Vermont treatment program for sexual aggressors. In D. R. Laws (Ed.), *Relapse prevention with sex offenders* (pp. 292–310). New York: Guilford Press.

Rasmussen, L. A., Burton, J. E., & Christopherson, B. (1990, October). *Interrupting precursors to perpetration in males ages four to twelve.* Paper presented at the annual conference of the National Adolescent Perpetrator Network, Albany, NY.

Index

321

DATE DUE

AG 22		

DEMCO 38-296